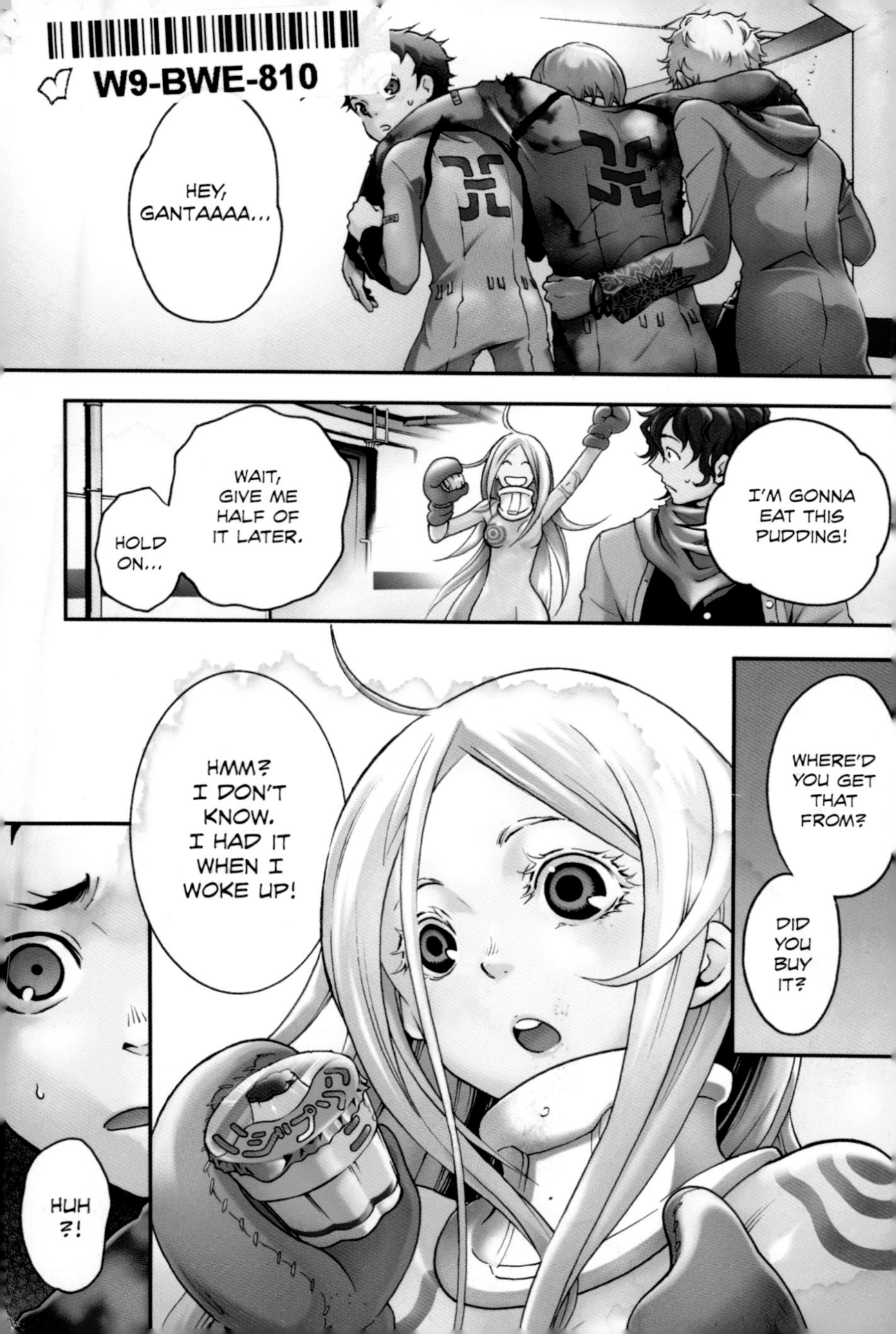
HEY, GANTAAAA...
I'M GONNA EAT THIS PUDDING!
WAIT, GIVE ME HALF OF IT LATER.
HOLD ON...
WHERE'D YOU GET THAT FROM?
DID YOU BUY IT?
HMM? I DON'T KNOW. I HAD IT WHEN I WOKE UP!
HUH?!

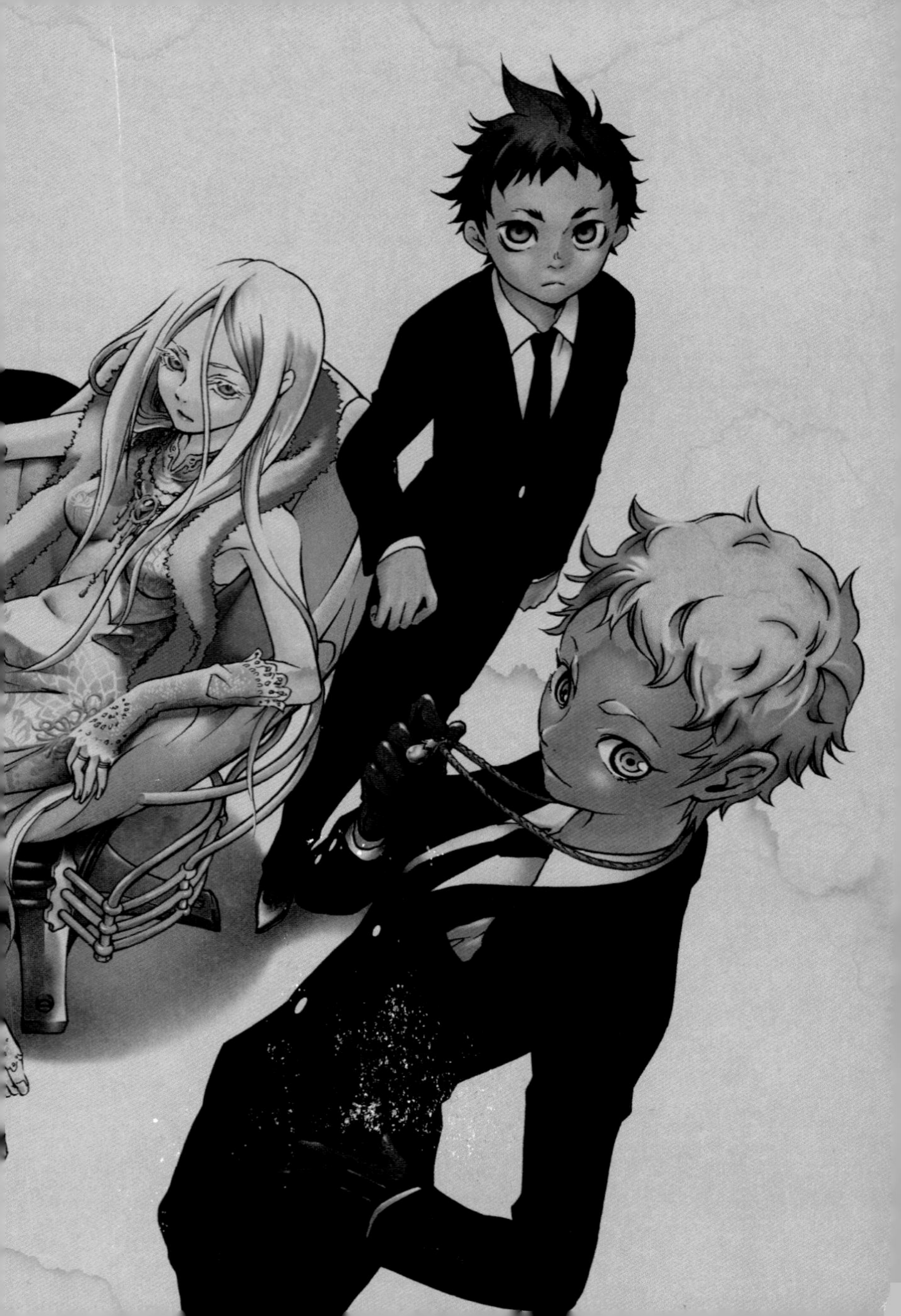

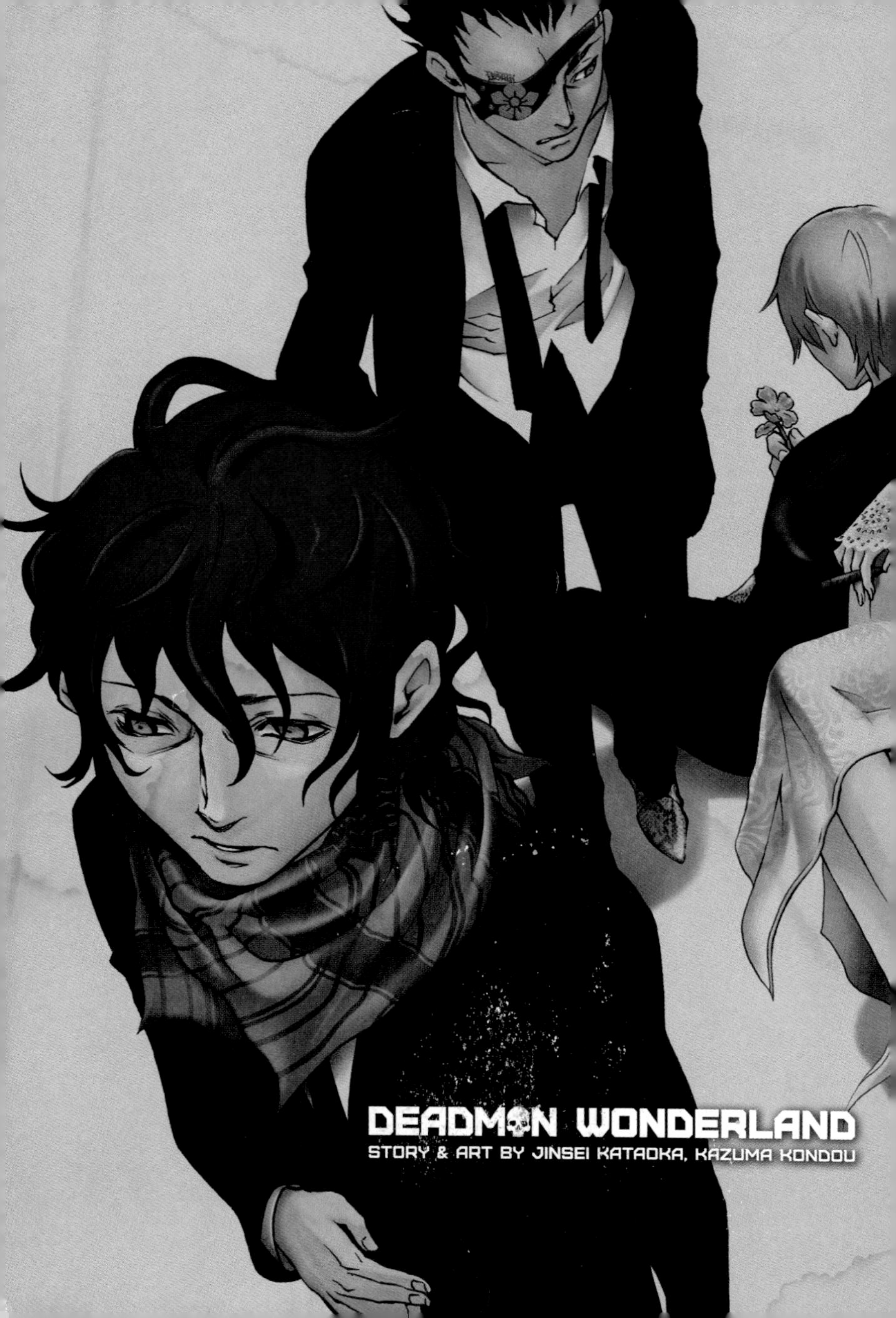
DEADMAN WONDERLAND
STORY & ART BY JINSEI KATAOKA, KAZUMA KONDOU

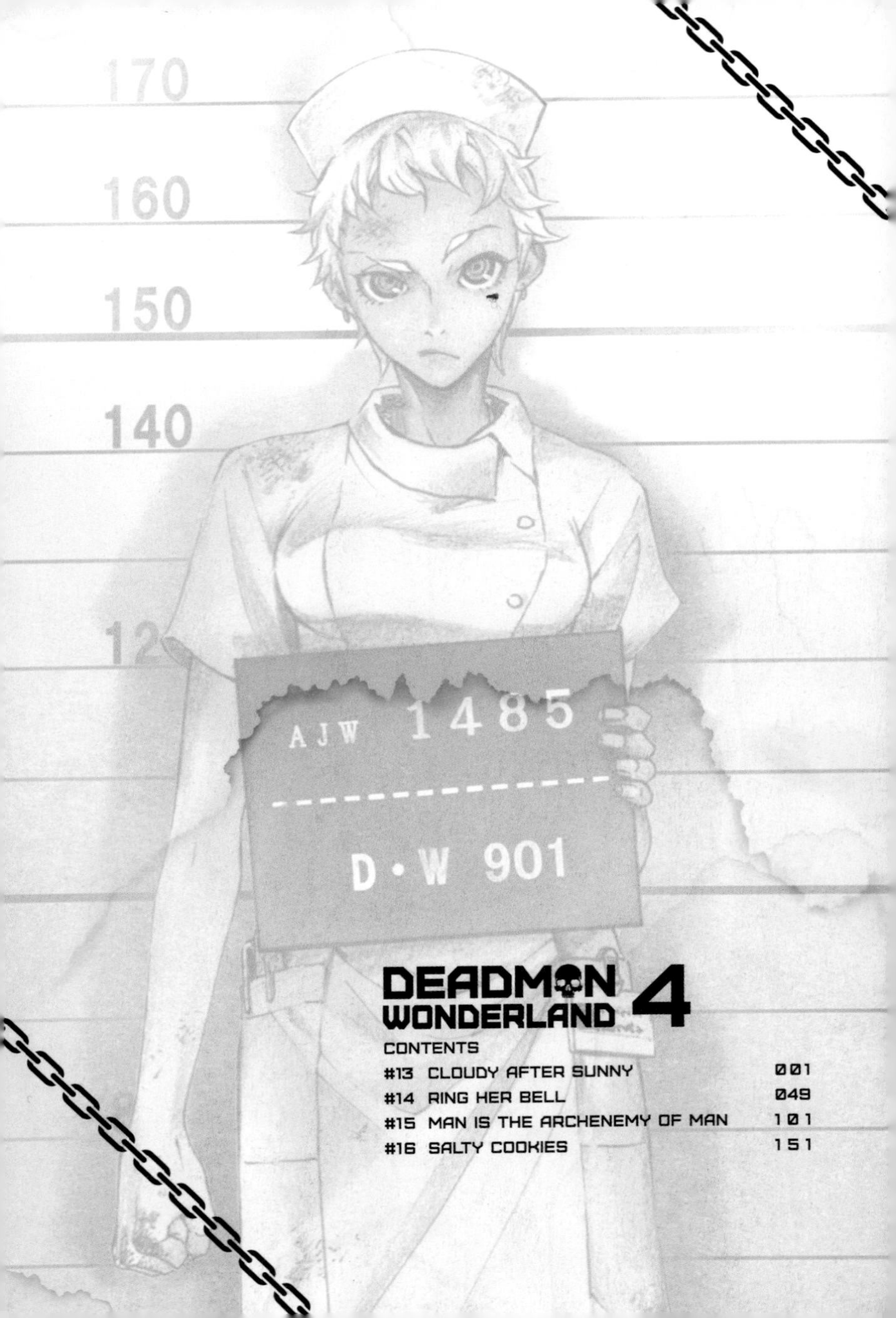
170
160
150
140
12
AJW 1485
D • W 901

DEADMAN WONDERLAND 4

CONTENTS

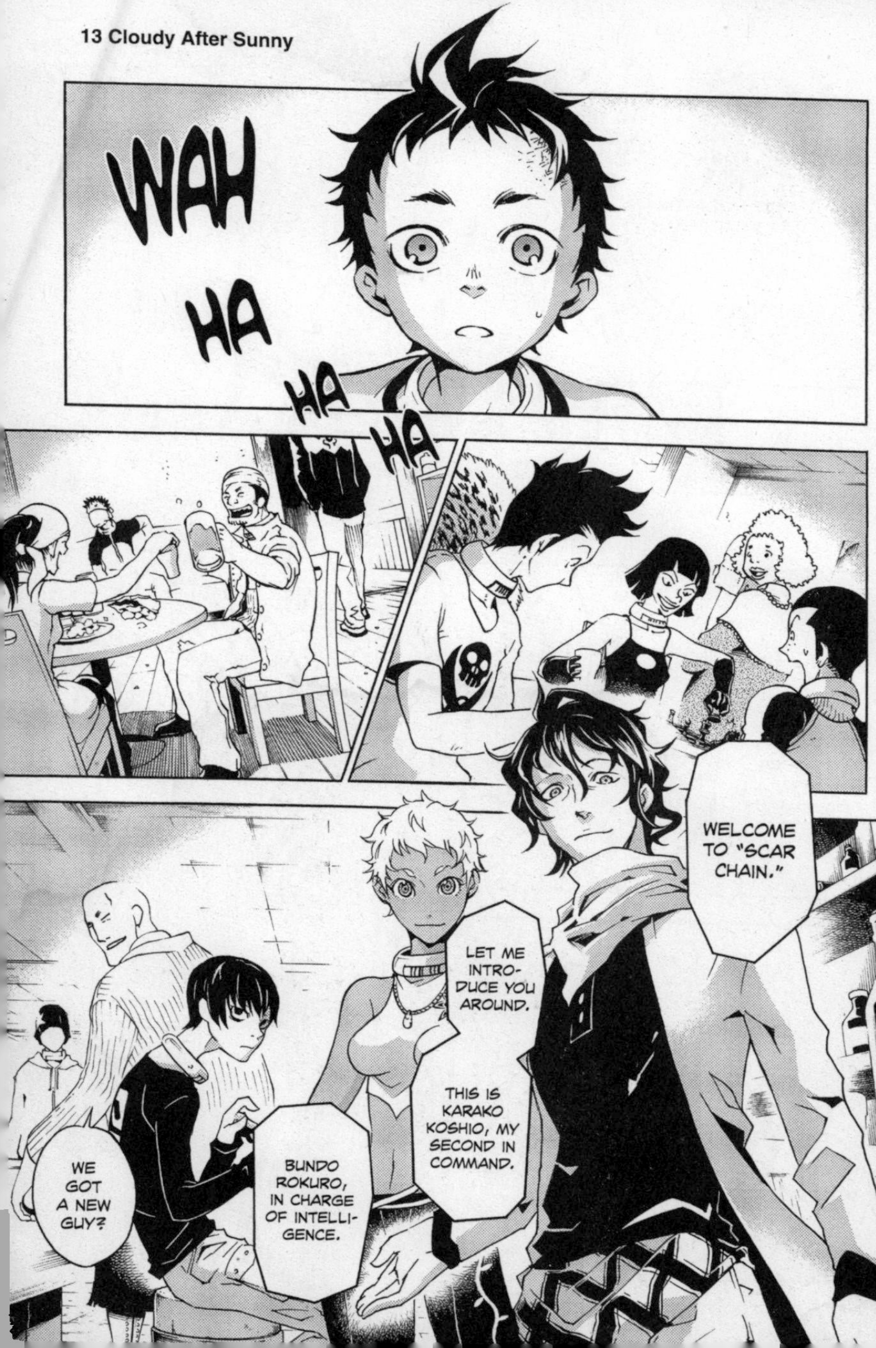
WAH
HA
HA
HA
WELCOME TO "SCAR CHAIN."
LET ME INTRODUCE YOU AROUND.
THIS IS KARAKO KOSHIO, MY SECOND IN COMMAND.
BUNDO ROKURO, IN CHARGE OF INTELLIGENCE.
WE GOT A NEW GUY?

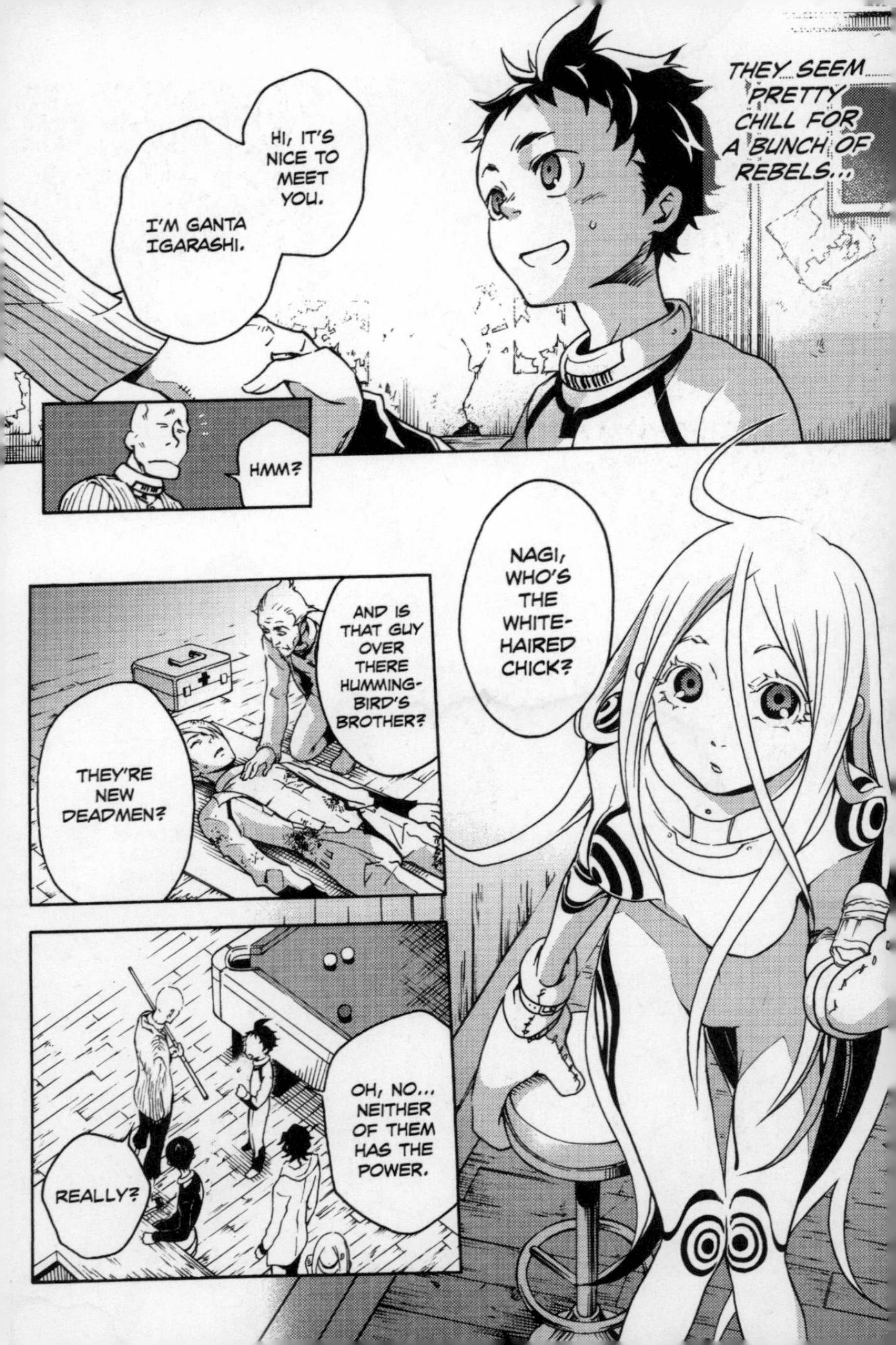
THEY SEEM... PRETTY CHILL FOR A BUNCH OF REBELS...
HI, IT'S NICE TO MEET YOU.
I'M GANTA IGARASHI.
HMM?
NAGI, WHO'S THE WHITE-HAIRED CHICK?
AND IS THAT GUY OVER THERE HUMMING-BIRD'S BROTHER?
THEY'RE NEW DEADMEN?
OH, NO... NEITHER OF THEM HAS THE POWER.
REALLY?

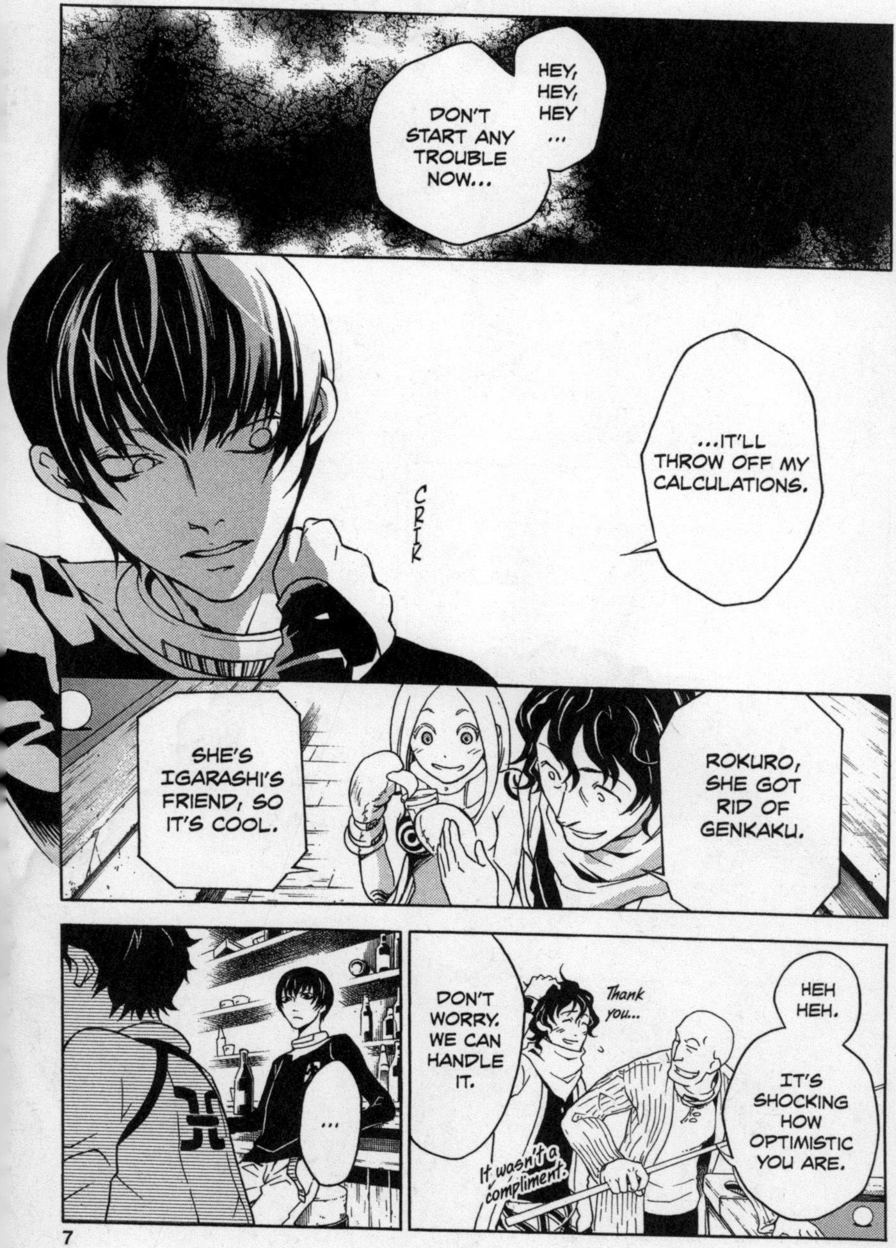
HEY, HEY, HEY...
DON'T START ANY TROUBLE NOW...
...IT'LL THROW OFF MY CALCULATIONS.
CRIK
ROKURO, SHE GOT RID OF GENKAKU.
SHE'S IGARASHI'S FRIEND, SO IT'S COOL.
HEH HEH.
IT'S SHOCKING HOW OPTIMISTIC YOU ARE.
Thank you...
DON'T WORRY. WE CAN HANDLE IT.
It wasn't a compliment.
...

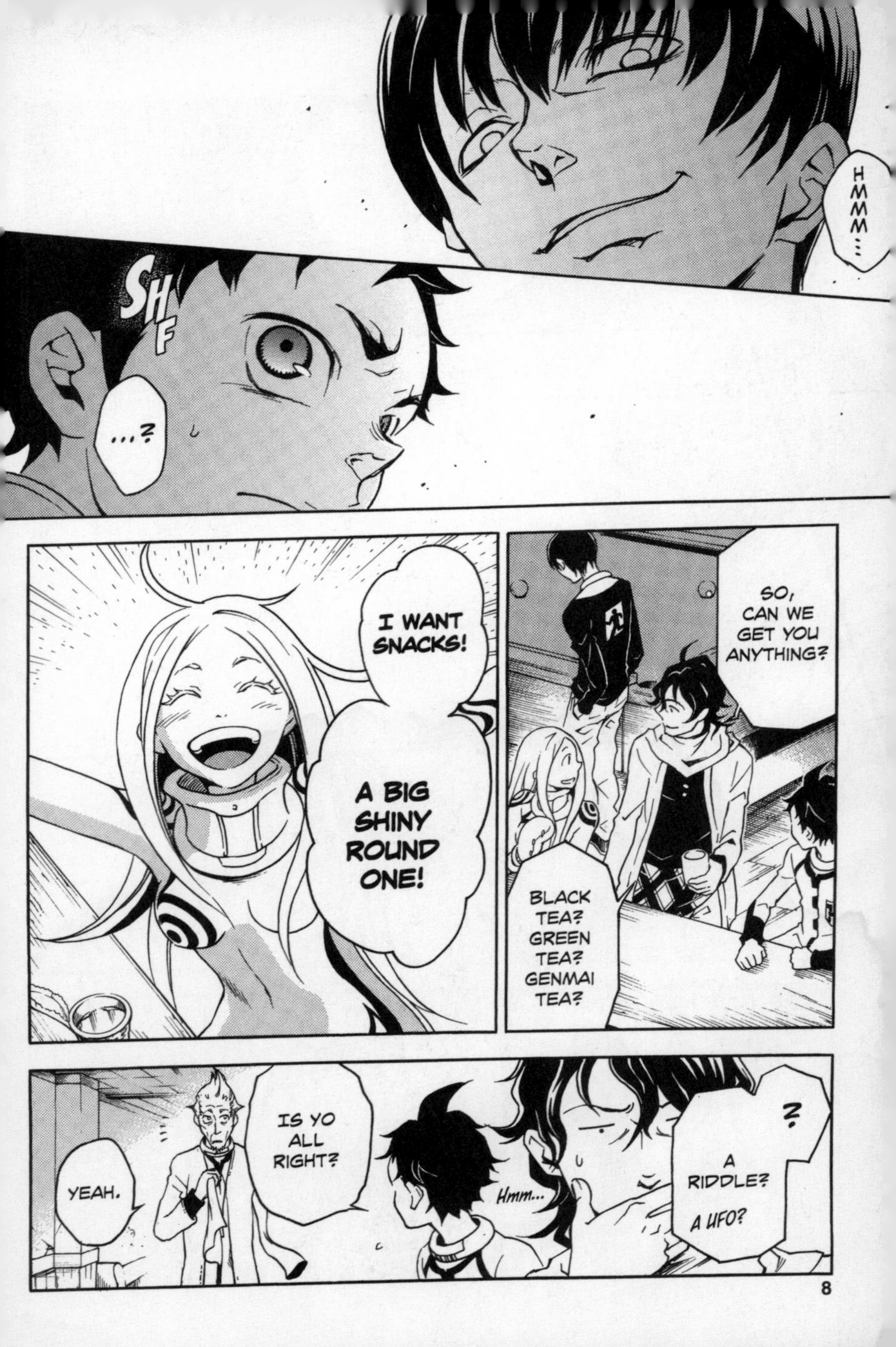
HMMM...
SHF
...?
SO, CAN WE GET YOU ANYTHING?
BLACK TEA? GREEN TEA? GENMAI TEA?
I WANT SNACKS!
A BIG SHINY ROUND ONE!
?
A RIDDLE?
A UFO?
Hmm...
IS YO ALL RIGHT?
YEAH.

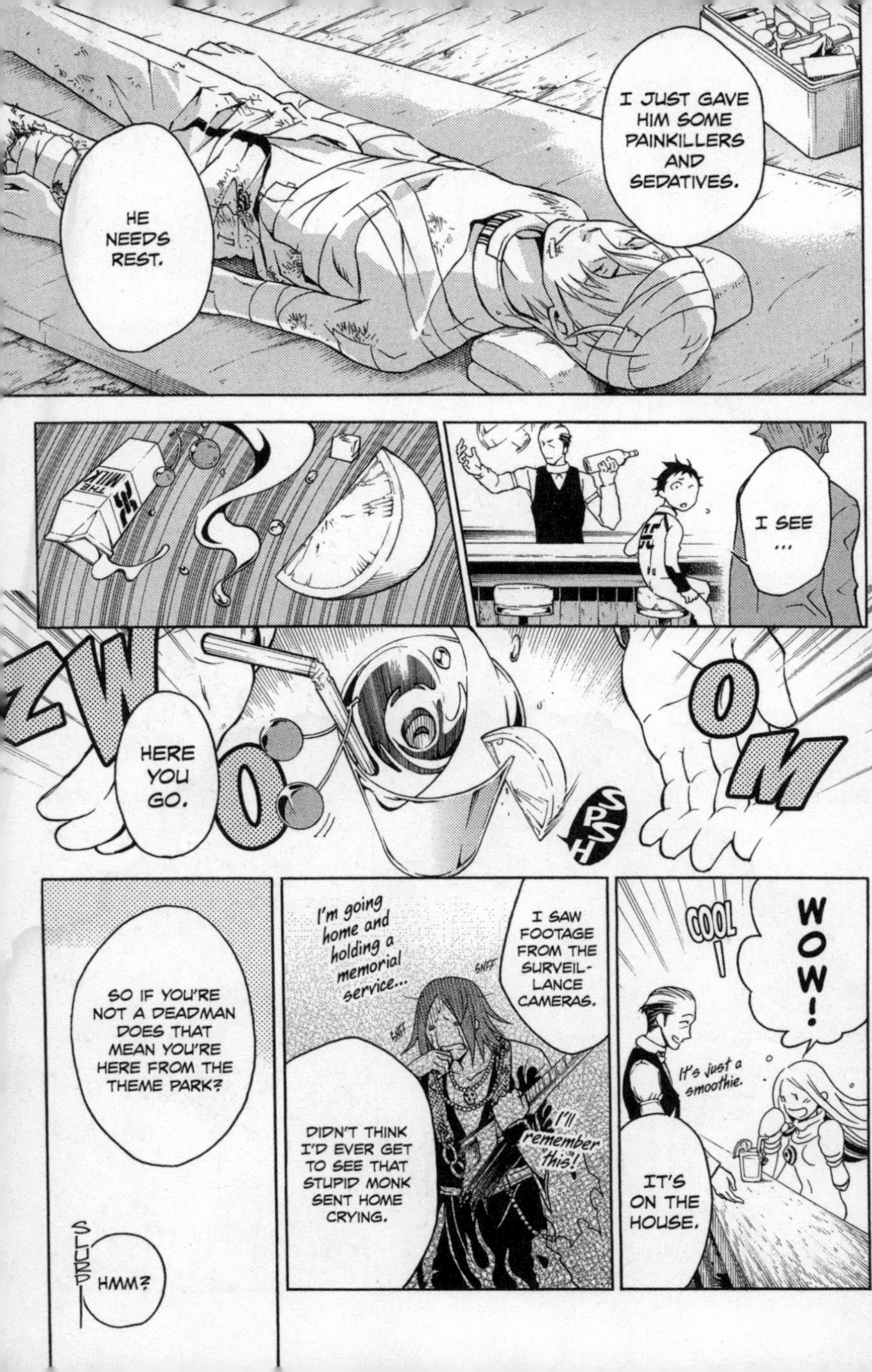
I JUST GAVE HIM SOME PAINKILLERS AND SEDATIVES.
HE NEEDS REST.
I SEE ...
THE MILK
ZWOOM
HERE YOU GO.
SPSH
WOW!
COOL!
It's just a smoothie.
IT'S ON THE HOUSE.
I SAW FOOTAGE FROM THE SURVEIL-LANCE CAMERAS.
I'm going home and holding a memorial service...
SNFF
SNFF
I'll remember this!
DIDN'T THINK I'D EVER GET TO SEE THAT STUPID MONK SENT HOME CRYING.
SO IF YOU'RE NOT A DEADMAN DOES THAT MEAN YOU'RE HERE FROM THE THEME PARK?
SLURP
HMM?

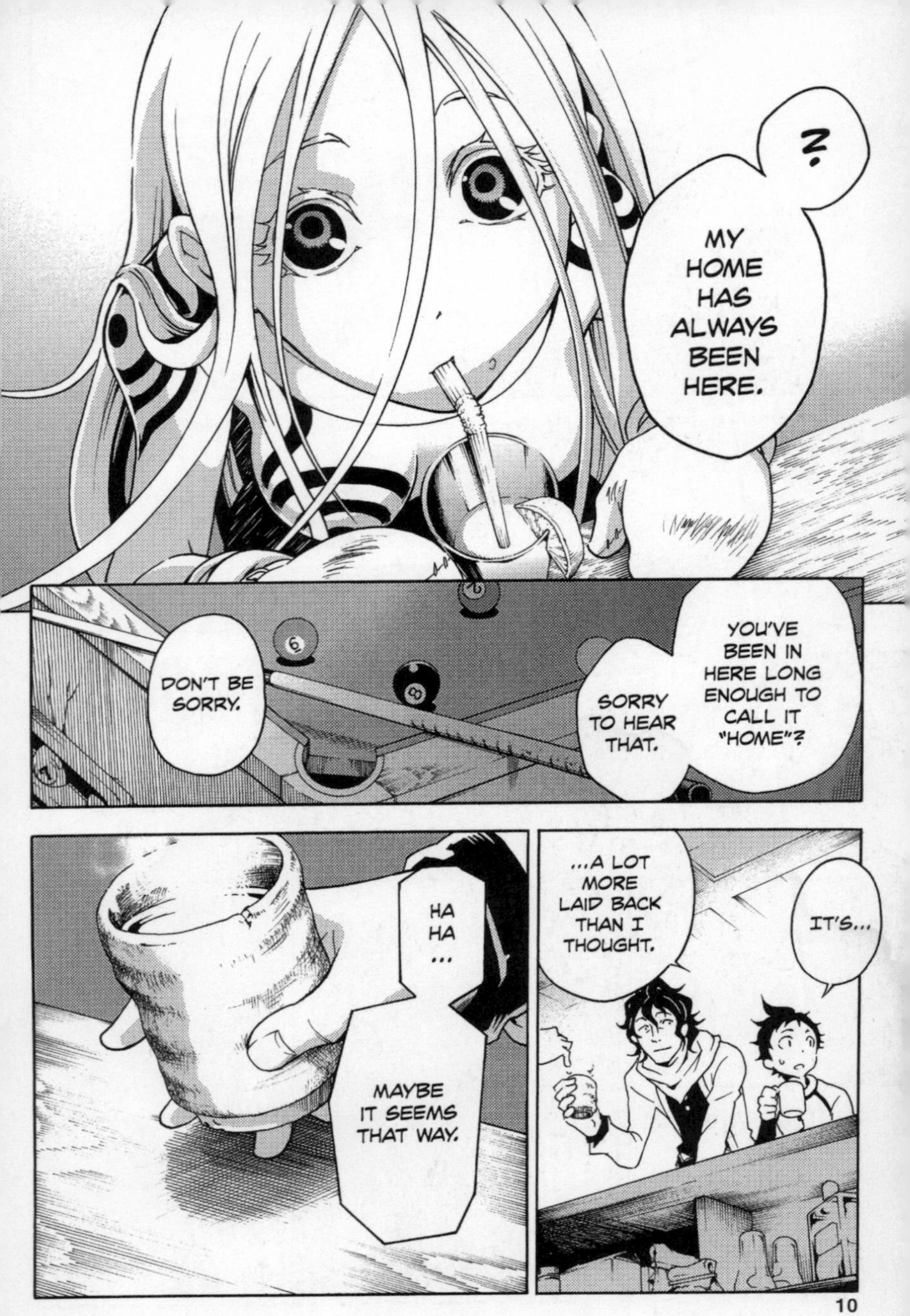
?
MY HOME HAS ALWAYS BEEN HERE.
YOU'VE BEEN IN HERE LONG ENOUGH TO CALL IT "HOME"?
SORRY TO HEAR THAT.
DON'T BE SORRY.
IT'S...
...A LOT MORE LAID BACK THAN I THOUGHT.
HA HA ...
MAYBE IT SEEMS THAT WAY.

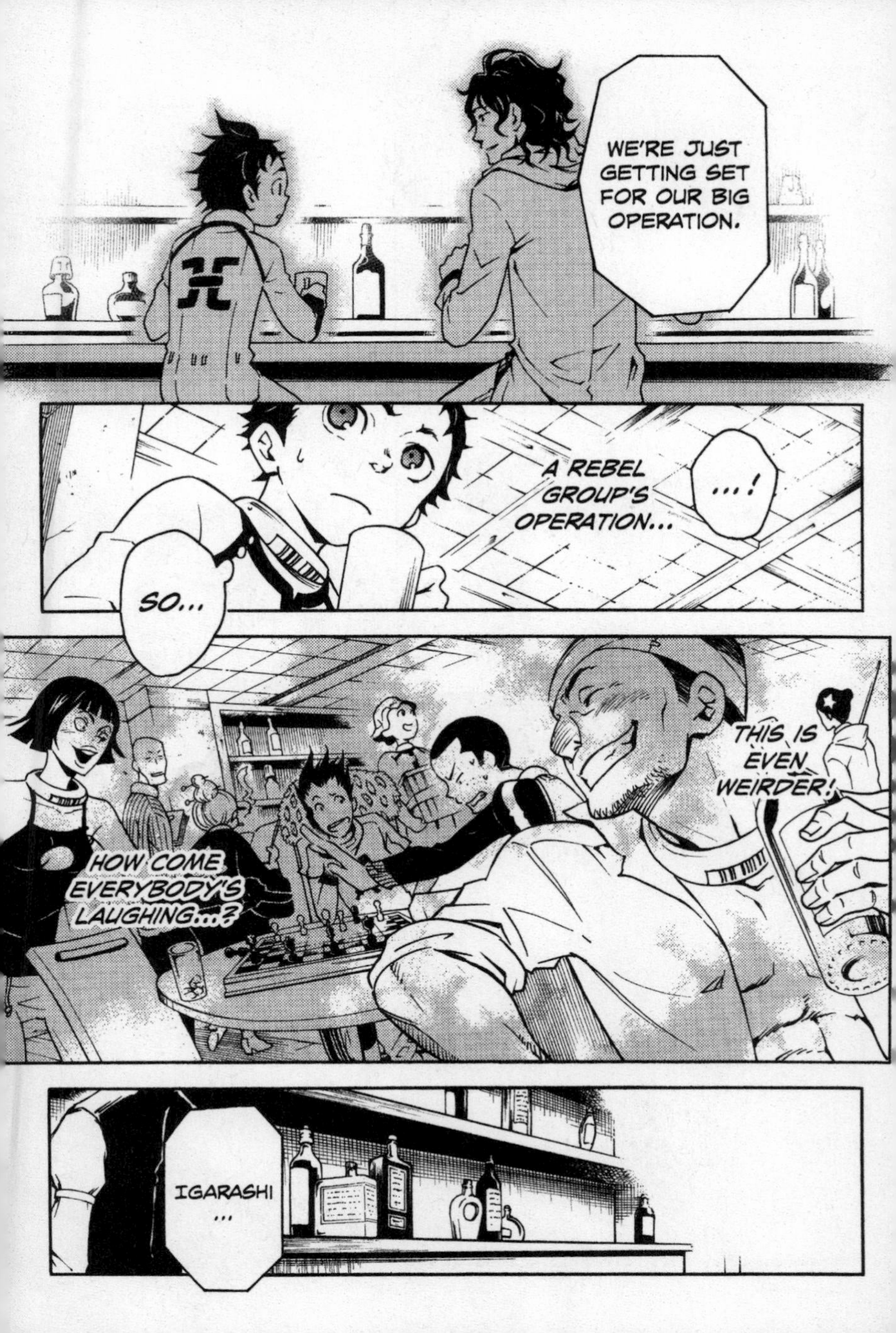
WE'RE JUST GETTING SET FOR OUR BIG OPERATION.
...!
A REBEL GROUP'S OPERATION...
SO...
THIS IS EVEN WEIRDER!
HOW COME EVERYBODY'S LAUGHING...?
IGARASHI ...

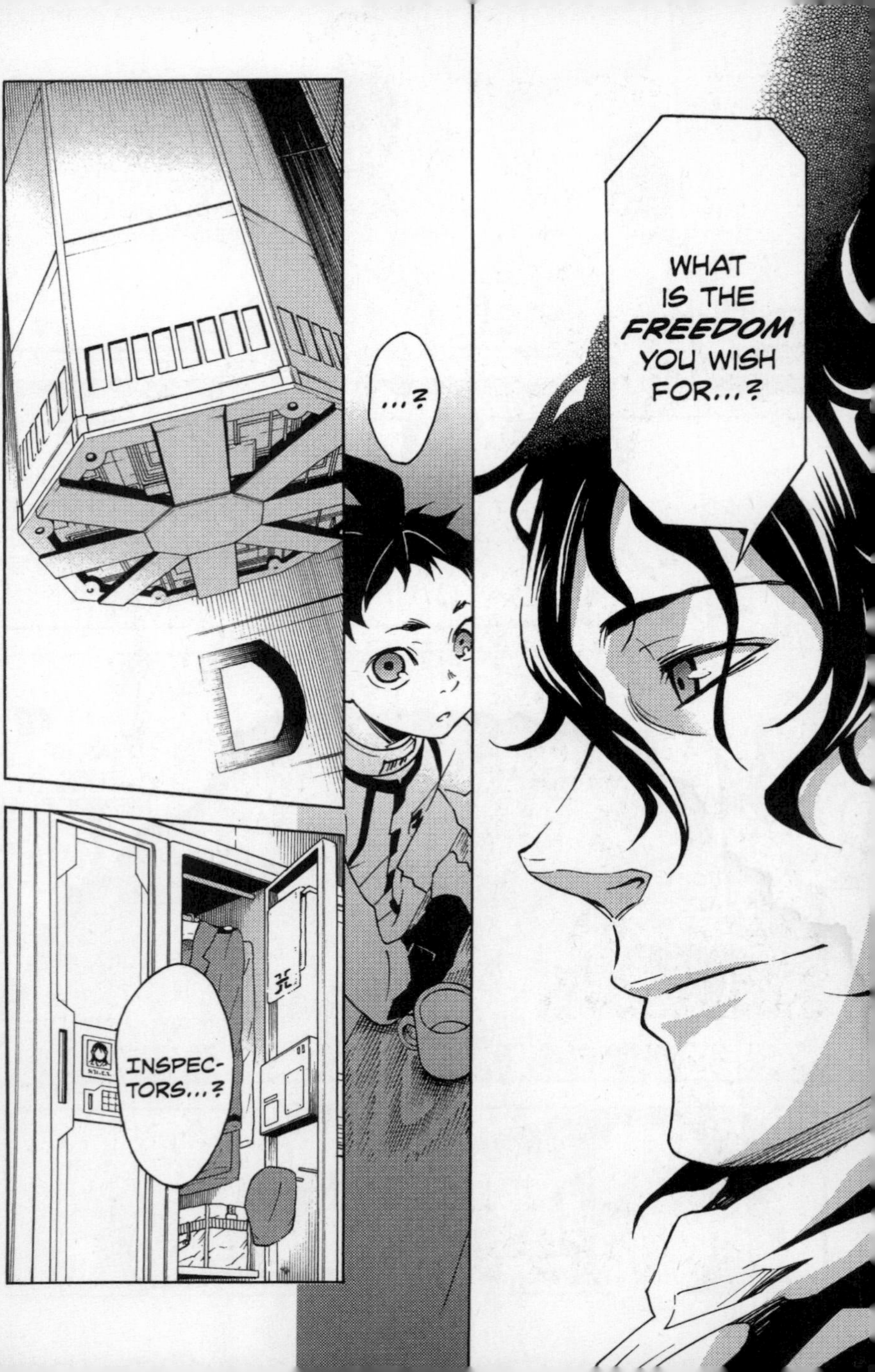
WHAT IS THE FREEDOM YOU WISH FOR...?
...?
INSPECTORS...?

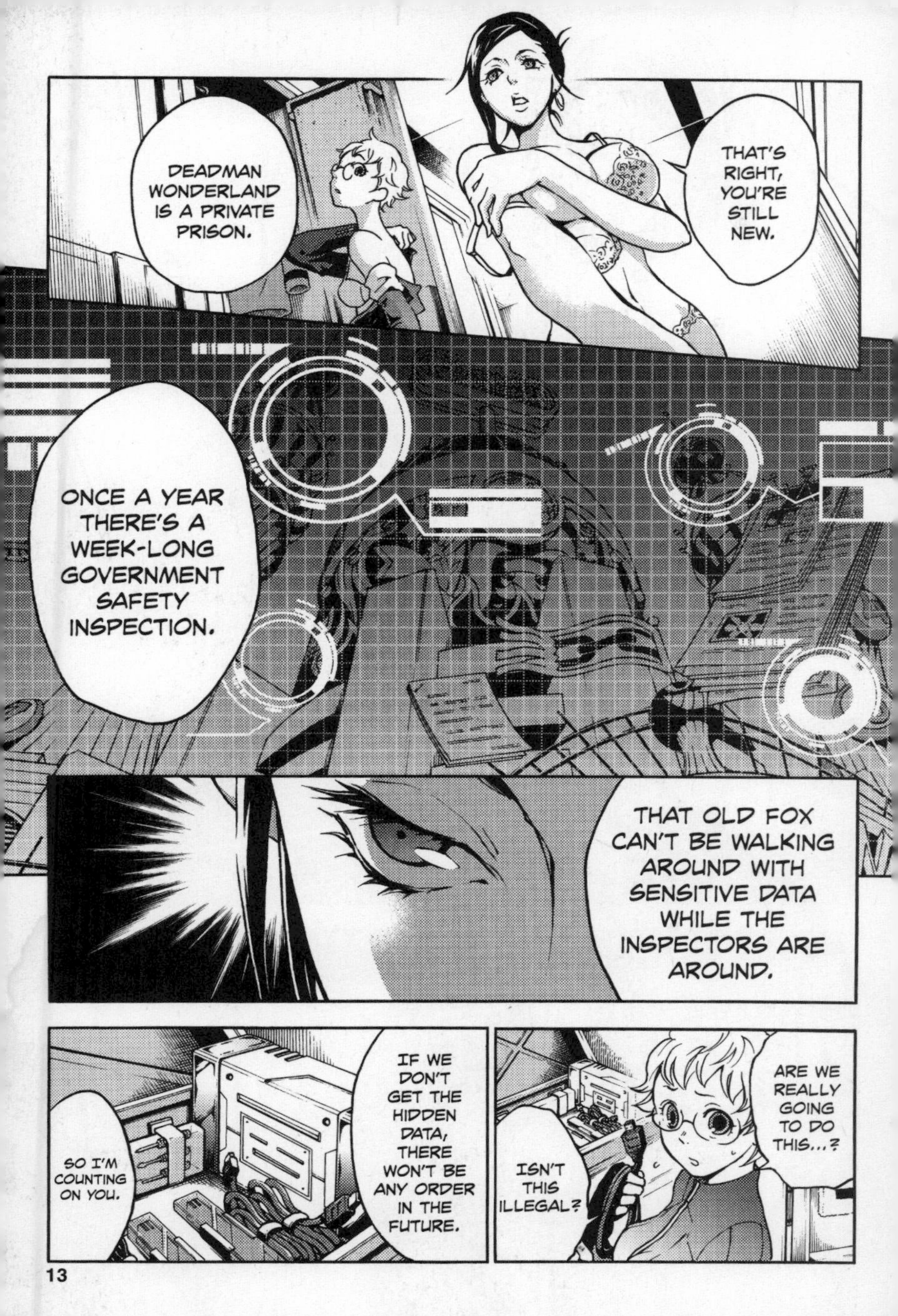
THAT'S RIGHT, YOU'RE STILL NEW.
DEADMAN WONDERLAND IS A PRIVATE PRISON.
ONCE A YEAR THERE'S A WEEK-LONG GOVERNMENT SAFETY INSPECTION.
THAT OLD FOX CAN'T BE WALKING AROUND WITH SENSITIVE DATA WHILE THE INSPECTORS ARE AROUND.
ARE WE REALLY GOING TO DO THIS...?
ISN'T THIS ILLEGAL?
IF WE DON'T GET THE HIDDEN DATA, THERE WON'T BE ANY ORDER IN THE FUTURE.
SO I'M COUNTING ON YOU.

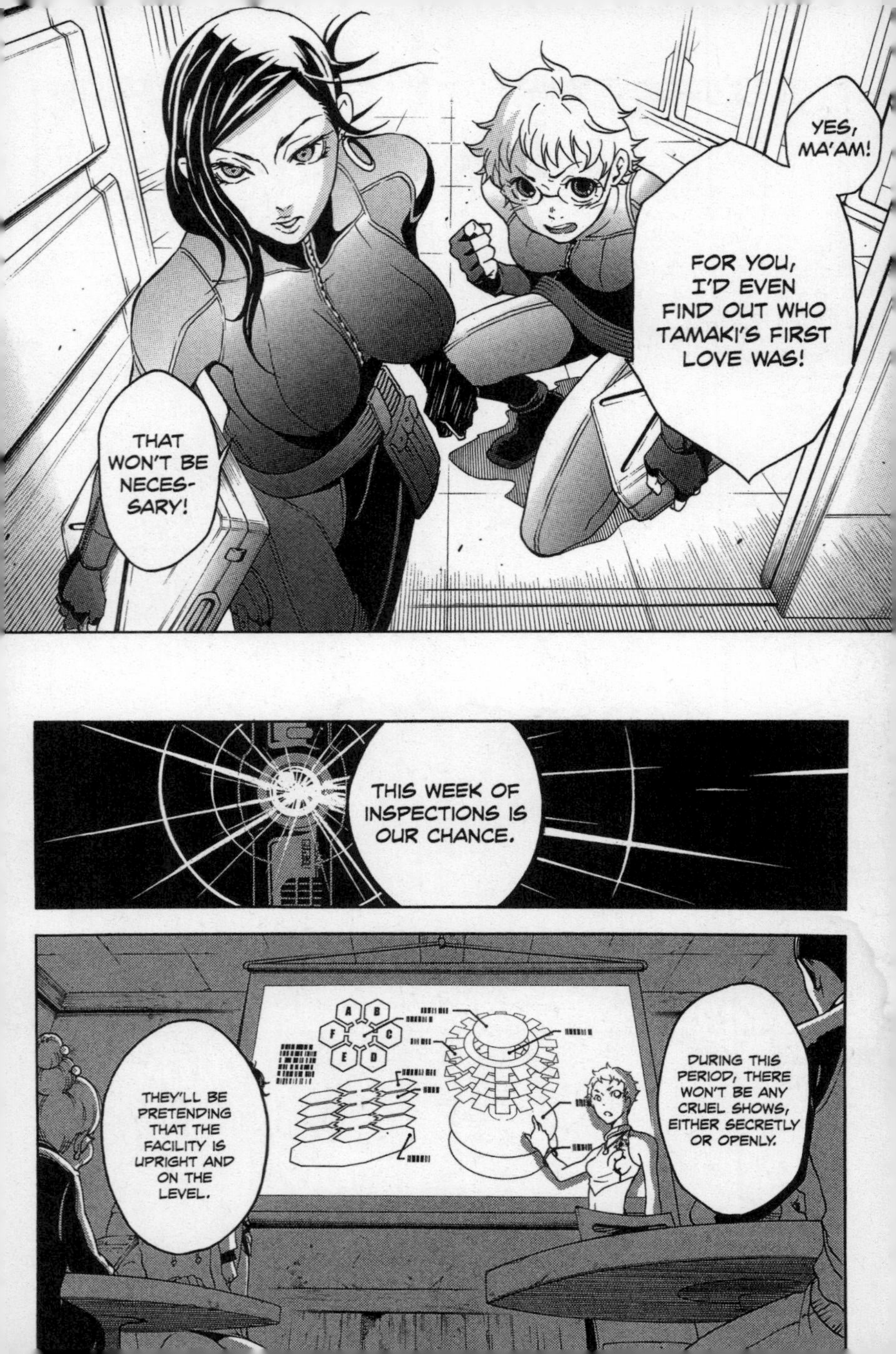
YES, MA'AM!
FOR YOU, I'D EVEN FIND OUT WHO TAMAKI'S FIRST LOVE WAS!
THAT WON'T BE NECES-SARY!
THIS WEEK OF INSPECTIONS IS OUR CHANCE.
DURING THIS PERIOD, THERE WON'T BE ANY CRUEL SHOWS, EITHER SECRETLY OR OPENLY.
THEY'LL BE PRETENDING THAT THE FACILITY IS UPRIGHT AND ON THE LEVEL.

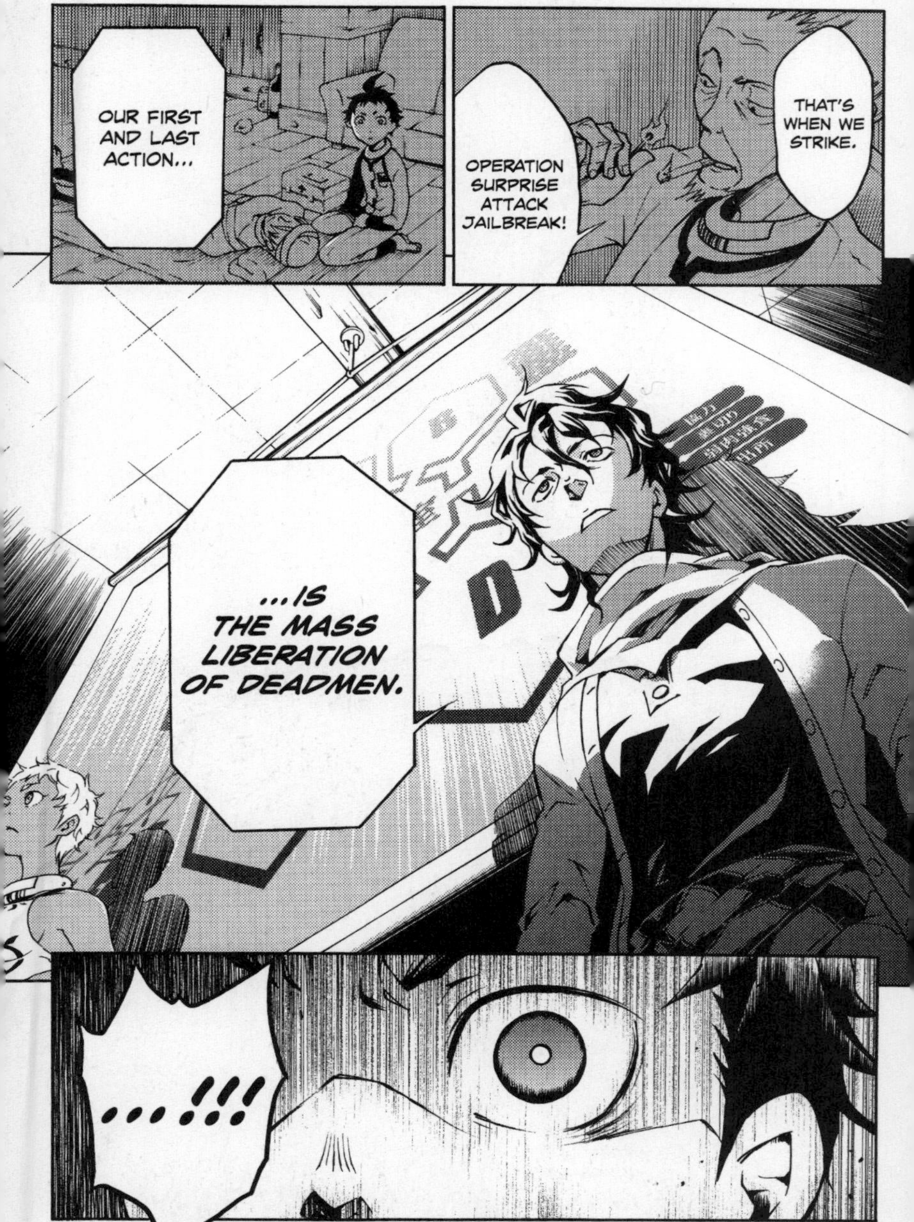
THAT'S WHEN WE STRIKE.
OPERATION SURPRISE ATTACK JAILBREAK!
OUR FIRST AND LAST ACTION...
...IS THE MASS LIBERATION OF DEADMEN.
...!!!

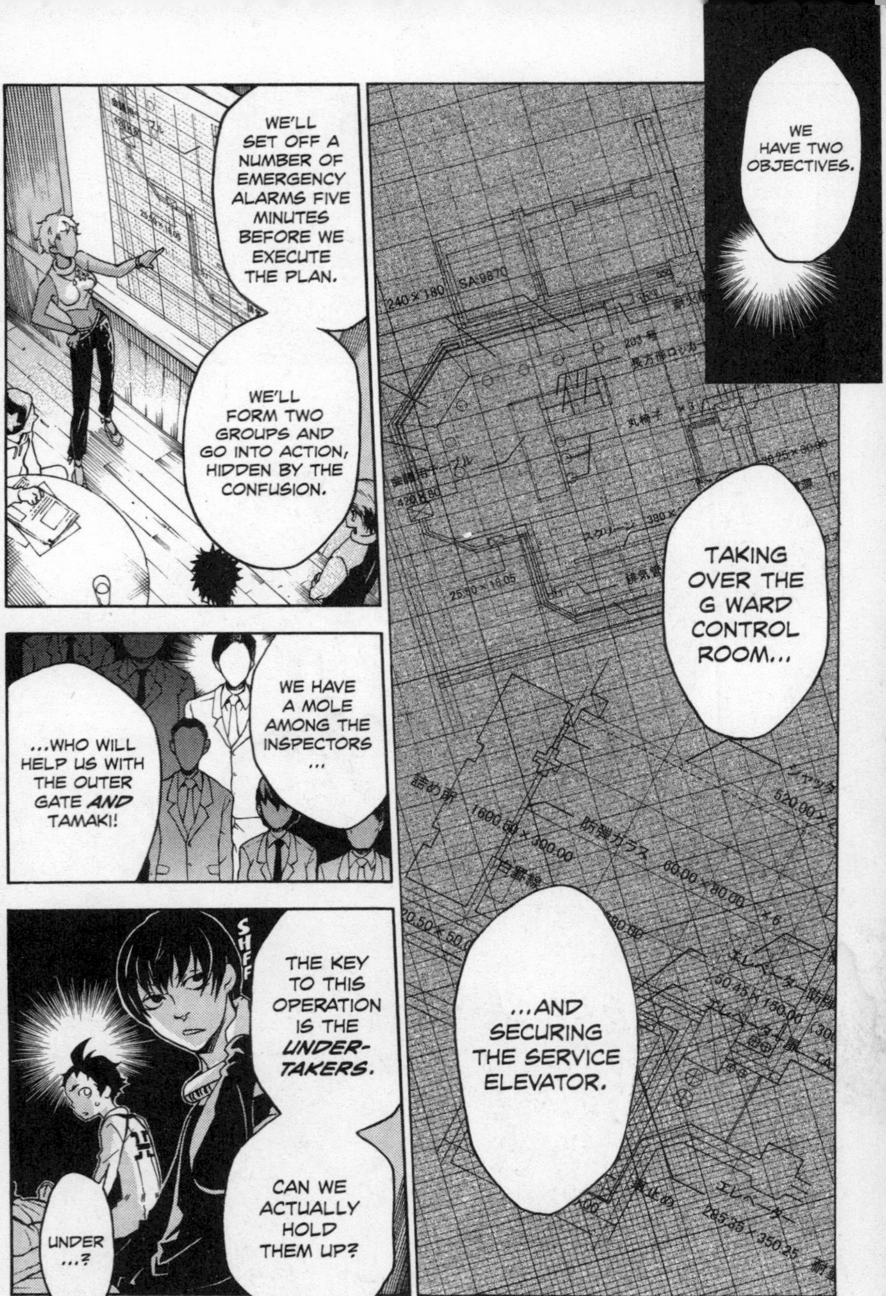
WE HAVE TWO OBJECTIVES.
TAKING OVER THE G WARD CONTROL ROOM...
...AND SECURING THE SERVICE ELEVATOR.
WE'LL SET OFF A NUMBER OF EMERGENCY ALARMS FIVE MINUTES BEFORE WE EXECUTE THE PLAN.
WE'LL FORM TWO GROUPS AND GO INTO ACTION, HIDDEN BY THE CONFUSION.
WE HAVE A MOLE AMONG THE INSPECTORS...
...WHO WILL HELP US WITH THE OUTER GATE *AND* TAMAKI!
SHFF
THE KEY TO THIS OPERATION IS THE ***UNDER-TAKERS***.
CAN WE ACTUALLY HOLD THEM UP?
UNDER...?

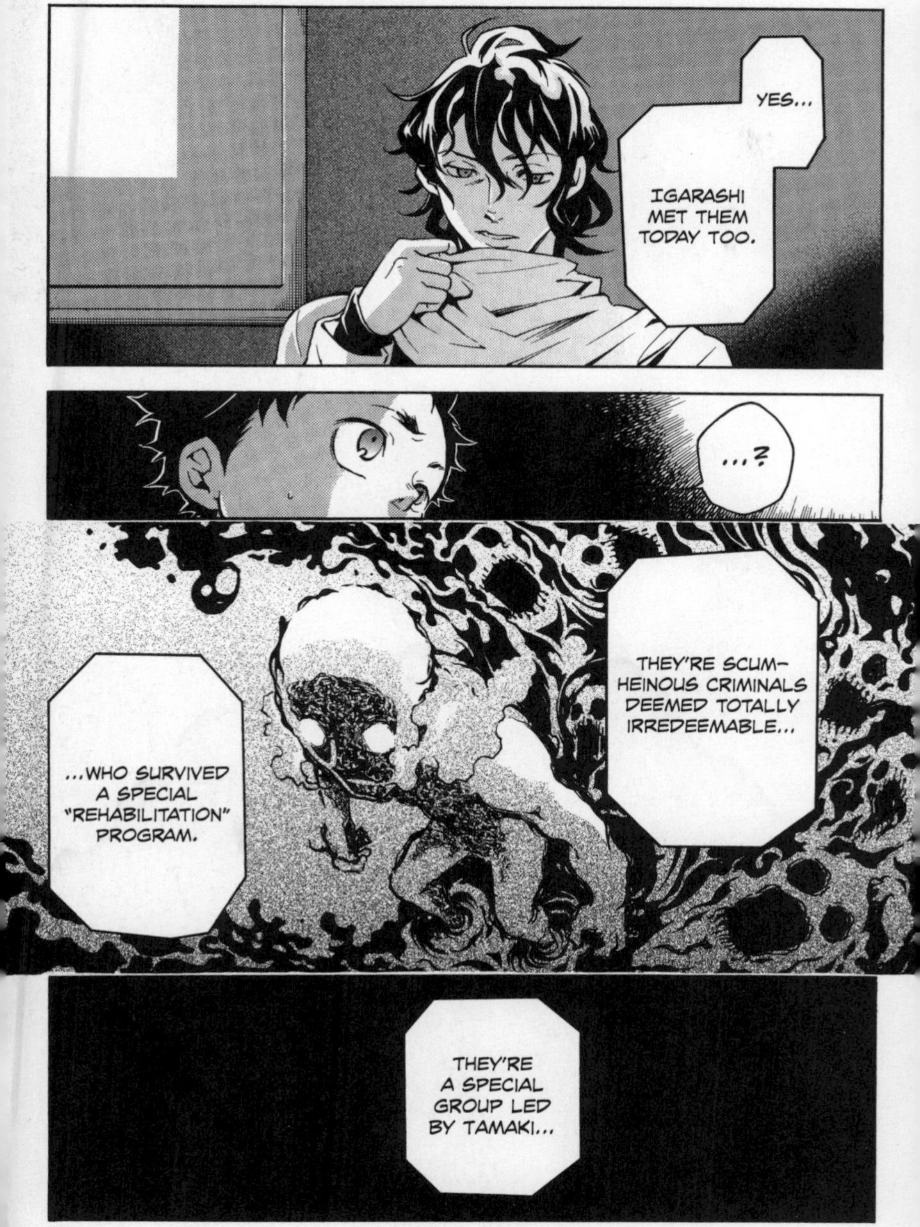
YES...
IGARASHI MET THEM TODAY TOO.
...?
THEY'RE SCUM—HEINOUS CRIMINALS DEEMED TOTALLY IRREDEEMABLE...
...WHO SURVIVED A SPECIAL "REHABILITATION" PROGRAM.
THEY'RE A SPECIAL GROUP LED BY TAMAKI...

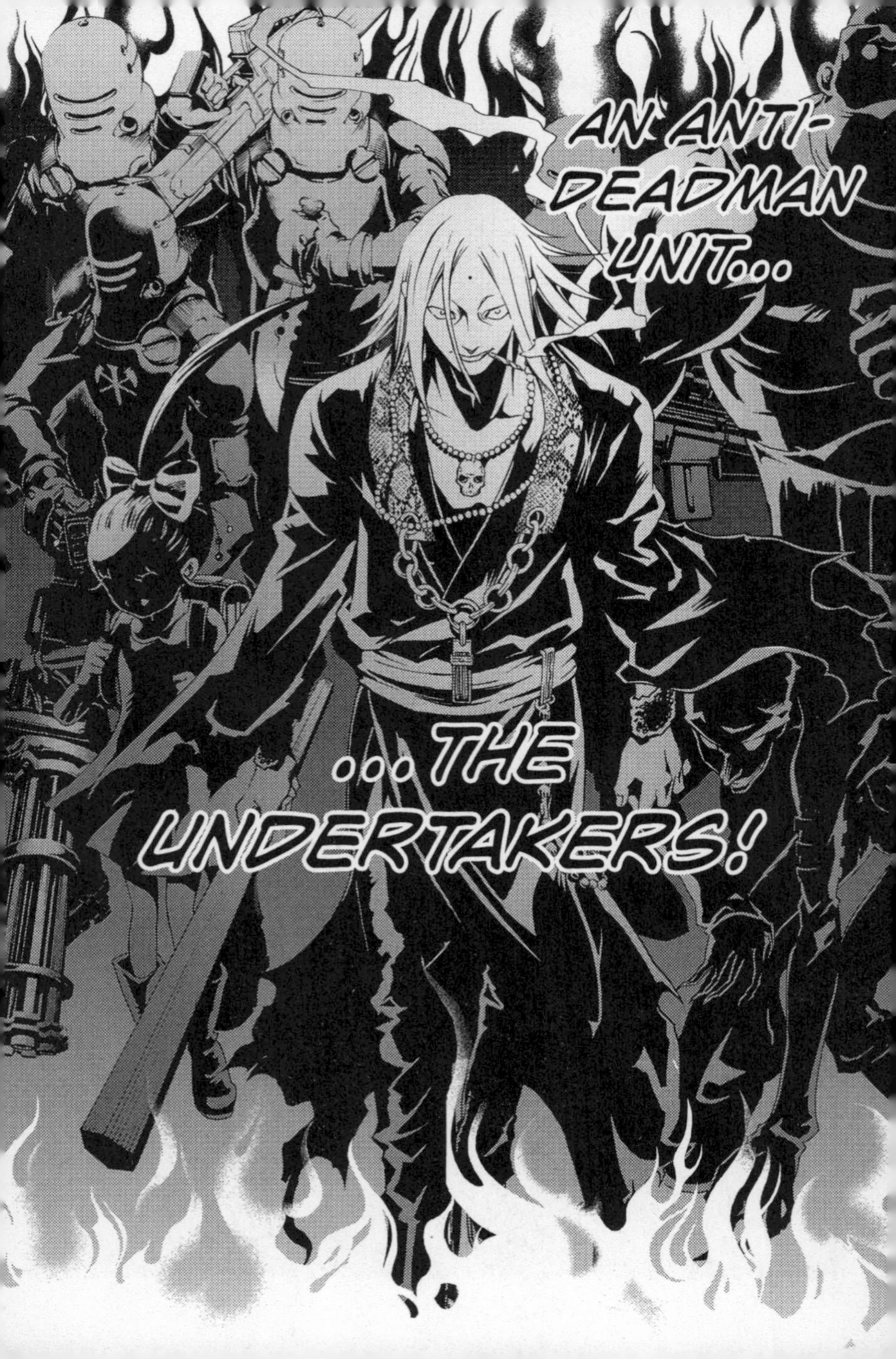
AN ANTI-DEADMAN UNIT...
...THE UNDERTAKERS!

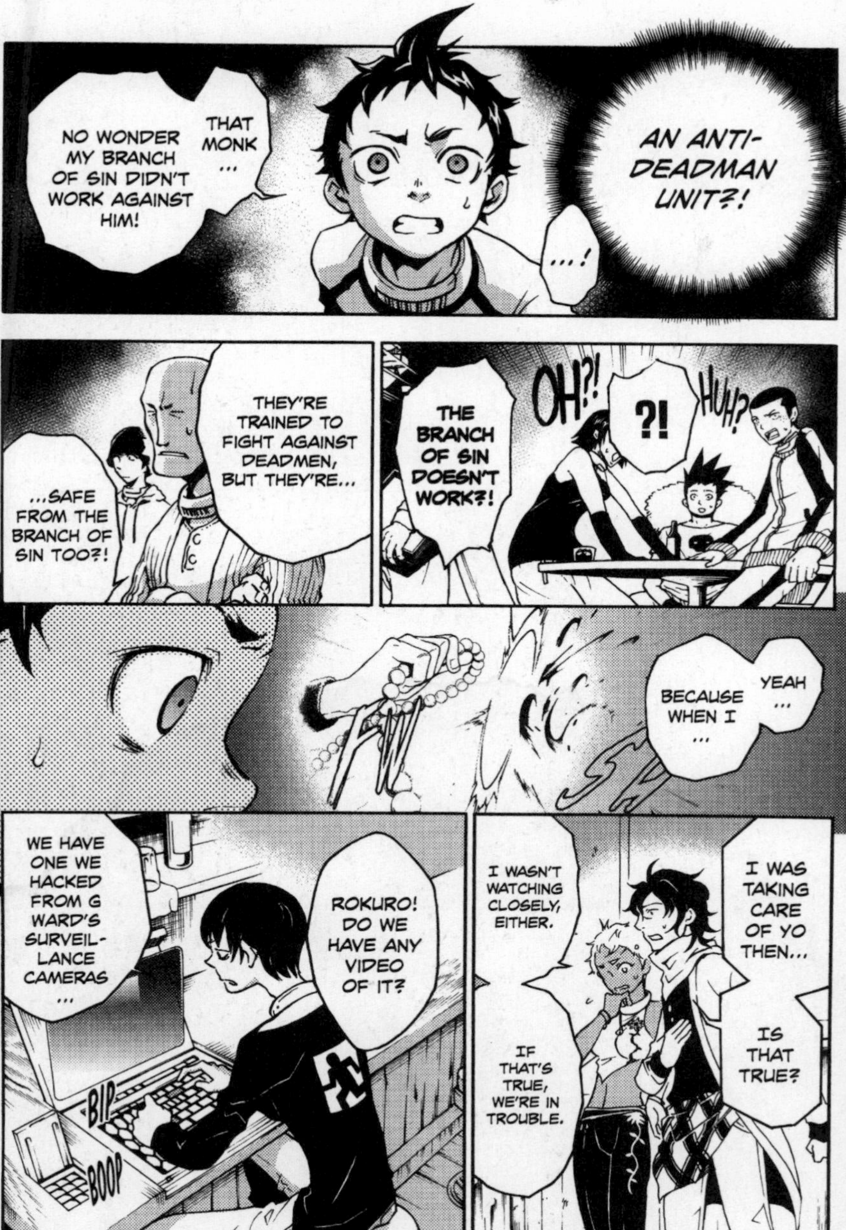
AN ANTI-DEADMAN UNIT?!
...!
THAT MONK ...
NO WONDER MY BRANCH OF SIN DIDN'T WORK AGAINST HIM!
HUH?
?!
OH?!
THE BRANCH OF SIN DOESN'T WORK?!
THEY'RE TRAINED TO FIGHT AGAINST DEADMEN, BUT THEY'RE...
...SAFE FROM THE BRANCH OF SIN TOO?!
YEAH ...
BECAUSE WHEN I ...
I WAS TAKING CARE OF YO THEN...
I WASN'T WATCHING CLOSELY, EITHER.
IS THAT TRUE?
IF THAT'S TRUE, WE'RE IN TROUBLE.
ROKURO! DO WE HAVE ANY VIDEO OF IT?
WE HAVE ONE WE HACKED FROM G WARD'S SURVEIL-LANCE CAMERAS ...
BIP
BOOP

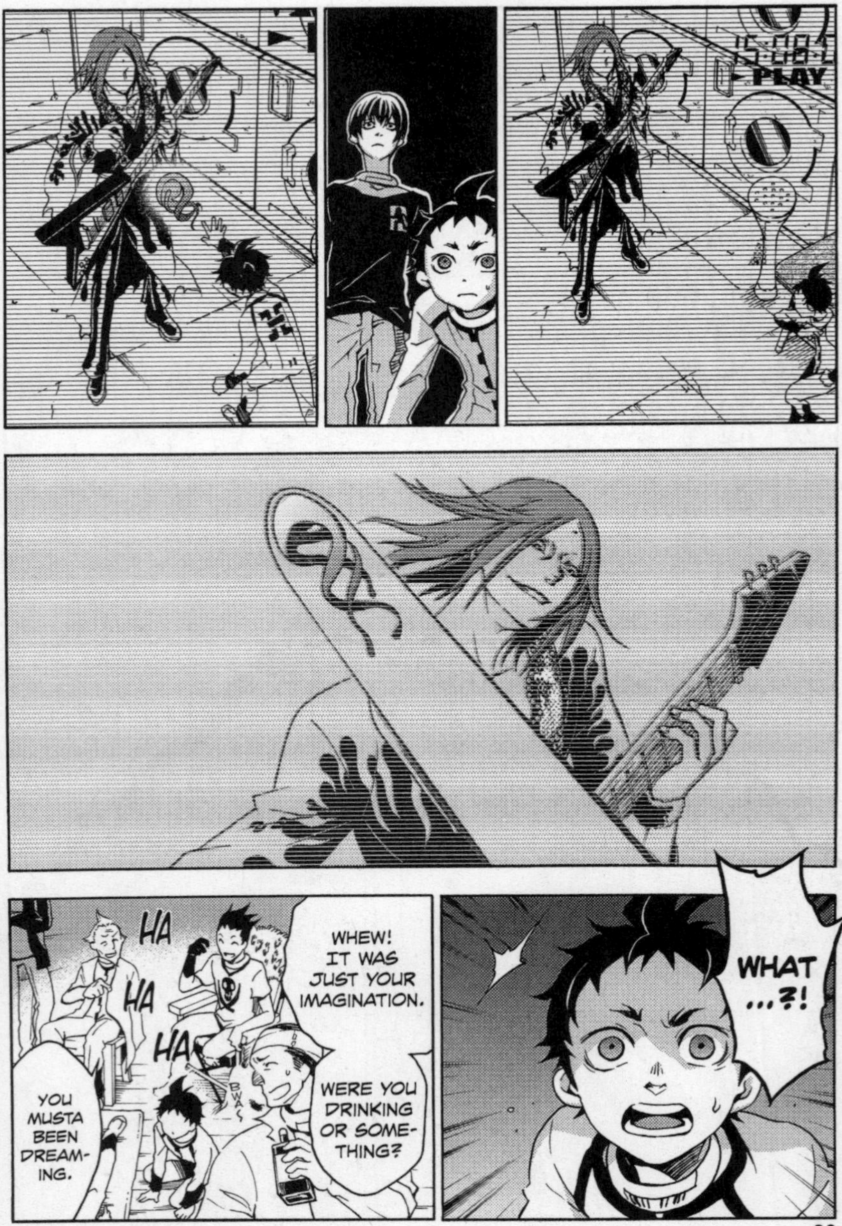
15:08
PLAY
WHAT ...?!
WHEW! IT WAS JUST YOUR IMAGINATION.
HA HA HA
WERE YOU DRINKING OR SOME-THING?
YOU MUSTA BEEN DREAM-ING.

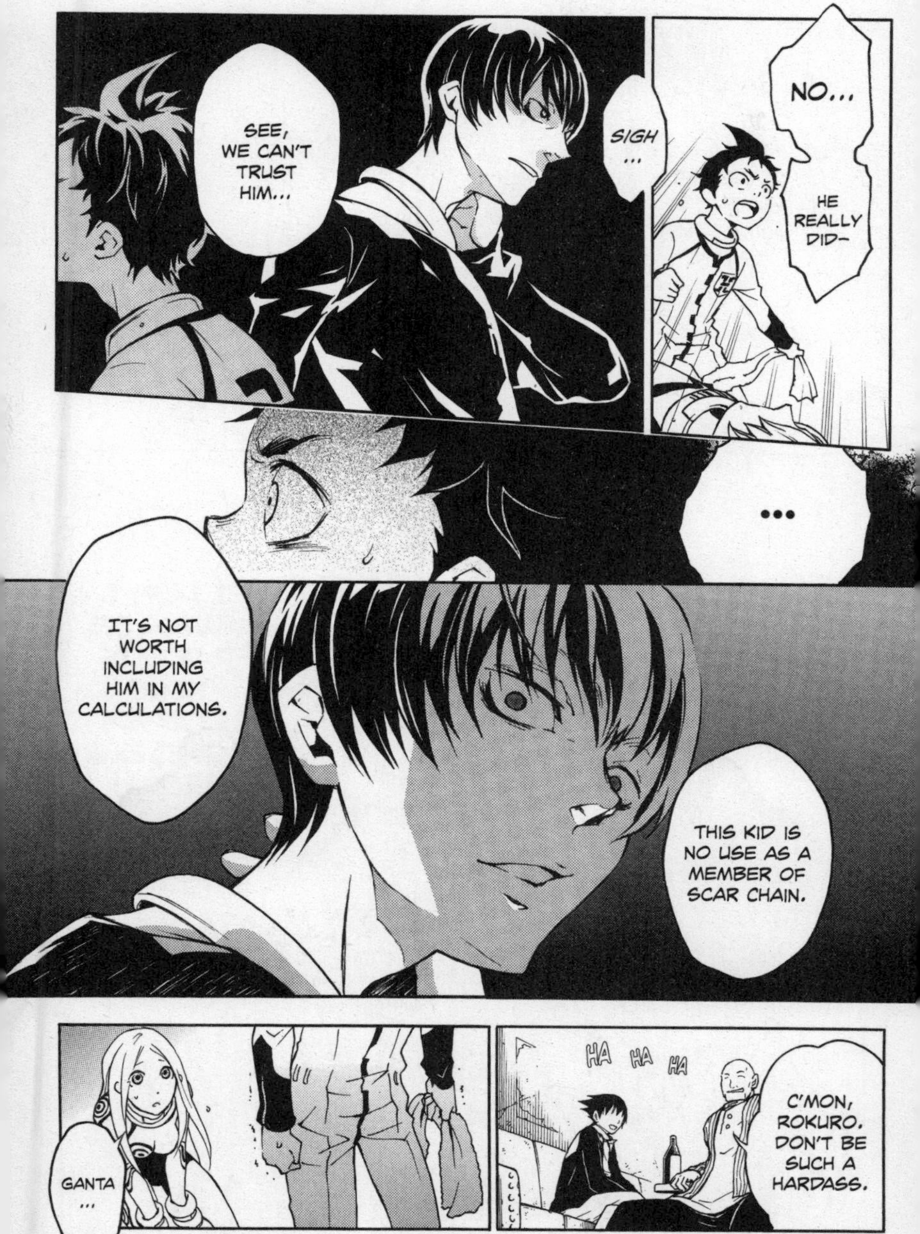
NO...
HE REALLY DID–
SIGH ...
SEE, WE CAN'T TRUST HIM...
...
IT'S NOT WORTH INCLUDING HIM IN MY CALCULATIONS.
THIS KID IS NO USE AS A MEMBER OF SCAR CHAIN.
HA HA HA
C'MON, ROKURO. DON'T BE SUCH A HARDASS.
GANTA ...

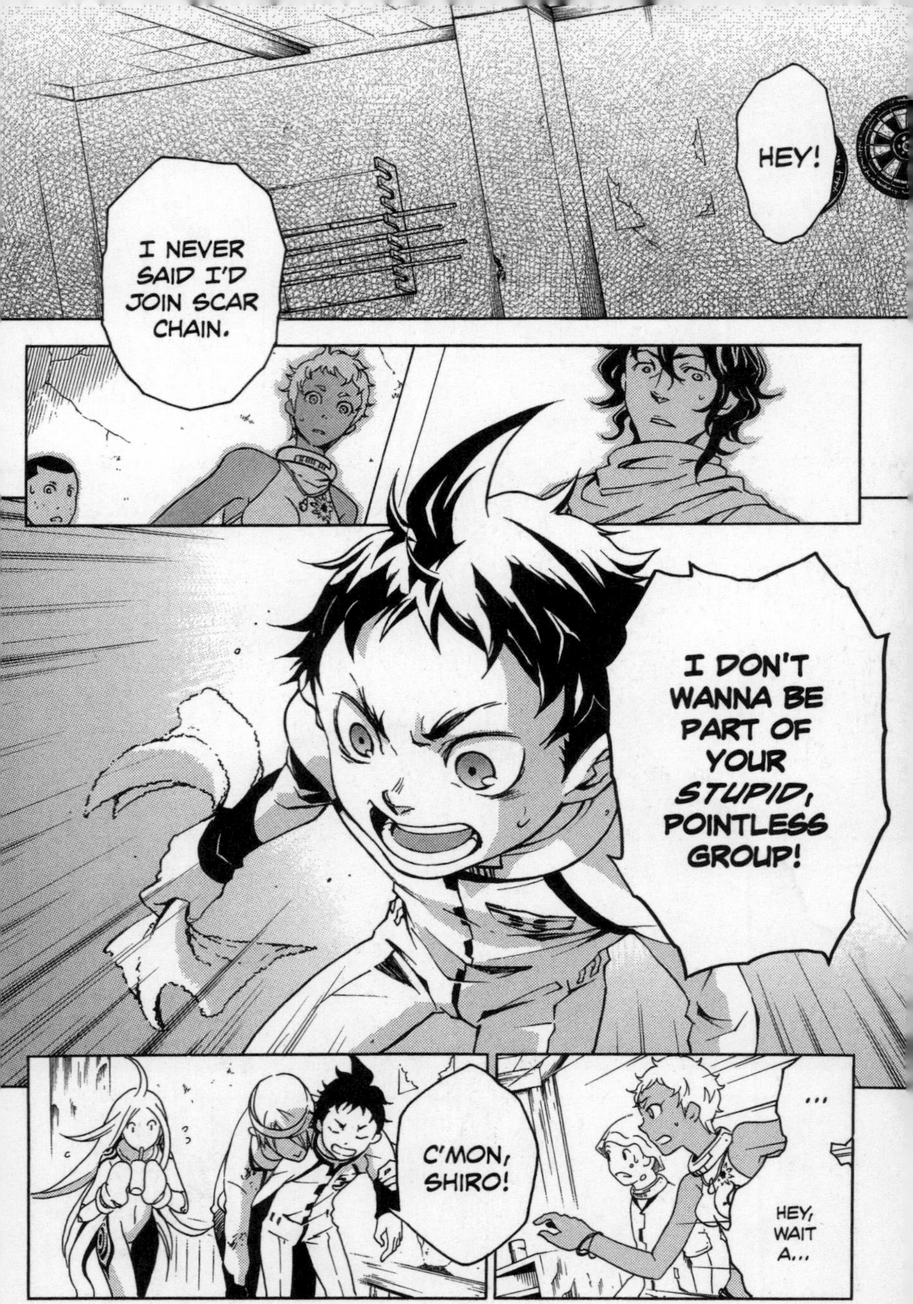
HEY!
I NEVER SAID I'D JOIN SCAR CHAIN.
I DON'T WANNA BE PART OF YOUR *STUPID*, POINTLESS GROUP!
...
HEY, WAIT A...
C'MON, SHIRO!

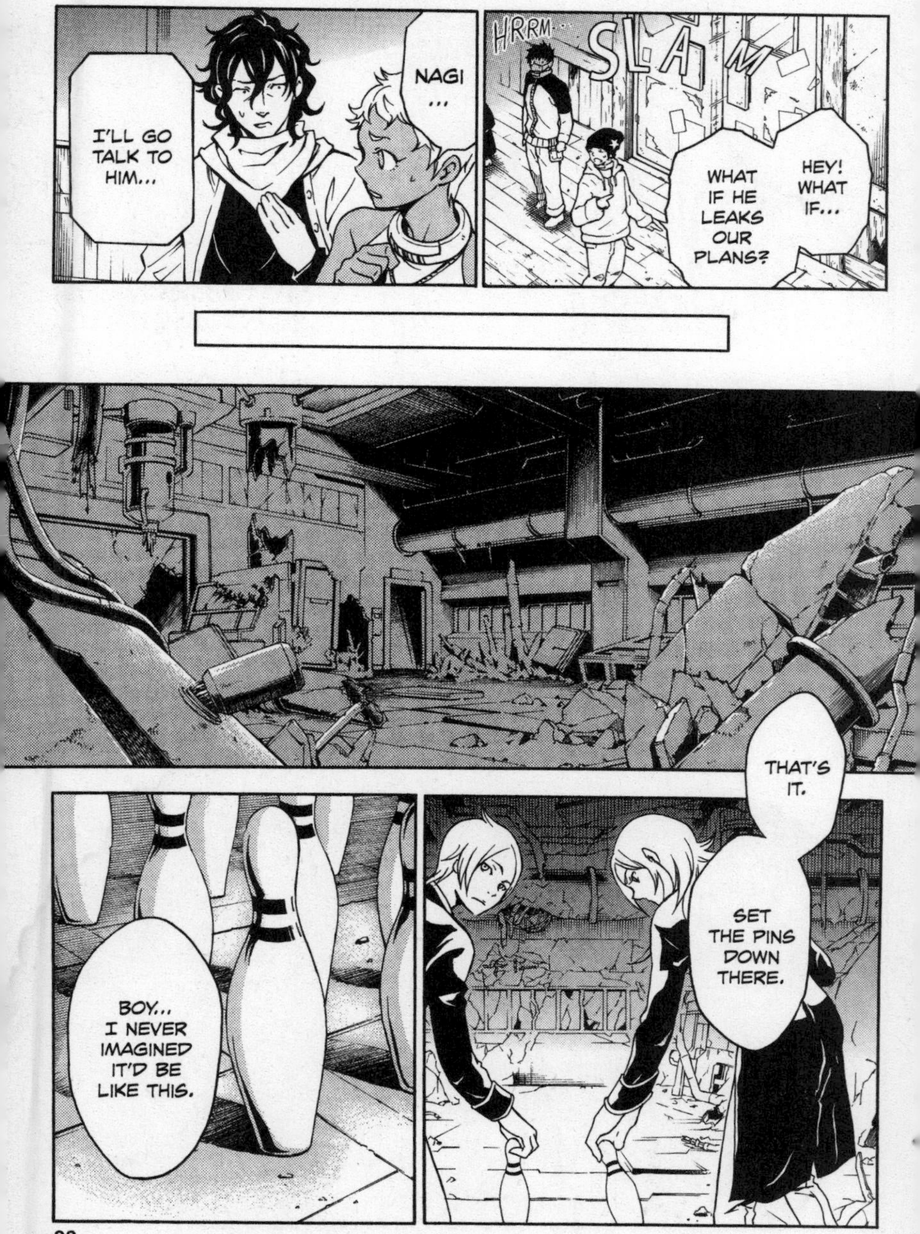
HRRM...
SLAM
HEY! WHAT IF...
WHAT IF HE LEAKS OUR PLANS?
NAGI ...
I'LL GO TALK TO HIM...
THAT'S IT.
SET THE PINS DOWN THERE.
BOY... I NEVER IMAGINED IT'D BE LIKE THIS.

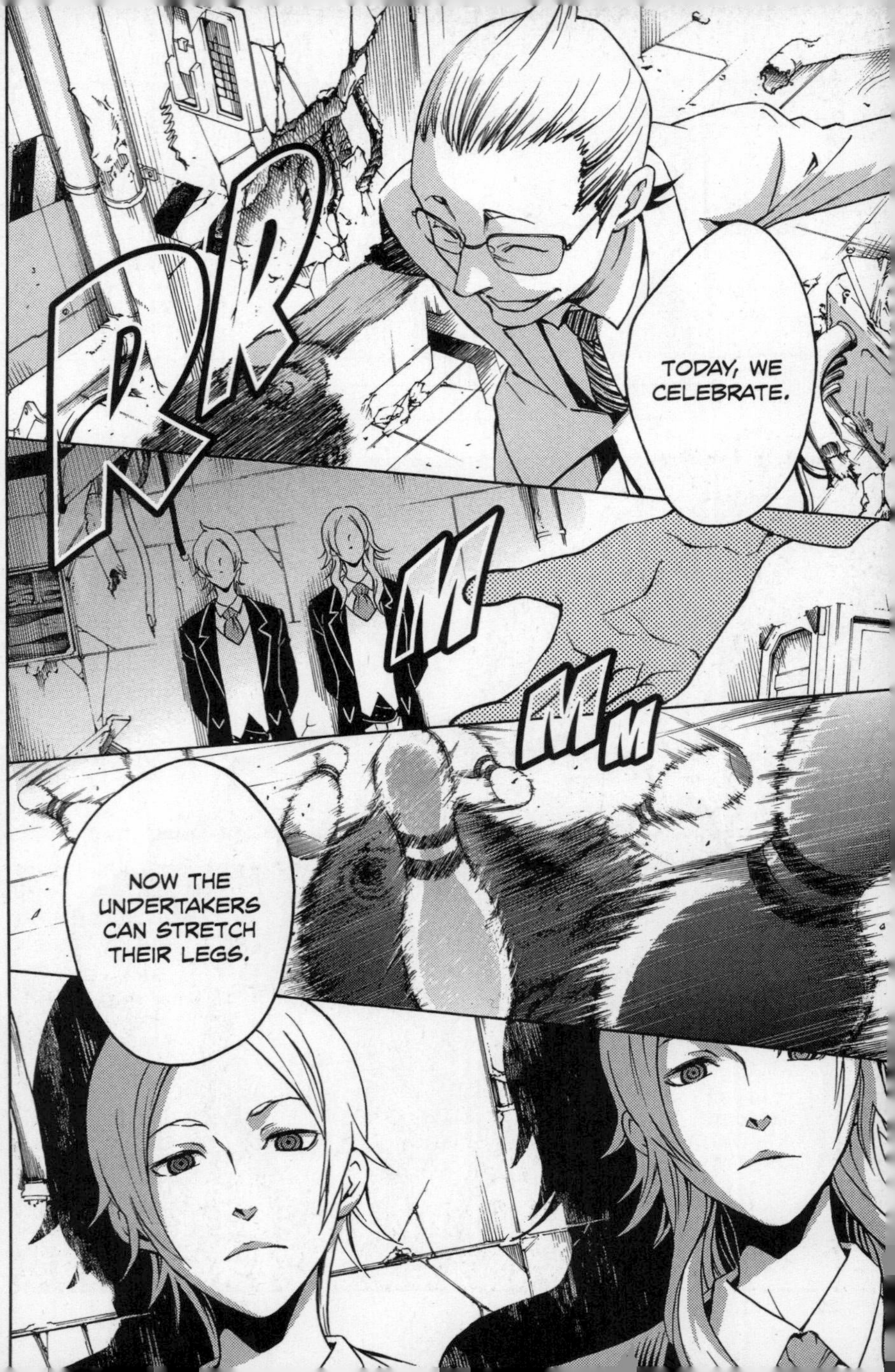
TODAY, WE CELEBRATE.
RRMMMM
NOW THE UNDERTAKERS CAN STRETCH THEIR LEGS.

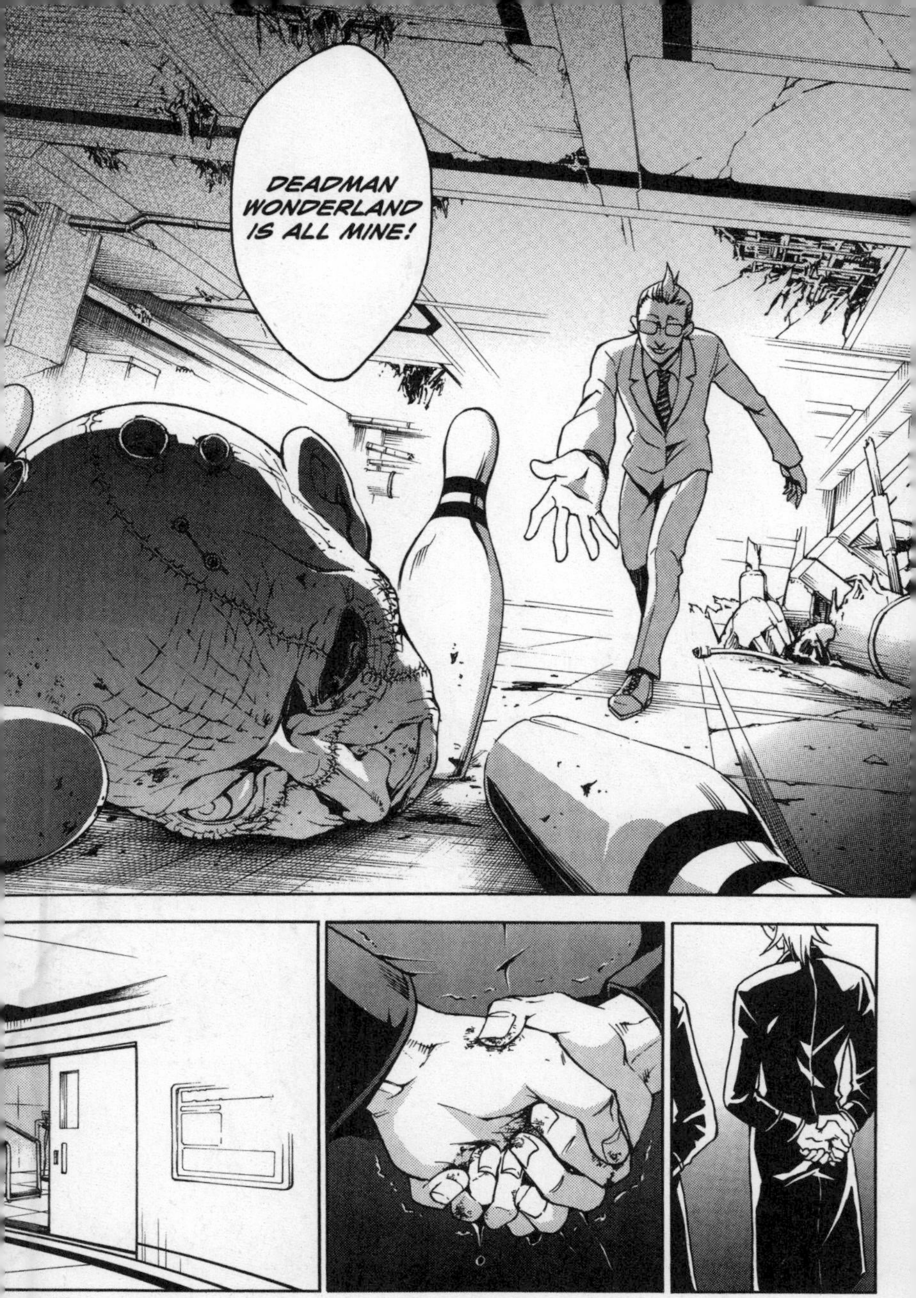
DEADMAN WONDERLAND IS ALL MINE!

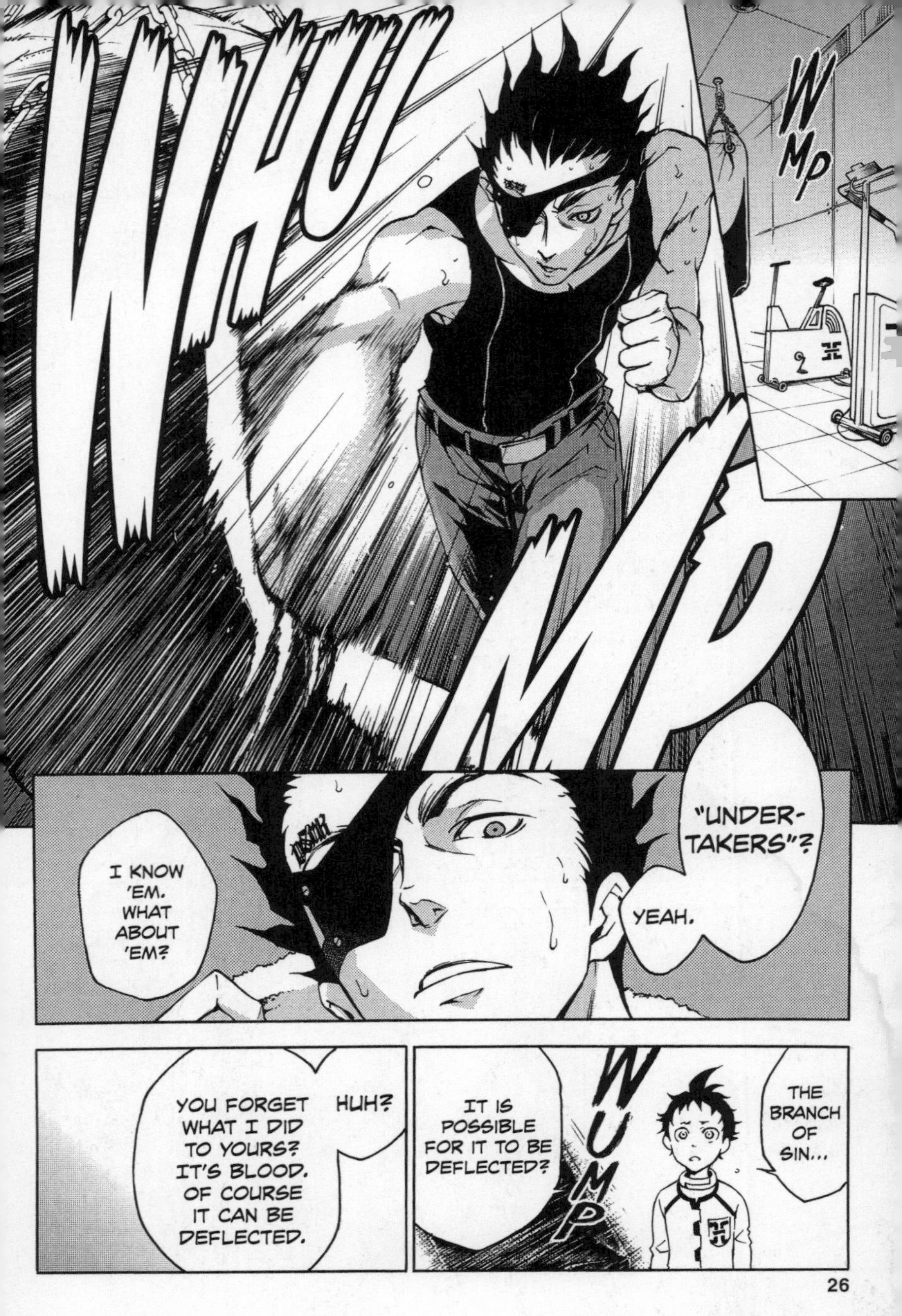
WMP
WHOMP
"UNDER-TAKERS"?
YEAH.
I KNOW 'EM. WHAT ABOUT 'EM?
THE BRANCH OF SIN...
WUMP
IT IS POSSIBLE FOR IT TO BE DEFLECTED?
HUH?
YOU FORGET WHAT I DID TO YOURS? IT'S BLOOD. OF COURSE IT CAN BE DEFLECTED.

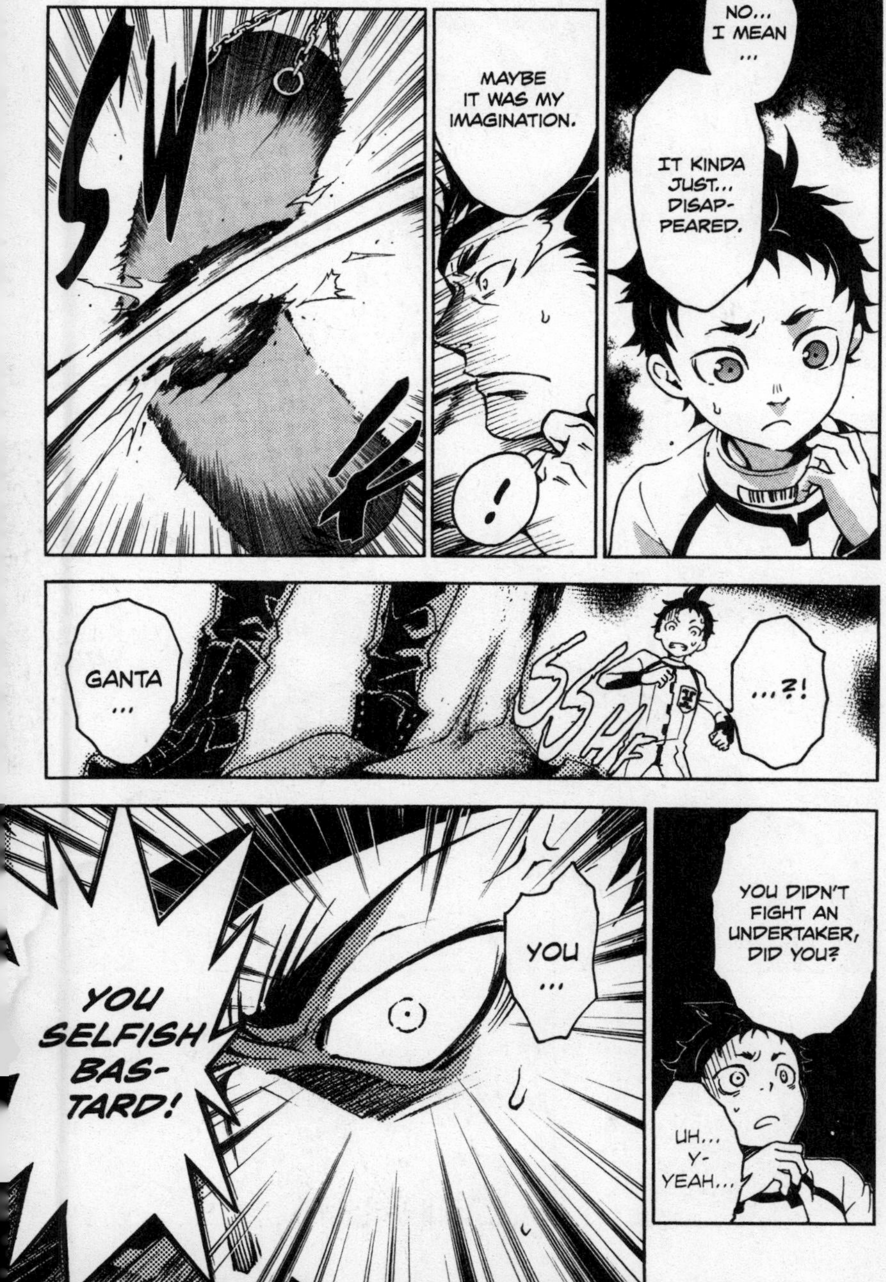
NO... I MEAN ...
IT KINDA JUST... DISAP-PEARED.
MAYBE IT WAS MY IMAGINATION.
!
...?!
GANTA ...
YOU DIDN'T FIGHT AN UNDERTAKER, DID YOU?
UH... Y-YEAH...
YOU ...
YOU SELFISH BAS-TARD!

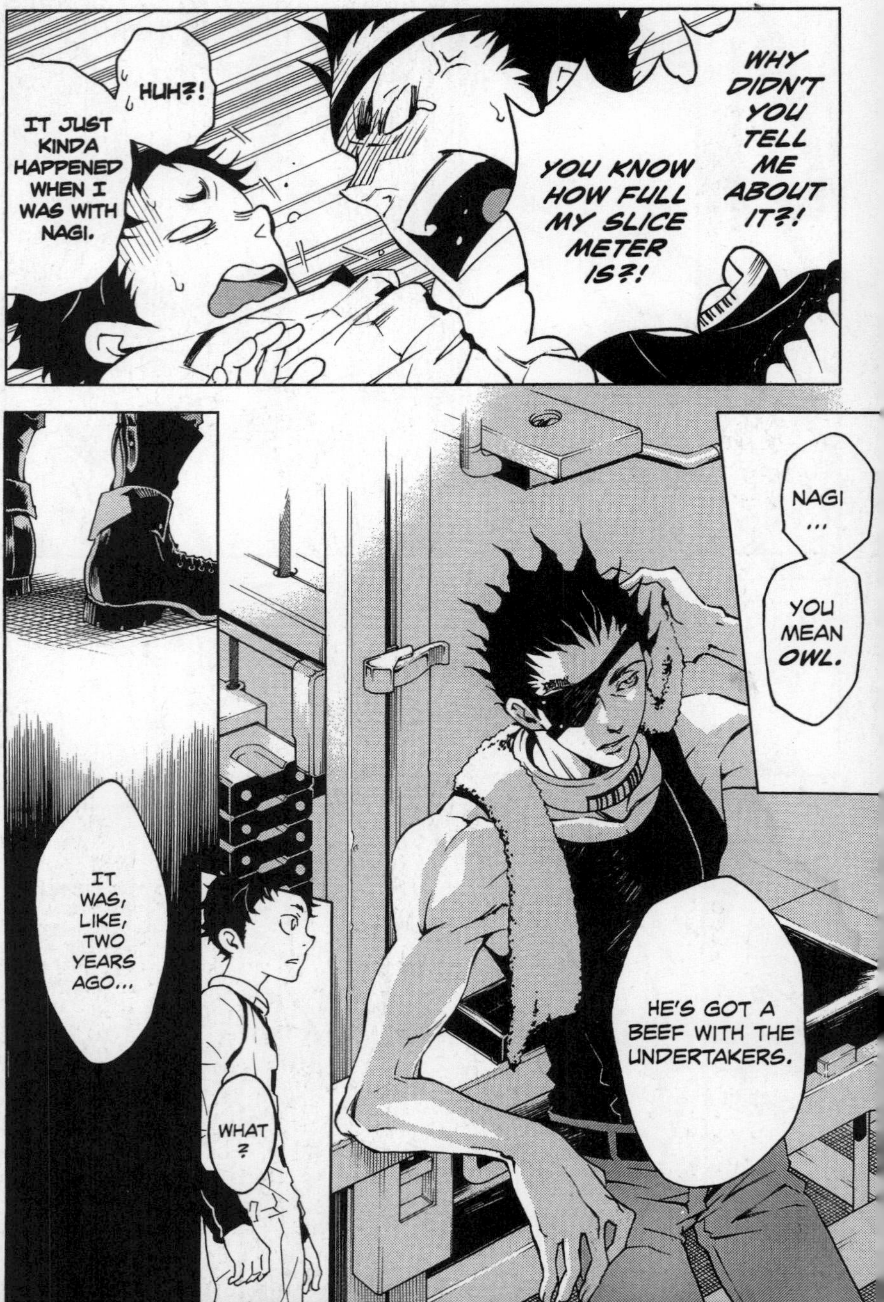
WHY DIDN'T YOU TELL ME ABOUT IT?!
YOU KNOW HOW FULL MY SLICE METER IS?!
HUH?!
IT JUST KINDA HAPPENED WHEN I WAS WITH NAGI.
NAGI...
YOU MEAN OWL.
HE'S GOT A BEEF WITH THE UNDERTAKERS.
IT WAS, LIKE, TWO YEARS AGO...
WHAT?

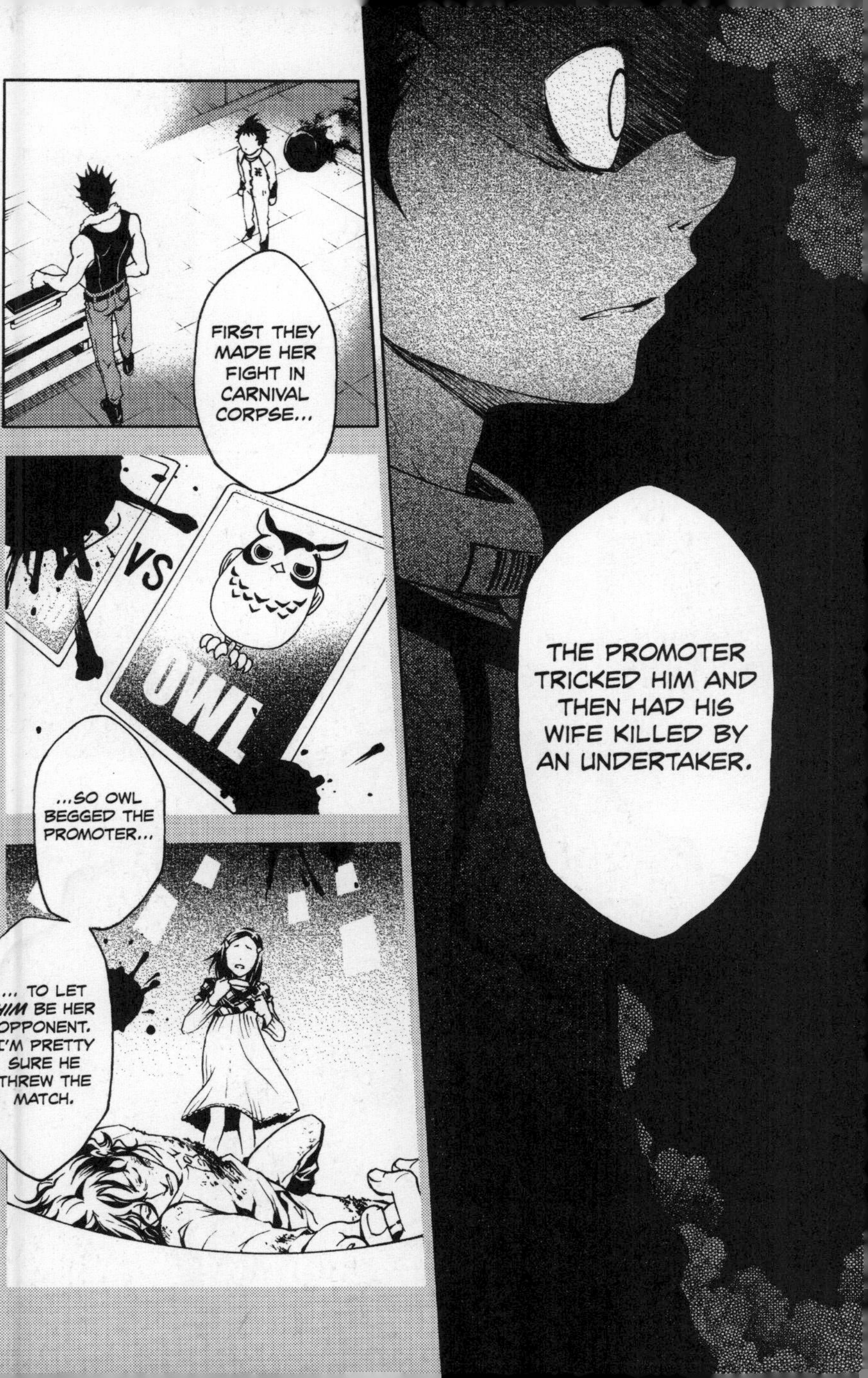
THE PROMOTER TRICKED HIM AND THEN HAD HIS WIFE KILLED BY AN UNDERTAKER.
FIRST THEY MADE HER FIGHT IN CARNIVAL CORPSE...
VS
OWL
...SO OWL BEGGED THE PROMOTER...
... TO LET *HIM* BE HER OPPONENT. I'M PRETTY SURE HE THREW THE MATCH.

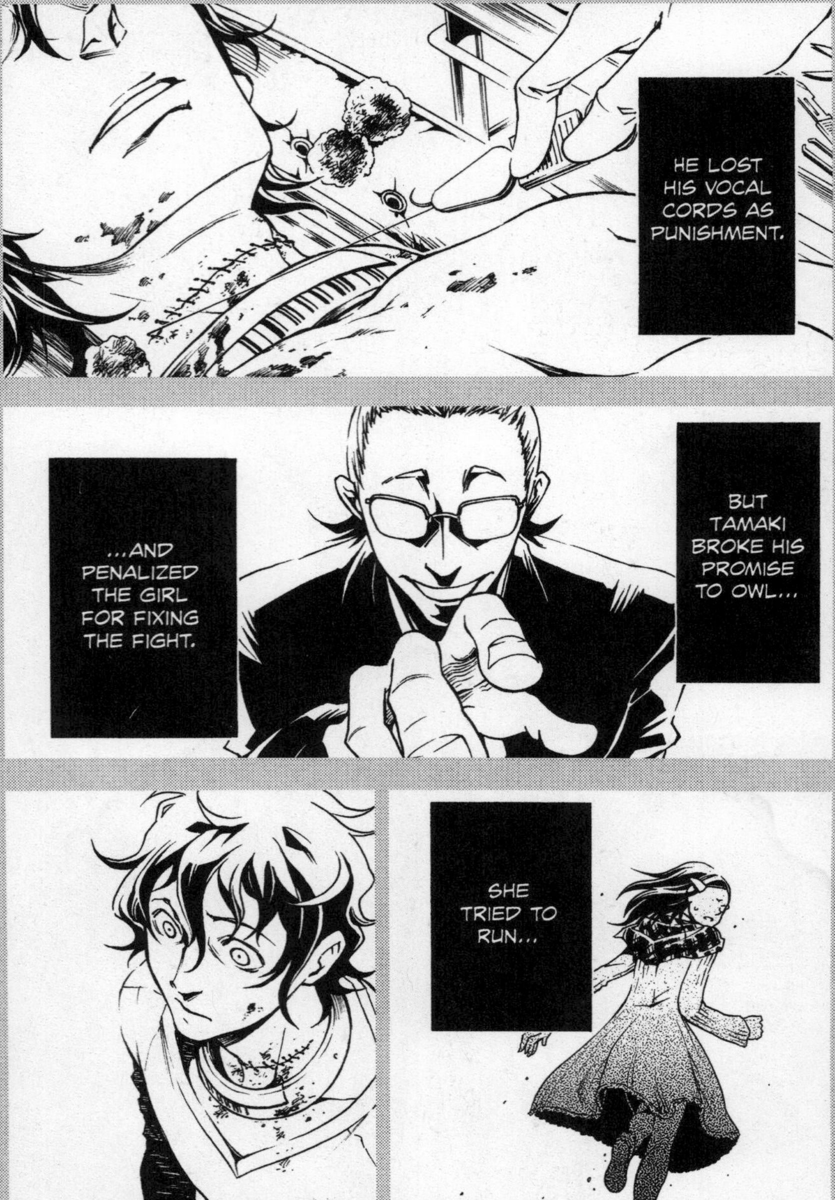
HE LOST HIS VOCAL CORDS AS PUNISHMENT.
BUT TAMAKI BROKE HIS PROMISE TO OWL...
...AND PENALIZED THE GIRL FOR FIXING THE FIGHT.
SHE TRIED TO RUN...

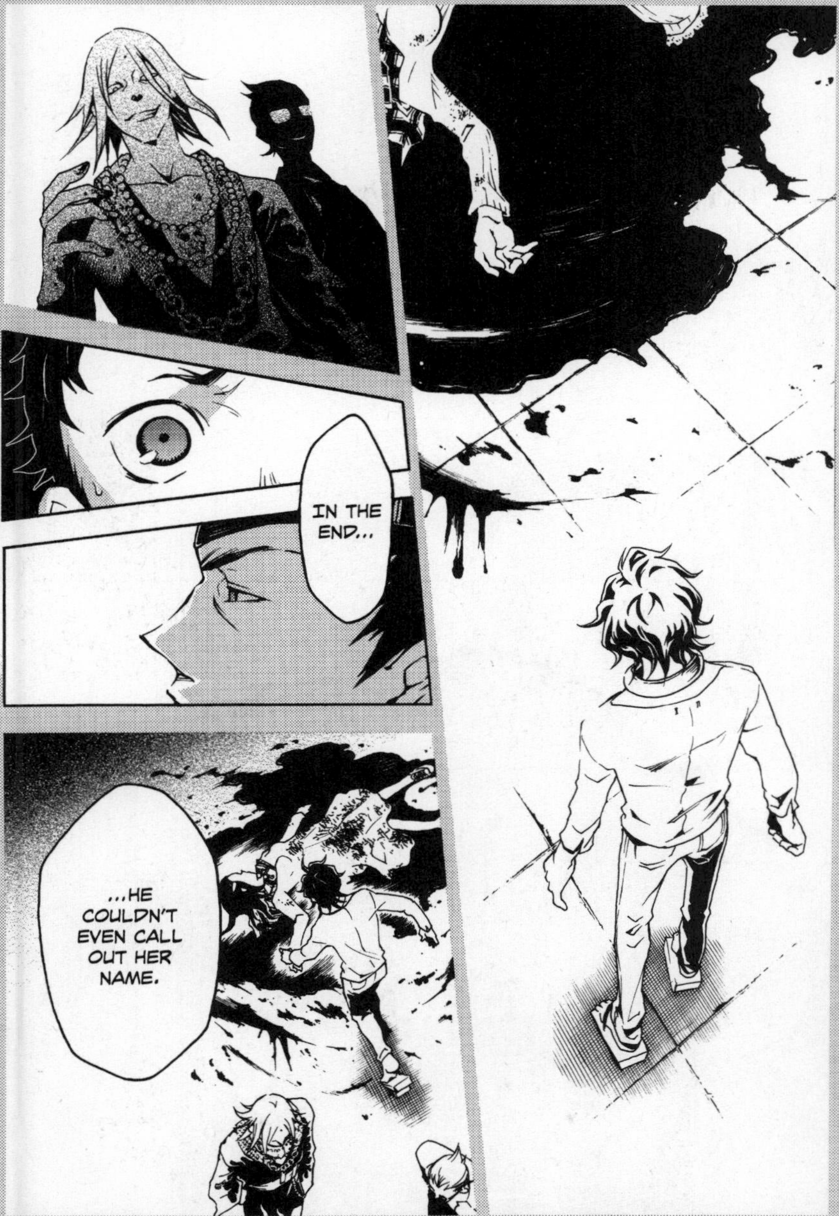
IN THE END...
...HE COULDN'T EVEN CALL OUT HER NAME.

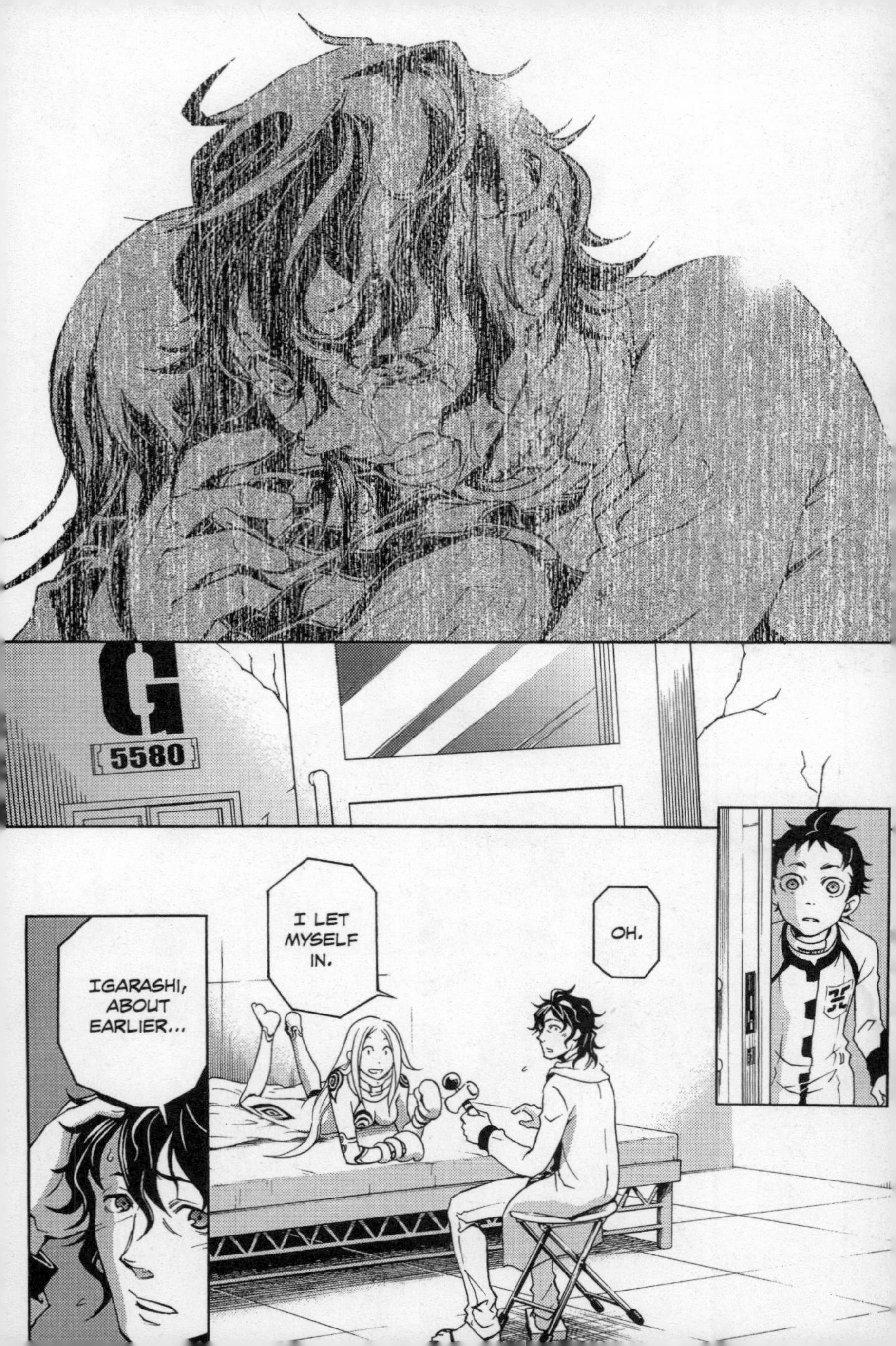
G
5580
OH.
I LET MYSELF IN.
IGARASHI, ABOUT EARLIER...

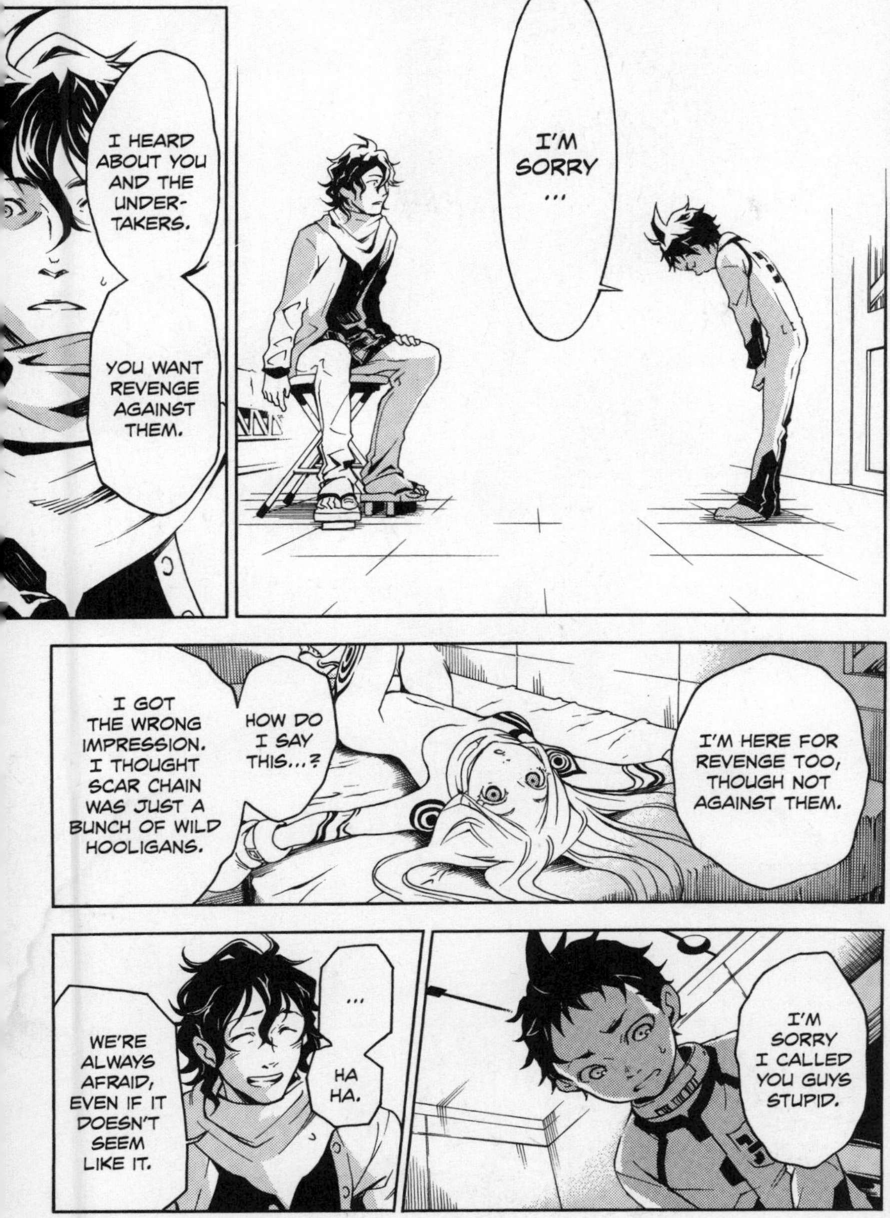
I'M SORRY ...
I HEARD ABOUT YOU AND THE UNDER-TAKERS.
YOU WANT REVENGE AGAINST THEM.
I'M HERE FOR REVENGE TOO, THOUGH NOT AGAINST THEM.
HOW DO I SAY THIS...?
I GOT THE WRONG IMPRESSION. I THOUGHT SCAR CHAIN WAS JUST A BUNCH OF WILD HOOLIGANS.
I'M SORRY I CALLED YOU GUYS STUPID.
...
HA HA.
WE'RE ALWAYS AFRAID, EVEN IF IT DOESN'T SEEM LIKE IT.

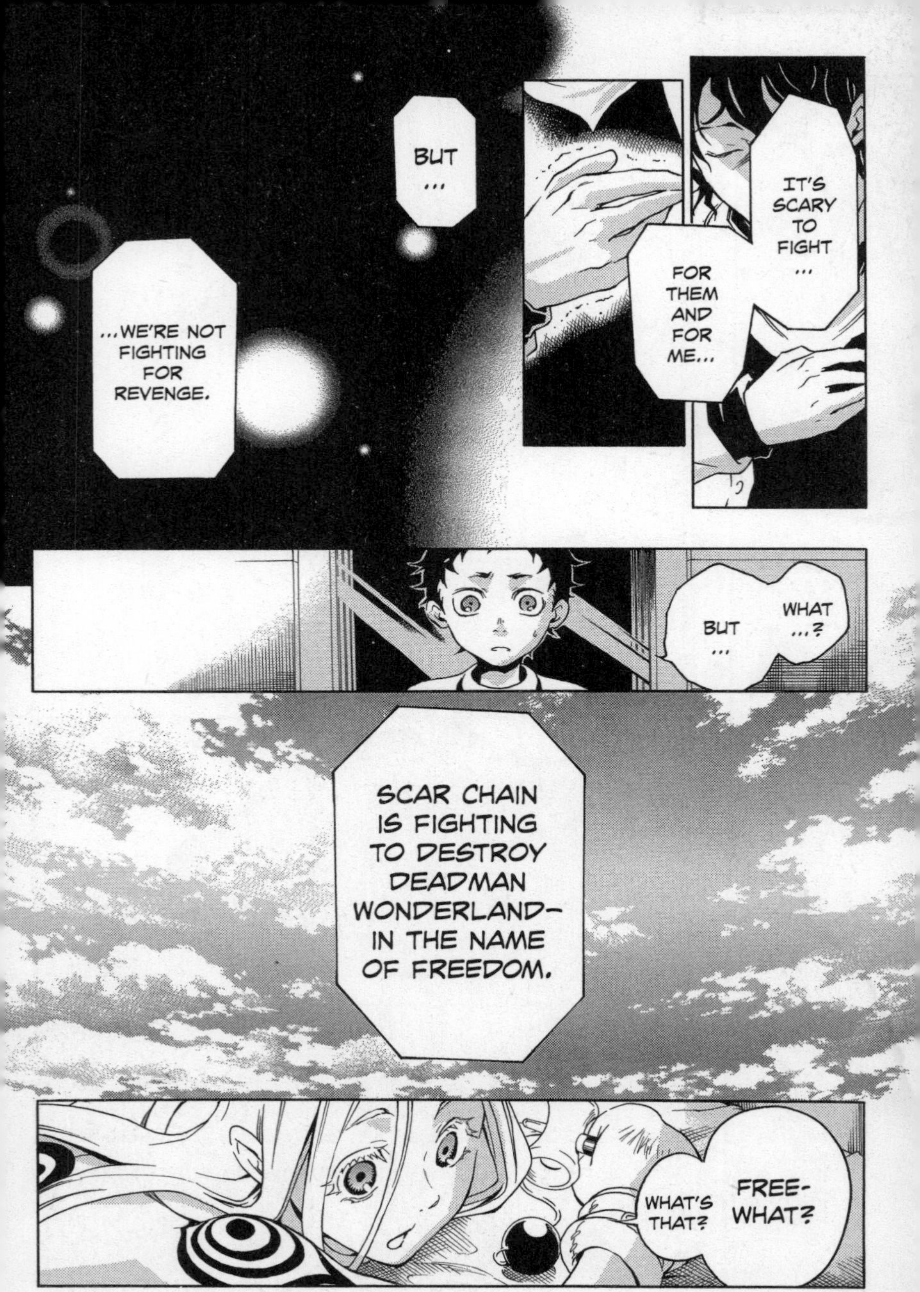
IT'S SCARY TO FIGHT...
FOR THEM AND FOR ME...
BUT...
...WE'RE NOT FIGHTING FOR REVENGE.
WHAT...?
BUT...
SCAR CHAIN IS FIGHTING TO DESTROY DEADMAN WONDERLAND—IN THE NAME OF FREEDOM.
FREE-WHAT?
WHAT'S THAT?

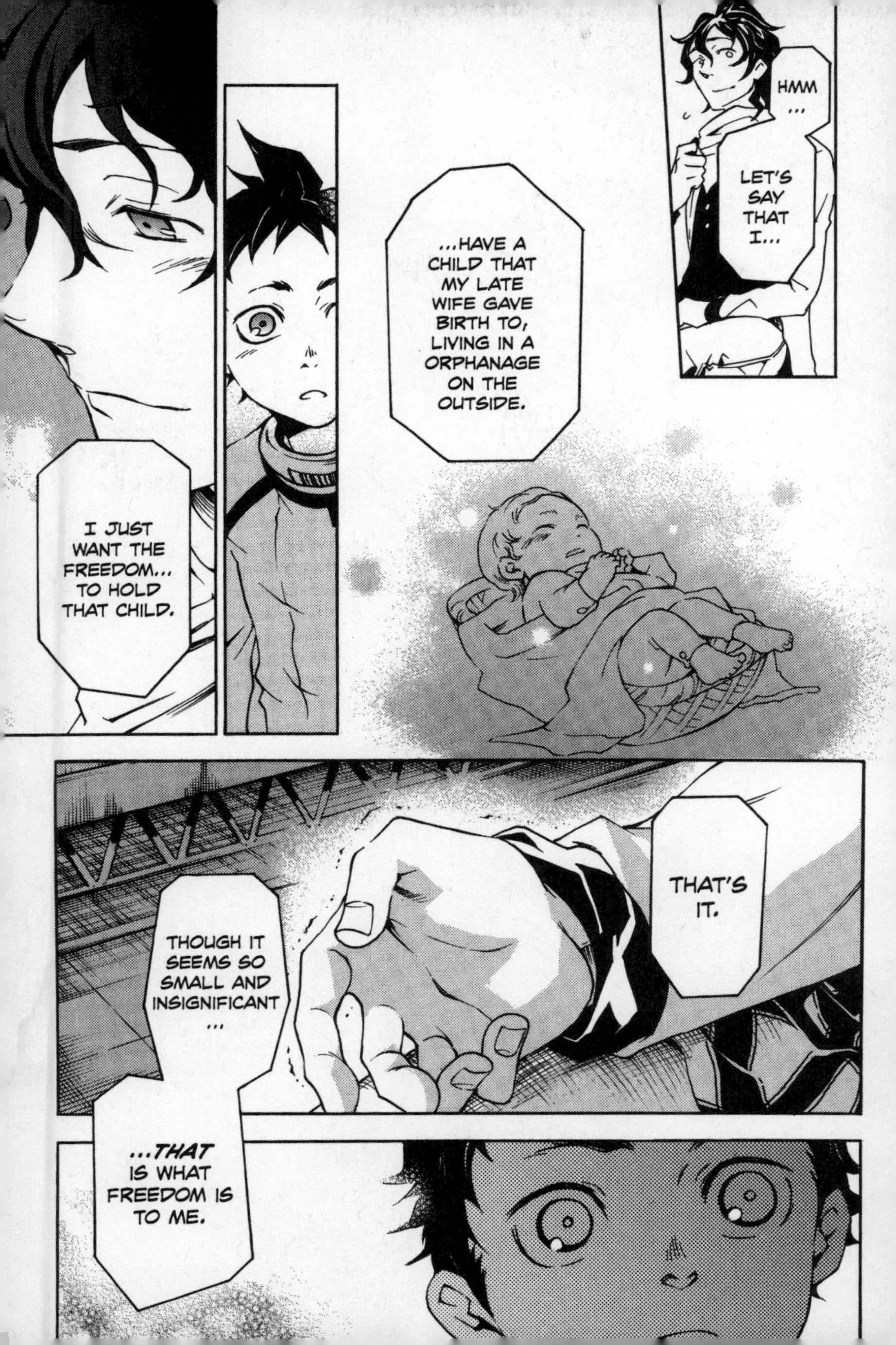
HMM ...
LET'S SAY THAT I...
...HAVE A CHILD THAT MY LATE WIFE GAVE BIRTH TO, LIVING IN A ORPHANAGE ON THE OUTSIDE.
I JUST WANT THE FREEDOM... TO HOLD THAT CHILD.
THAT'S IT.
THOUGH IT SEEMS SO SMALL AND INSIGNIFICANT ...
...THAT IS WHAT FREEDOM IS TO ME.

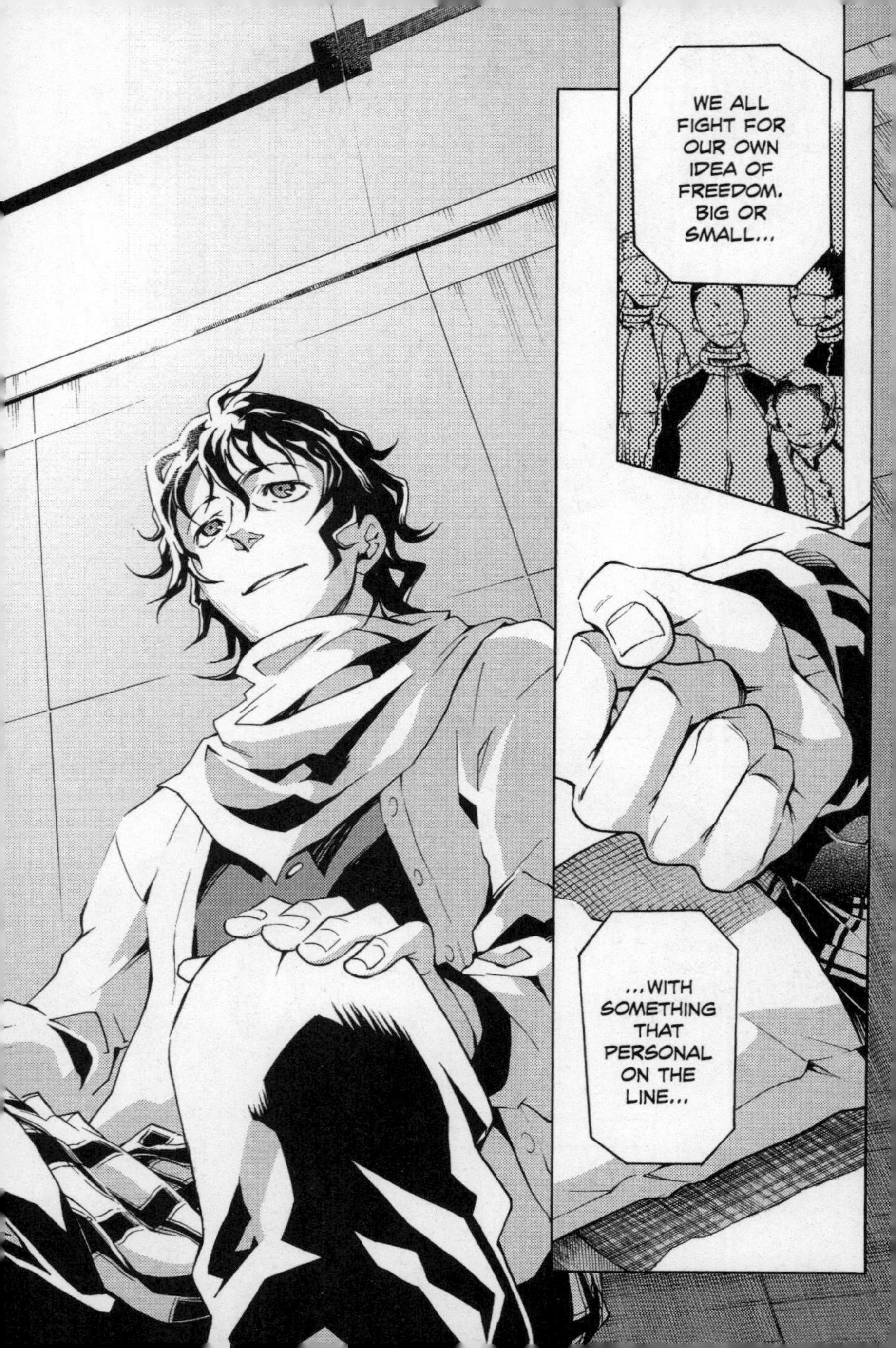
WE ALL FIGHT FOR OUR OWN IDEA OF FREEDOM. BIG OR SMALL...
...WITH SOMETHING THAT PERSONAL ON THE LINE...

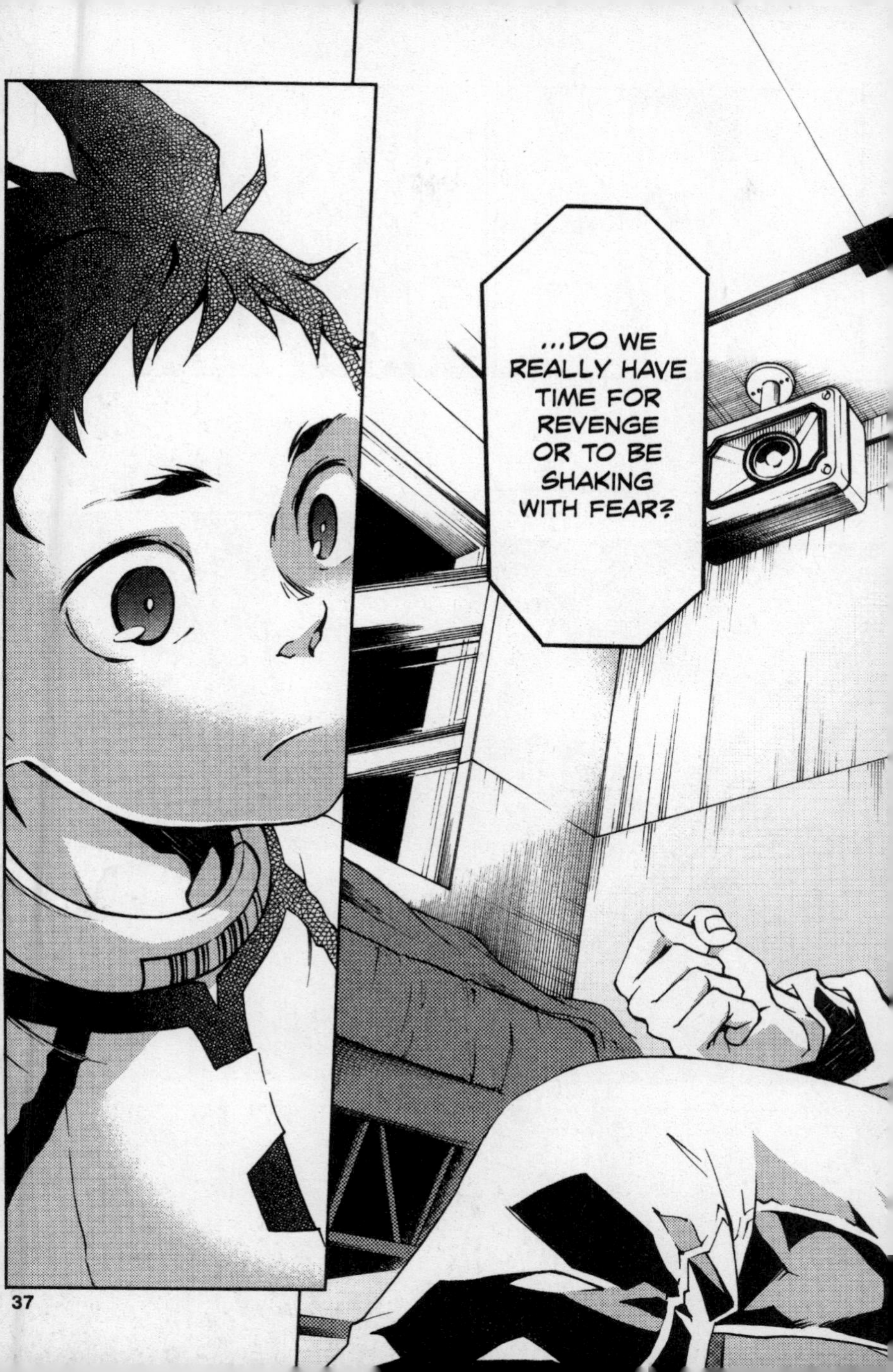
...DO WE REALLY HAVE TIME FOR REVENGE OR TO BE SHAKING WITH FEAR?

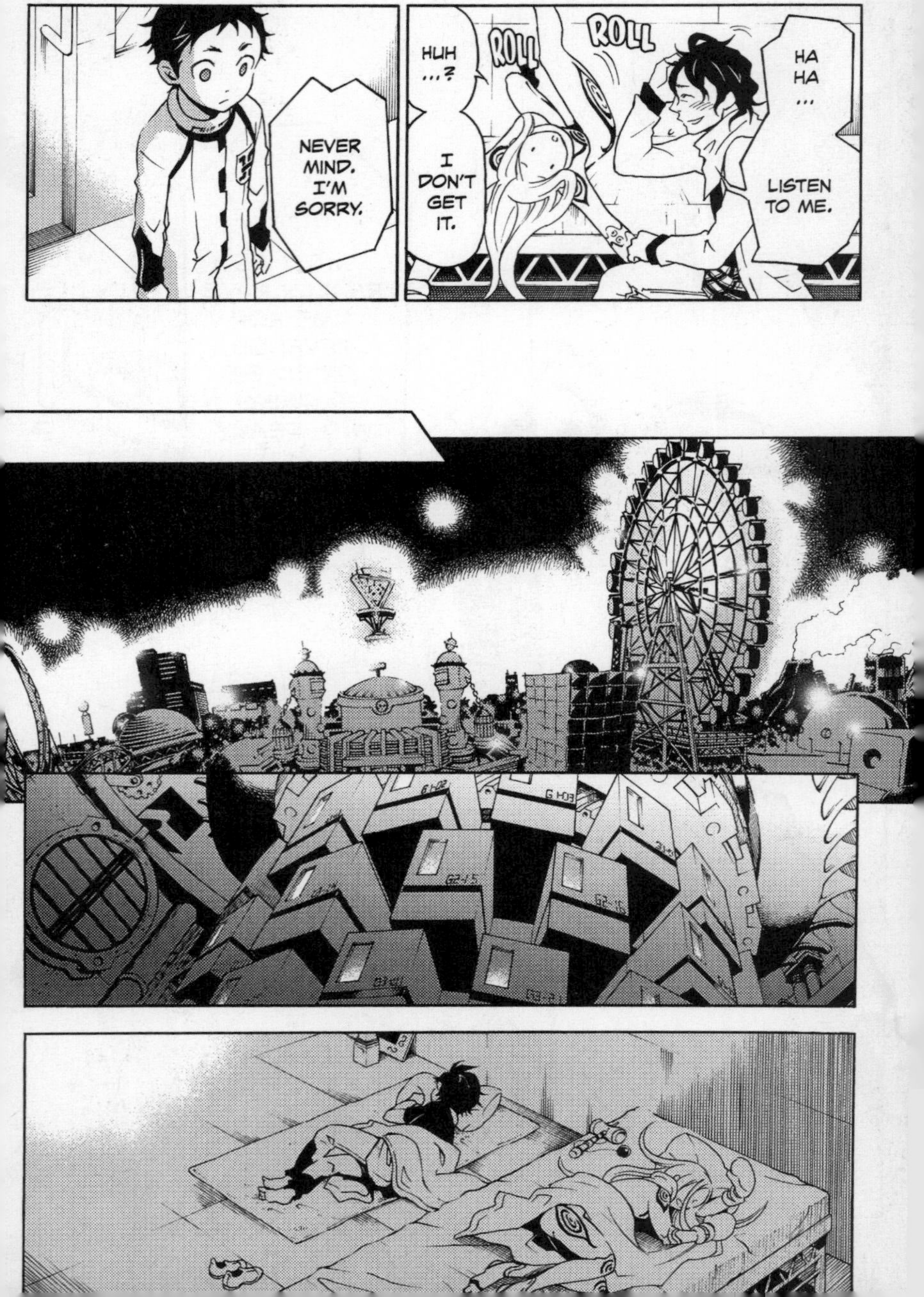
HA HA ...
ROLL
ROLL
HUH ...?
LISTEN TO ME.
I DON'T GET IT.
NEVER MIND. I'M SORRY.

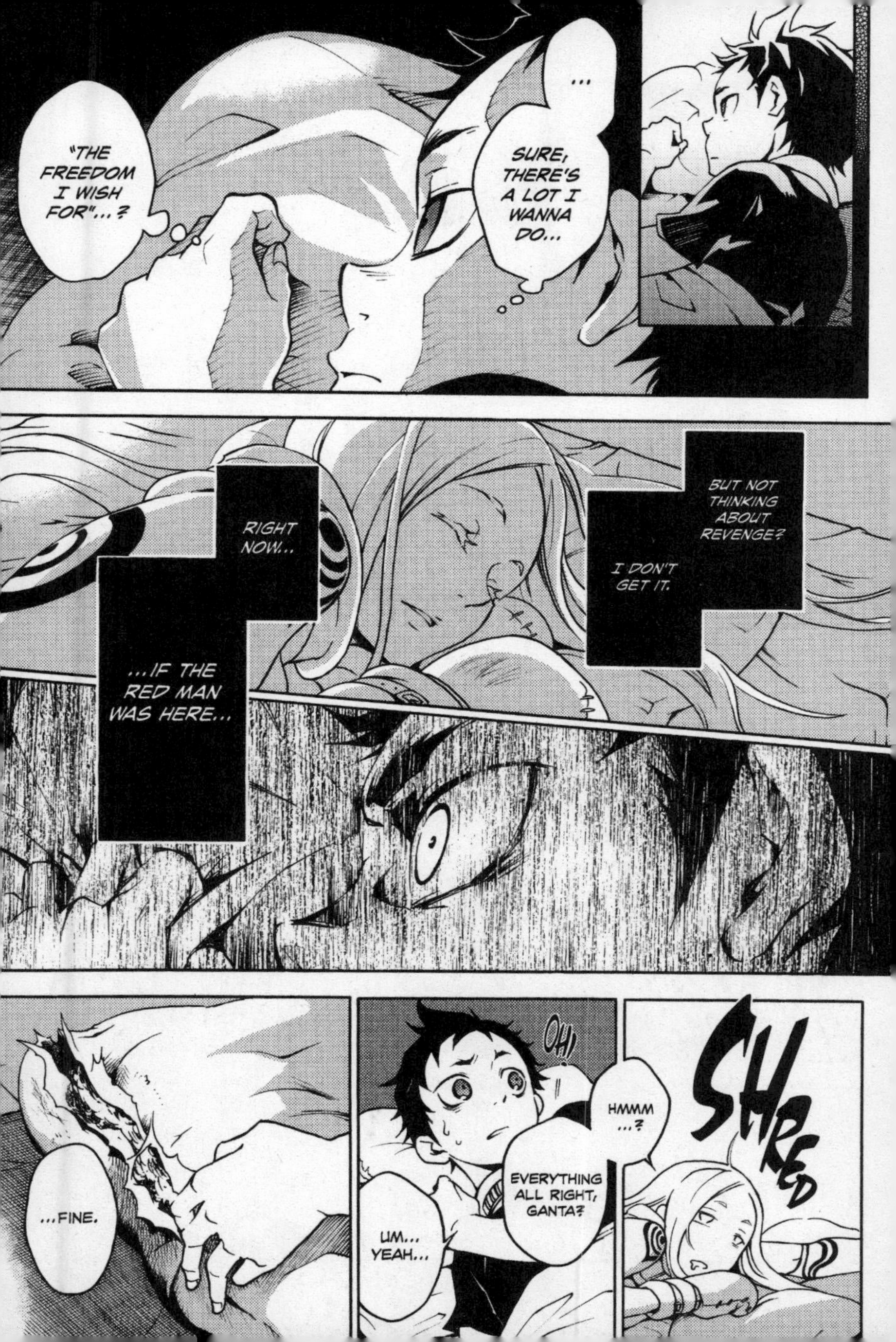
...
SURE, THERE'S A LOT I WANNA DO...
"THE FREEDOM I WISH FOR"...?
BUT NOT THINKING ABOUT REVENGE?
I DON'T GET IT.
RIGHT NOW...
...IF THE RED MAN WAS HERE...
SHRED
OH!
HMMM ...?
EVERYTHING ALL RIGHT, GANTA?
UM... YEAH...
...FINE.

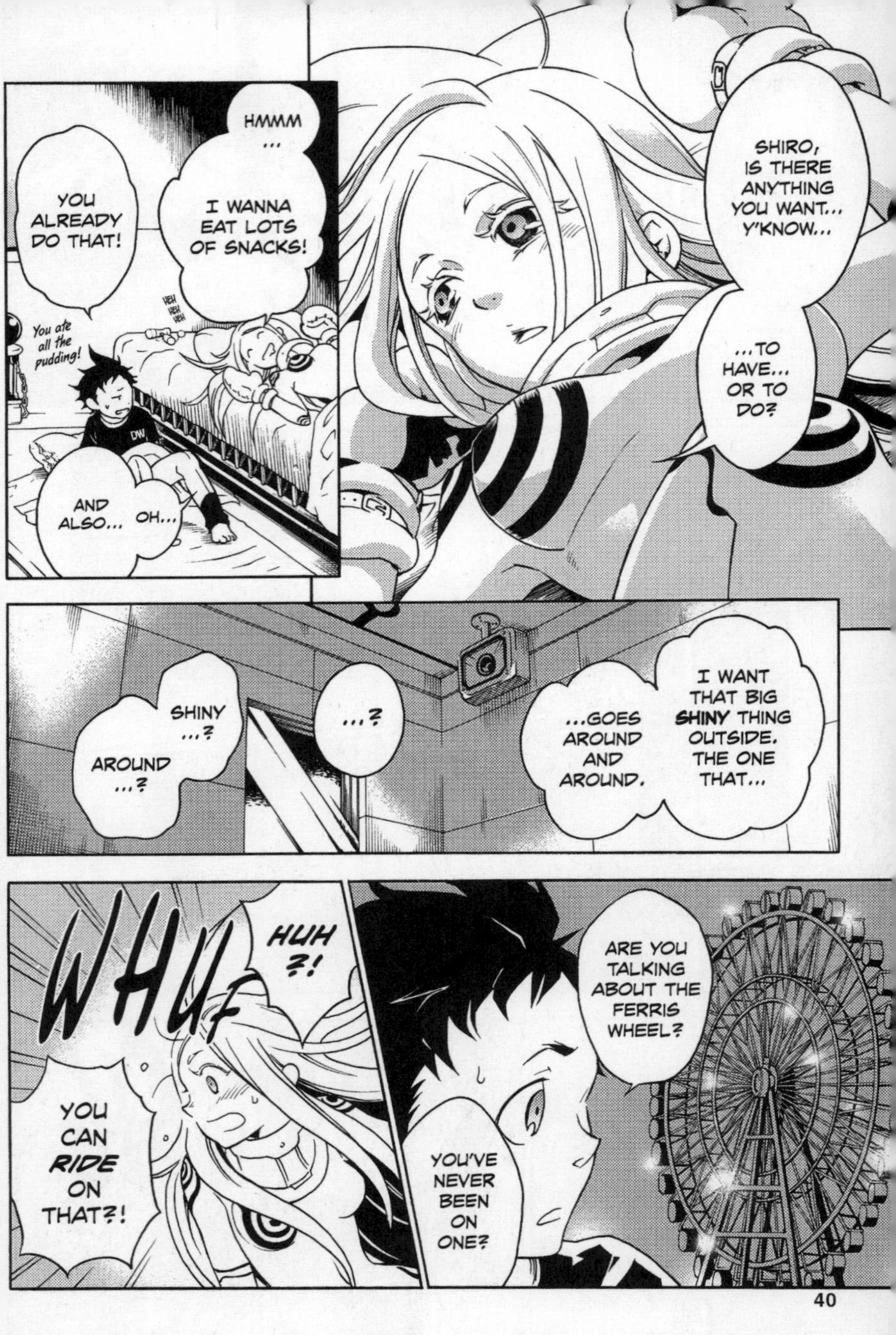
SHIRO, IS THERE ANYTHING YOU WANT... Y'KNOW...
...TO HAVE... OR TO DO?
HMMM...
I WANNA EAT LOTS OF SNACKS!
YOU ALREADY DO THAT!
YEH YEH YEH
You ate all the pudding!
AND ALSO... OH...
I WANT THAT BIG **SHINY** THING OUTSIDE. THE ONE THAT...
...GOES AROUND AND AROUND.
...?
SHINY ...?
AROUND ...?
ARE YOU TALKING ABOUT THE FERRIS WHEEL?
YOU'VE NEVER BEEN ON ONE?
HUH ?!
WHUF
YOU CAN ***RIDE*** ON THAT?!

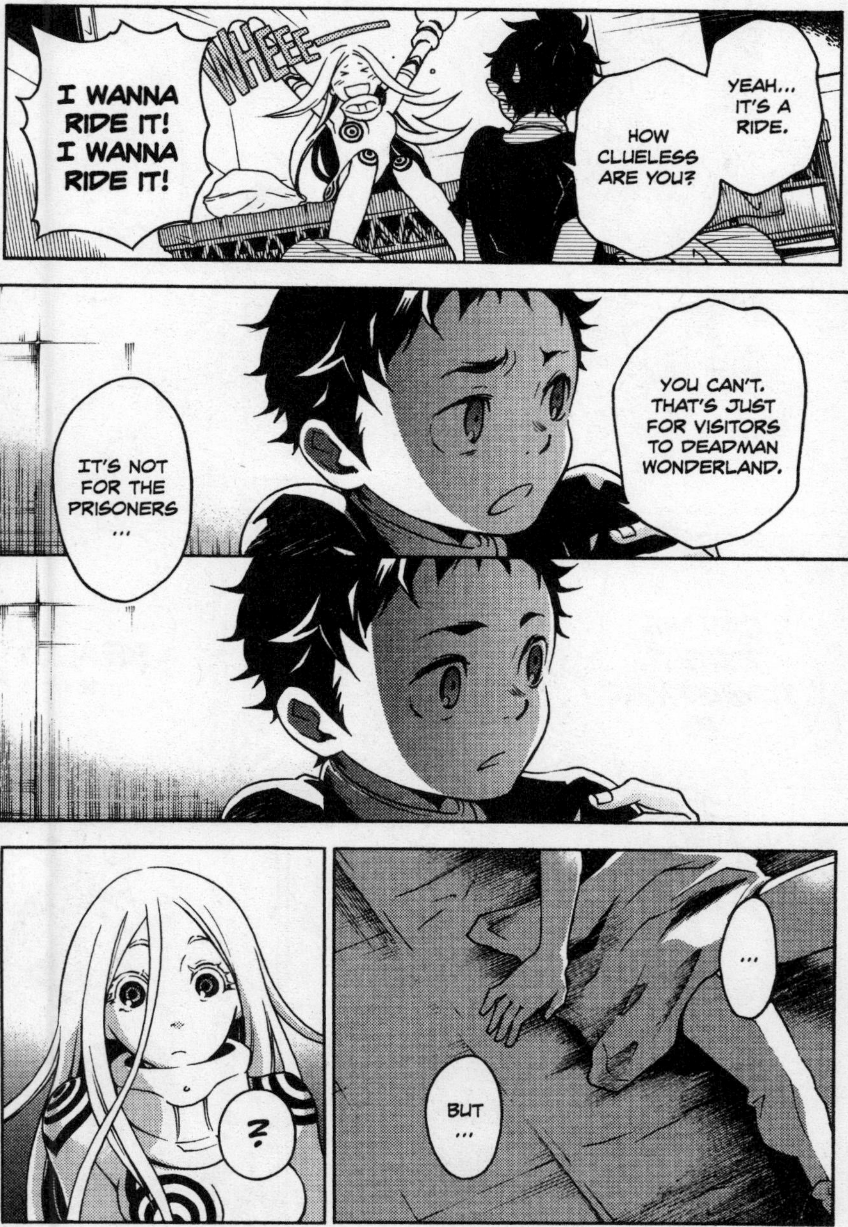
YEAH... IT'S A RIDE.
HOW CLUELESS ARE YOU?
WHEEE
I WANNA RIDE IT! I WANNA RIDE IT!
YOU CAN'T. THAT'S JUST FOR VISITORS TO DEADMAN WONDERLAND.
IT'S NOT FOR THE PRISONERS ...
...
BUT ...
?

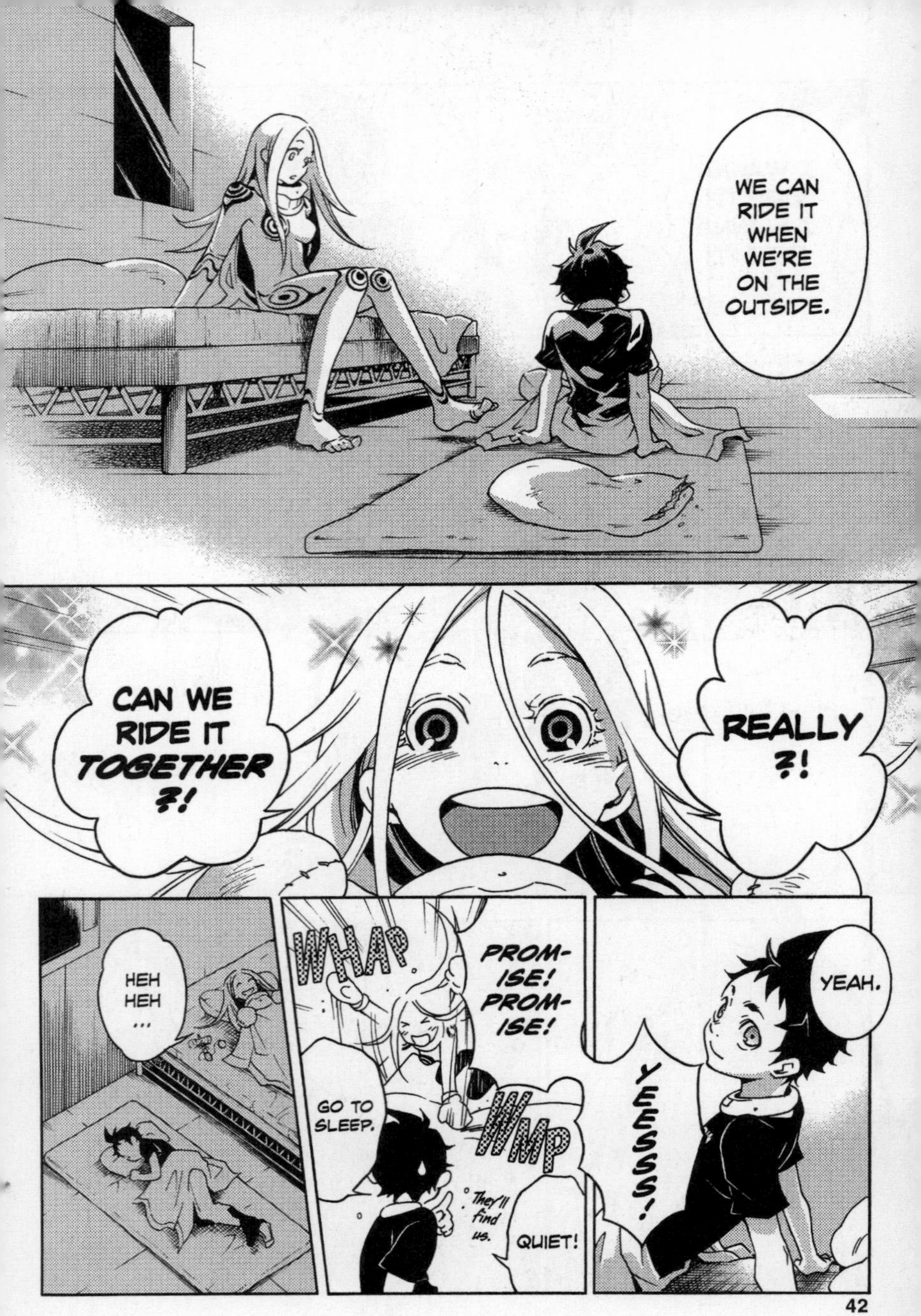
WE CAN RIDE IT WHEN WE'RE ON THE OUTSIDE.
REALLY ?!
CAN WE RIDE IT *TOGETHER* ?!
YEAH.
YEESSS!
PROMISE! PROMISE!
WHAP
WMP
QUIET!
They'll find us.
GO TO SLEEP.
HEH HEH ...

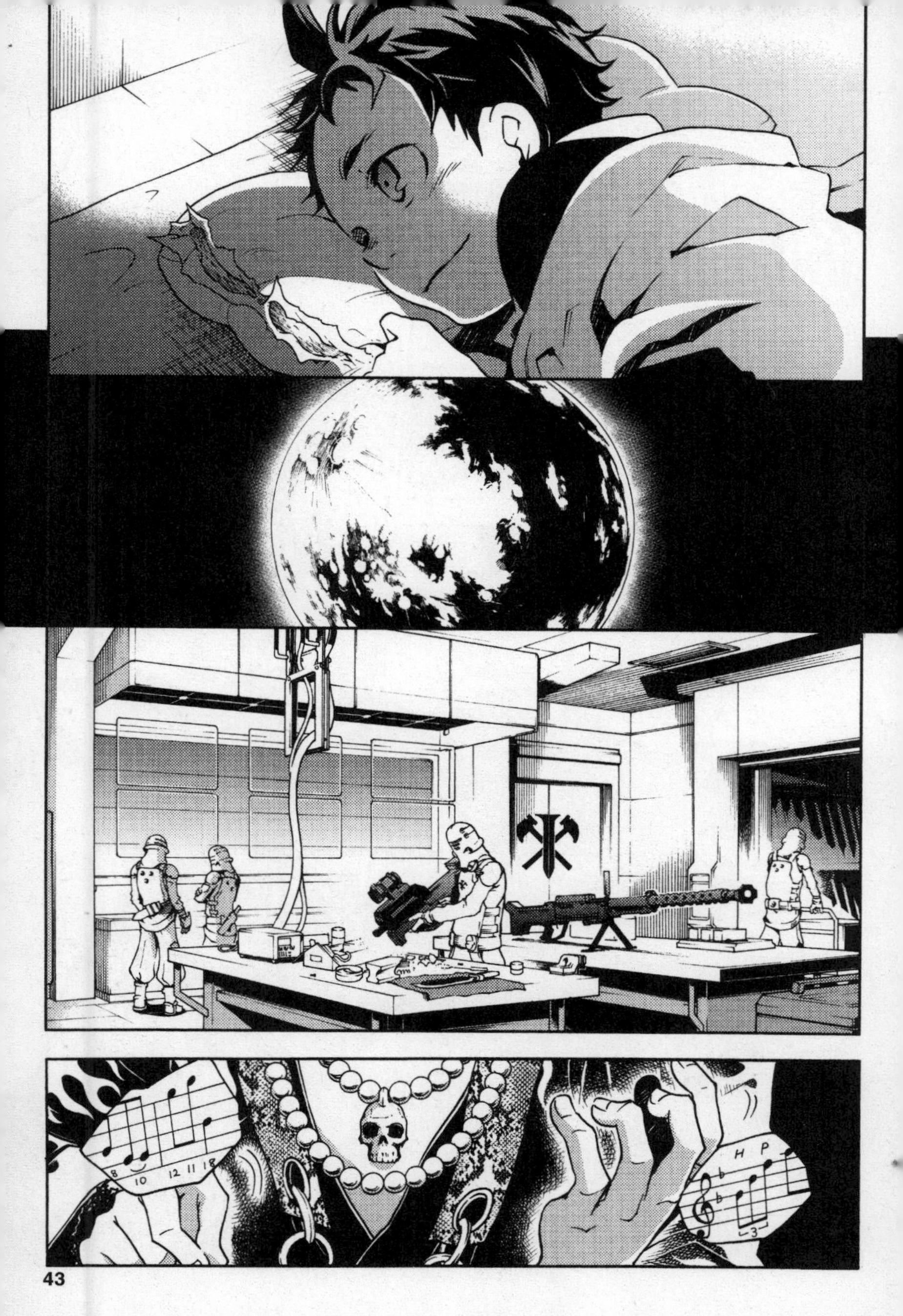
H P
3
8 10 12 11 18

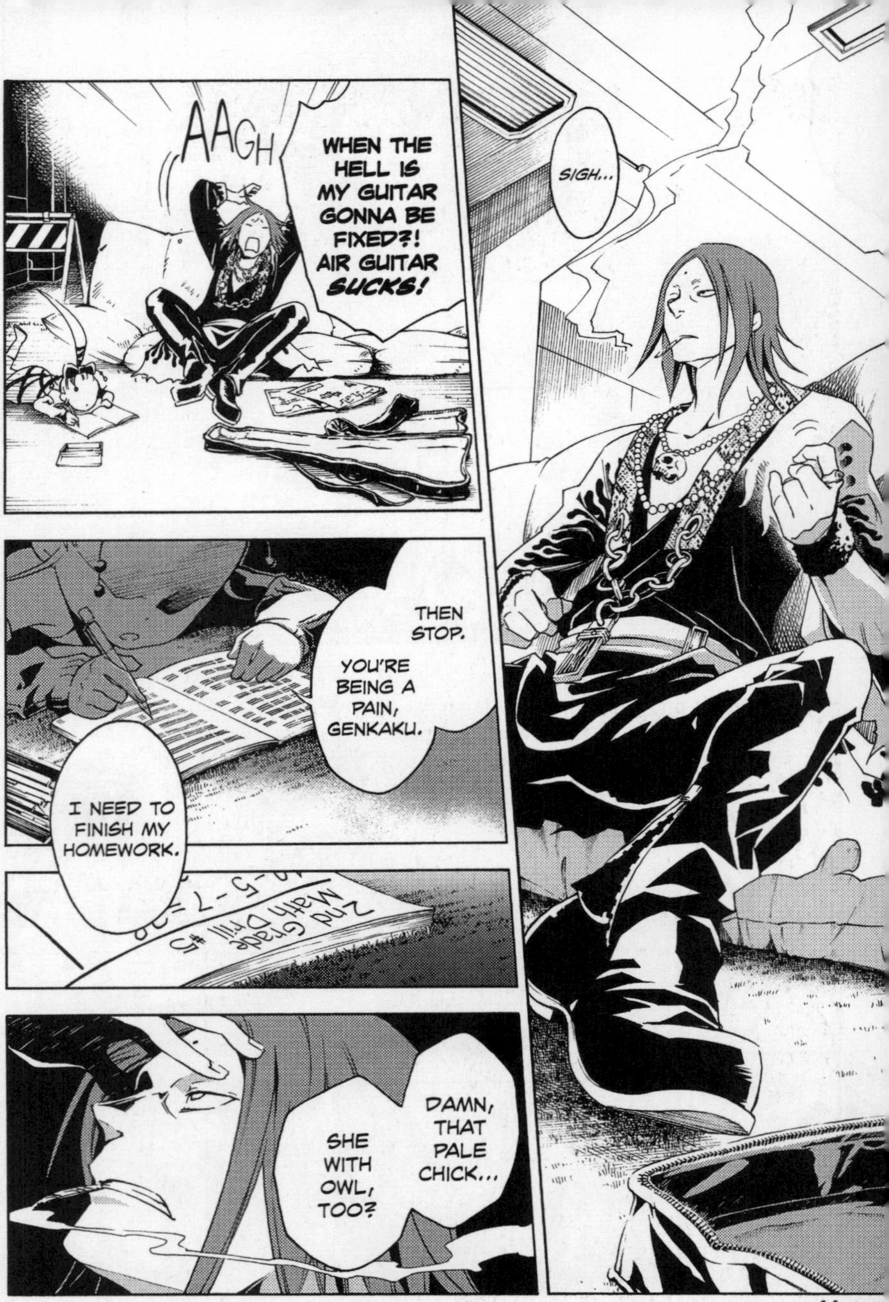
SIGH...
AAGH
WHEN THE HELL IS MY GUITAR GONNA BE FIXED?! AIR GUITAR SUCKS!
THEN STOP.
YOU'RE BEING A PAIN, GENKAKU.
I NEED TO FINISH MY HOMEWORK.
2nd Grade Math Drill #5
DAMN, THAT PALE CHICK...
SHE WITH OWL, TOO?

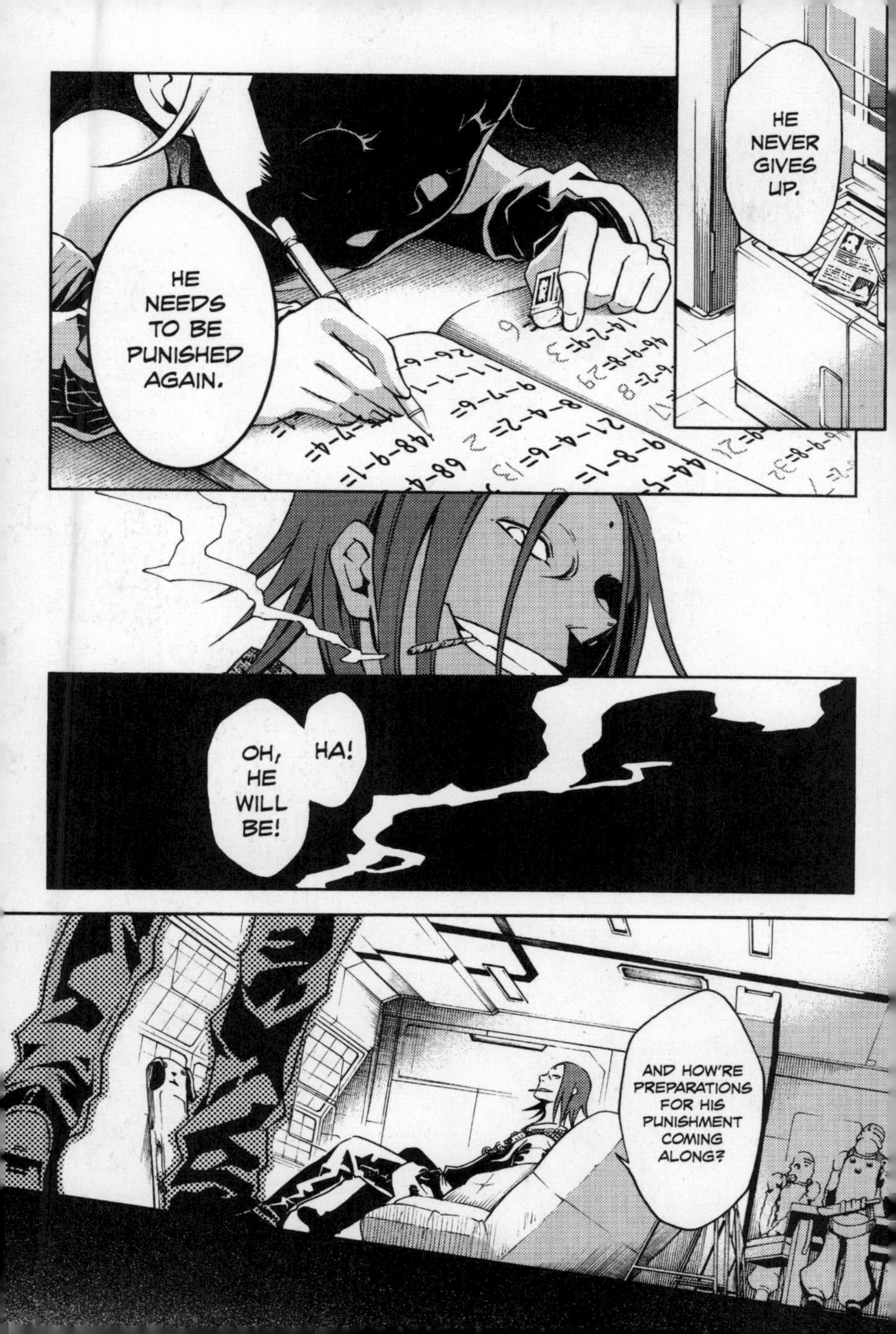
HE NEVER GIVES UP.
HE NEEDS TO BE PUNISHED AGAIN.
HA!
OH, HE WILL BE!
AND HOW'RE PREPARATIONS FOR HIS PUNISHMENT COMING ALONG?

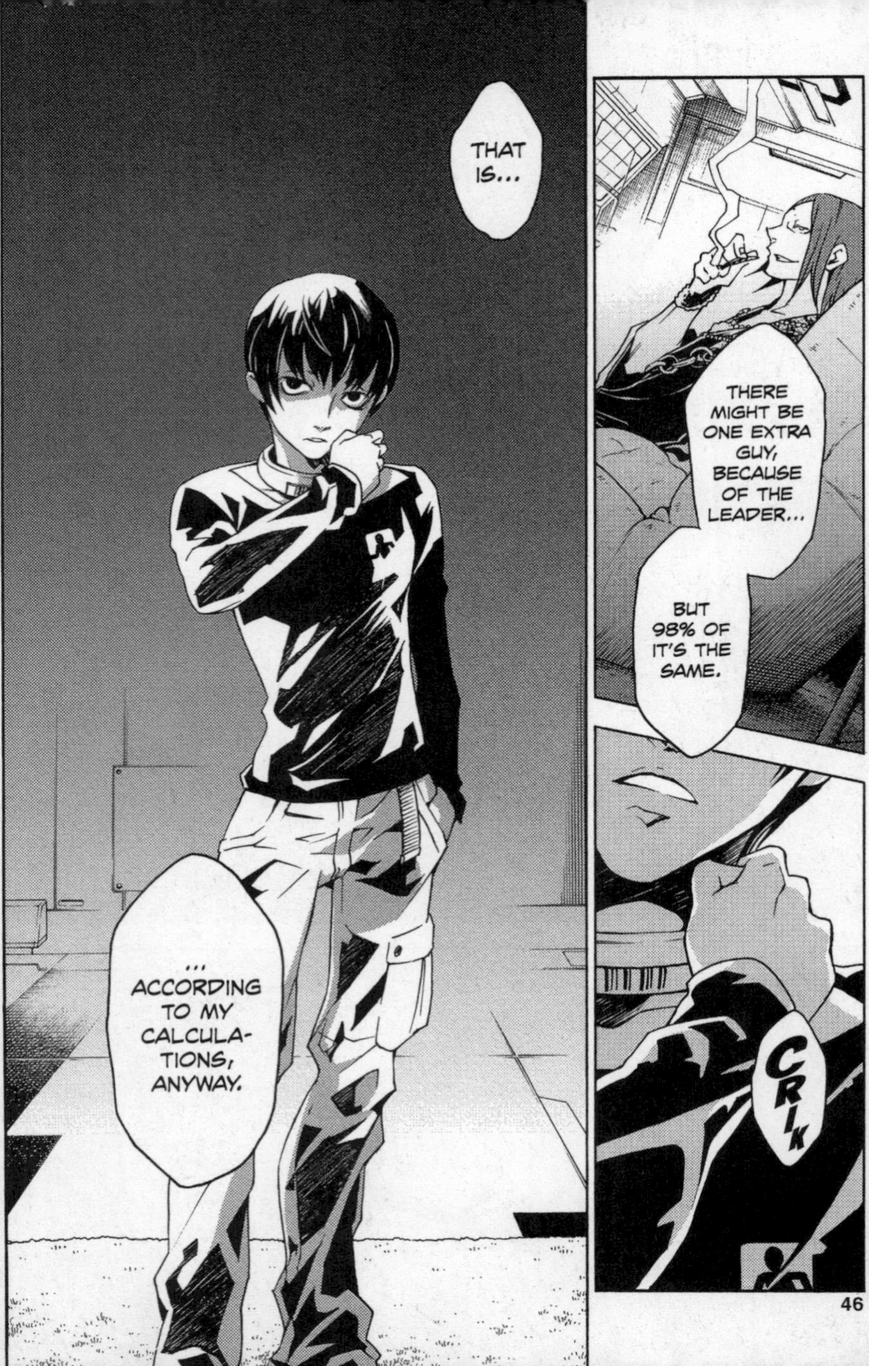
THERE MIGHT BE ONE EXTRA GUY, BECAUSE OF THE LEADER...
BUT 98% OF IT'S THE SAME.
CRIK
THAT IS...
...ACCORDING TO MY CALCULA-TIONS, ANYWAY.

DEAD MAN WONDER LAND DEAD MAN WONDER LAND DE
DEAD MAN WONDER LAND DEAD MAN WONDER LAND DE
DEAD MAN WONDER LAND DEAD MAN WONDER LAND DE
DEAD MAN WONDER LAND DEAD MAN WONDER LAND DE
DEAD MAN WONDER LAND DEAD MAN WONDER LAND DE
DEAD MAN WONDER LAND DEAD MAN WONDER LAND DE
DEAD MAN WONDER LAND DEAD MAN WONDER LAND DE

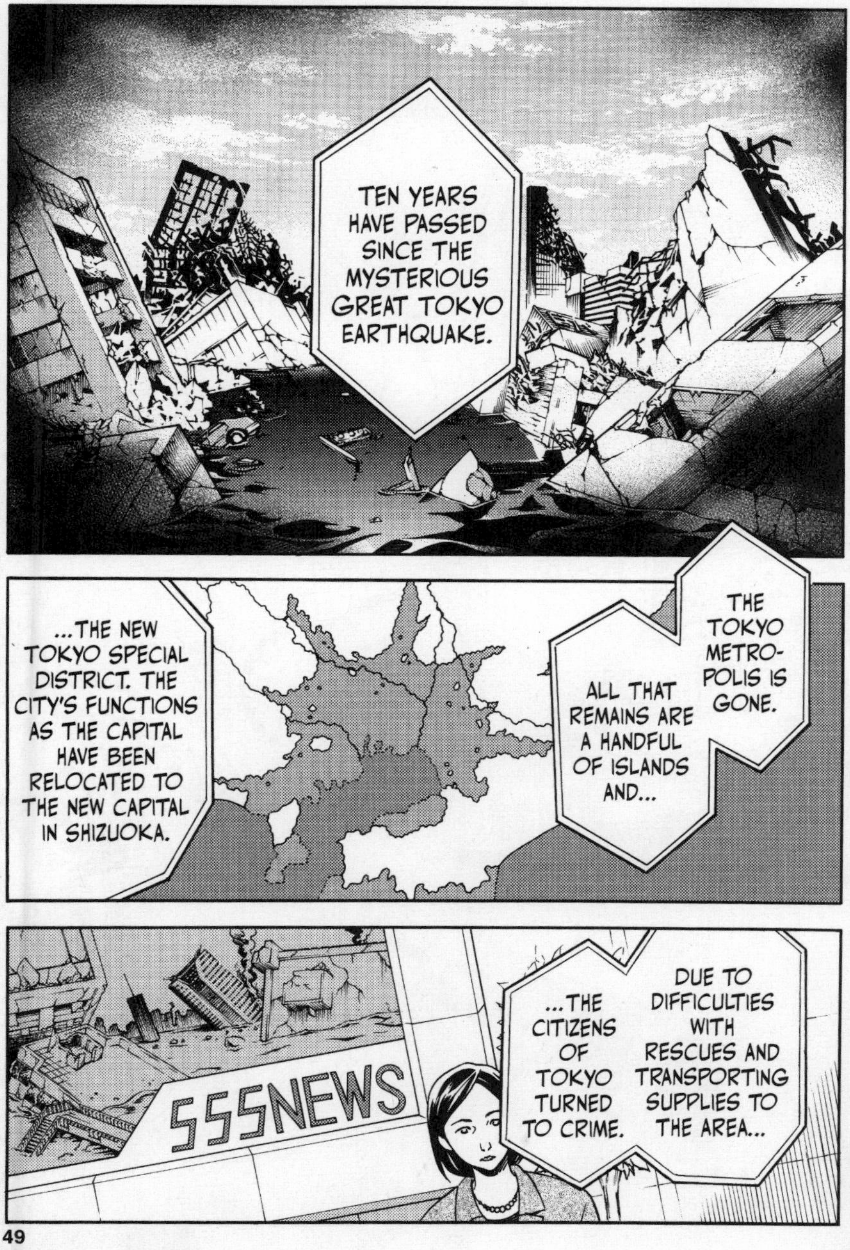
TEN YEARS HAVE PASSED SINCE THE MYSTERIOUS GREAT TOKYO EARTHQUAKE.
THE TOKYO METRO-POLIS IS GONE.
ALL THAT REMAINS ARE A HANDFUL OF ISLANDS AND...
...THE NEW TOKYO SPECIAL DISTRICT. THE CITY'S FUNCTIONS AS THE CAPITAL HAVE BEEN RELOCATED TO THE NEW CAPITAL IN SHIZUOKA.
DUE TO DIFFICULTIES WITH RESCUES AND TRANSPORTING SUPPLIES TO THE AREA...
...THE CITIZENS OF TOKYO TURNED TO CRIME.
555NEWS

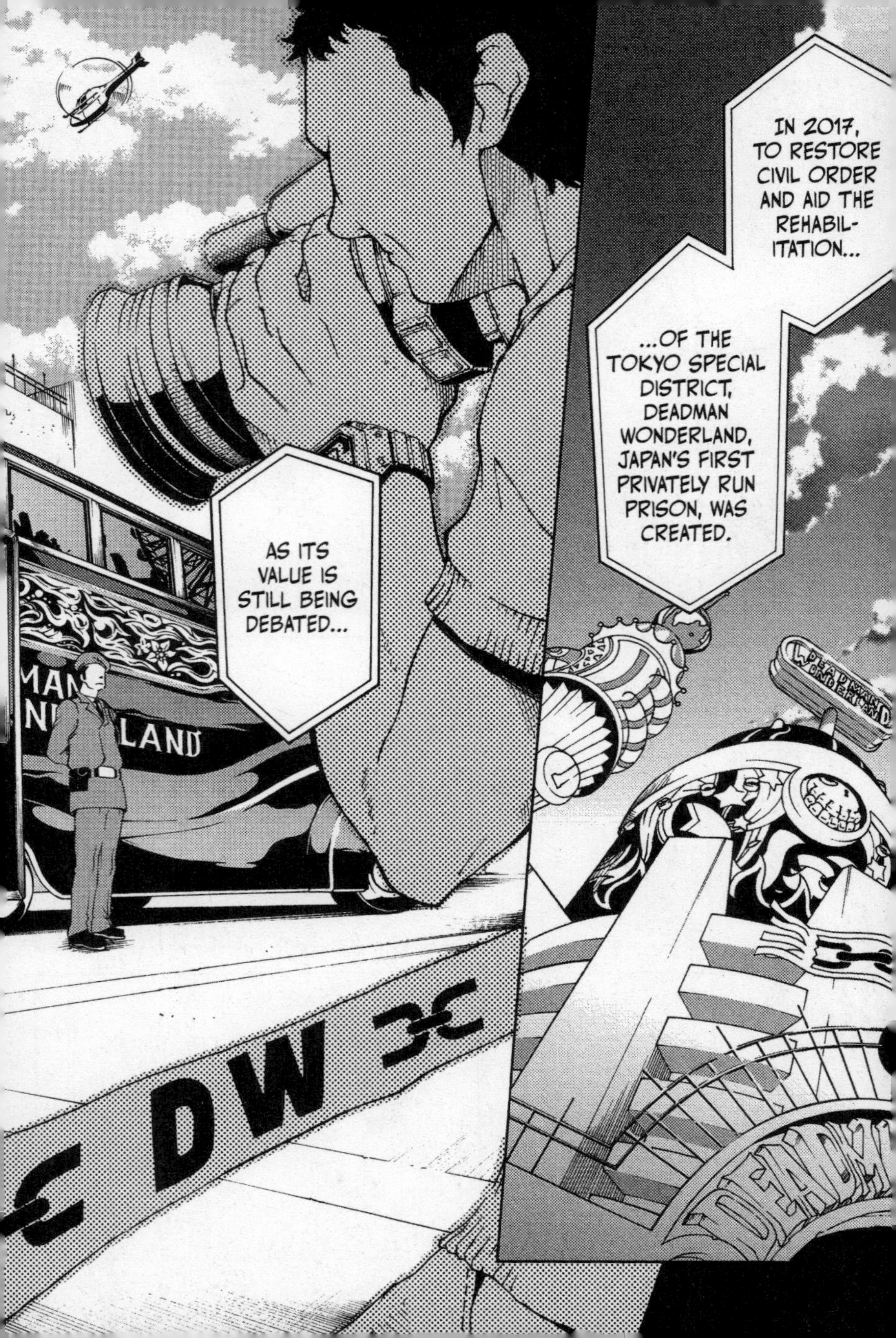
IN 2017, TO RESTORE CIVIL ORDER AND AID THE REHABIL-ITATION...
...OF THE TOKYO SPECIAL DISTRICT, DEADMAN WONDERLAND, JAPAN'S FIRST PRIVATELY RUN PRISON, WAS CREATED.
AS ITS VALUE IS STILL BEING DEBATED...

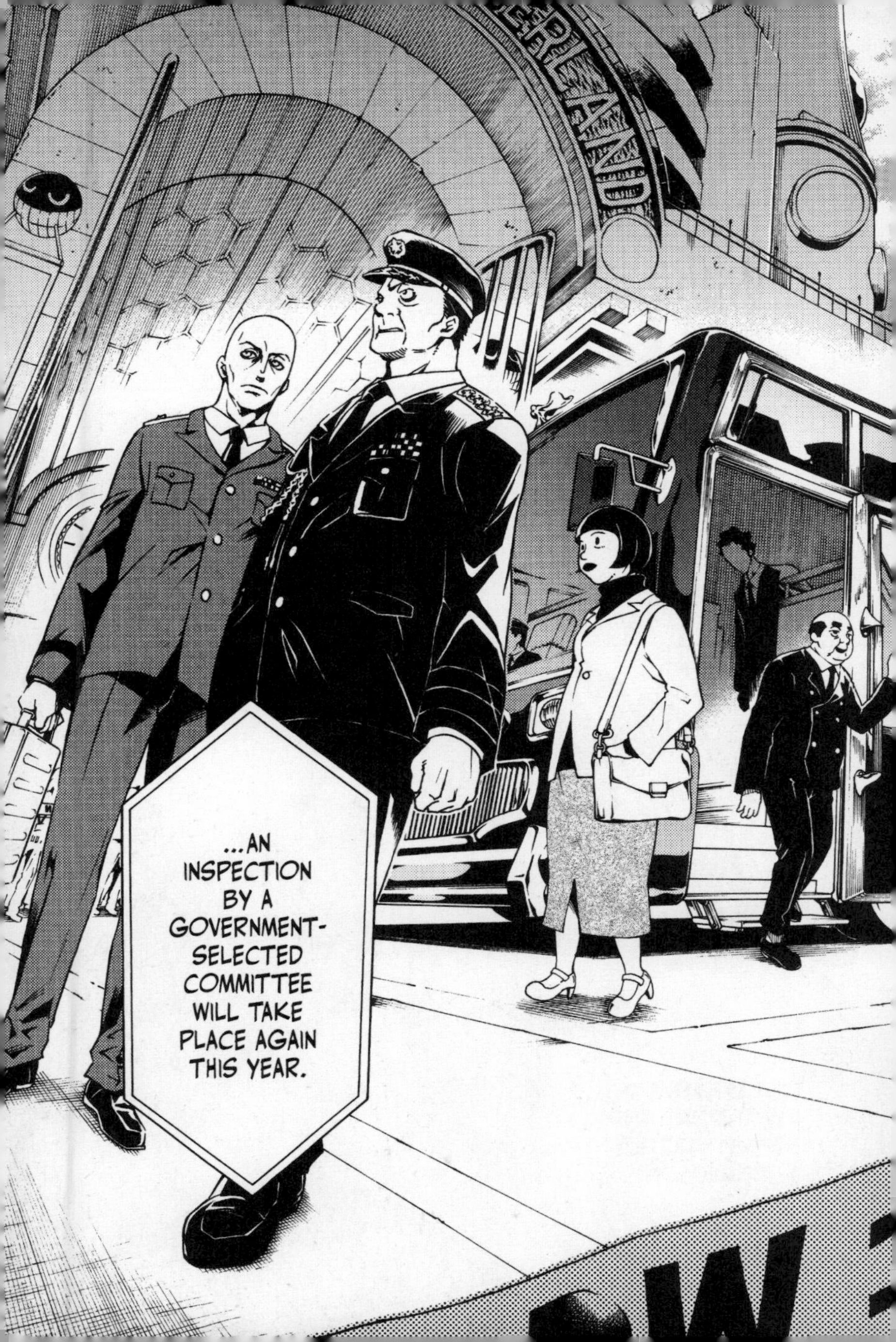
...AN INSPECTION BY A GOVERNMENT-SELECTED COMMITTEE WILL TAKE PLACE AGAIN THIS YEAR.

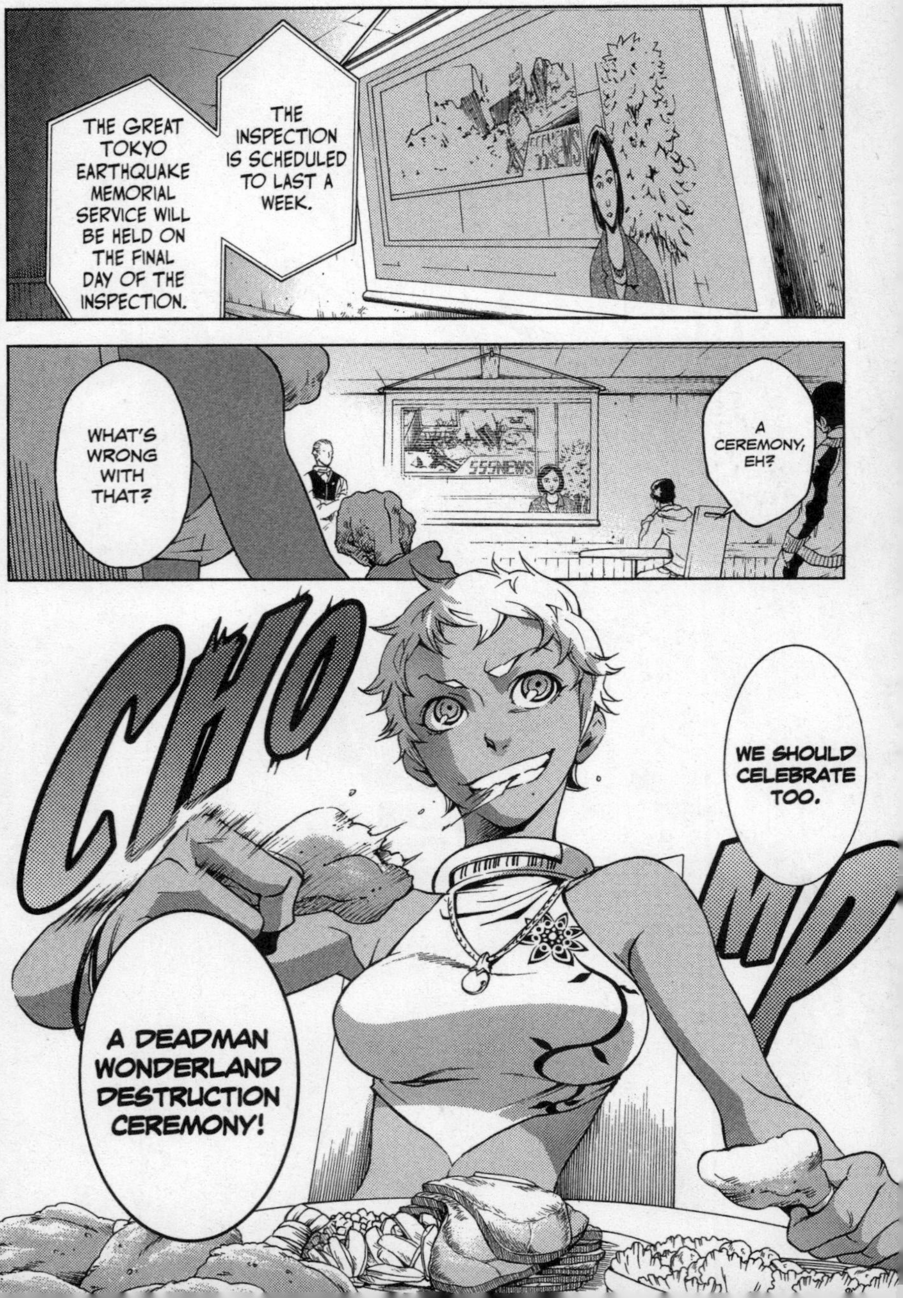
THE INSPECTION IS SCHEDULED TO LAST A WEEK.
THE GREAT TOKYO EARTHQUAKE MEMORIAL SERVICE WILL BE HELD ON THE FINAL DAY OF THE INSPECTION.
A CEREMONY, EH?
555NEWS
WHAT'S WRONG WITH THAT?
WE SHOULD CELEBRATE TOO.
CHOMP
A DEADMAN WONDERLAND DESTRUCTION CEREMONY!

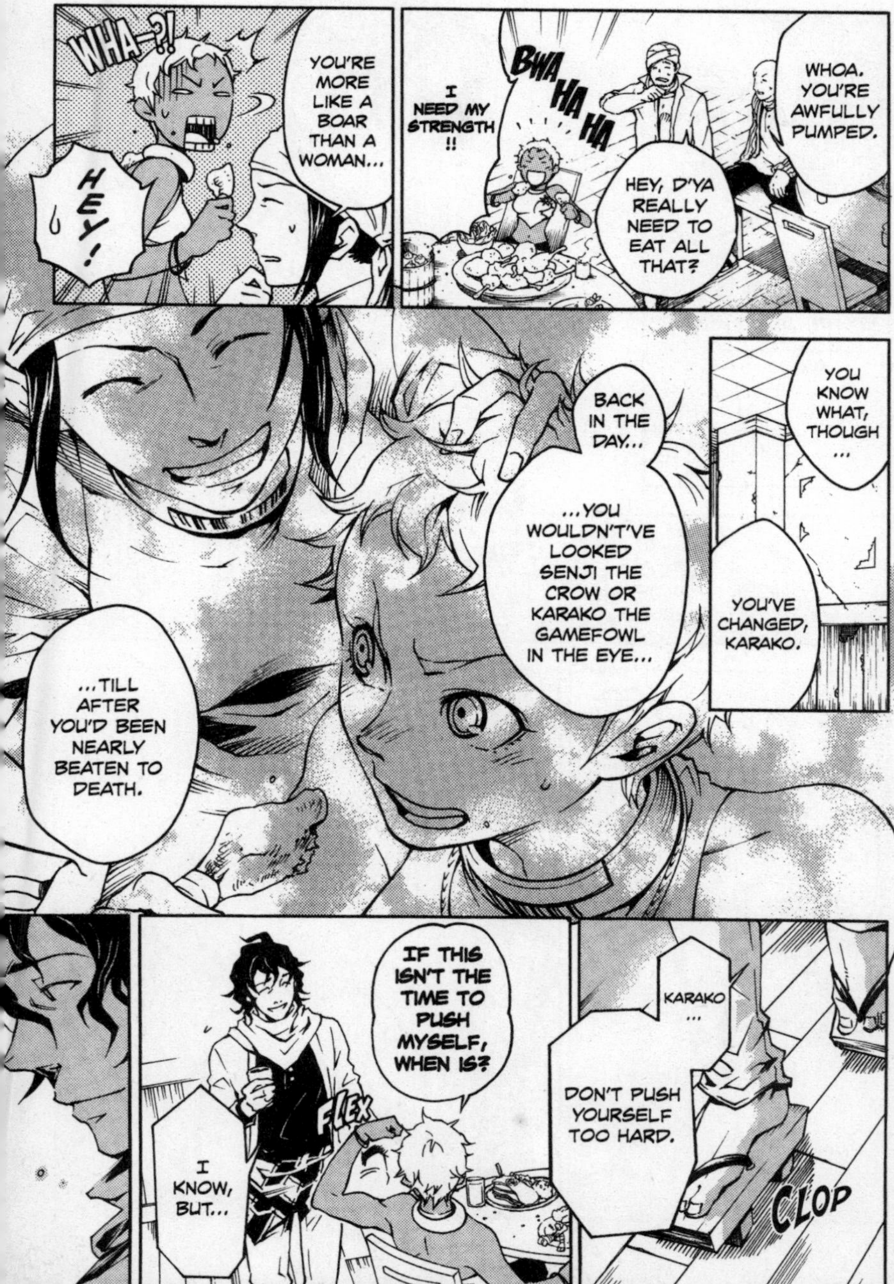
WHOA. YOU'RE AWFULLY PUMPED.
BWA HA HA
HEY, D'YA REALLY NEED TO EAT ALL THAT?
I NEED MY STRENGTH!!
YOU'RE MORE LIKE A BOAR THAN A WOMAN...
WHA-?!
HEY!
YOU KNOW WHAT, THOUGH...
YOU'VE CHANGED, KARAKO.
BACK IN THE DAY...
...YOU WOULDN'T'VE LOOKED SENJI THE CROW OR KARAKO THE GAMEFOWL IN THE EYE...
...TILL AFTER YOU'D BEEN NEARLY BEATEN TO DEATH.
KARAKO...
DON'T PUSH YOURSELF TOO HARD.
CLOP
IF THIS ISN'T THE TIME TO PUSH MYSELF, WHEN IS?
FLEX
I KNOW, BUT...

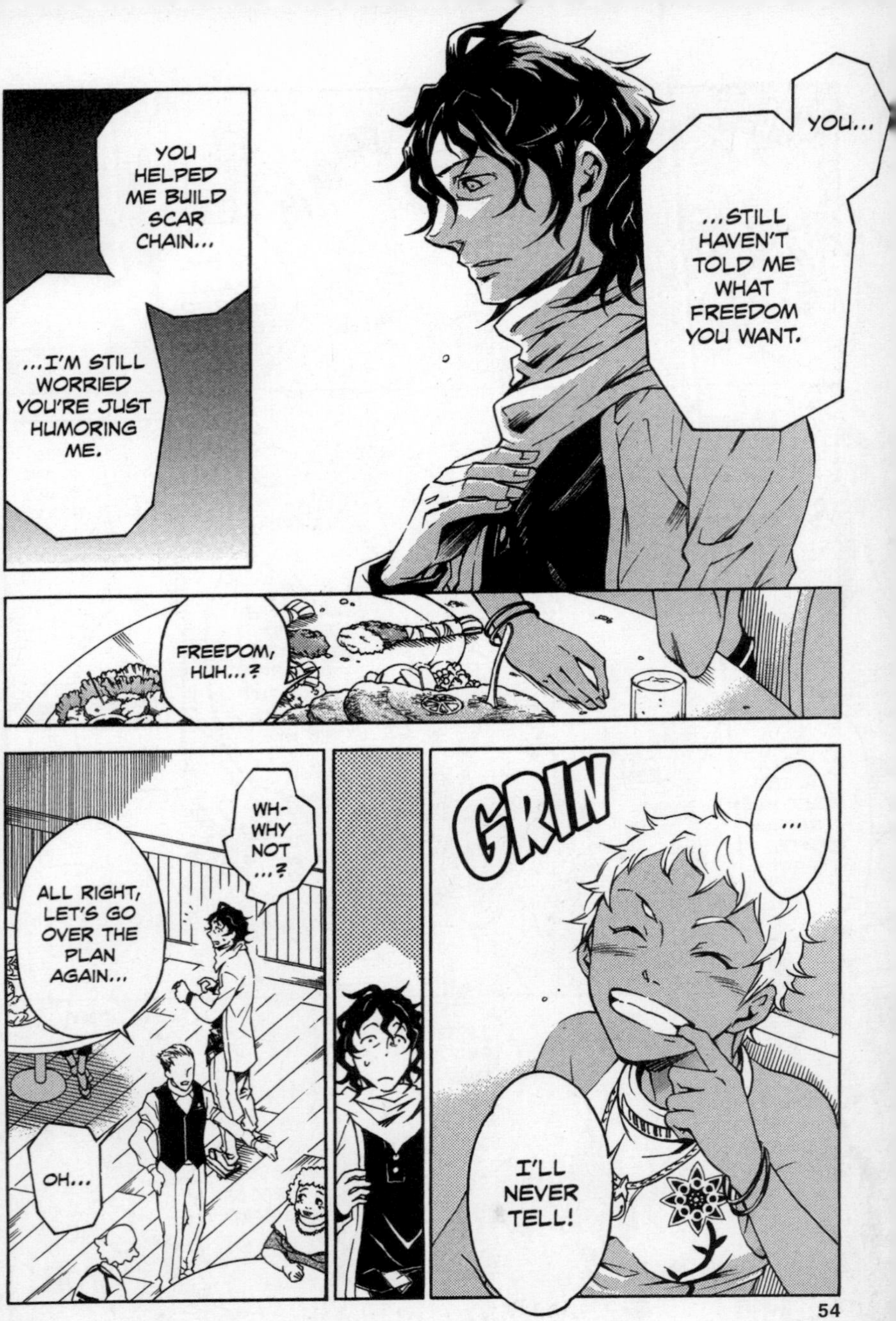
YOU...
...STILL HAVEN'T TOLD ME WHAT FREEDOM YOU WANT.
YOU HELPED ME BUILD SCAR CHAIN...
...I'M STILL WORRIED YOU'RE JUST HUMORING ME.
FREEDOM, HUH...?
GRIN
...
I'LL NEVER TELL!
WH- WHY NOT ...?
ALL RIGHT, LET'S GO OVER THE PLAN AGAIN...
OH...

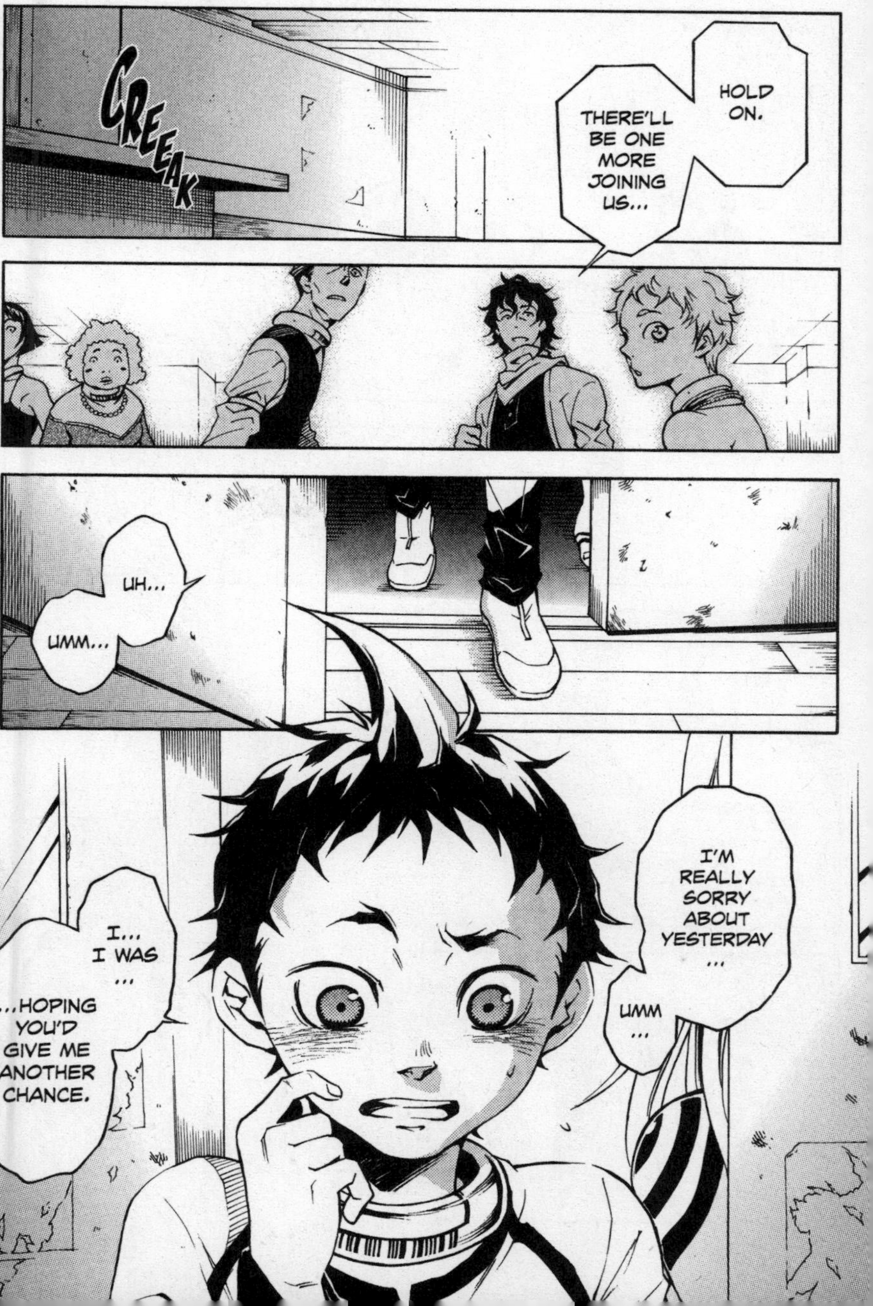
HOLD ON.
THERE'LL BE ONE MORE JOINING US...
CREEAK
UH...
UMM...
I'M REALLY SORRY ABOUT YESTERDAY...
UMM...
I... I WAS...
...HOPING YOU'D GIVE ME ANOTHER CHANCE.

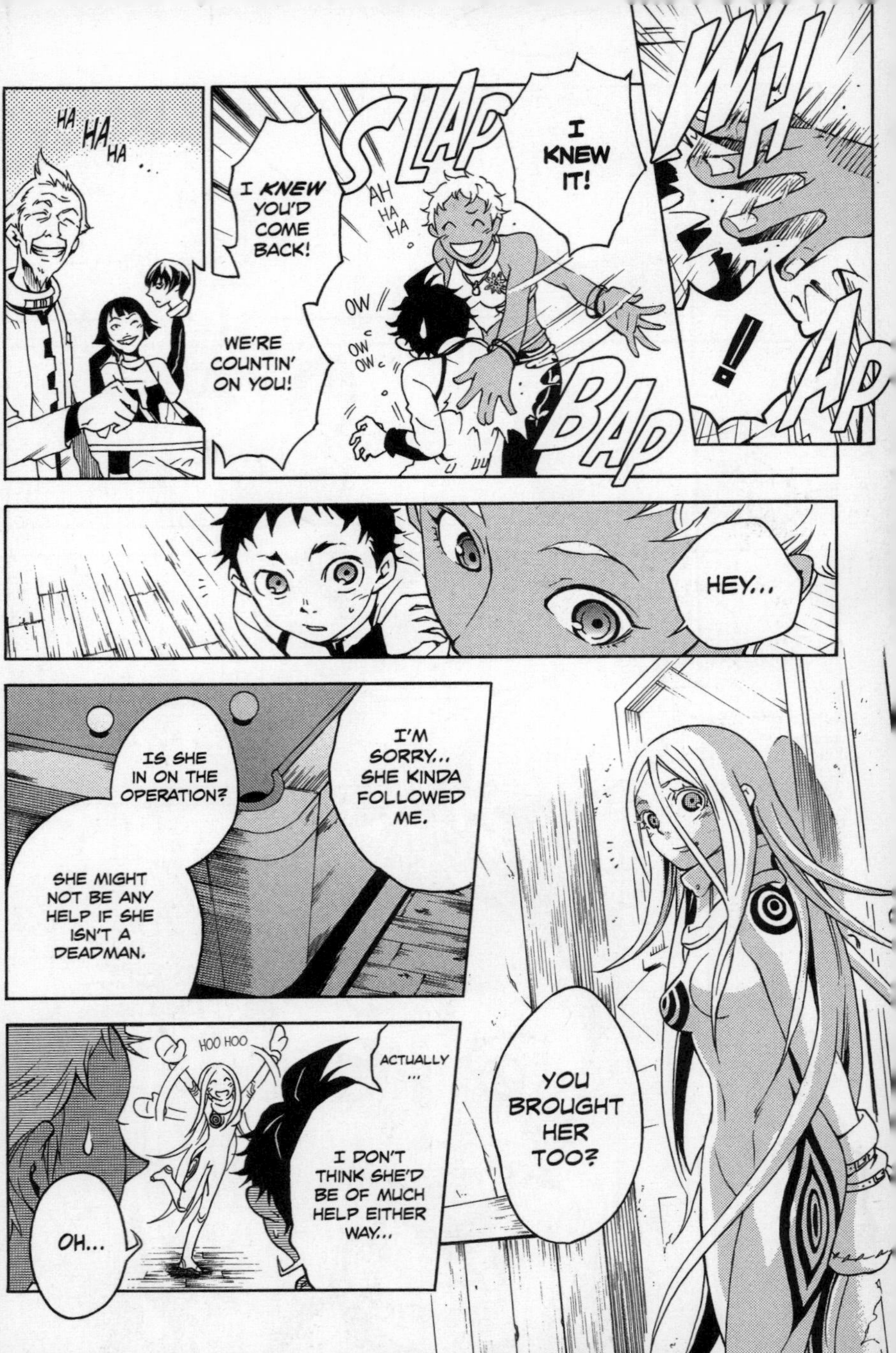
WHAP
!
I KNEW IT!
SLAP
BAP
AH HA HA
I KNEW YOU'D COME BACK!
OW OW OW
WE'RE COUNTIN' ON YOU!
HA HA HA ...
HEY...
YOU BROUGHT HER TOO?
I'M SORRY... SHE KINDA FOLLOWED ME.
IS SHE IN ON THE OPERATION?
SHE MIGHT NOT BE ANY HELP IF SHE ISN'T A DEADMAN.
ACTUALLY ...
HOO HOO
I DON'T THINK SHE'D BE OF MUCH HELP EITHER WAY...
OH...

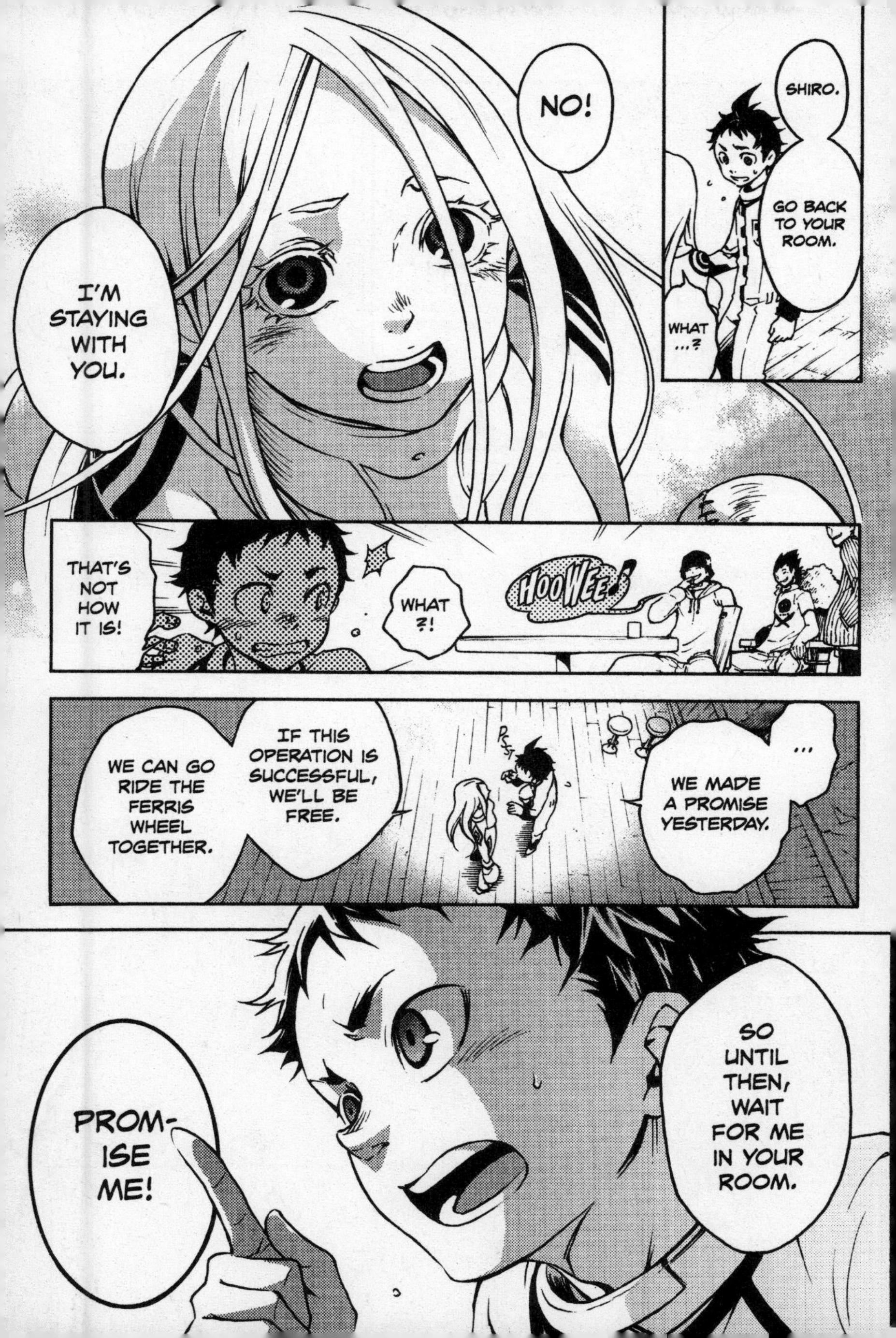
SHIRO.
GO BACK TO YOUR ROOM.
WHAT ...?
NO!
I'M STAYING WITH YOU.
HOOWEE!
WHAT?!
THAT'S NOT HOW IT IS!
...
WE MADE A PROMISE YESTERDAY.
PSST
IF THIS OPERATION IS SUCCESSFUL, WE'LL BE FREE.
WE CAN GO RIDE THE FERRIS WHEEL TOGETHER.
SO UNTIL THEN, WAIT FOR ME IN YOUR ROOM.
PROM-ISE ME!

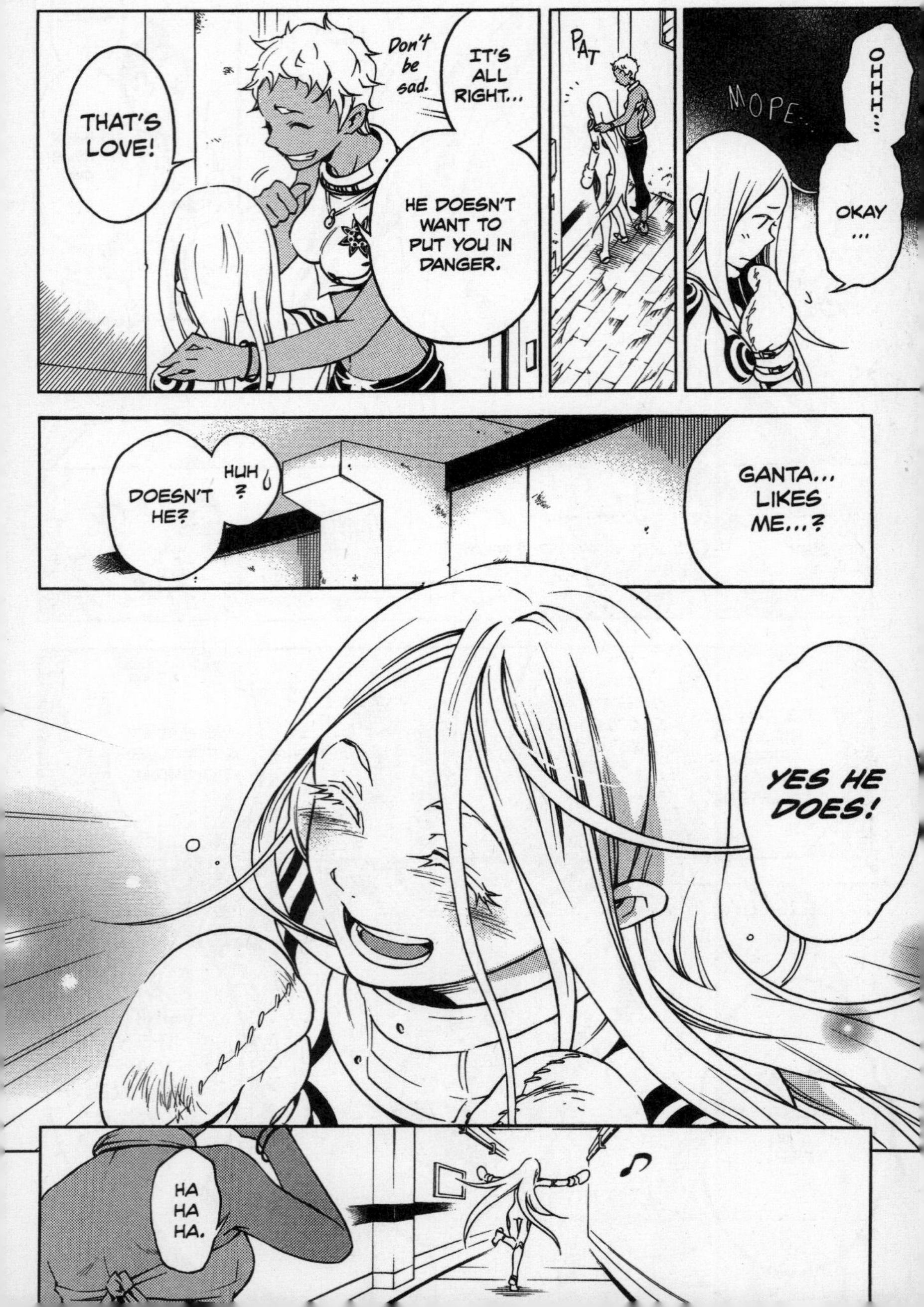
OHHH...
MOPE...
OKAY...
PAT
IT'S ALL RIGHT...
Don't be sad.
HE DOESN'T WANT TO PUT YOU IN DANGER.
THAT'S LOVE!
GANTA... LIKES ME...?
HUH?
DOESN'T HE?
YES HE DOES!
HA HA HA.

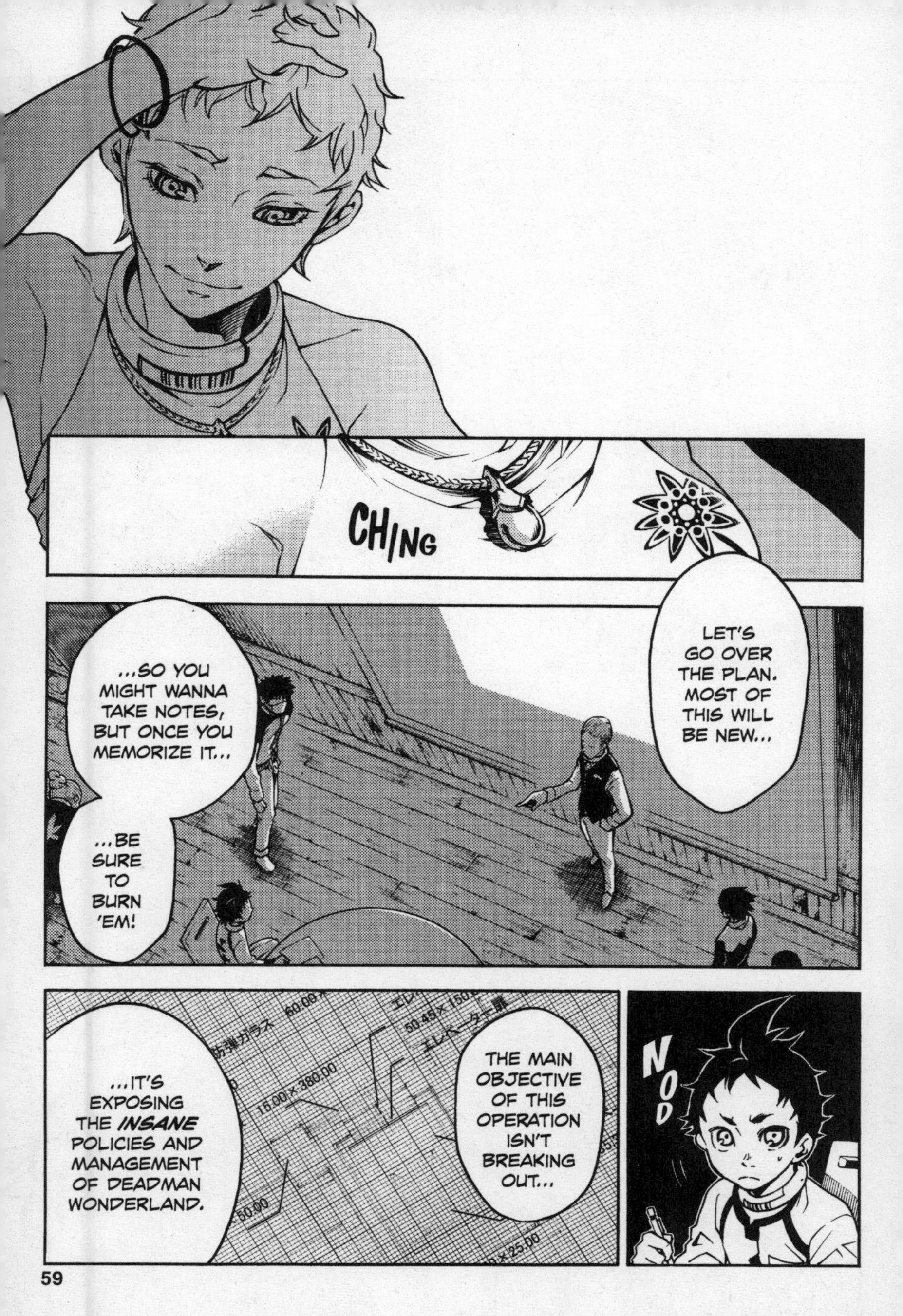
CHING
LET'S GO OVER THE PLAN. MOST OF THIS WILL BE NEW...
...SO YOU MIGHT WANNA TAKE NOTES, BUT ONCE YOU MEMORIZE IT...
...BE SURE TO BURN 'EM!
NOD
THE MAIN OBJECTIVE OF THIS OPERATION ISN'T BREAKING OUT...
...IT'S EXPOSING THE *INSANE* POLICIES AND MANAGEMENT OF DEADMAN WONDERLAND.

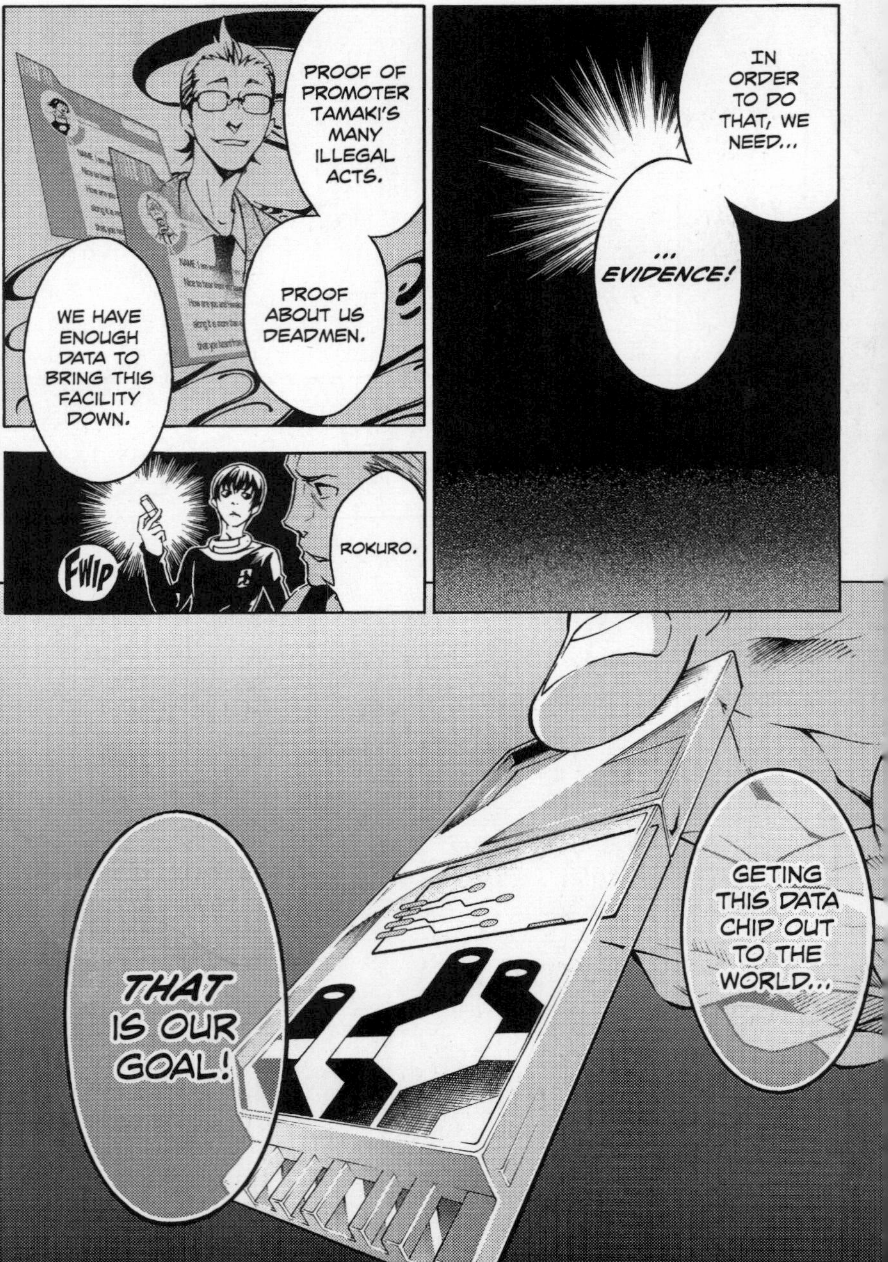
IN ORDER TO DO THAT, WE NEED...
...EVIDENCE!
PROOF OF PROMOTER TAMAKI'S MANY ILLEGAL ACTS.
PROOF ABOUT US DEADMEN.
WE HAVE ENOUGH DATA TO BRING THIS FACILITY DOWN.
ROKURO.
FWIP
GETING THIS DATA CHIP OUT TO THE WORLD...
THAT IS OUR GOAL!

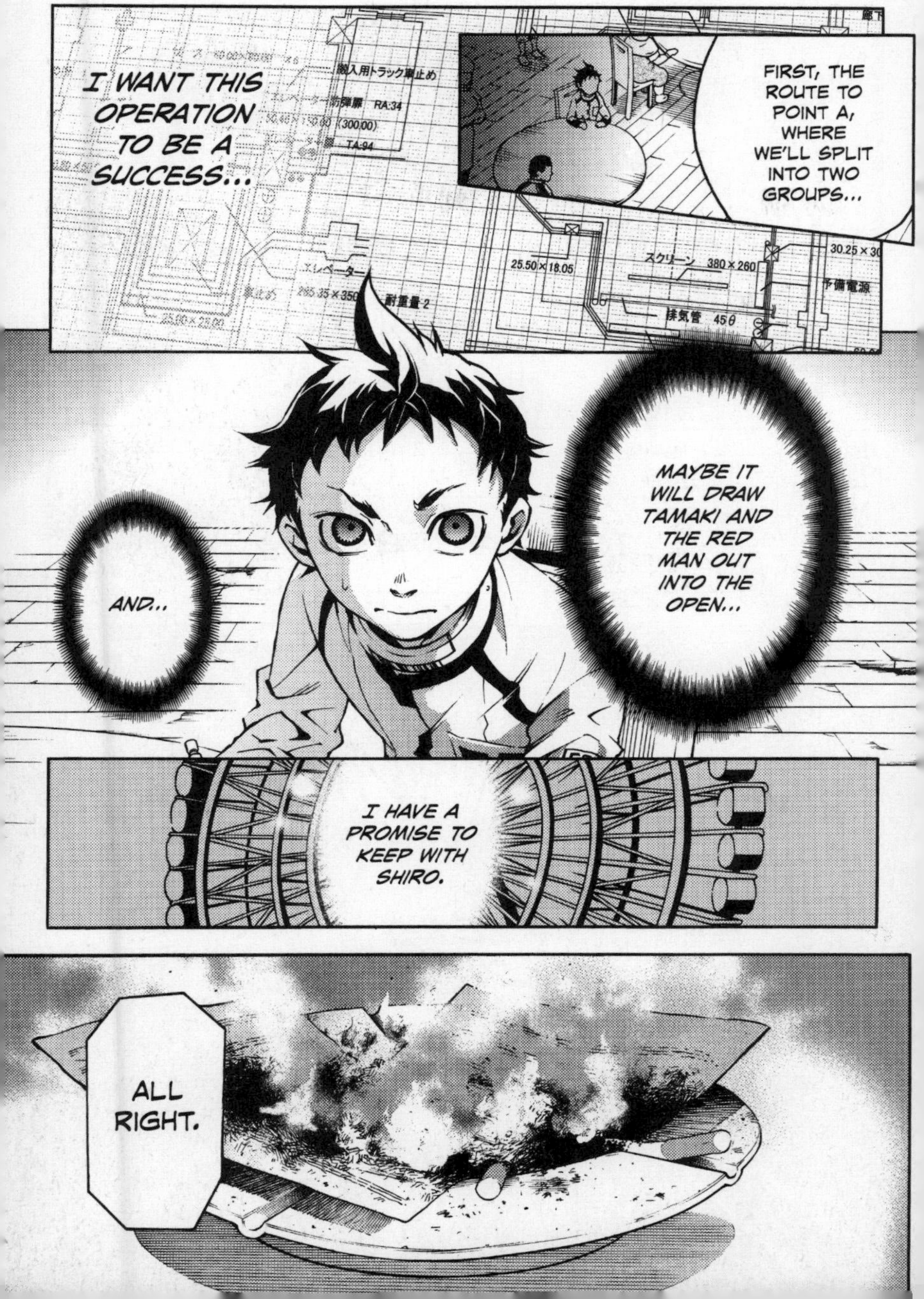
FIRST, THE ROUTE TO POINT A, WHERE WE'LL SPLIT INTO TWO GROUPS...
I WANT THIS OPERATION TO BE A SUCCESS...
MAYBE IT WILL DRAW TAMAKI AND THE RED MAN OUT INTO THE OPEN...
AND...
I HAVE A PROMISE TO KEEP WITH SHIRO.
ALL RIGHT.

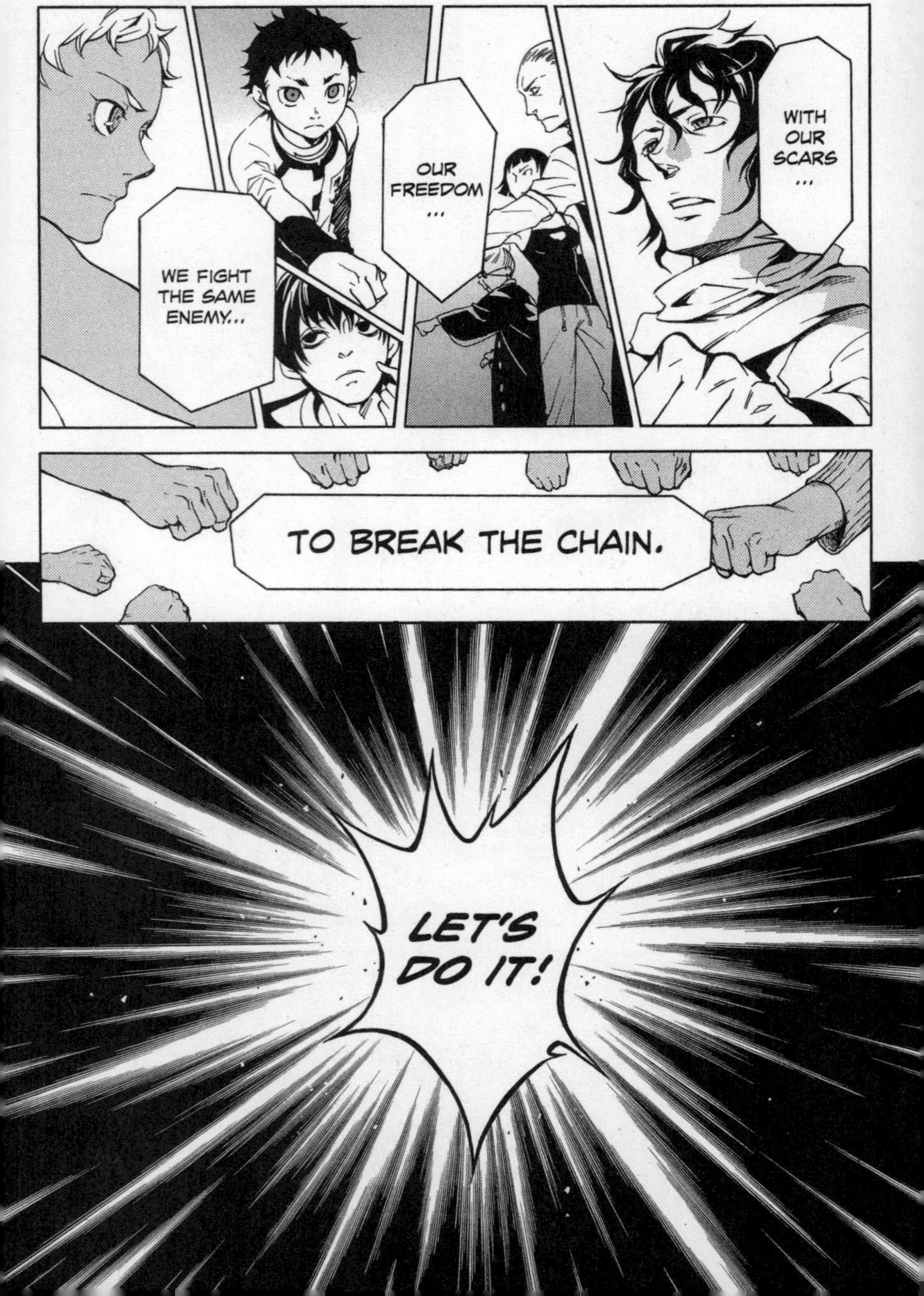
WITH OUR SCARS ...
OUR FREEDOM ...
WE FIGHT THE SAME ENEMY...
TO BREAK THE CHAIN.
LET'S DO IT!

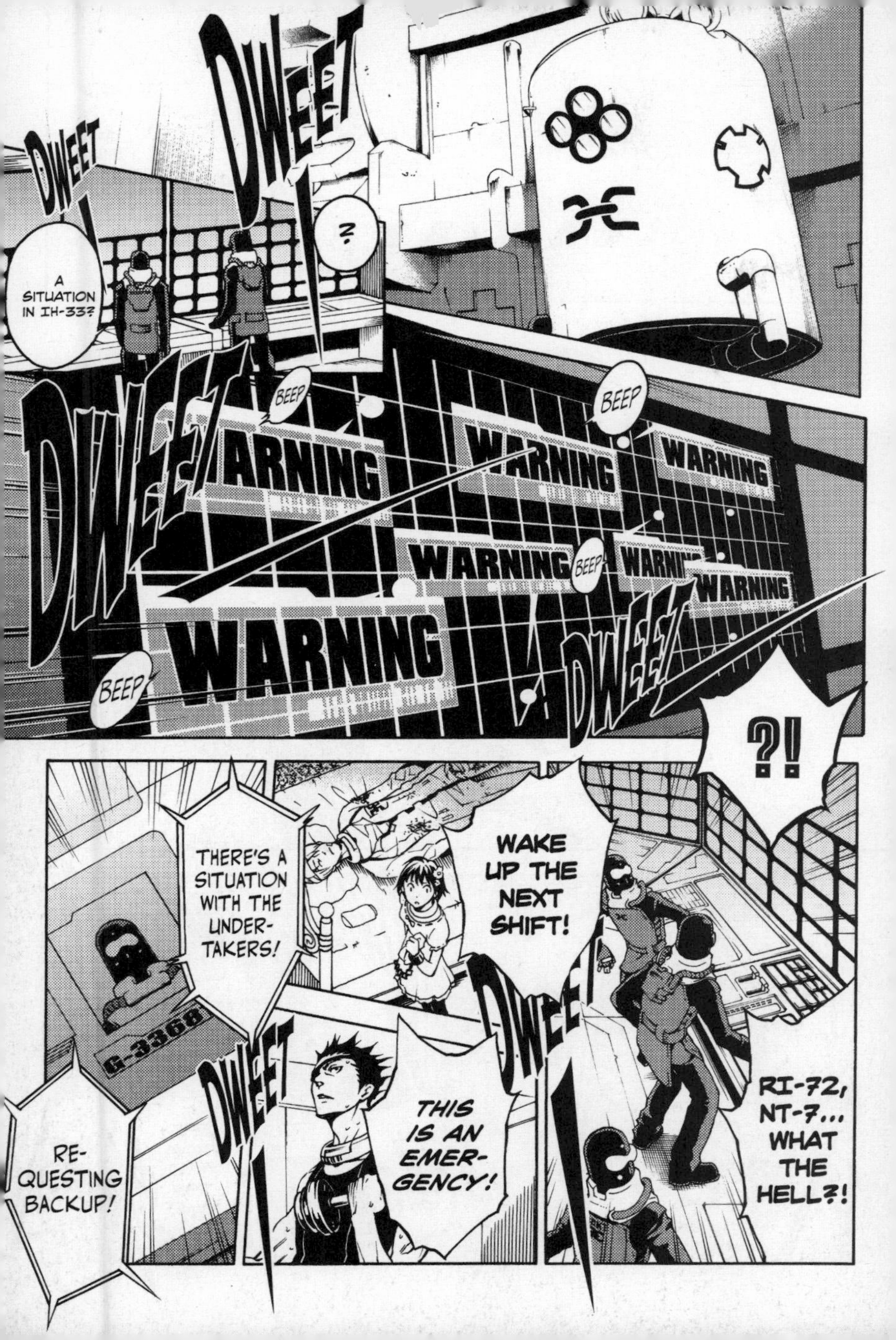
DWEET
DWEET
?
DWEET
A SITUATION IN IH-33?
BEEP
WARNING
WARNING
WARNING
BEEP
WARNING
WARNING
WARNING
DWEET
BEEP
WARNING
BEEP
DWEET
?!
WAKE UP THE NEXT SHIFT!
RI-72, NT-7... WHAT THE HELL?!
DWEET
THIS IS AN EMER-GENCY!
DWEET
THERE'S A SITUATION WITH THE UNDER-TAKERS!
G-3368
RE-QUESTING BACKUP!

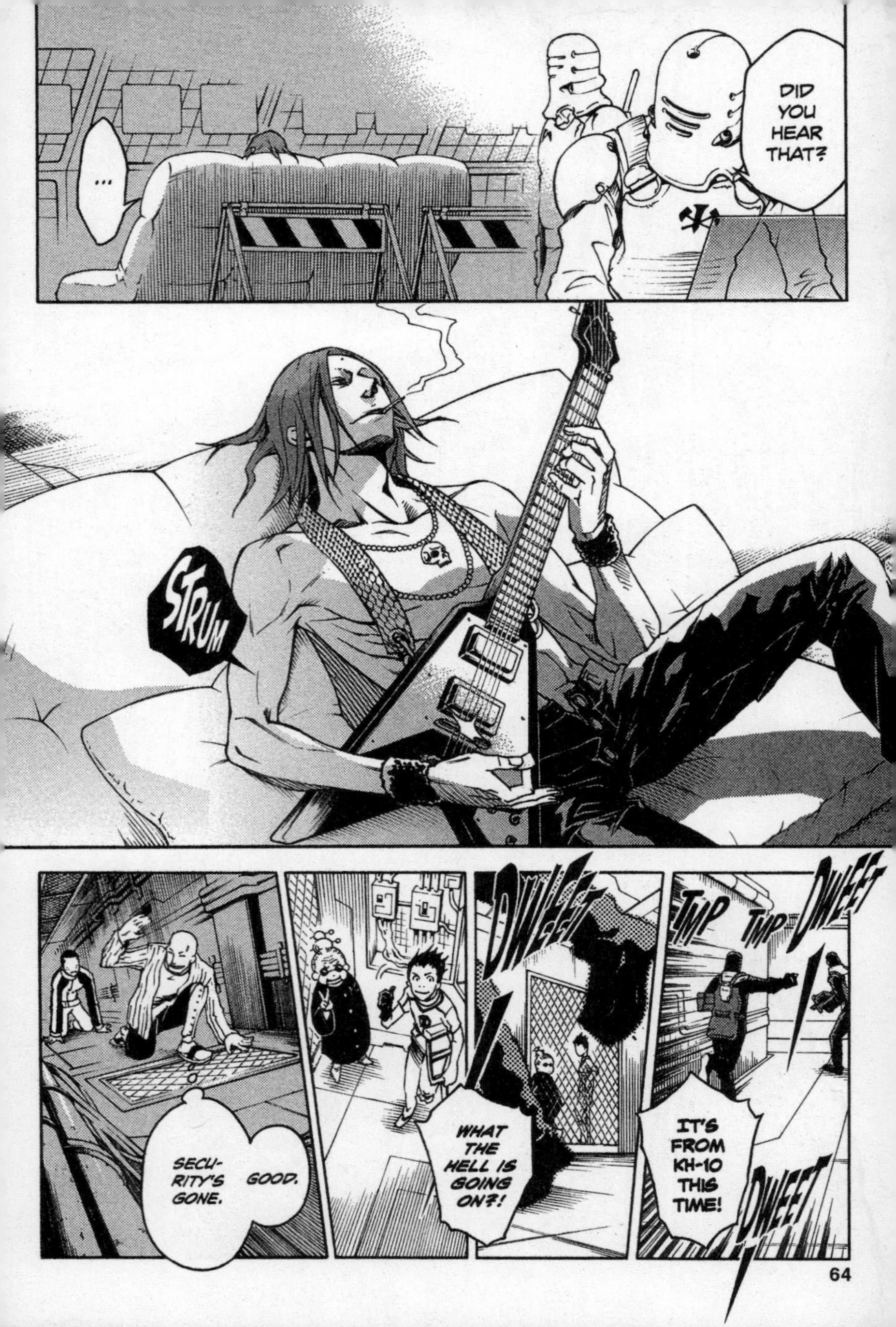
DID YOU HEAR THAT?
...
STRUM
TMP TMP
DWEET
IT'S FROM KH-10 THIS TIME!
DWEET
DWEET
WHAT THE HELL IS GOING ON?!
SECU-RITY'S GONE.
GOOD.

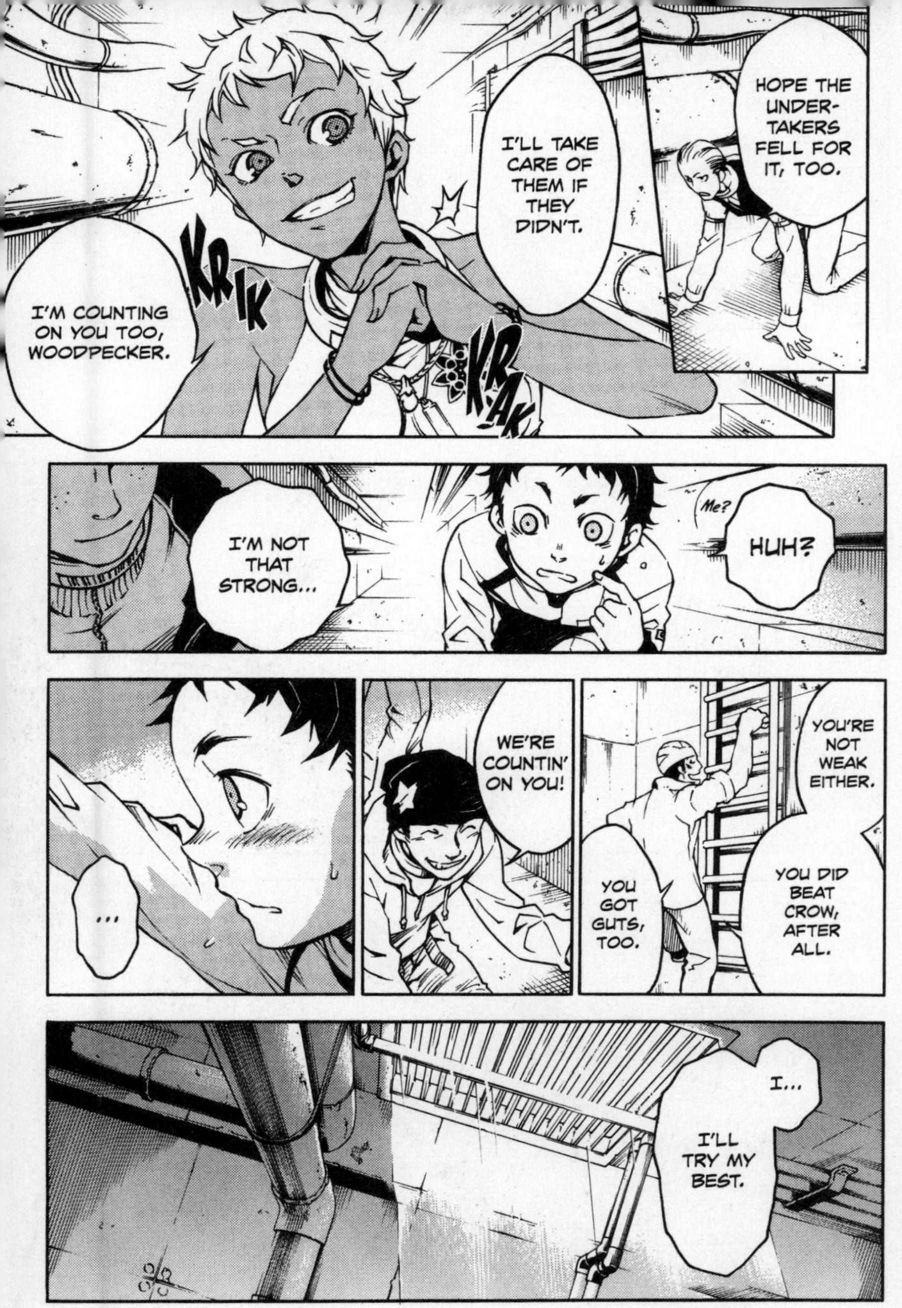
HOPE THE UNDER-TAKERS FELL FOR IT, TOO.
I'LL TAKE CARE OF THEM IF THEY DIDN'T.
KRIK
KRAK
I'M COUNTING ON YOU TOO, WOODPECKER.
HUH?
Me?
I'M NOT THAT STRONG...
YOU'RE NOT WEAK EITHER.
YOU DID BEAT CROW, AFTER ALL.
YOU GOT GUTS, TOO.
WE'RE COUNTIN' ON YOU!
...
I...
I'LL TRY MY BEST.

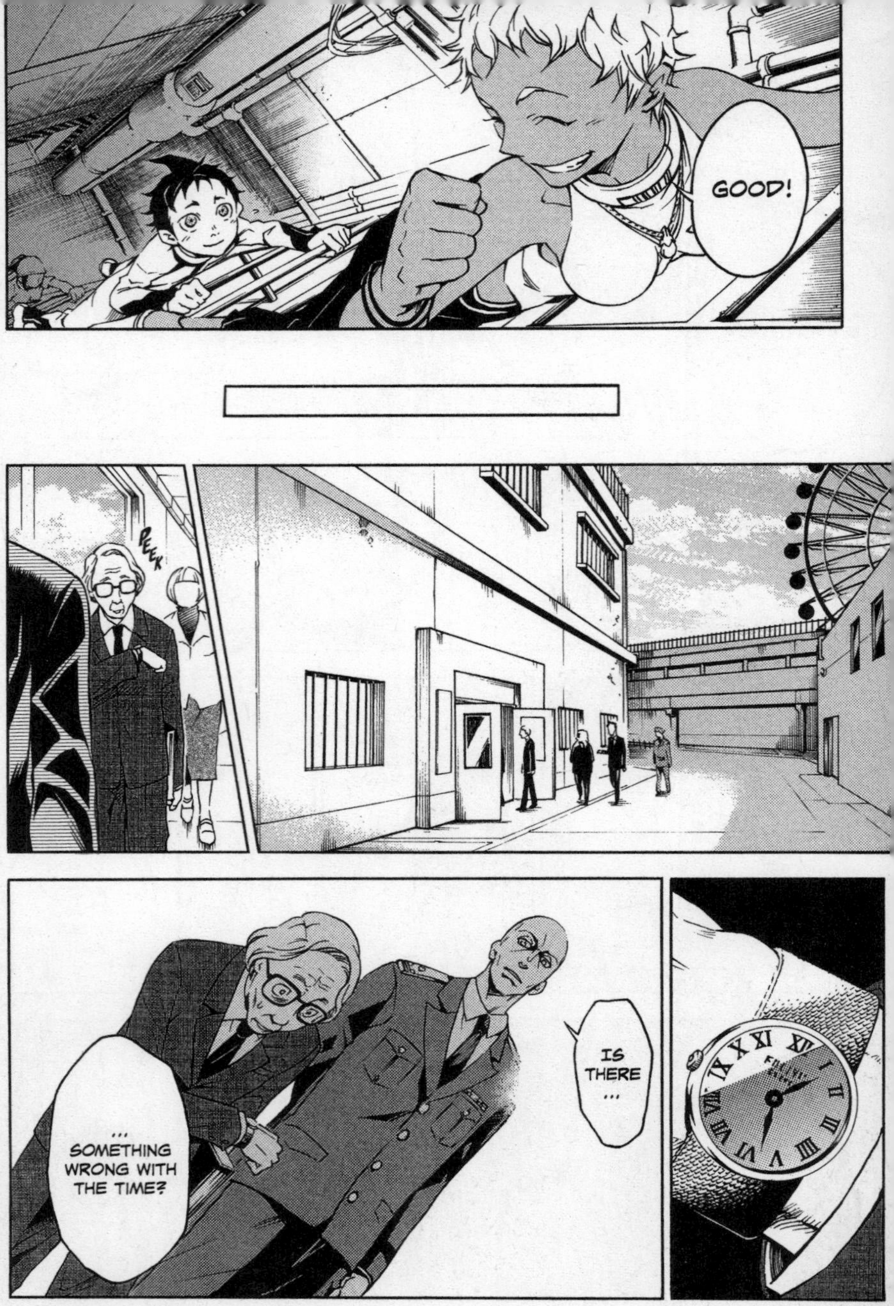
GOOD!
PEEK
IS THERE ...
... SOMETHING WRONG WITH THE TIME?

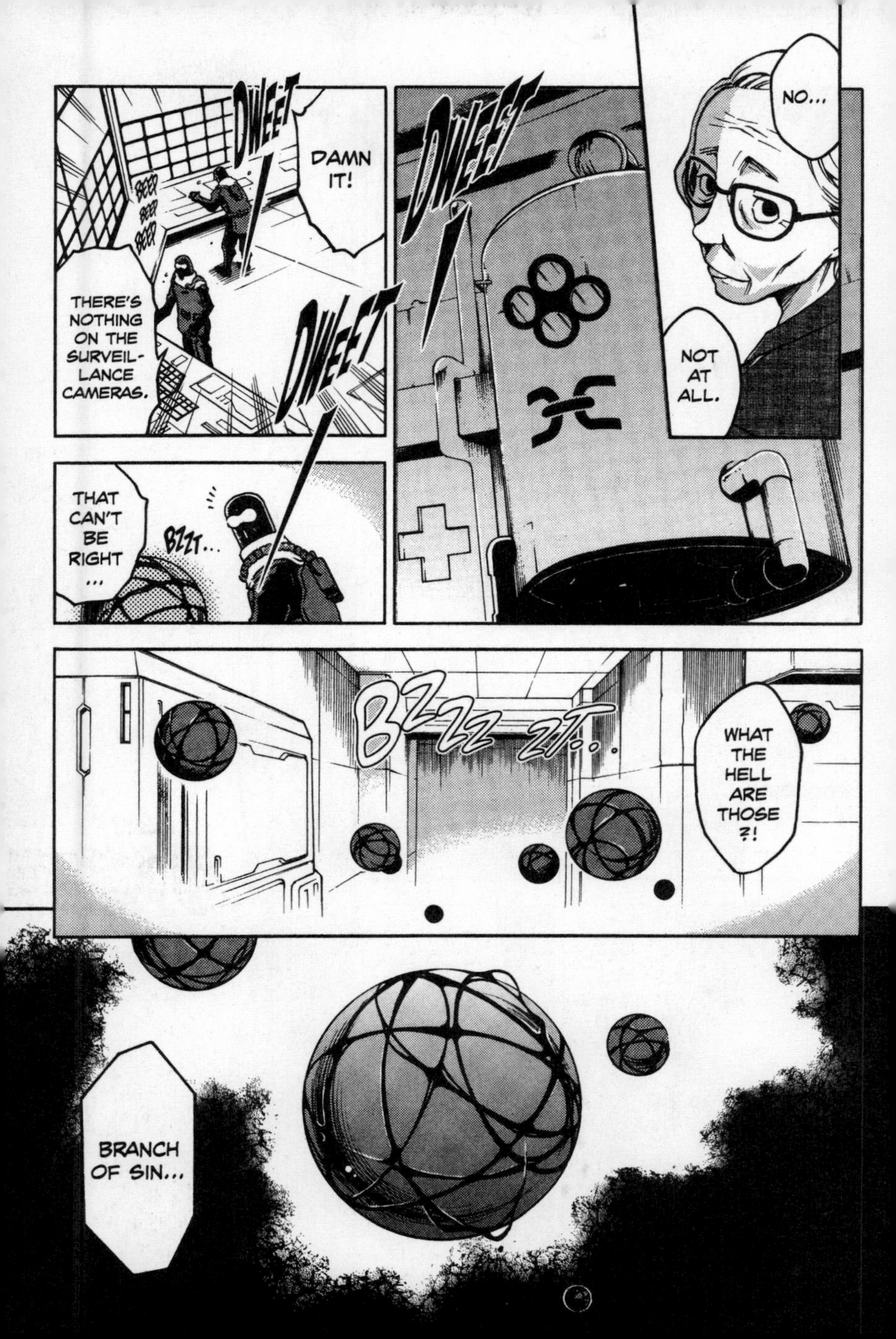
NO...
NOT AT ALL.
DWEET
DWEET
DWEET
DAMN IT!
BEEP BEEP BEEP
THERE'S NOTHING ON THE SURVEIL-LANCE CAMERAS.
THAT CAN'T BE RIGHT...
BZZT...
BZZZZT...
WHAT THE HELL ARE THOSE?!
BRANCH OF SIN...

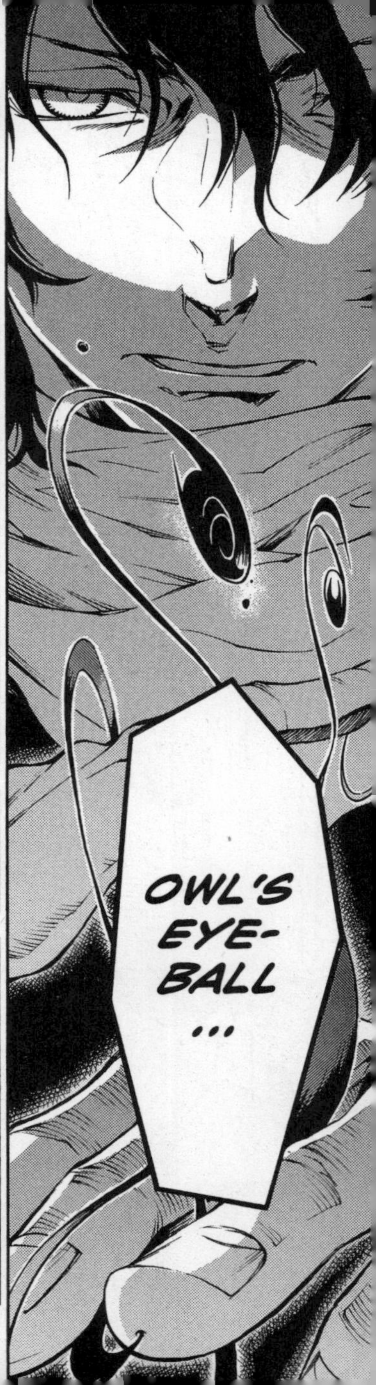
OWL'S EYE-BALL ...

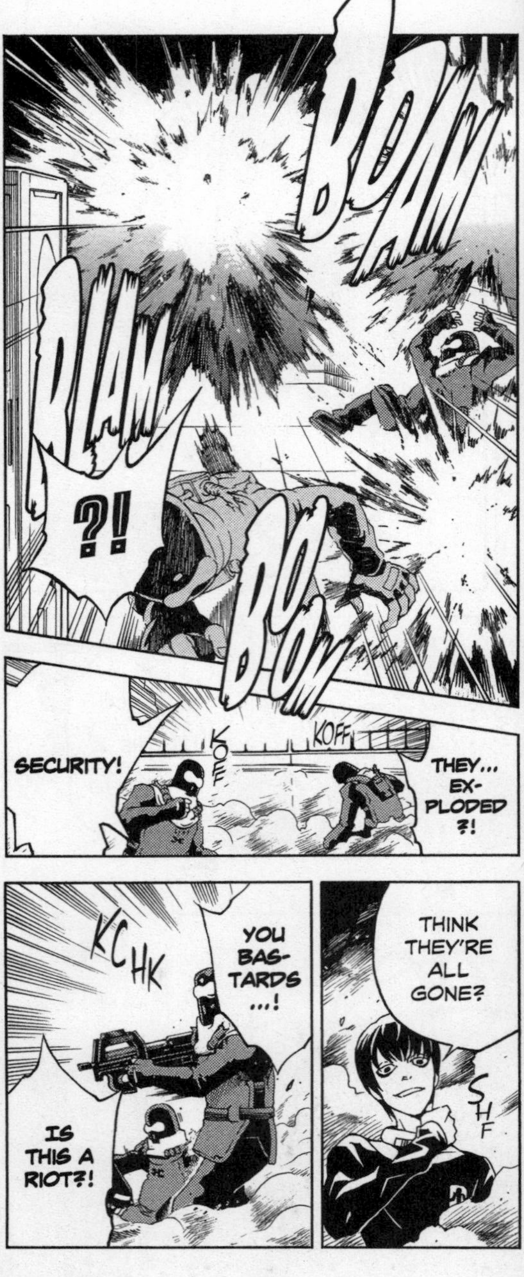
BOOM
BLAM
?!
BOOM
THEY... EX-PLODED ?!
KOFF
KOFF
SECURITY!
THINK THEY'RE ALL GONE?
SHF
YOU BAS-TARDS ...!
KCHK
IS THIS A RIOT?!

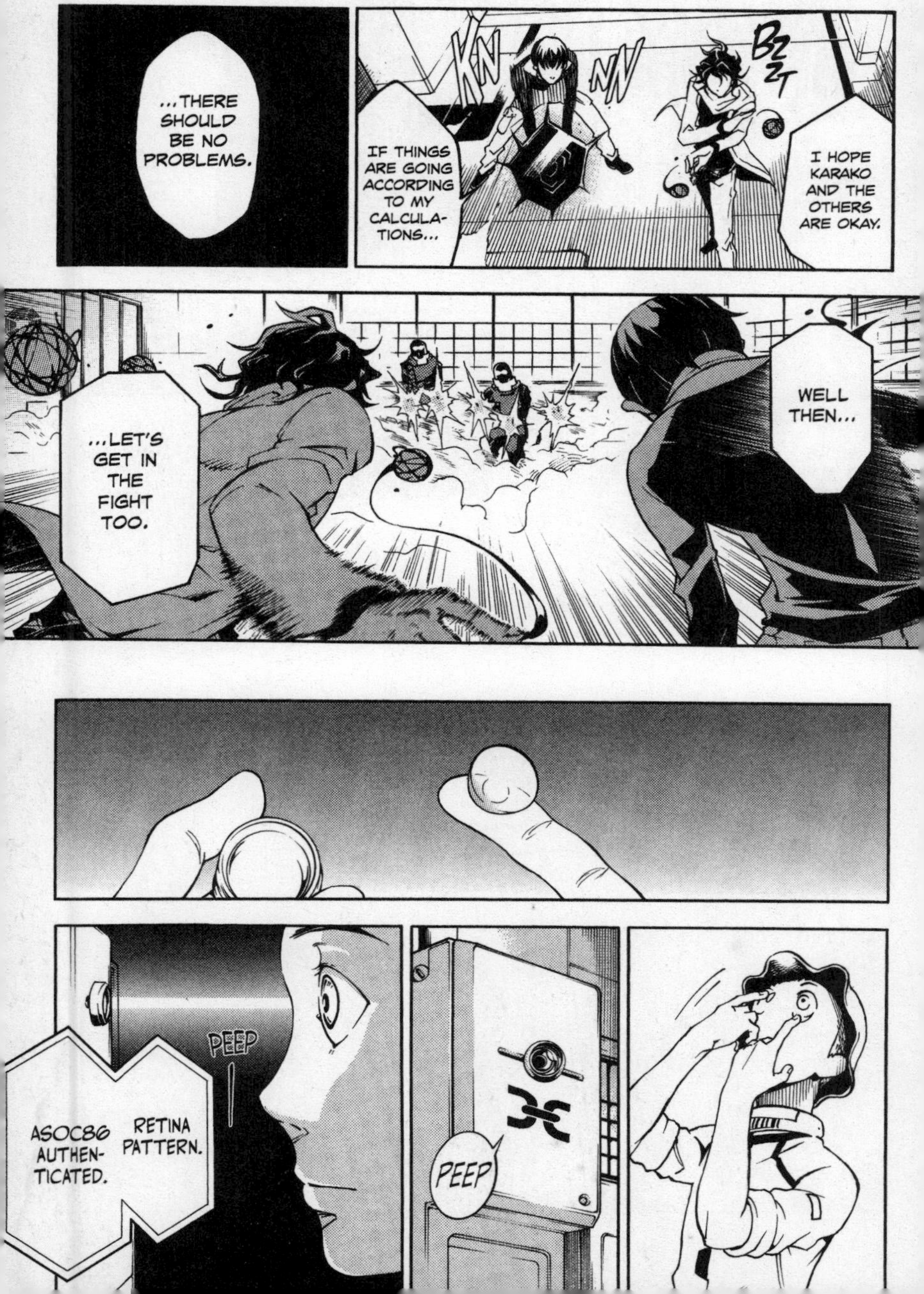
I HOPE KARAKO AND THE OTHERS ARE OKAY.
BZZT
IF THINGS ARE GOING ACCORDING TO MY CALCULATIONS...
KNNN
...THERE SHOULD BE NO PROBLEMS.
WELL THEN...
...LET'S GET IN THE FIGHT TOO.
PEEP
RETINA PATTERN.
ASOC86 AUTHENTICATED.
PEEP

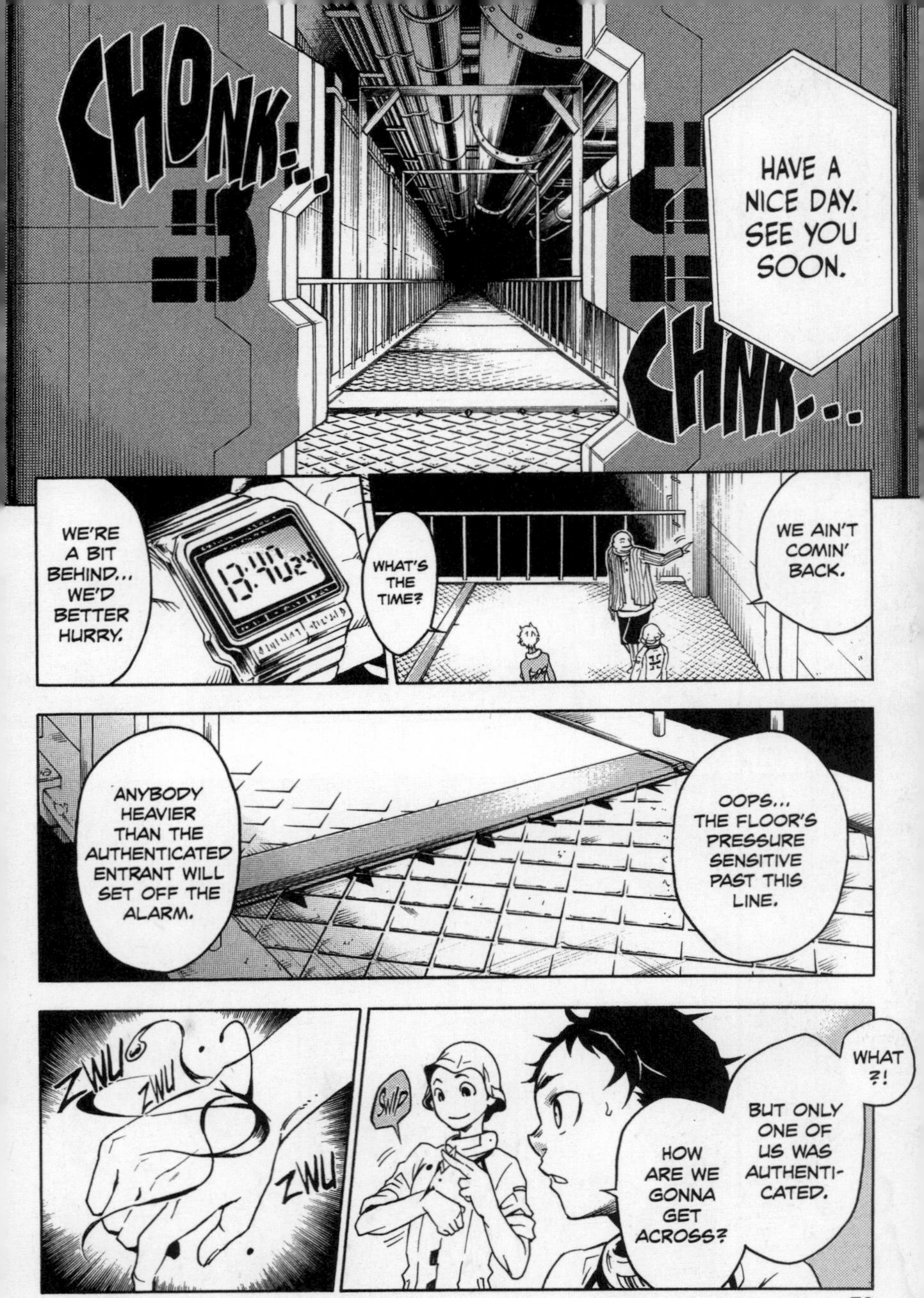
HAVE A NICE DAY. SEE YOU SOON.
CHONK...
CHNK...
WE AIN'T COMIN' BACK.
WHAT'S THE TIME?
WE'RE A BIT BEHIND... WE'D BETTER HURRY.
OOPS... THE FLOOR'S PRESSURE SENSITIVE PAST THIS LINE.
ANYBODY HEAVIER THAN THE AUTHENTICATED ENTRANT WILL SET OFF THE ALARM.
WHAT?!
BUT ONLY ONE OF US WAS AUTHENTI-CATED.
HOW ARE WE GONNA GET ACROSS?
SWIP
ZWU
ZWU
ZWU

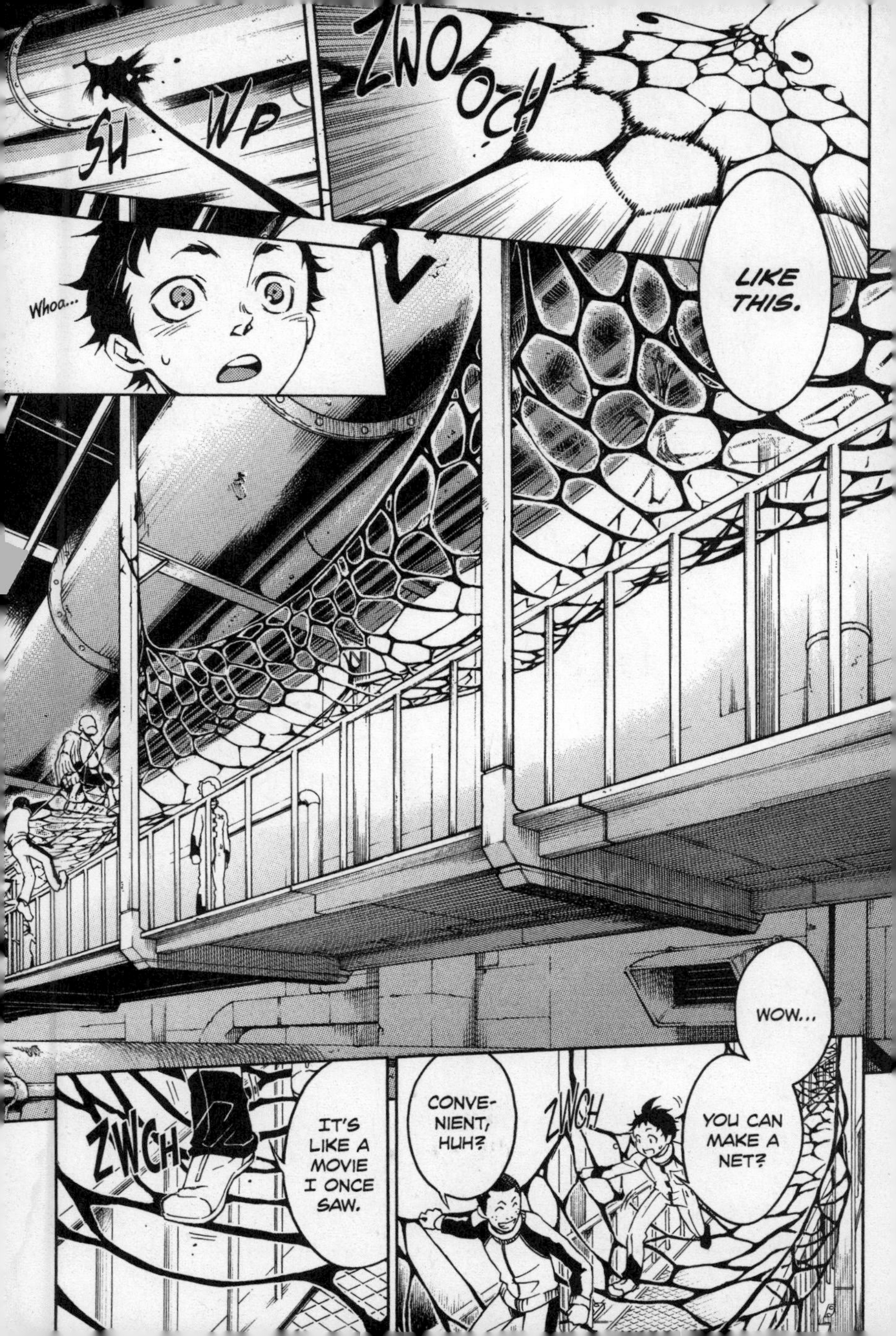
ZWOOCH
SH WP
LIKE THIS.
Whoa...
WOW...
YOU CAN MAKE A NET?
ZWCH
CONVE-NIENT, HUH?
IT'S LIKE A MOVIE I ONCE SAW.
ZWCH

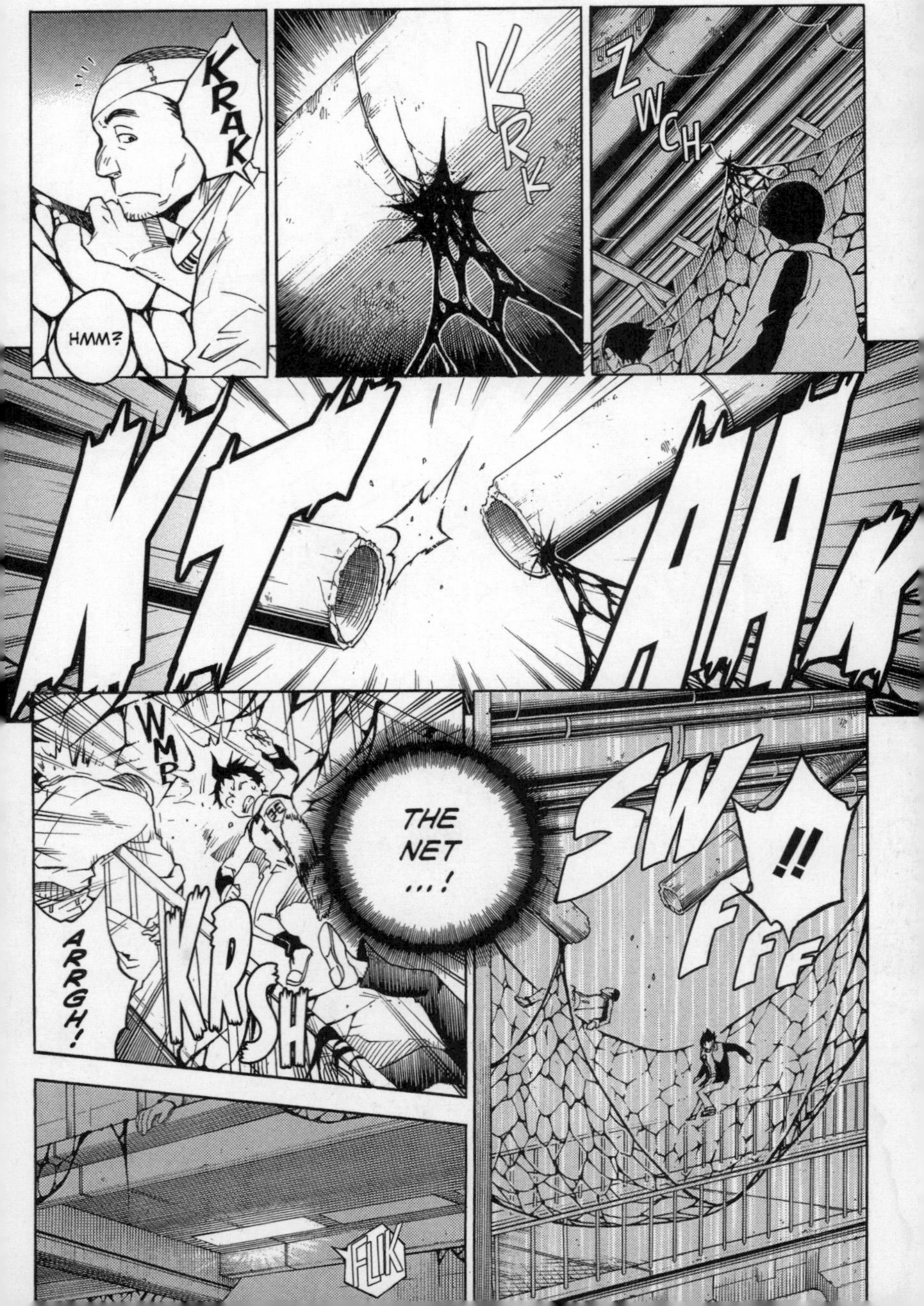
ZWCH
KRRK
KRAK
HMM?
SWFFF
!!
THE NET ...!
WMP
KRSH
ARRGH!
FLIK

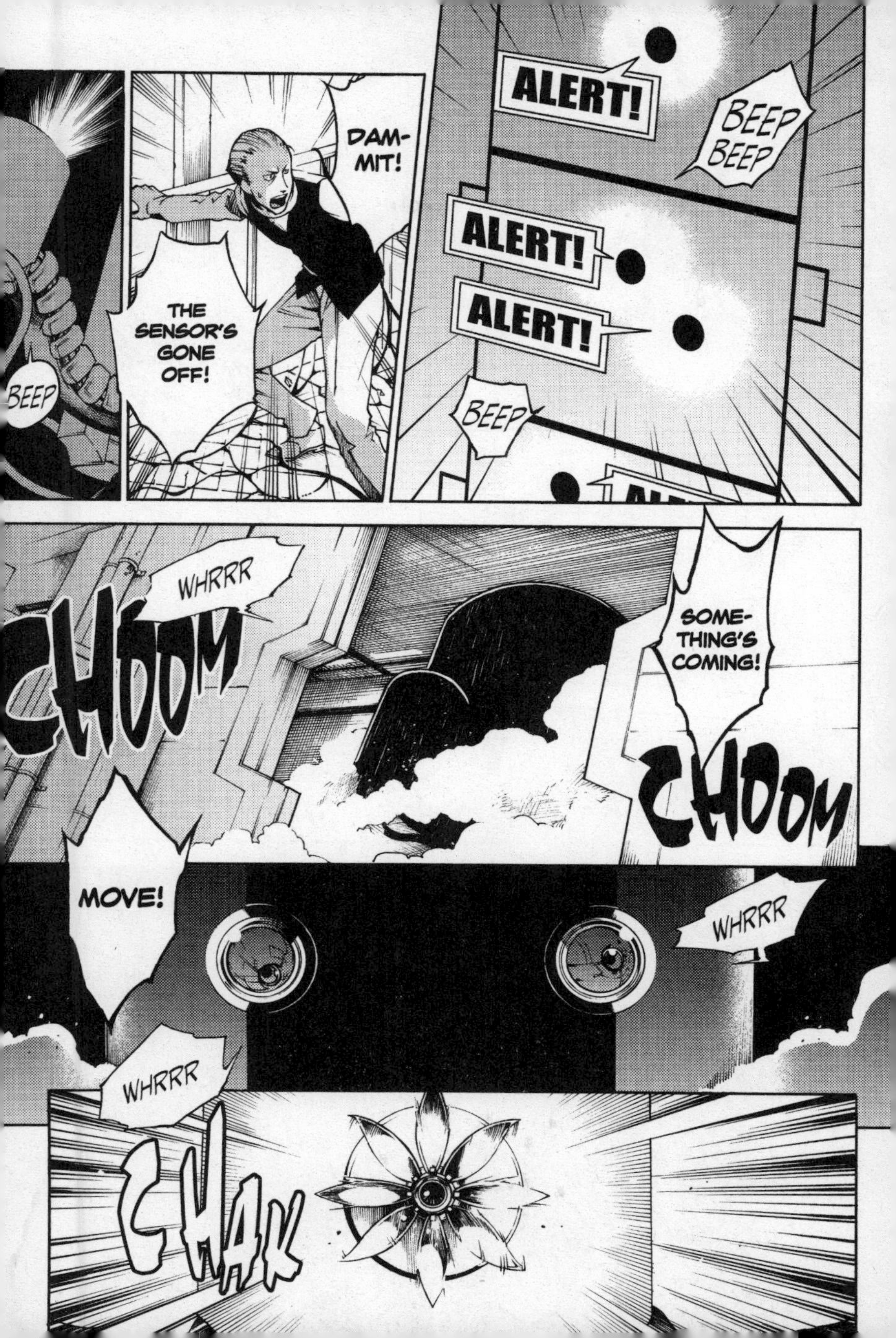
ALERT!
BEEP BEEP
ALERT!
ALERT!
BEEP
DAM-MIT!
THE SENSOR'S GONE OFF!
BEEP
SOME-THING'S COMING!
WHRRR
CHOOM
CHOOM
WHRRR
MOVE!
WHRRR
CHAK

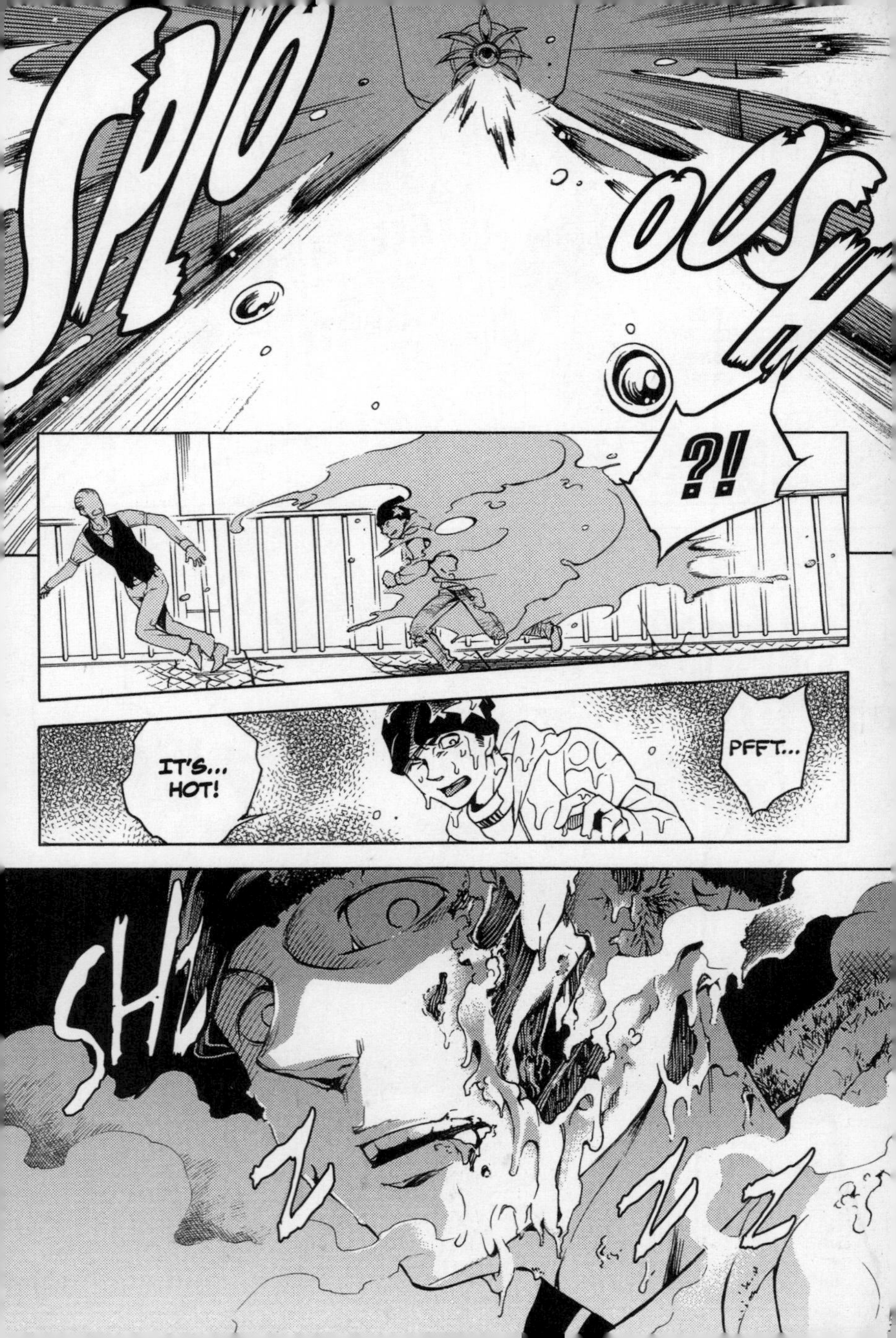
SPLO
OOSH
?!
PFFT...
IT'S... HOT!
SHZ
ZZZ

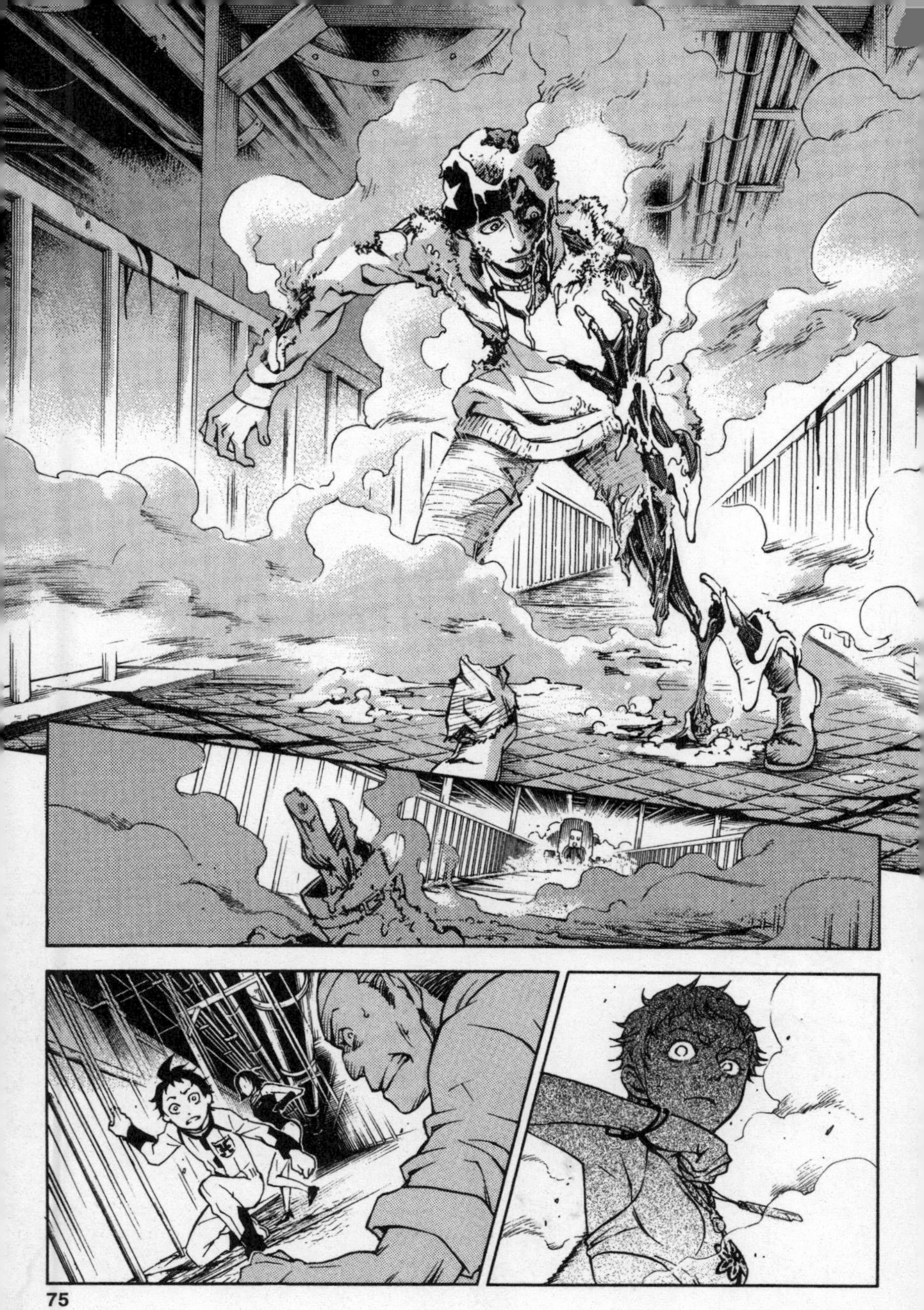

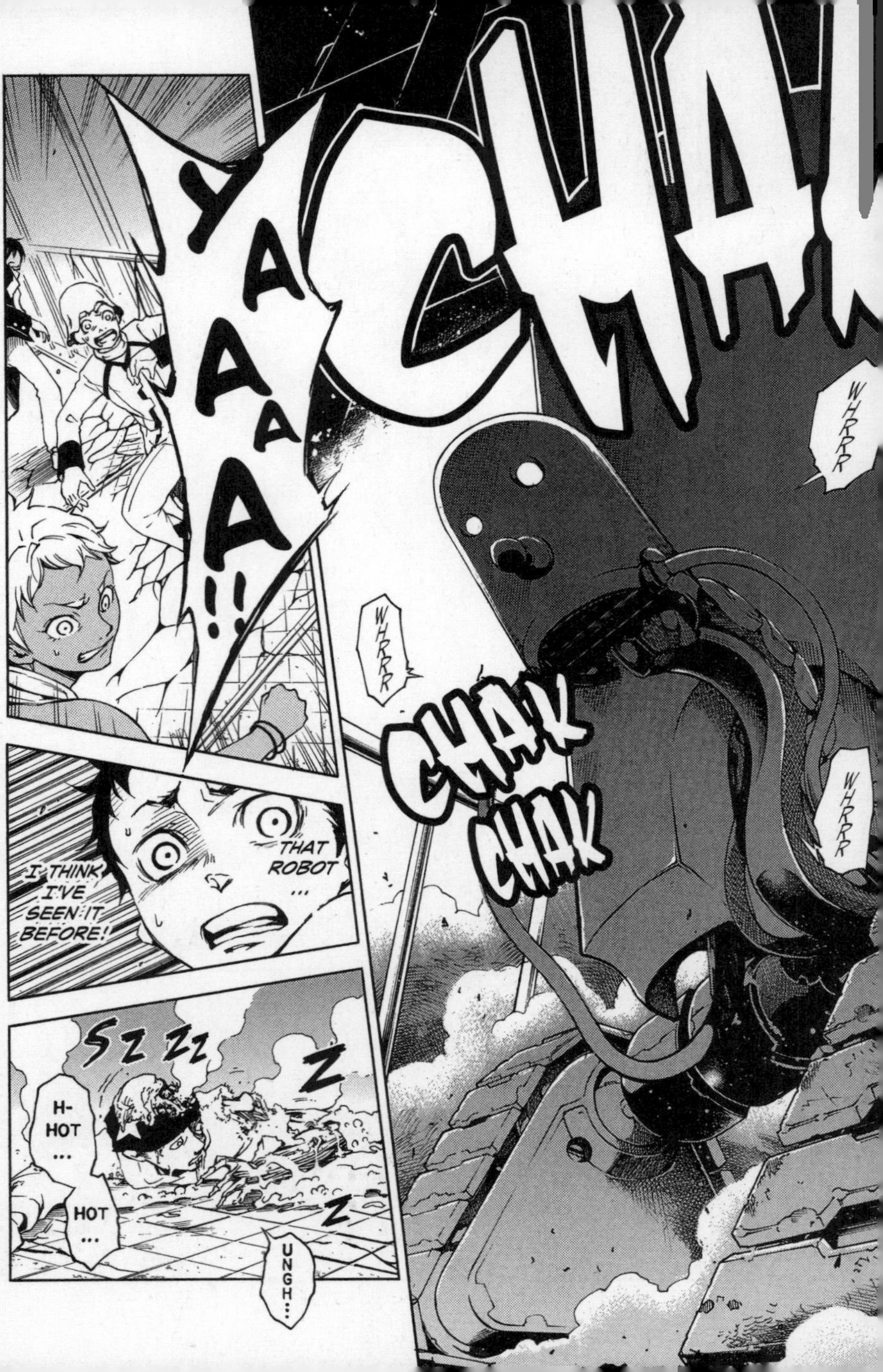
CHA
WHRRR
WHRRR
CHAK CHAK
WHRRR
YAAAAA!!
THAT ROBOT...
I THINK I'VE SEEN IT BEFORE!
SZZZZ
Z
Z
H-HOT...
HOT...
UNGH...

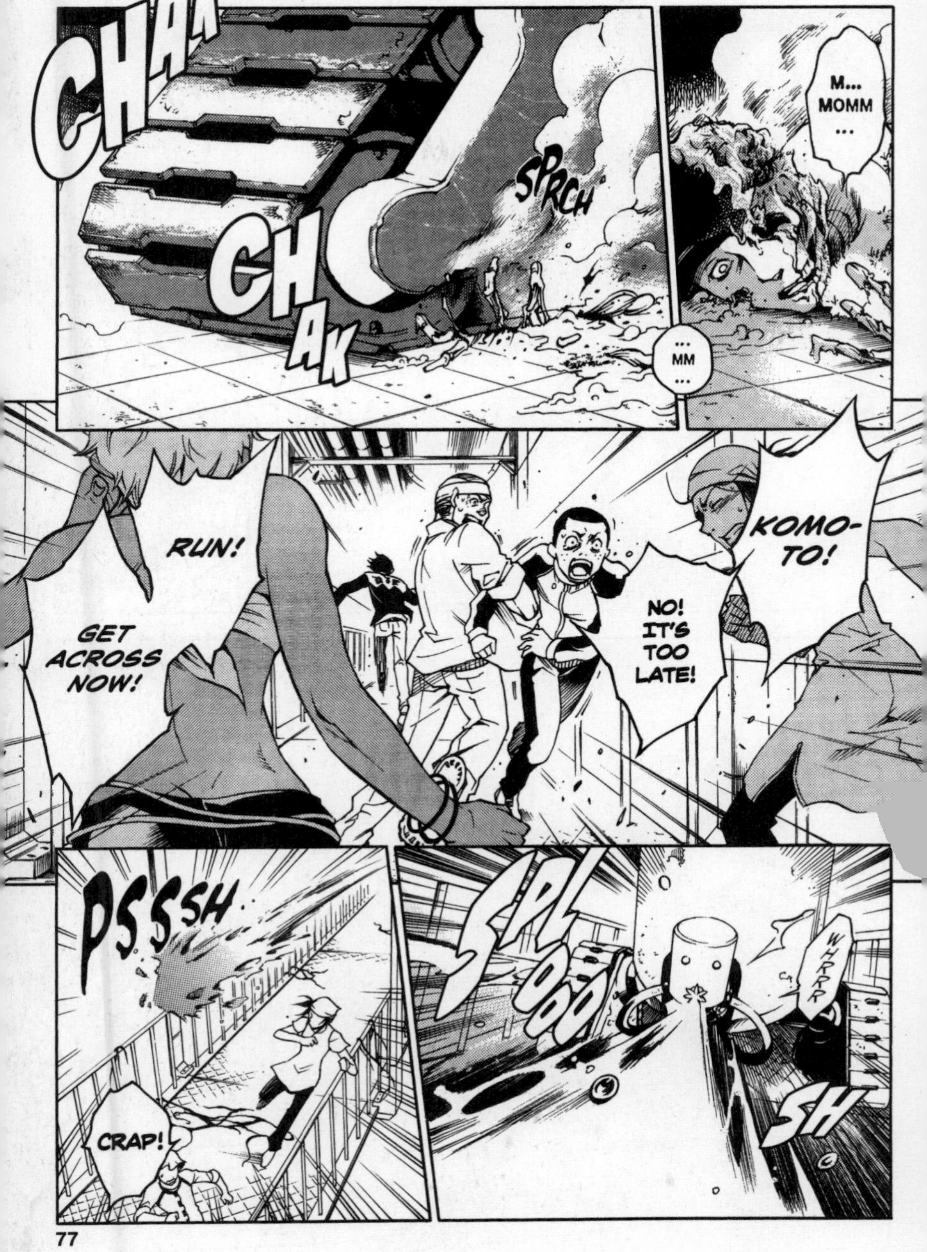
M... MOMM ...
... MM ...
CHAK
SPRCH
CHAK
KOMO-TO!
NO! IT'S TOO LATE!
RUN!
GET ACROSS NOW!
SPLOOO
WHRRR
SH
PSSSH
CRAP!

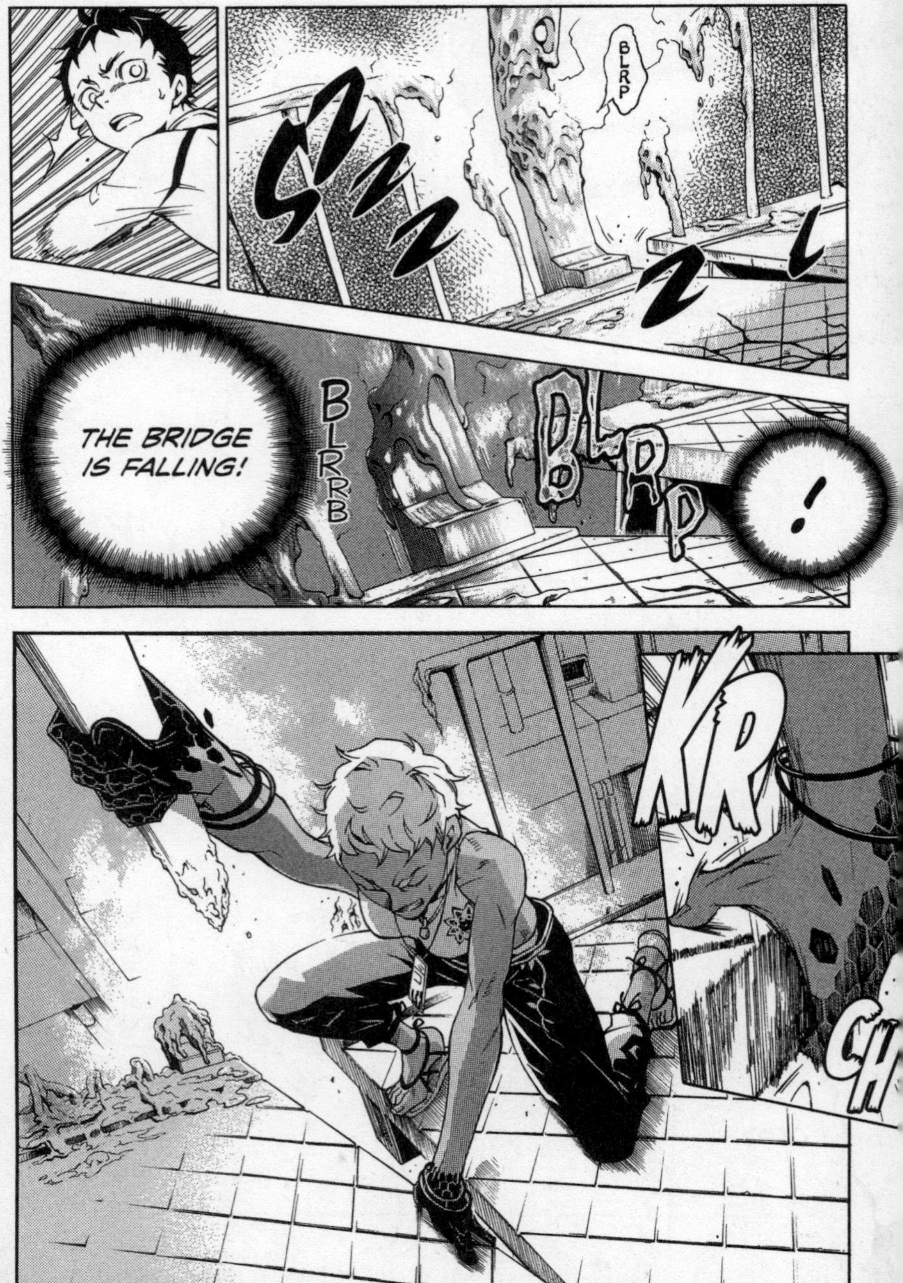
BLRP
BLRP
BLRRB
THE BRIDGE IS FALLING!
KR
CH

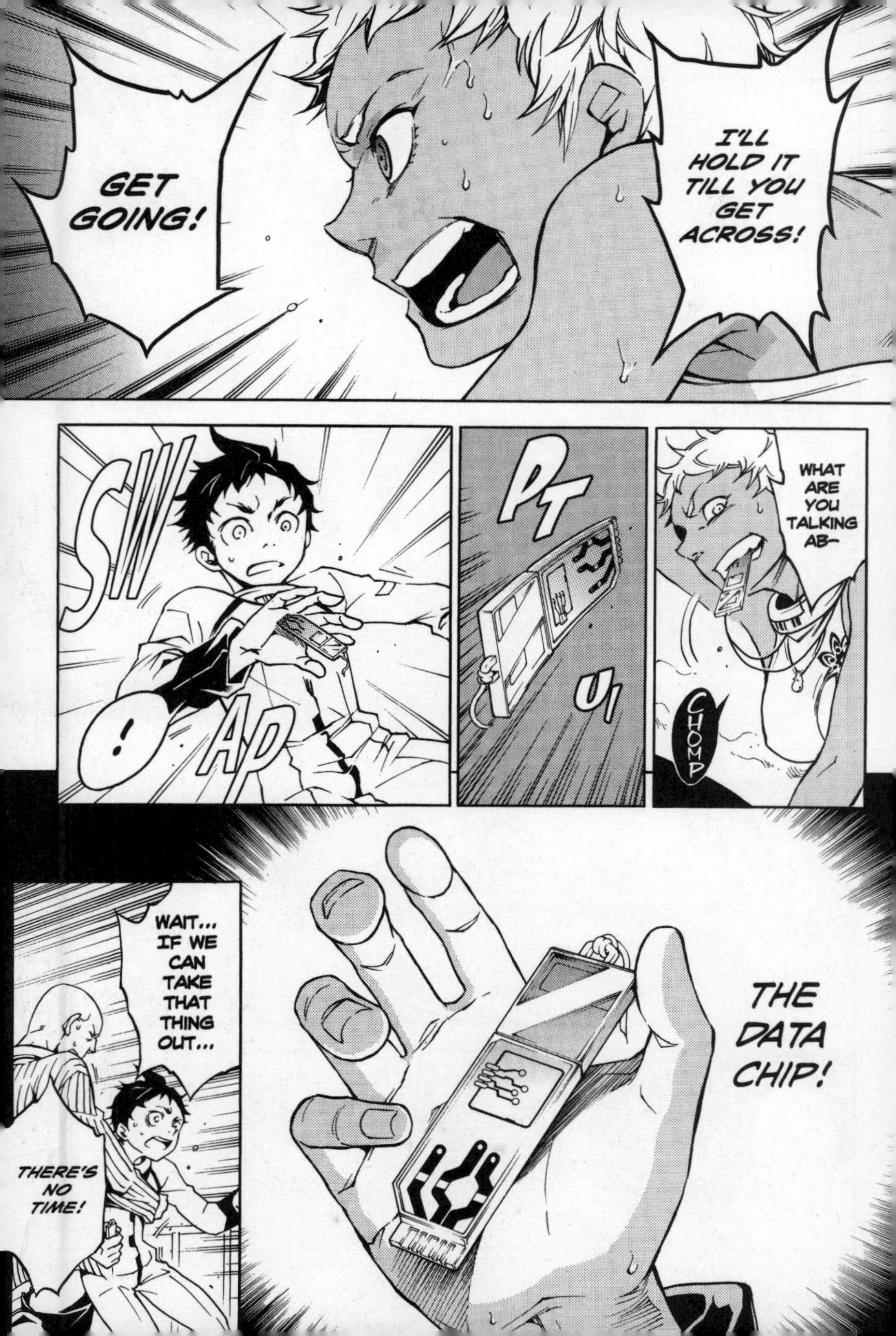
I'LL HOLD IT TILL YOU GET ACROSS!
GET GOING!
WHAT ARE YOU TALKING AB—
CHOMP
PT
UI
SW
AP
!
THE DATA CHIP!
WAIT... IF WE CAN TAKE THAT THING OUT...
THERE'S NO TIME!

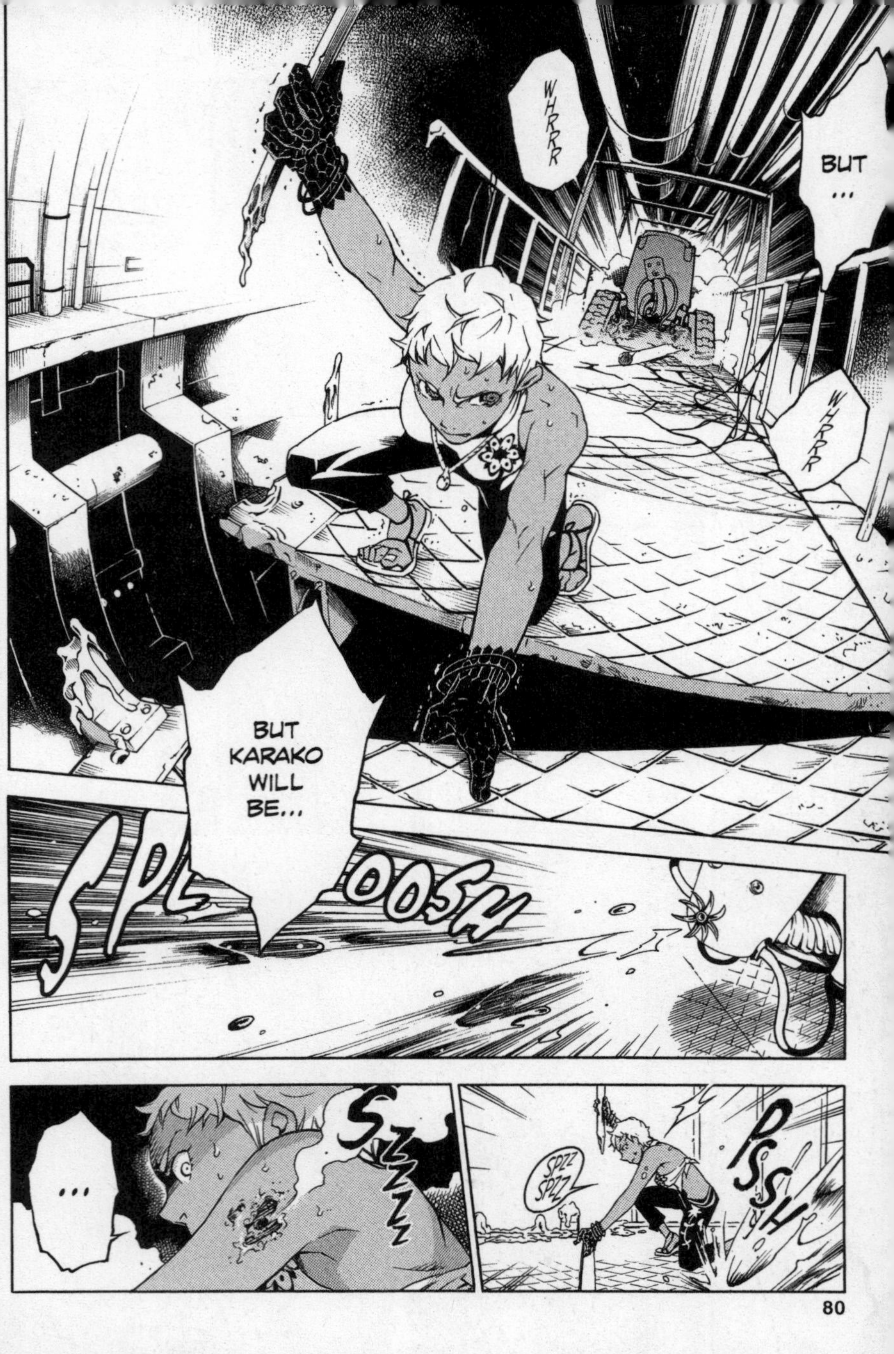
BUT ...
WHRRR
WHRRR
BUT KARAKO WILL BE...
SPLOOSH
PSSH
SPZZ SPZZ
SZZZ
...

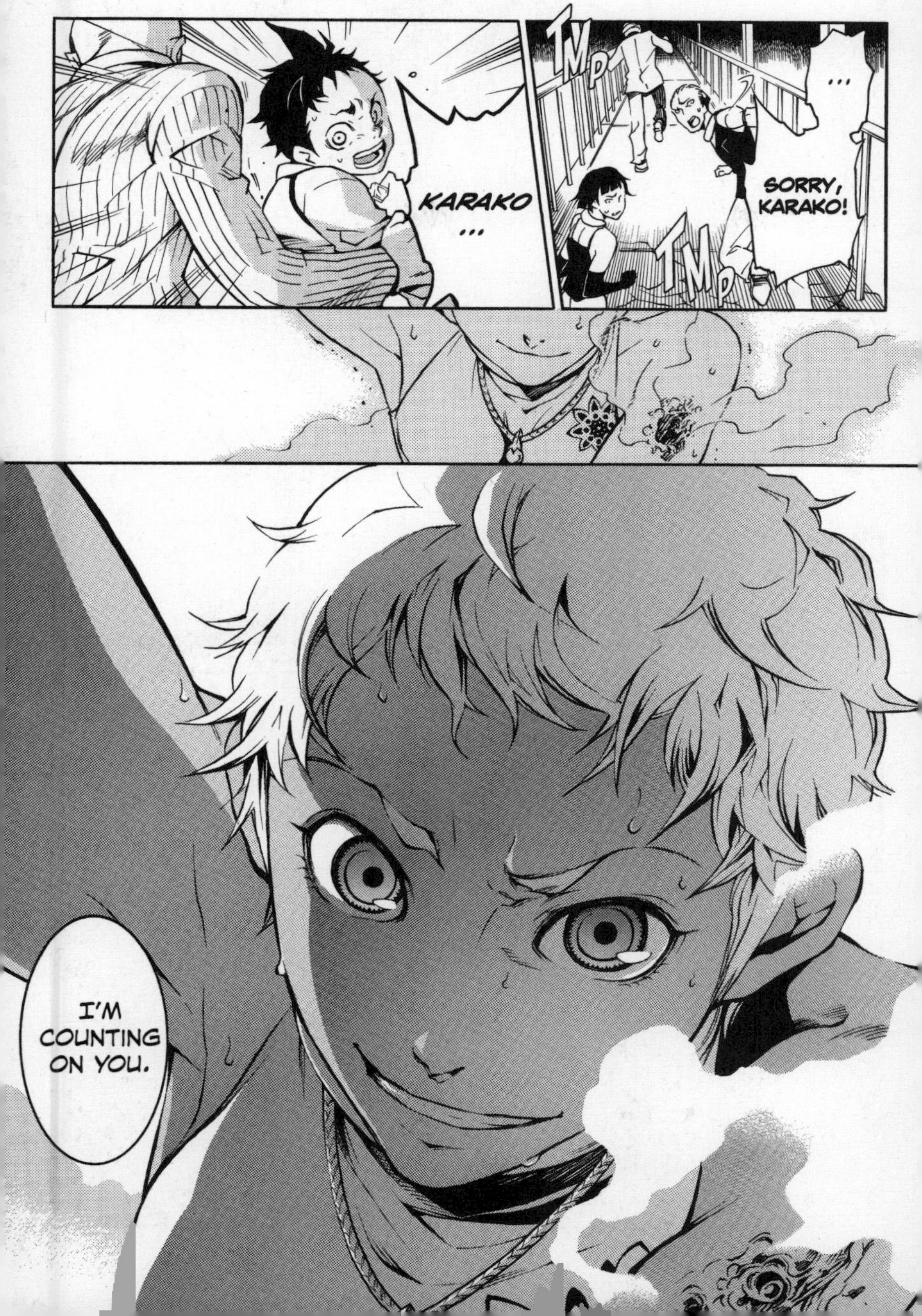
...
TMP
SORRY, KARAKO!
TMP
KARAKO ...
I'M COUNTING ON YOU.

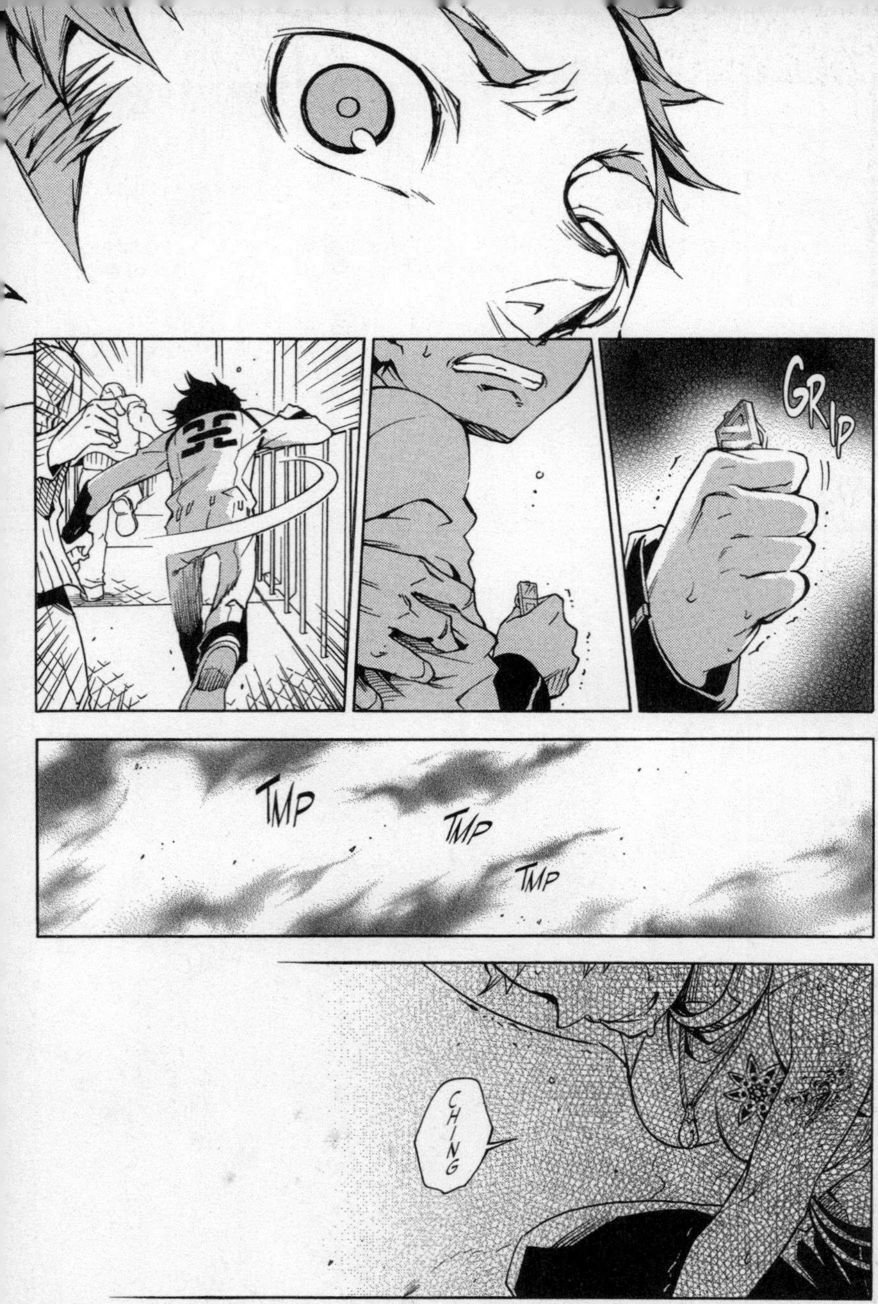
GRIP
TMP
TMP
TMP
CHING

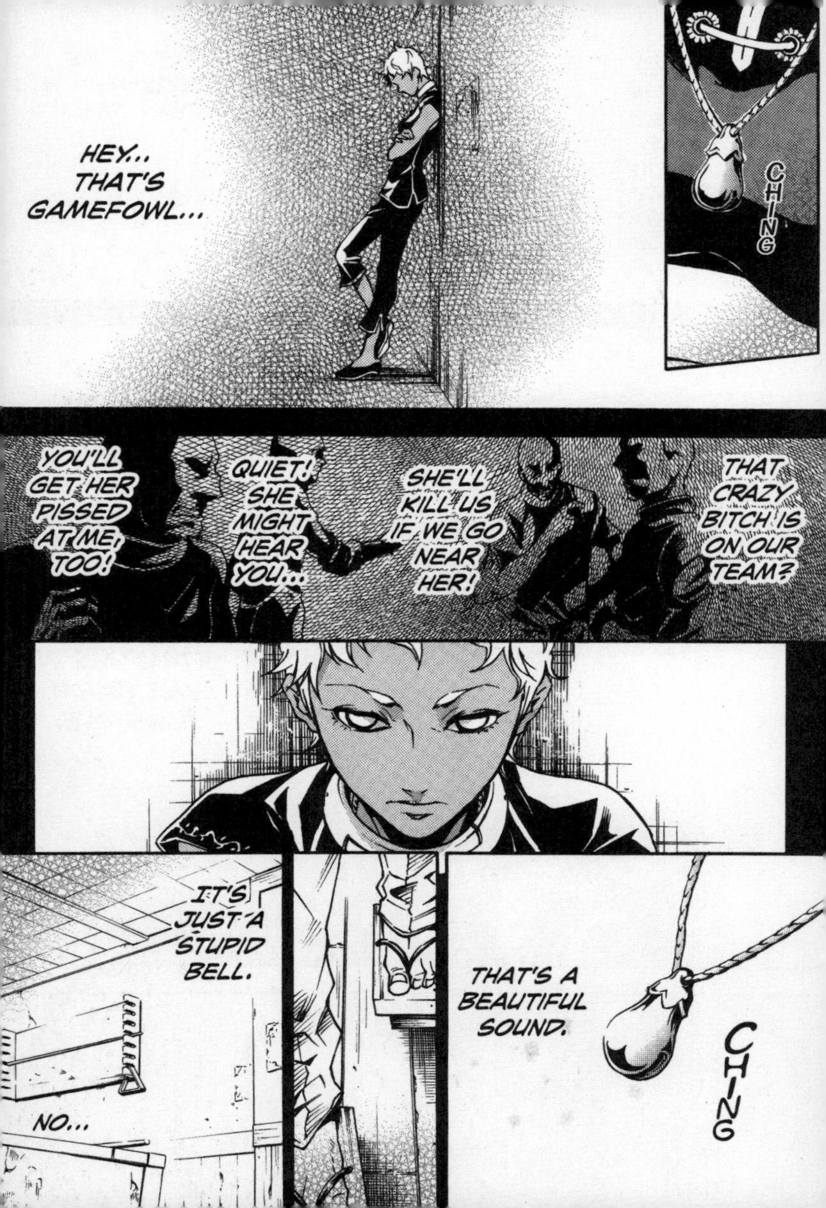
CHING
HEY... THAT'S GAMEFOWL...
THAT CRAZY BITCH IS ON OUR TEAM?
SHE'LL KILL US IF WE GO NEAR HER!
QUIET! SHE MIGHT HEAR YOU...
YOU'LL GET HER PISSED AT ME, TOO!
CHING
THAT'S A BEAUTIFUL SOUND.
IT'S JUST A STUPID BELL.
NO...

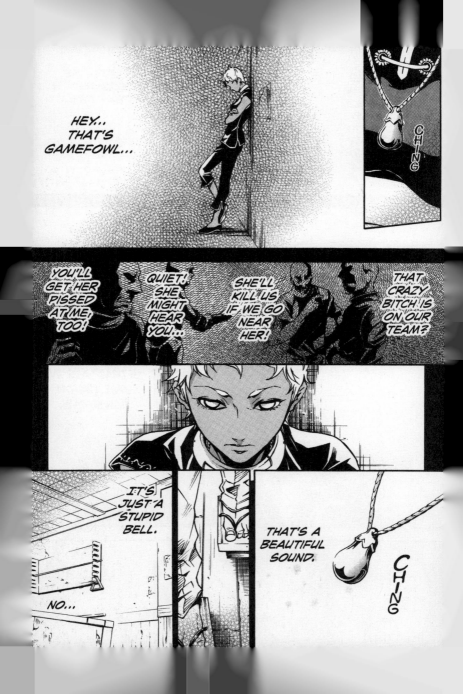

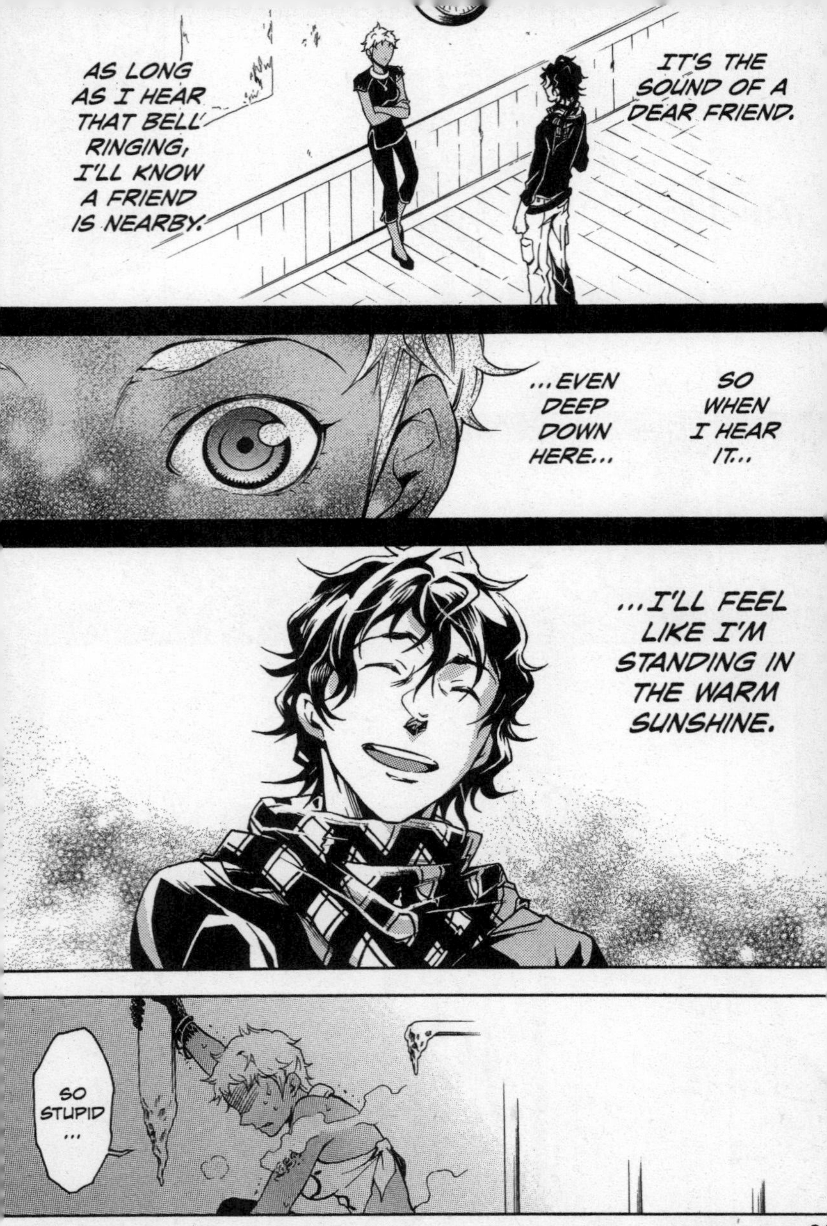
IT'S THE SOUND OF A DEAR FRIEND.
AS LONG AS I HEAR THAT BELL RINGING, I'LL KNOW A FRIEND IS NEARBY.
SO WHEN I HEAR IT...
...EVEN DEEP DOWN HERE...
...I'LL FEEL LIKE I'M STANDING IN THE WARM SUNSHINE.
SO STUPID ...

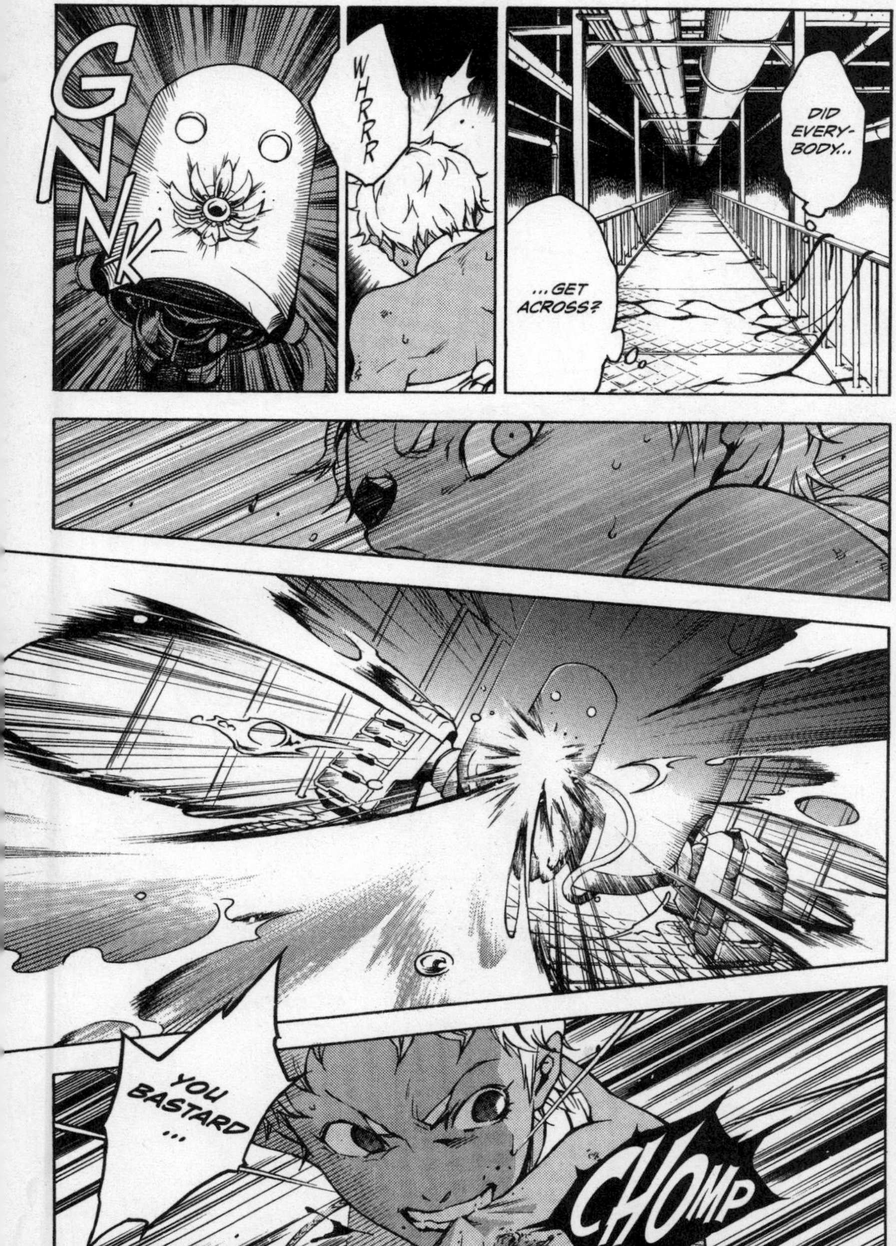
DID EVERY-BODY...
...GET ACROSS?
WHRRR
GNNK
YOU BASTARD ...
CHOMP

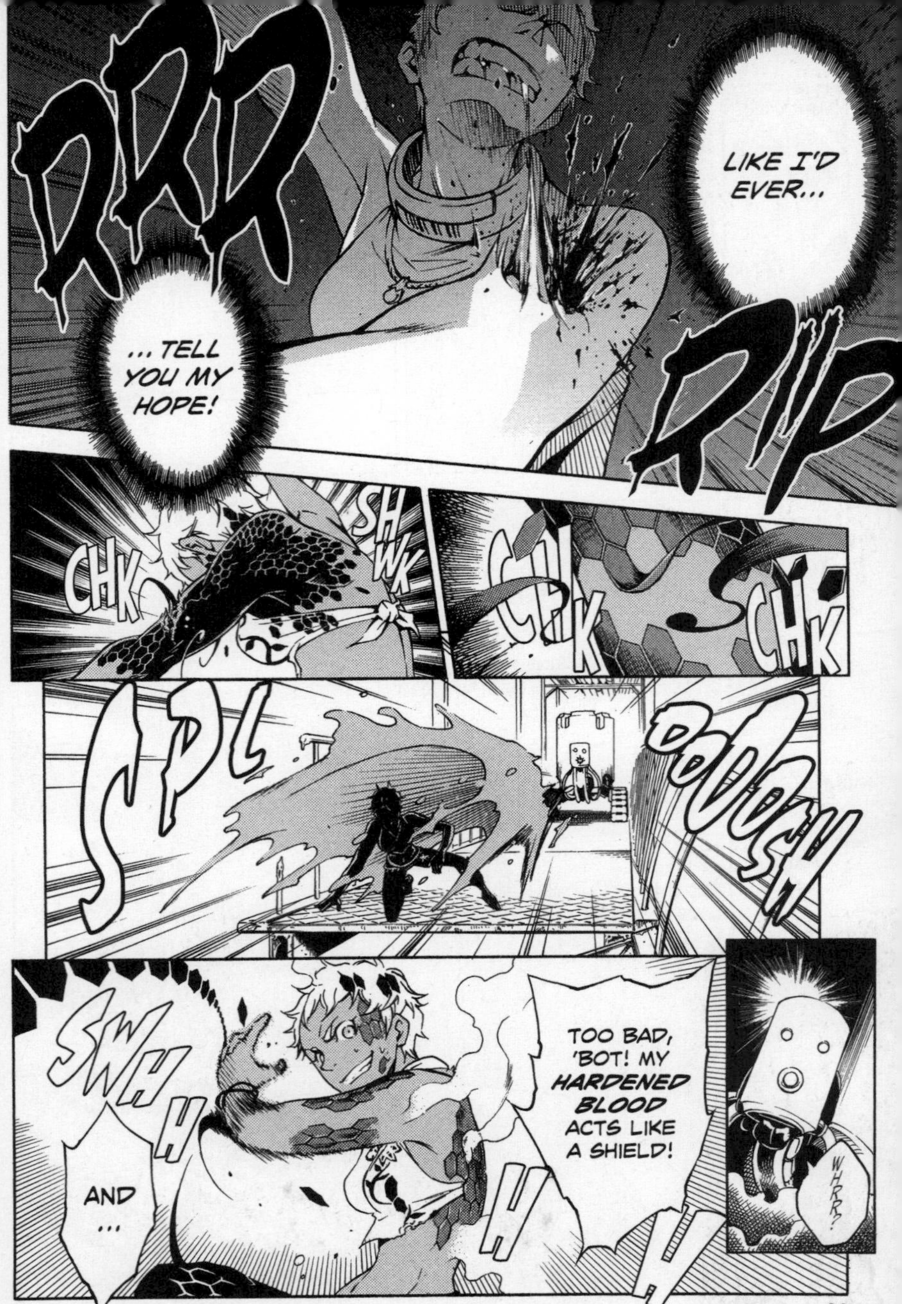

DRIP
LIKE I'D EVER...
...TELL YOU MY HOPE!
DRIP
CHK
CHK
CHK
SHWK
CHK
WHRR?
TOO BAD, 'BOT! MY HARDENED BLOOD ACTS LIKE A SHIELD!
SWHHHHH
AND ...

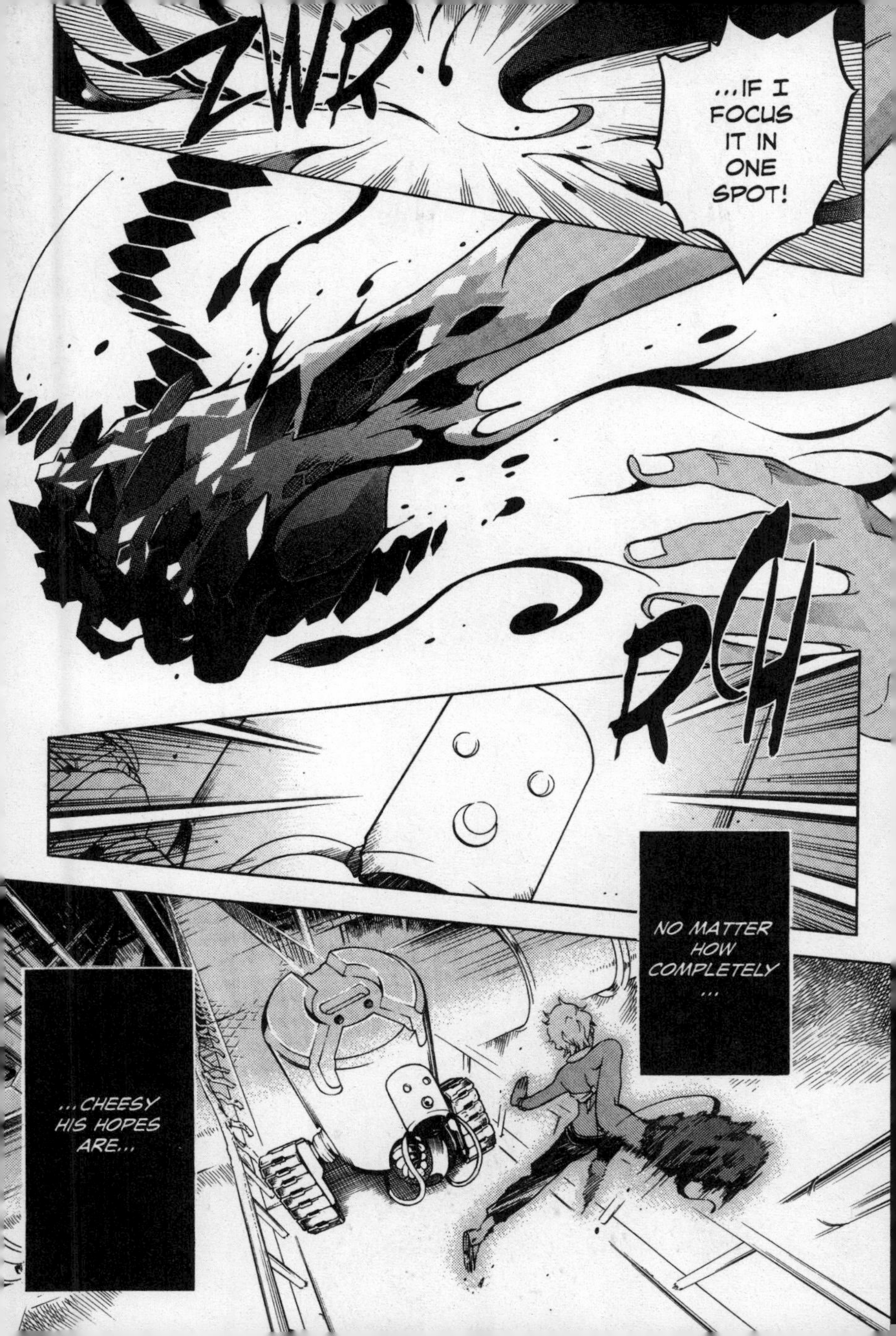
...IF I FOCUS IT IN ONE SPOT!
ZWR
RCH
NO MATTER HOW COMPLETELY ...
...CHEESY HIS HOPES ARE...

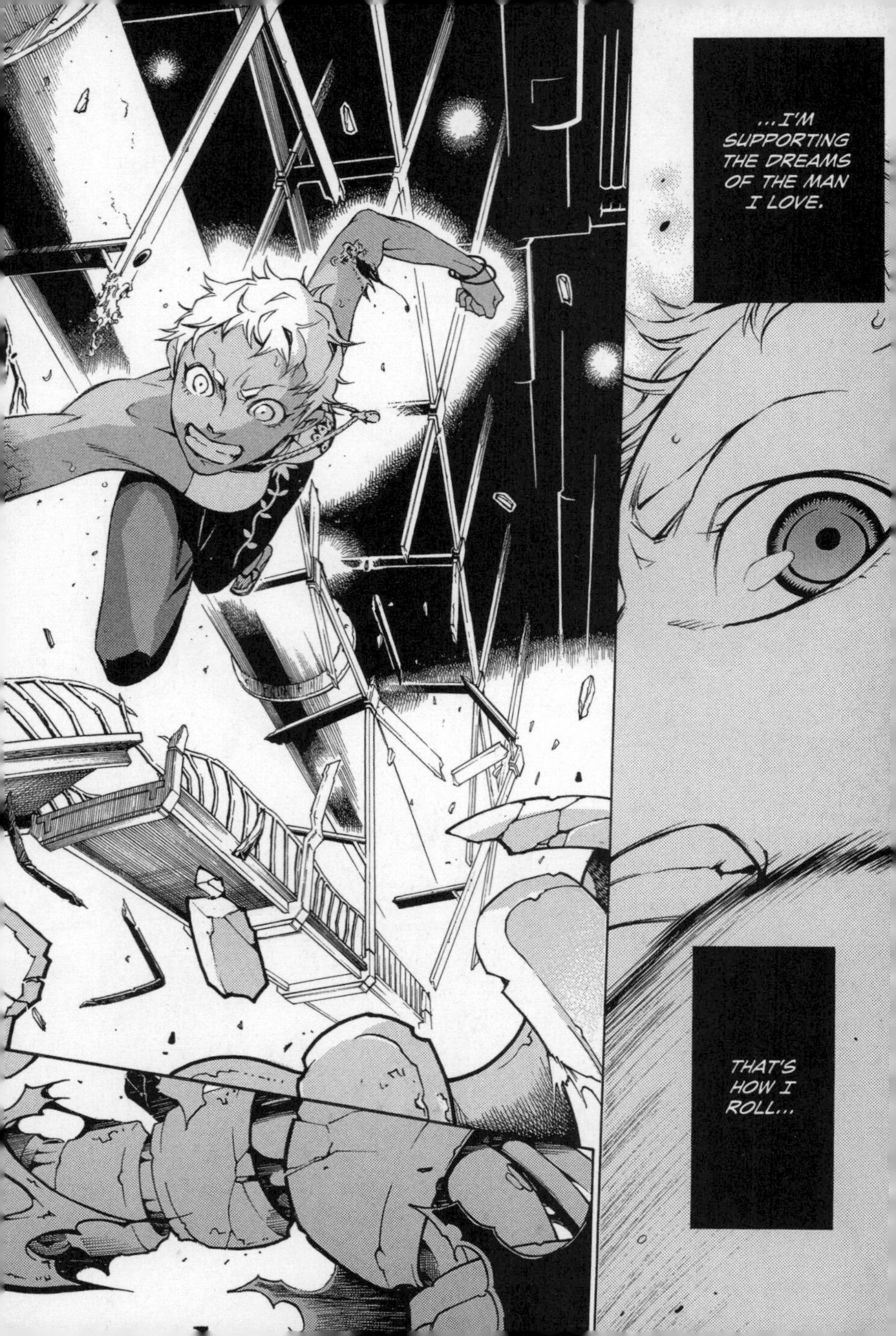
...I'M SUPPORTING THE DREAMS OF THE MAN I LOVE.
THAT'S HOW I ROLL...

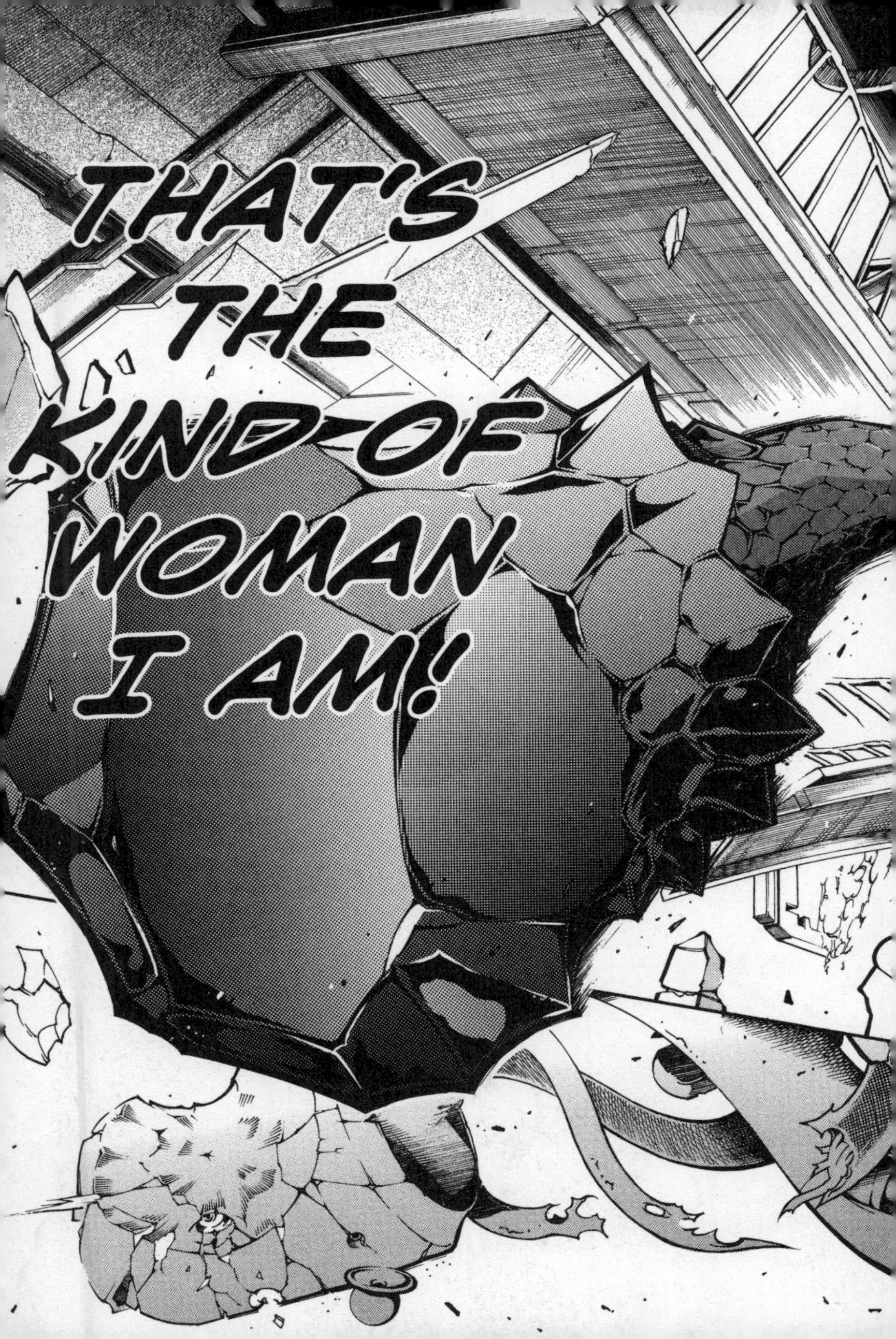
THAT'S THE KIND OF WOMAN I AM!

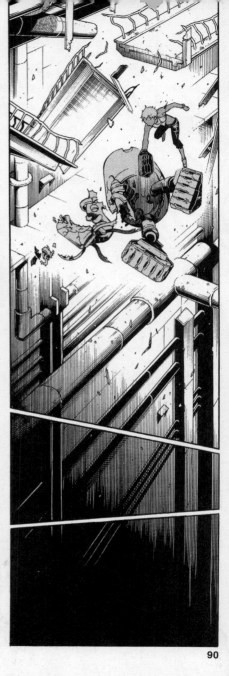

KARAKO...
SHE'LL BE
OKAY...

...WON'T
SHE?

CHN K

WE
CAN'T
GO
BACK.

MAYBE
THE
UNDER-
TAKERS
ARE ON
TO US.

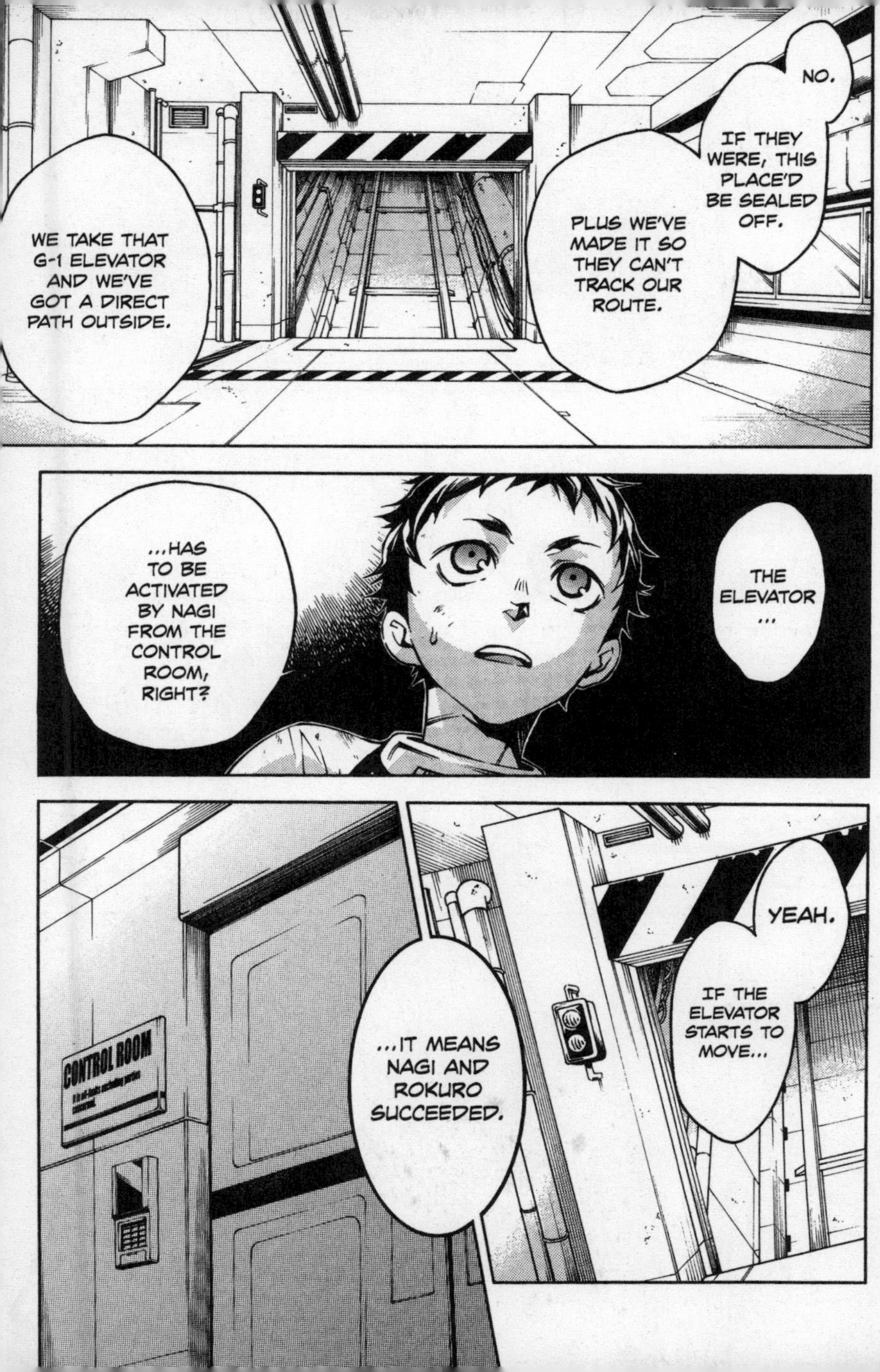
NO.
IF THEY WERE, THIS PLACE'D BE SEALED OFF.
PLUS WE'VE MADE IT SO THEY CAN'T TRACK OUR ROUTE.
WE TAKE THAT G-1 ELEVATOR AND WE'VE GOT A DIRECT PATH OUTSIDE.
THE ELEVATOR...
...HAS TO BE ACTIVATED BY NAGI FROM THE CONTROL ROOM, RIGHT?
YEAH.
IF THE ELEVATOR STARTS TO MOVE...
...IT MEANS NAGI AND ROKURO SUCCEEDED.
CONTROL ROOM

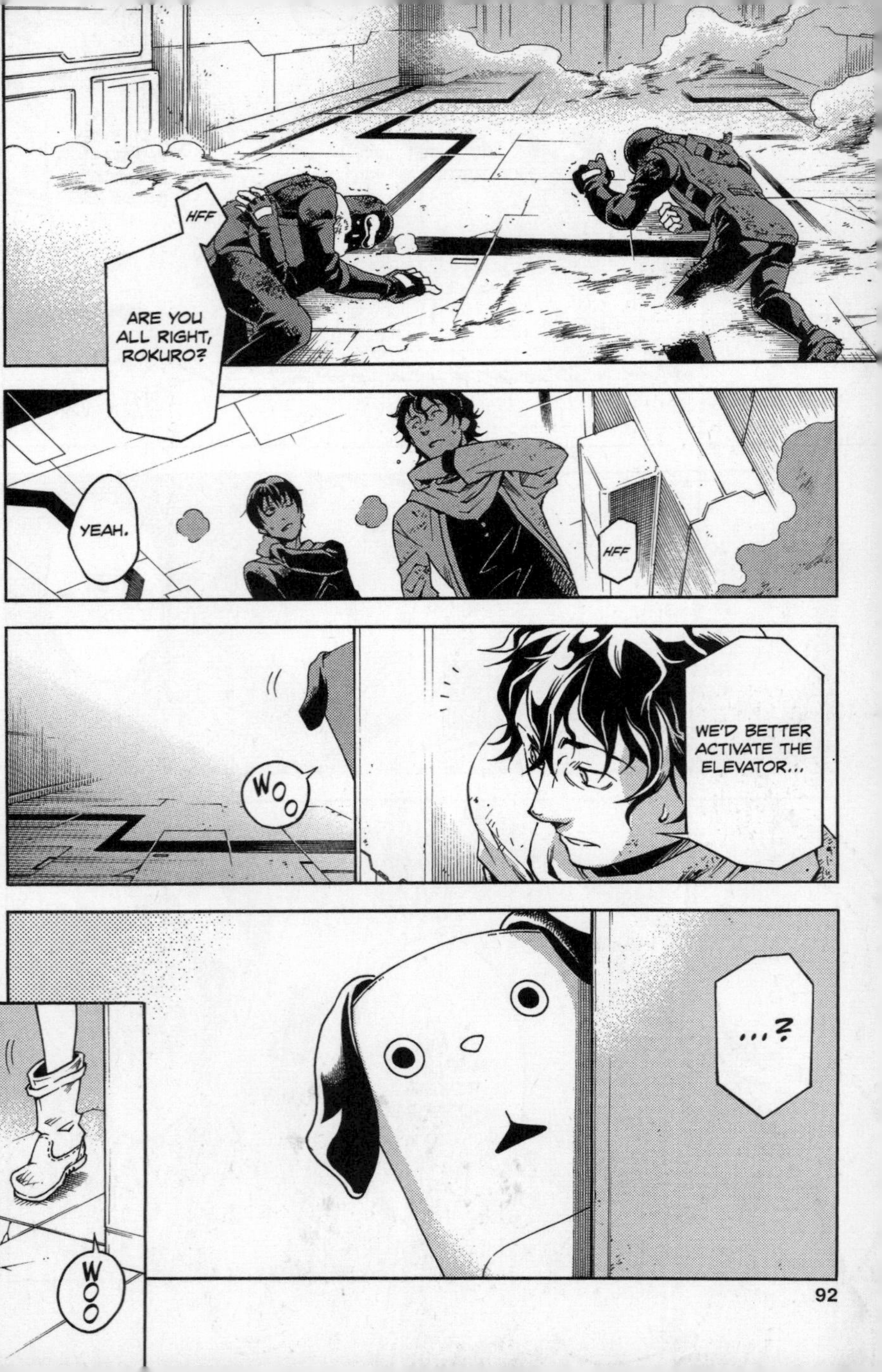
HFF
ARE YOU ALL RIGHT, ROKURO?
HFF
YEAH.
WE'D BETTER ACTIVATE THE ELEVATOR...
WOO
...?
WOO

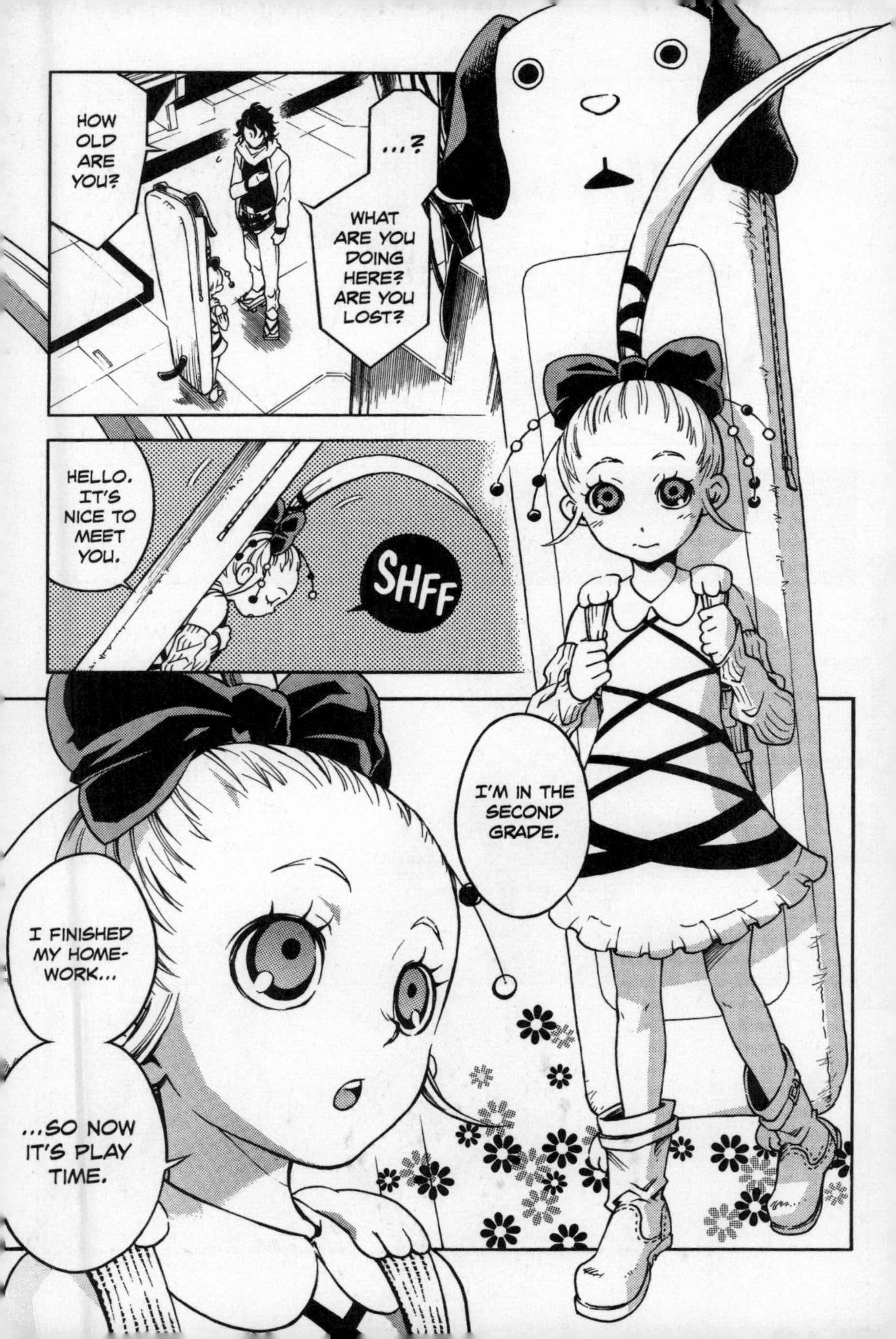
I'M IN THE SECOND GRADE.
...?
WHAT ARE YOU DOING HERE? ARE YOU LOST?
HOW OLD ARE YOU?
SHFF
HELLO. IT'S NICE TO MEET YOU.
I FINISHED MY HOME-WORK...
...SO NOW IT'S PLAY TIME.

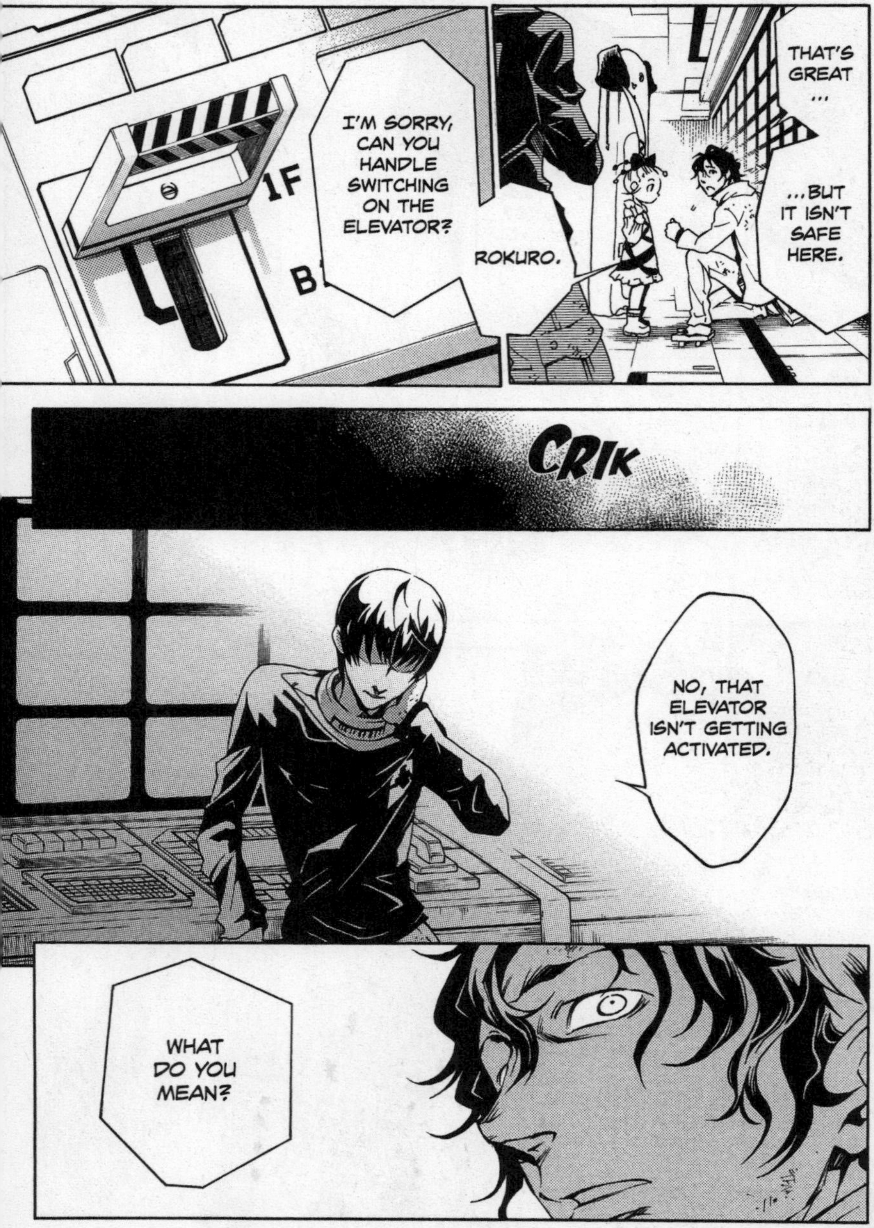
THAT'S GREAT ...
...BUT IT ISN'T SAFE HERE.
ROKURO.
I'M SORRY, CAN YOU HANDLE SWITCHING ON THE ELEVATOR?
1F
B
CRIK
NO, THAT ELEVATOR ISN'T GETTING ACTIVATED.
WHAT DO YOU MEAN?

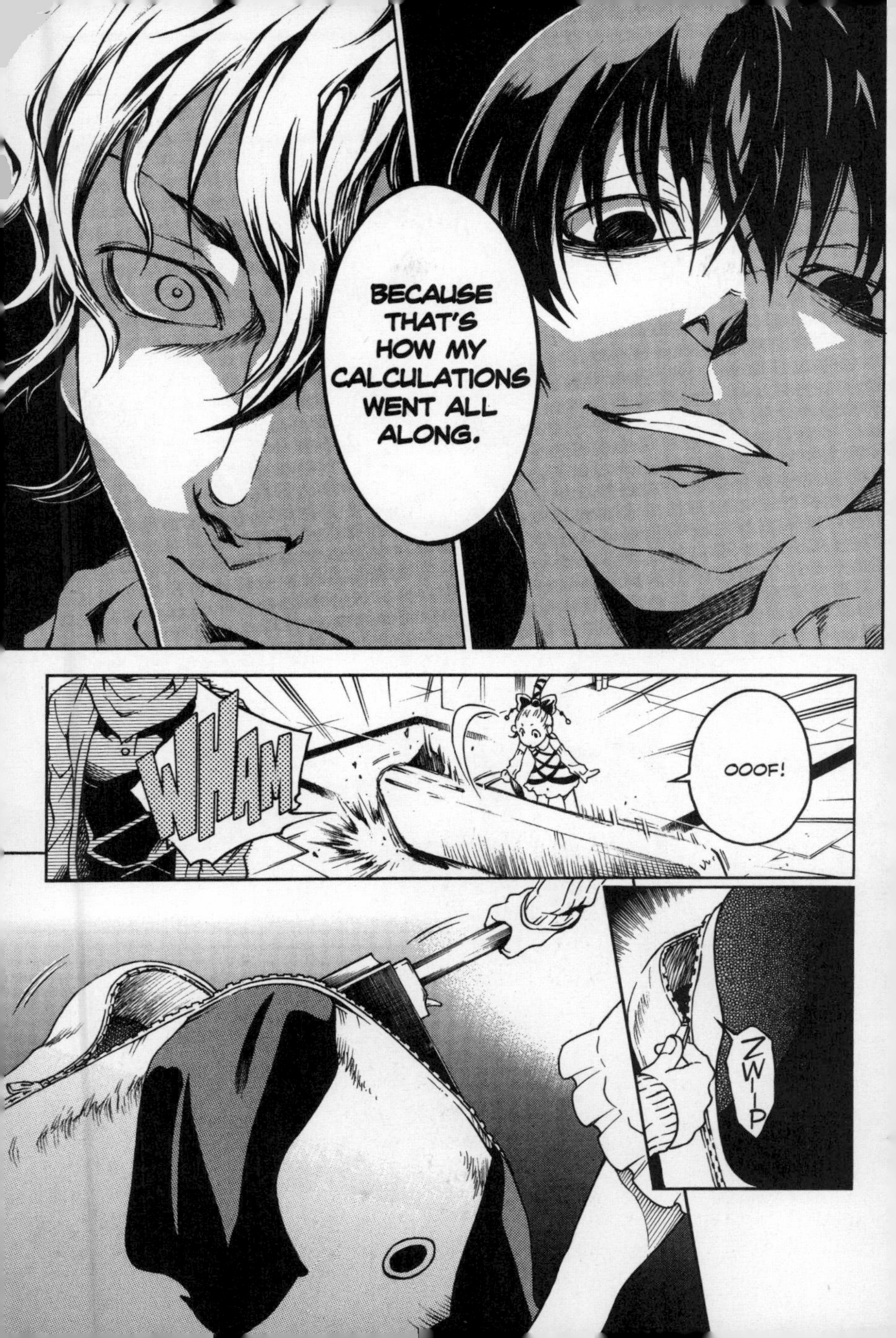
BECAUSE THAT'S HOW MY CALCULATIONS WENT ALL ALONG.
OOOF!
WHAM
ZWIP

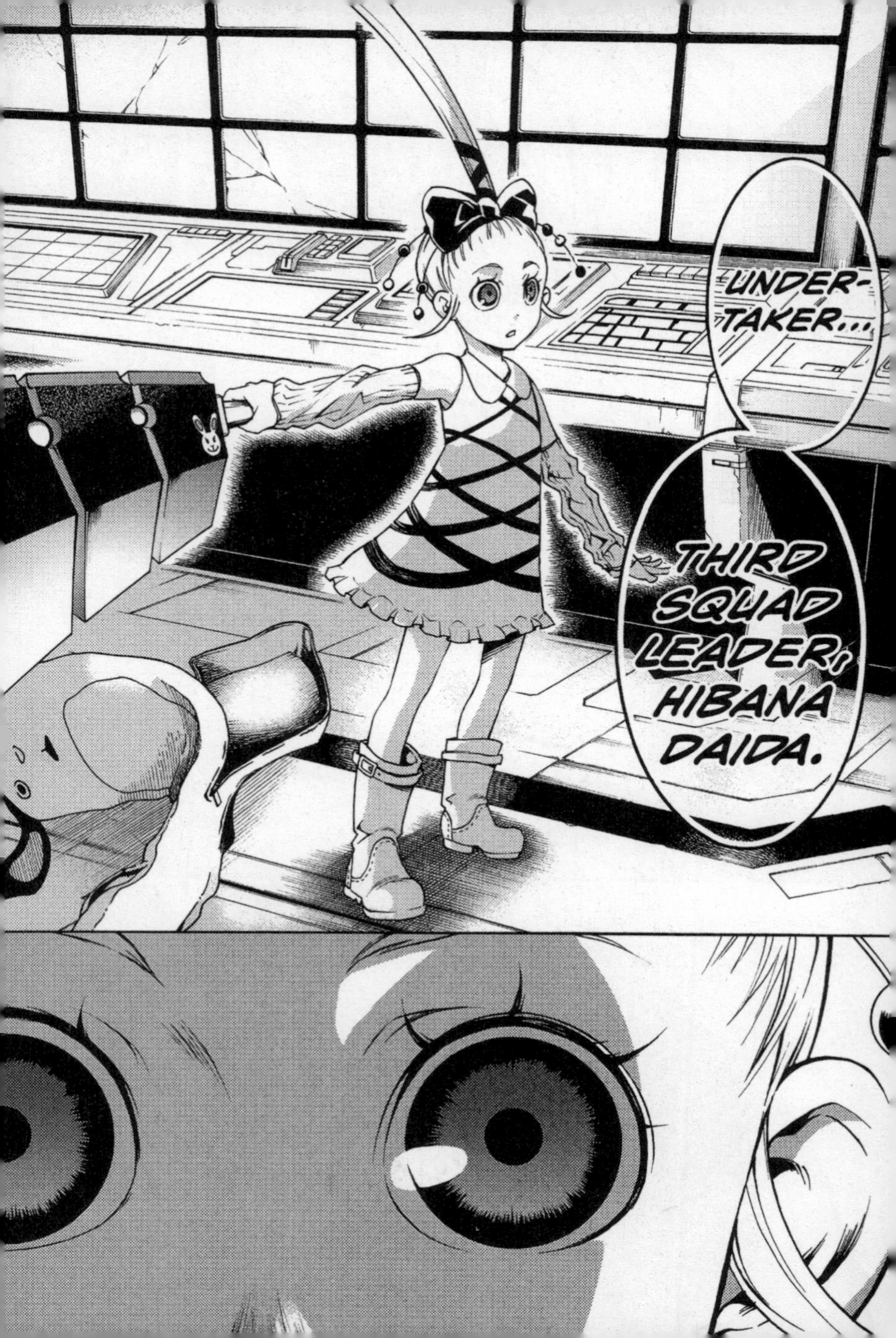
UNDER-TAKER...
THIRD SQUAD LEADER, HIBANA DAIDA.

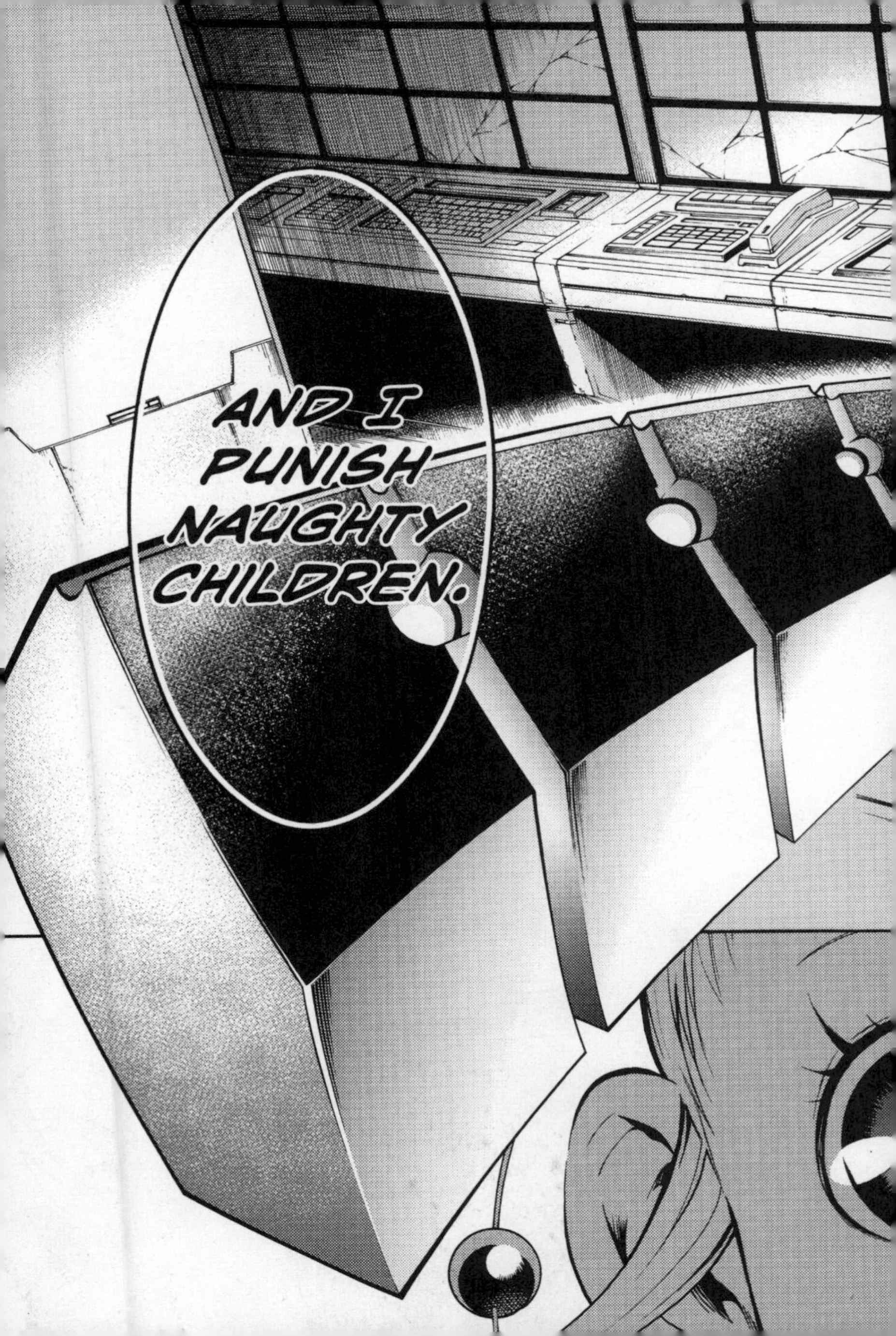
AND I PUNISH NAUGHTY CHILDREN.

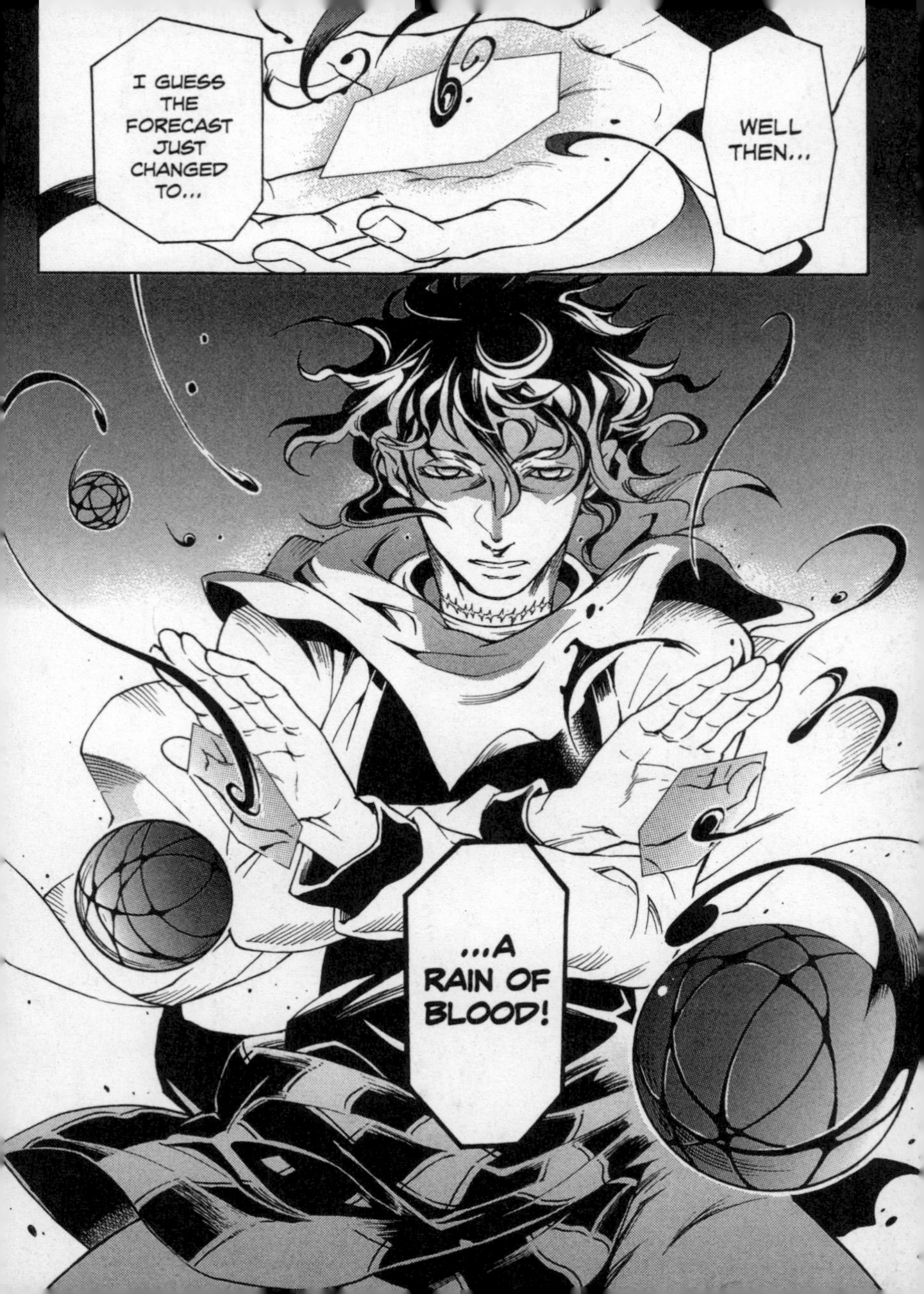
WELL THEN...
I GUESS THE FORECAST JUST CHANGED TO...
...A RAIN OF BLOOD!

WONDER

DEADMAN WONDER LAND

WONDER

DEADMAN WONDER LAND

WONDER

DEADMAN WONDER LAND

WONDER

DEADMAN WONDER LAND

WONDER

DEADMAN WONDER LAND

WONDER

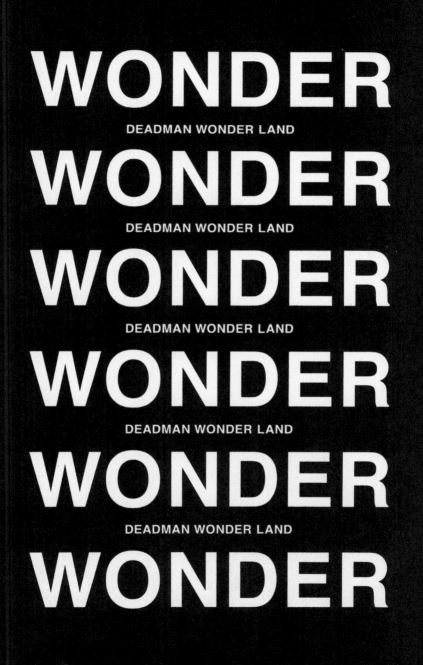

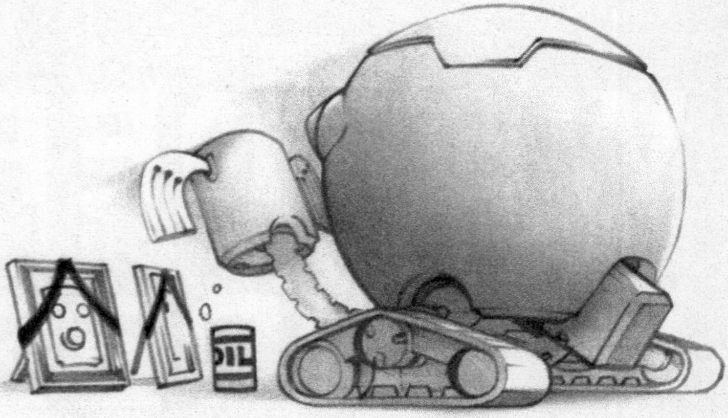
OIL

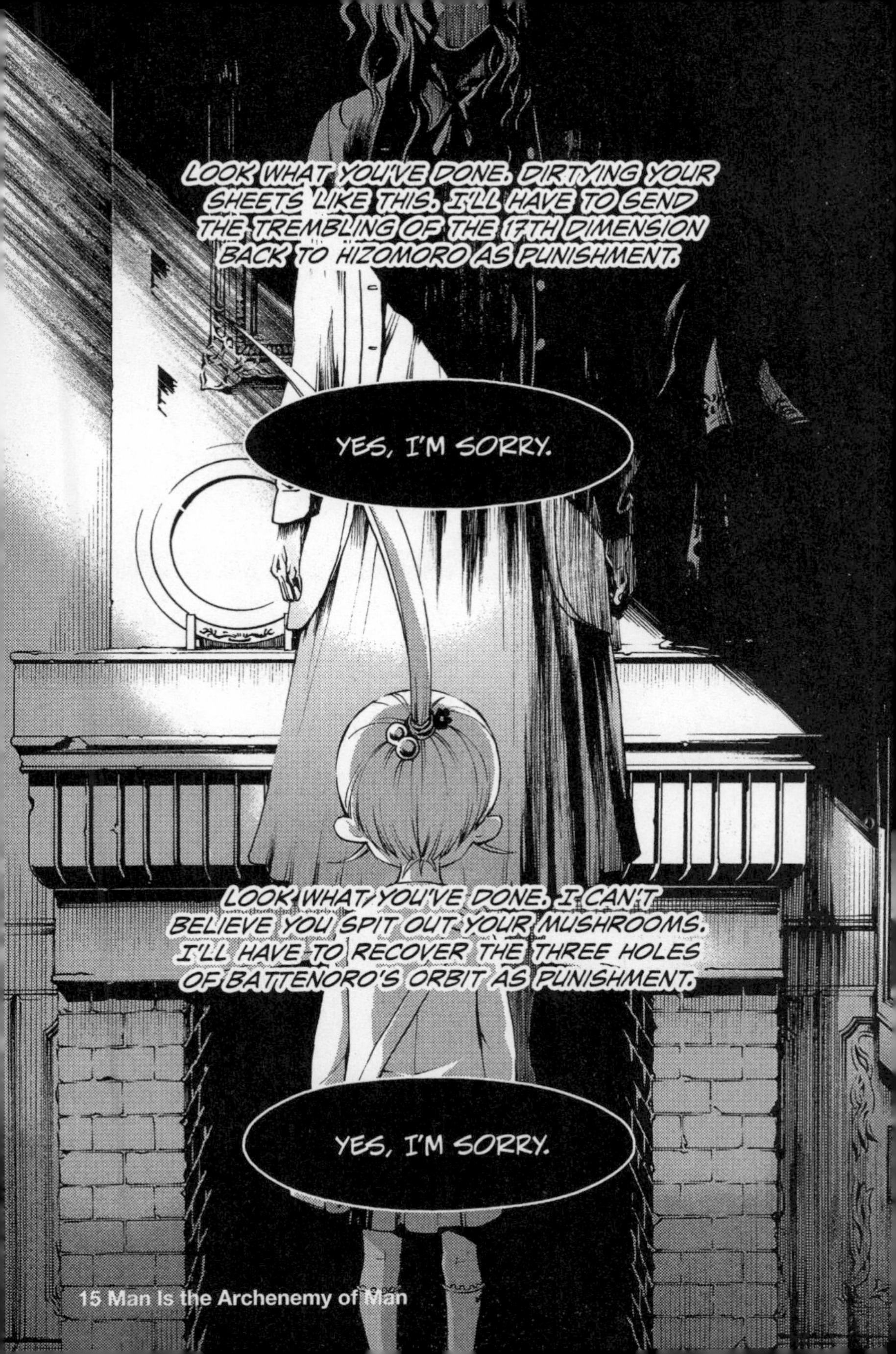
LOOK WHAT YOU'VE DONE. DIRTYING YOUR SHEETS LIKE THIS. I'LL HAVE TO SEND THE TREMBLING OF THE 17TH DIMENSION BACK TO HIZOMORO AS PUNISHMENT.
YES, I'M SORRY.
LOOK WHAT YOU'VE DONE. I CAN'T BELIEVE YOU SPIT OUT YOUR MUSHROOMS. I'LL HAVE TO RECOVER THE THREE HOLES OF BATTENORO'S ORBIT AS PUNISHMENT.
YES, I'M SORRY.

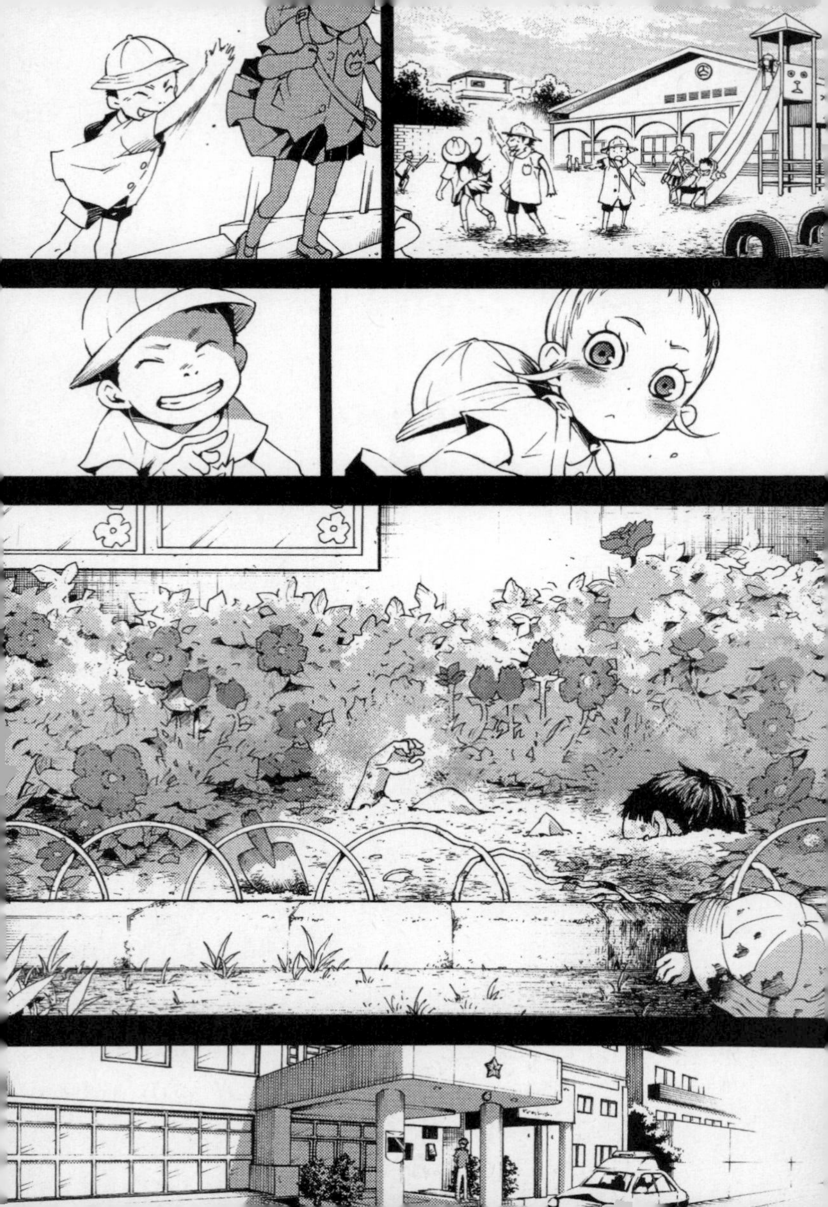

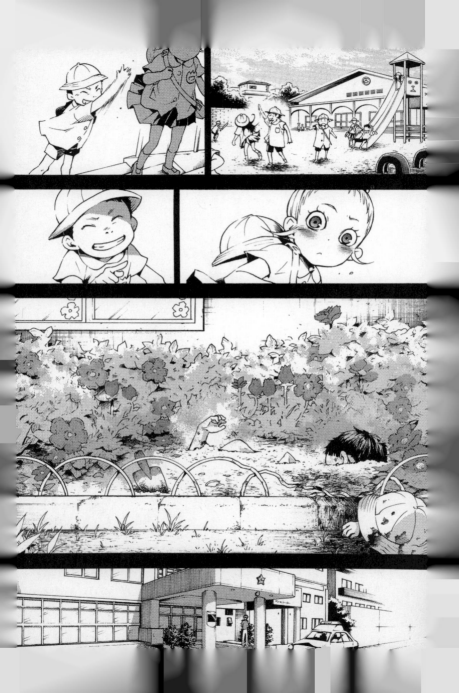

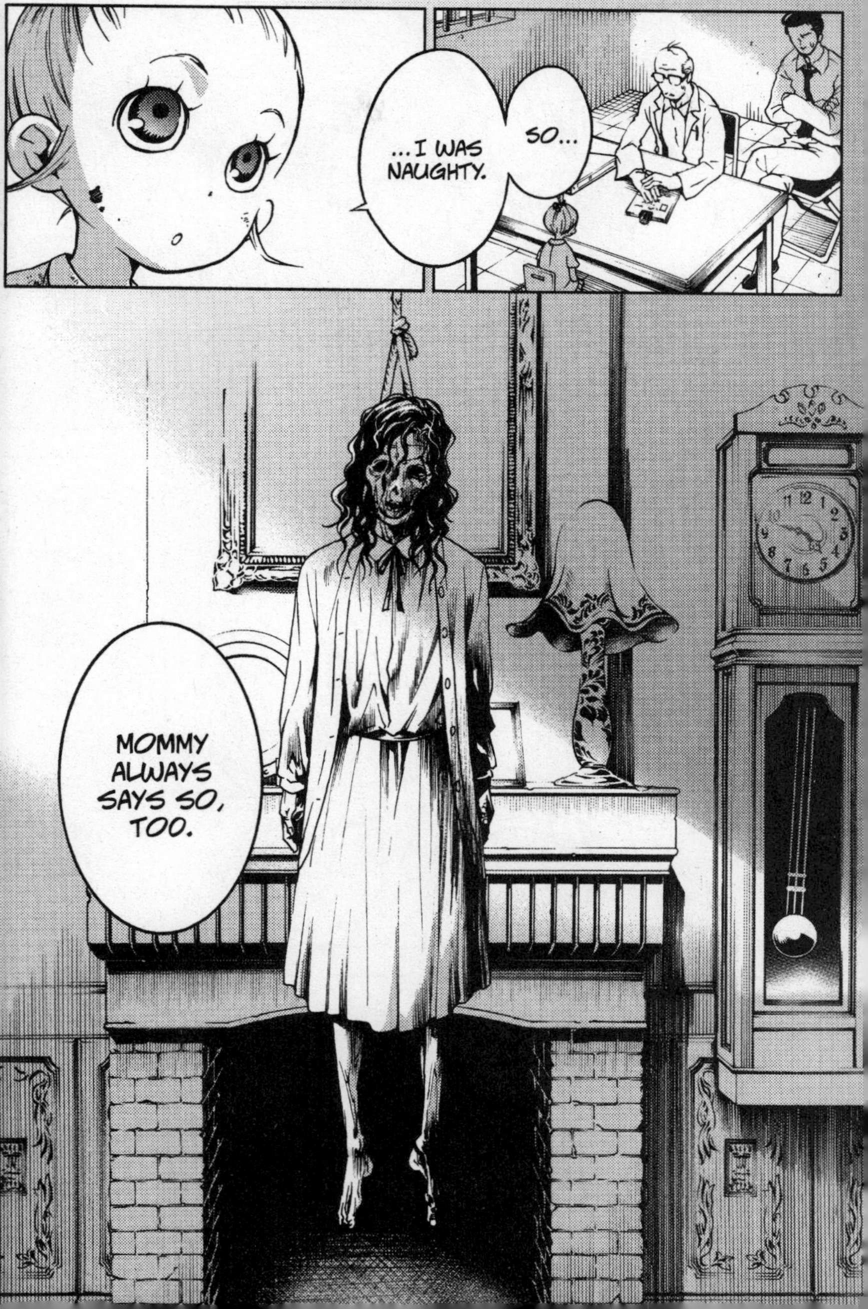
SO...
...I WAS NAUGHTY.
MOMMY ALWAYS SAYS SO, TOO.

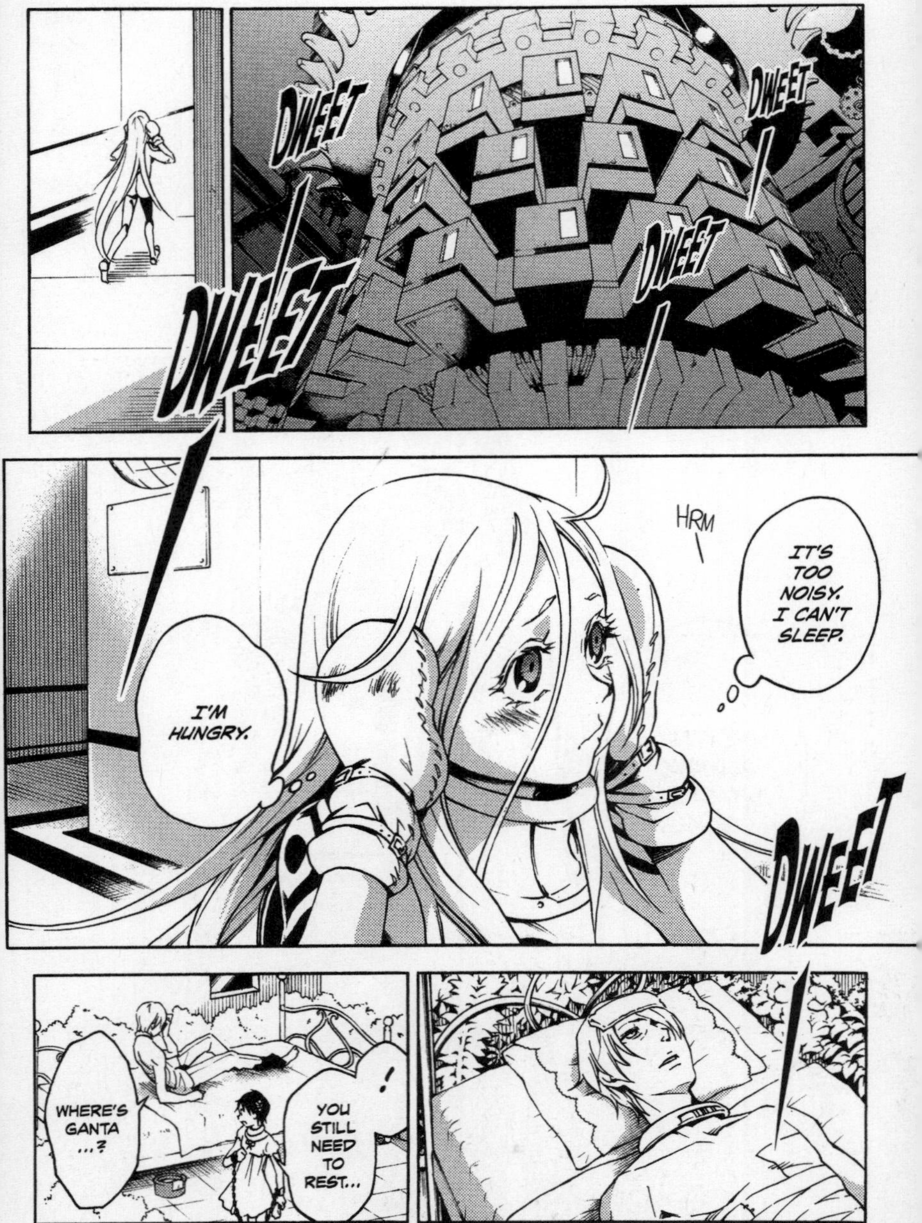
DWEET
DWEET
DWEET
DWEET
HRM
IT'S TOO NOISY. I CAN'T SLEEP.
I'M HUNGRY.
DWEET
!
YOU STILL NEED TO REST...
WHERE'S GANTA ...?

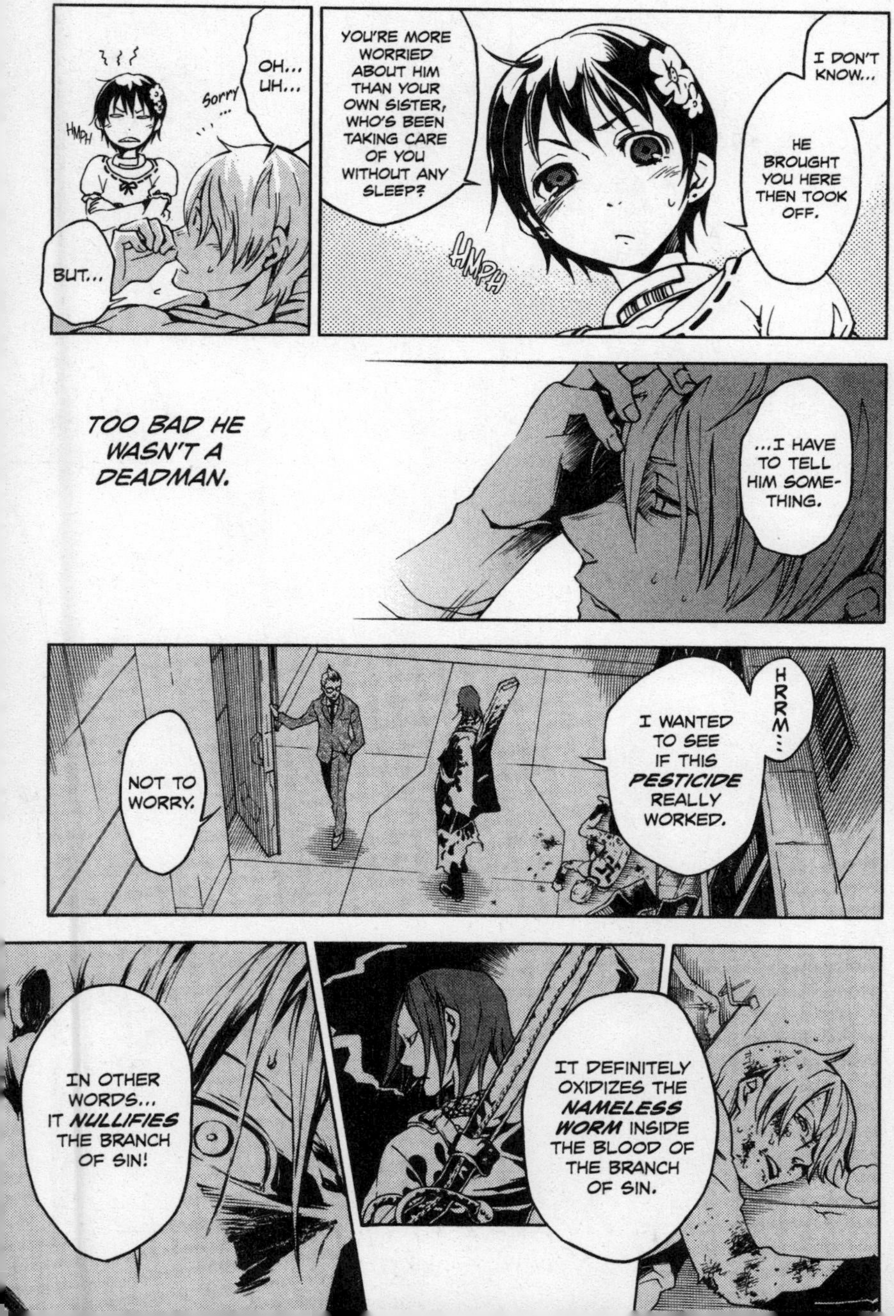
I DON'T KNOW...
HE BROUGHT YOU HERE THEN TOOK OFF.
YOU'RE MORE WORRIED ABOUT HIM THAN YOUR OWN SISTER, WHO'S BEEN TAKING CARE OF YOU WITHOUT ANY SLEEP?
HMPH
OH... UH...
Sorry...
HMPH
BUT...
...I HAVE TO TELL HIM SOMETHING.
TOO BAD HE WASN'T A DEADMAN.
HRRM...
I WANTED TO SEE IF THIS PESTICIDE REALLY WORKED.
NOT TO WORRY.
IT DEFINITELY OXIDIZES THE NAMELESS WORM INSIDE THE BLOOD OF THE BRANCH OF SIN.
IN OTHER WORDS... IT NULLIFIES THE BRANCH OF SIN!

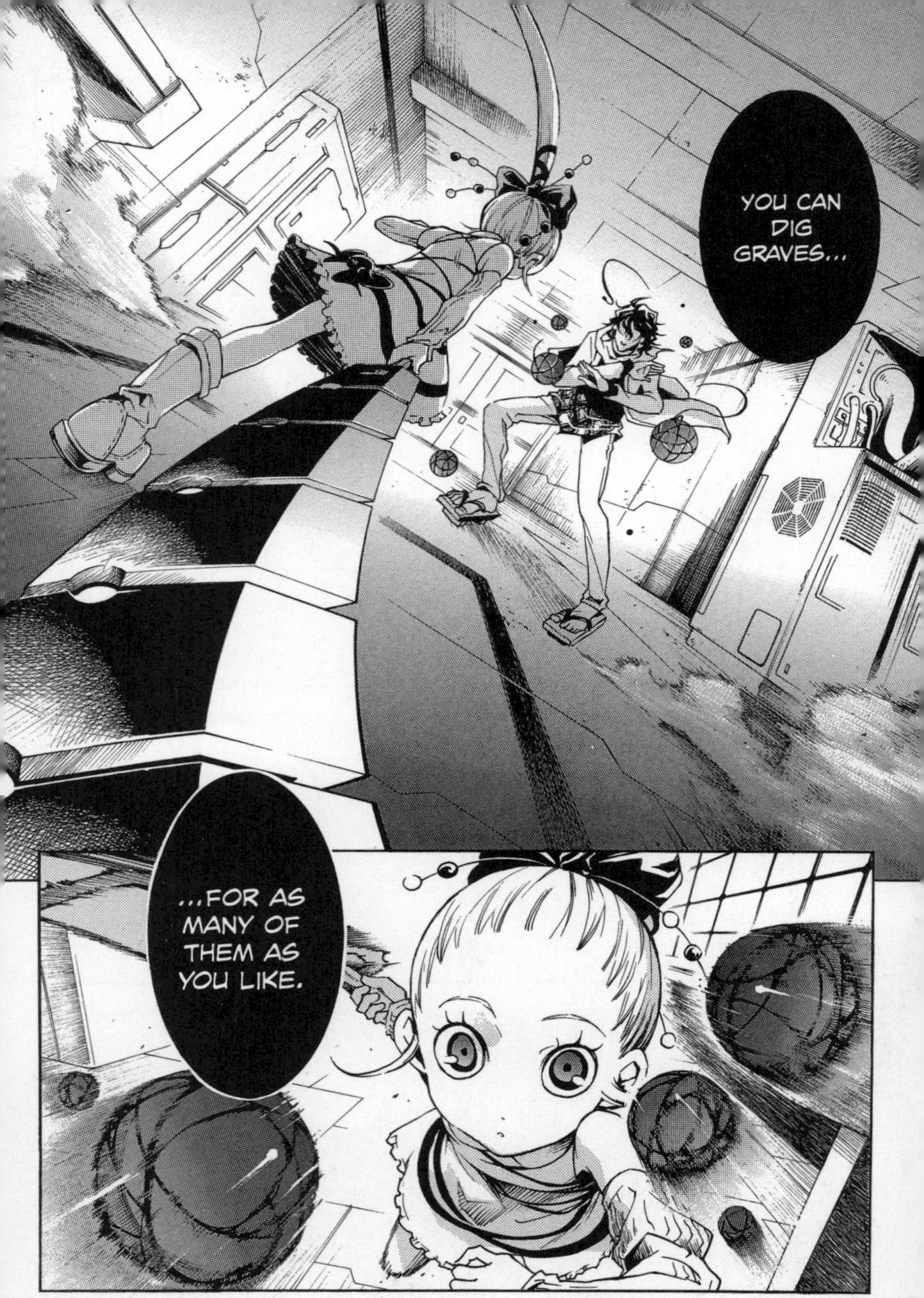
YOU CAN DIG GRAVES...
...FOR AS MANY OF THEM AS YOU LIKE.

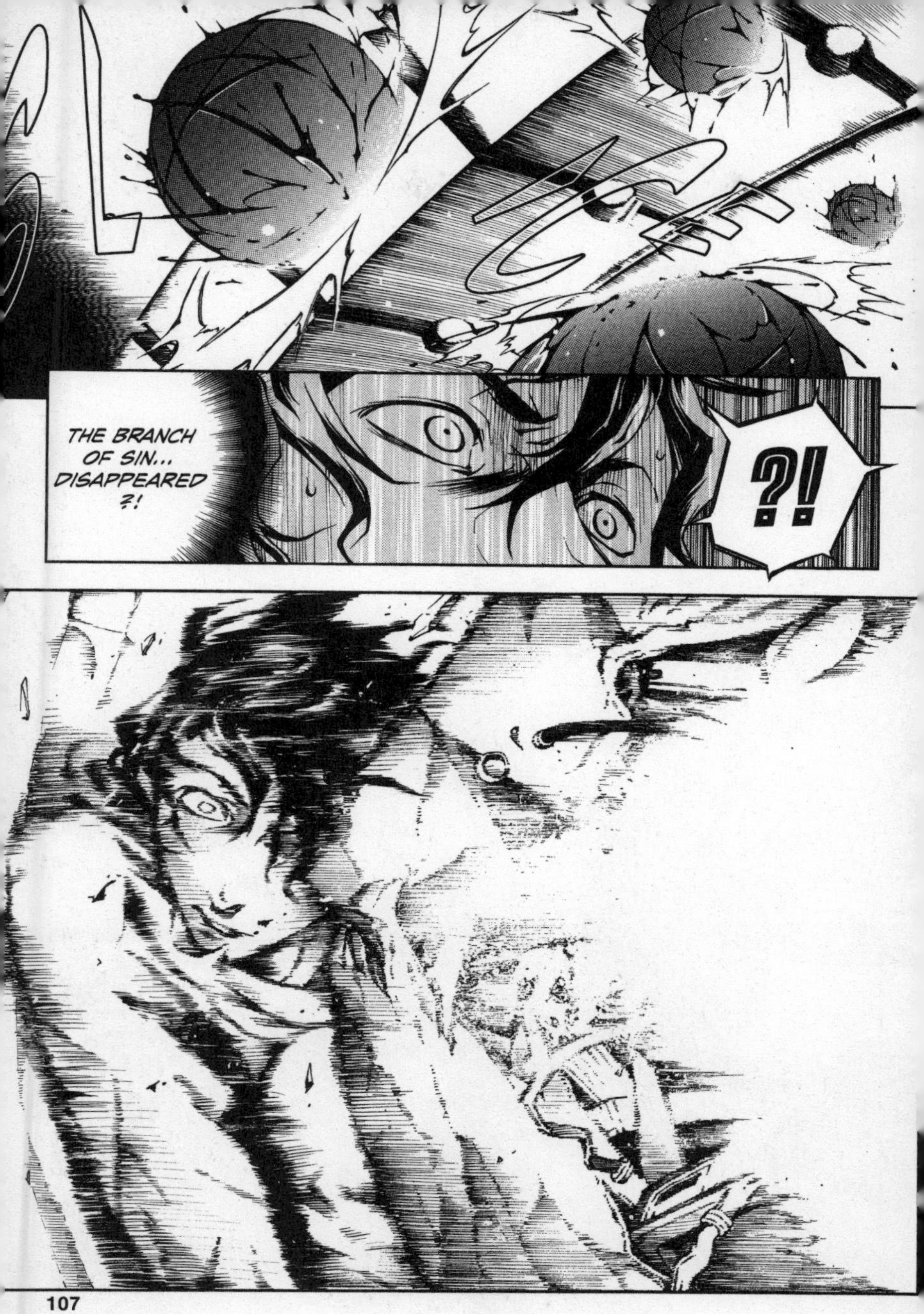
?!
THE BRANCH OF SIN... DISAPPEARED ?!

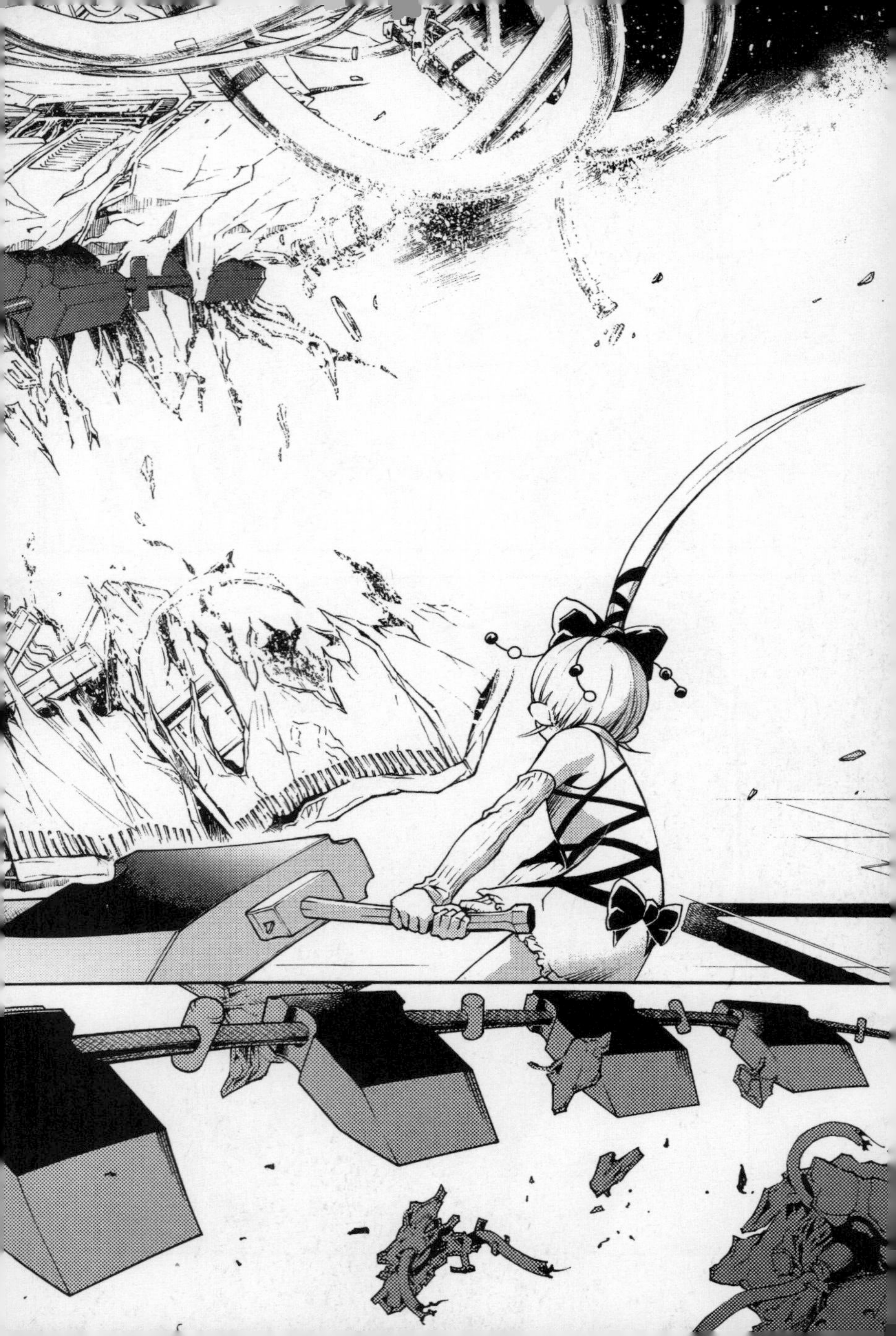

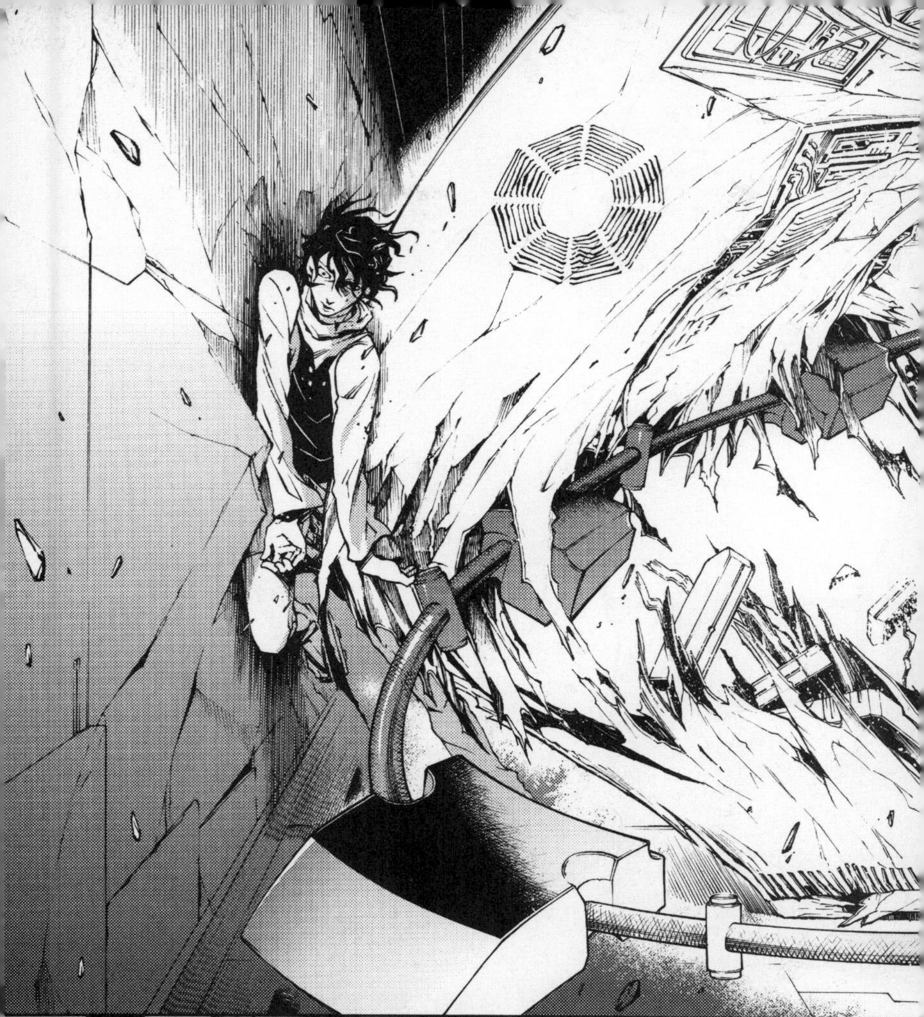
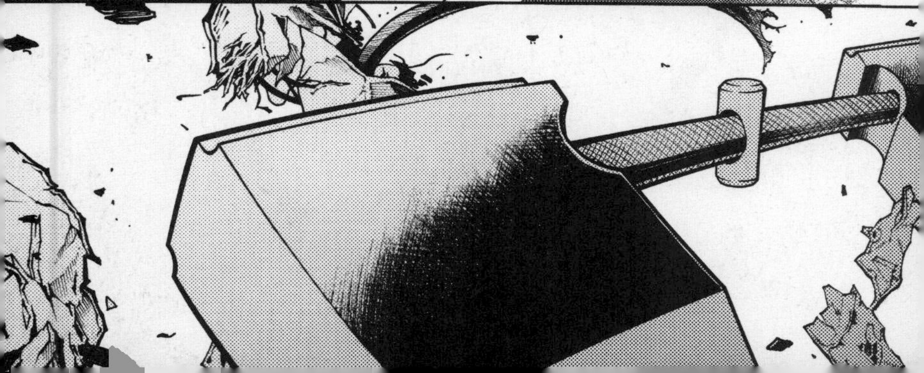

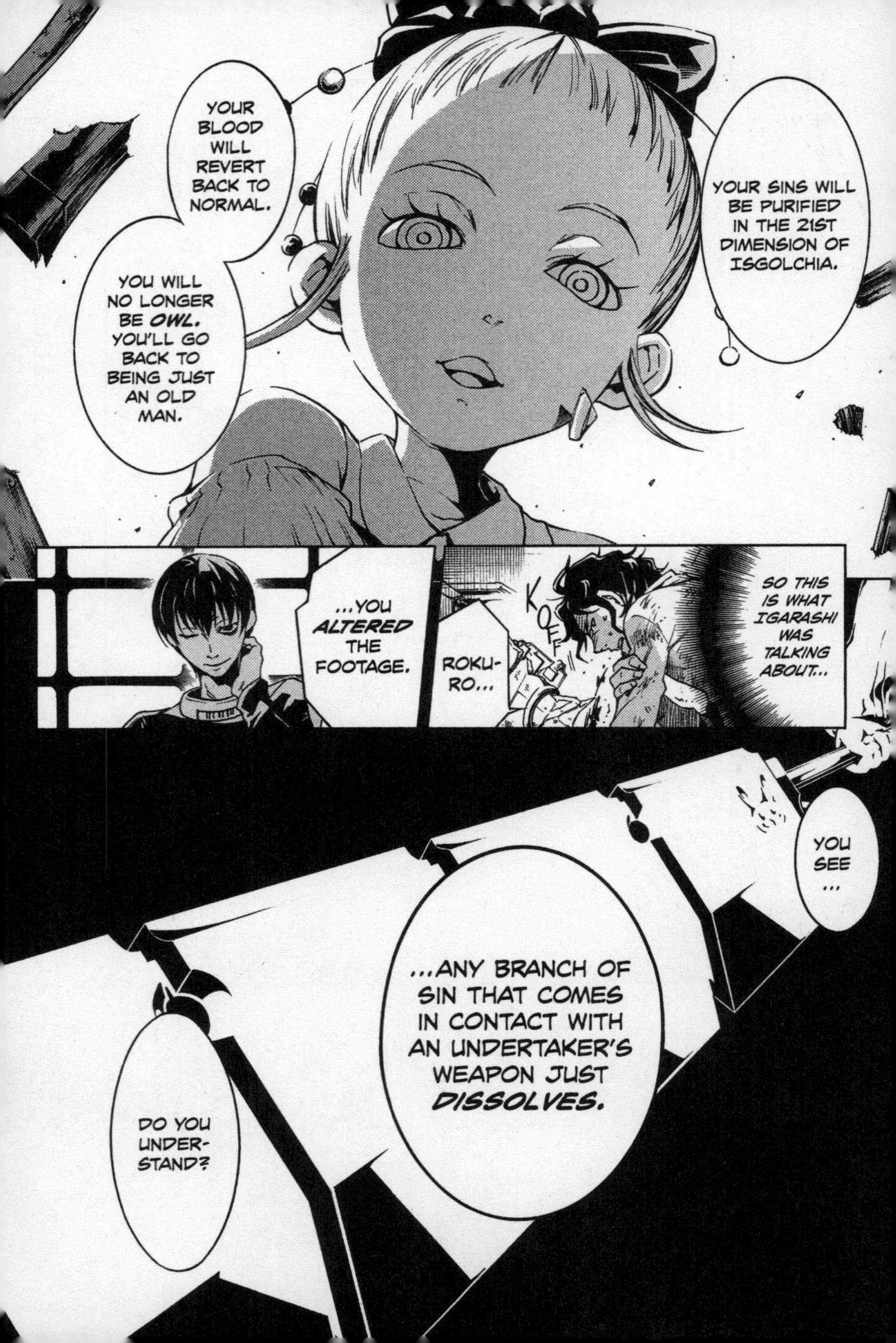
YOUR SINS WILL BE PURIFIED IN THE 21ST DIMENSION OF ISGOLCHIA.
YOUR BLOOD WILL REVERT BACK TO NORMAL.
YOU WILL NO LONGER BE OWL. YOU'LL GO BACK TO BEING JUST AN OLD MAN.
SO THIS IS WHAT IGARASHI WAS TALKING ABOUT...
KOFF
ROKU-RO...
...YOU ALTERED THE FOOTAGE.
YOU SEE ...
...ANY BRANCH OF SIN THAT COMES IN CONTACT WITH AN UNDERTAKER'S WEAPON JUST DISSOLVES.
DO YOU UNDER-STAND?

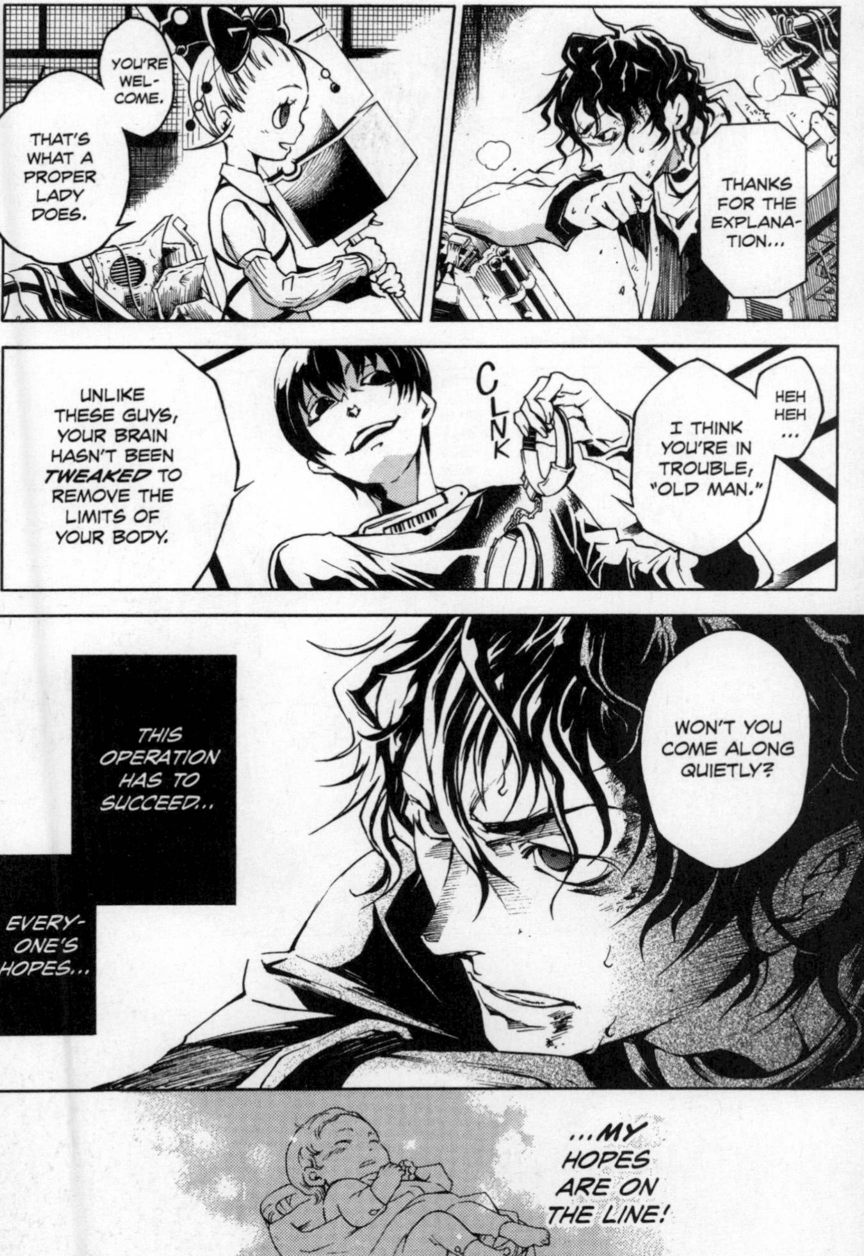
THANKS FOR THE EXPLANATION...
YOU'RE WELCOME.
THAT'S WHAT A PROPER LADY DOES.
HEH HEH...
I THINK YOU'RE IN TROUBLE, "OLD MAN."
CLNK
UNLIKE THESE GUYS, YOUR BRAIN HASN'T BEEN ***TWEAKED*** TO REMOVE THE LIMITS OF YOUR BODY.
WON'T YOU COME ALONG QUIETLY?
THIS OPERATION HAS TO SUCCEED...
EVERYONE'S HOPES...
...MY HOPES ARE ON THE LINE!

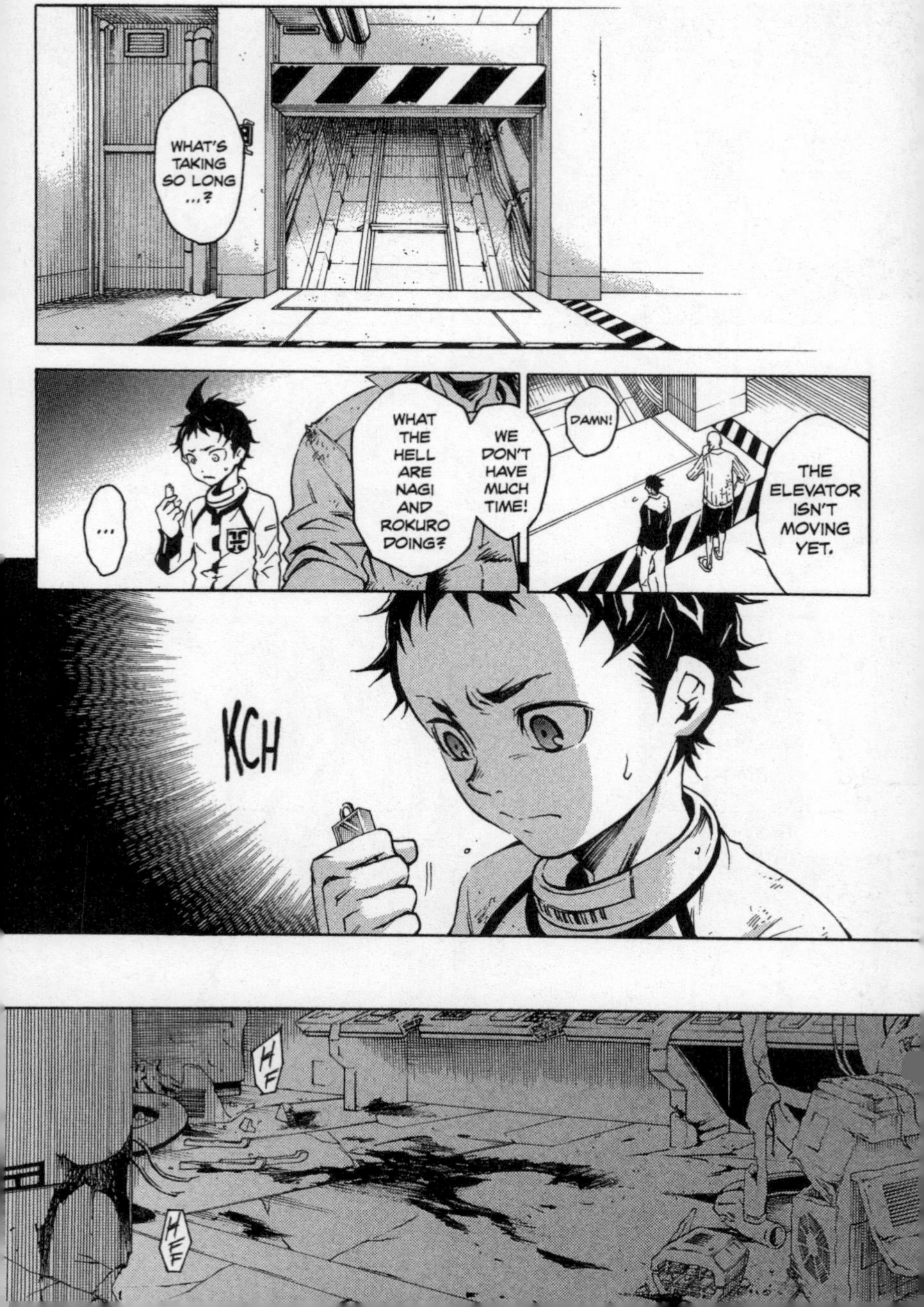
WHAT'S TAKING SO LONG ...?
THE ELEVATOR ISN'T MOVING YET.
DAMN!
WE DON'T HAVE MUCH TIME!
WHAT THE HELL ARE NAGI AND ROKURO DOING?
...
KCH
HF
HFF

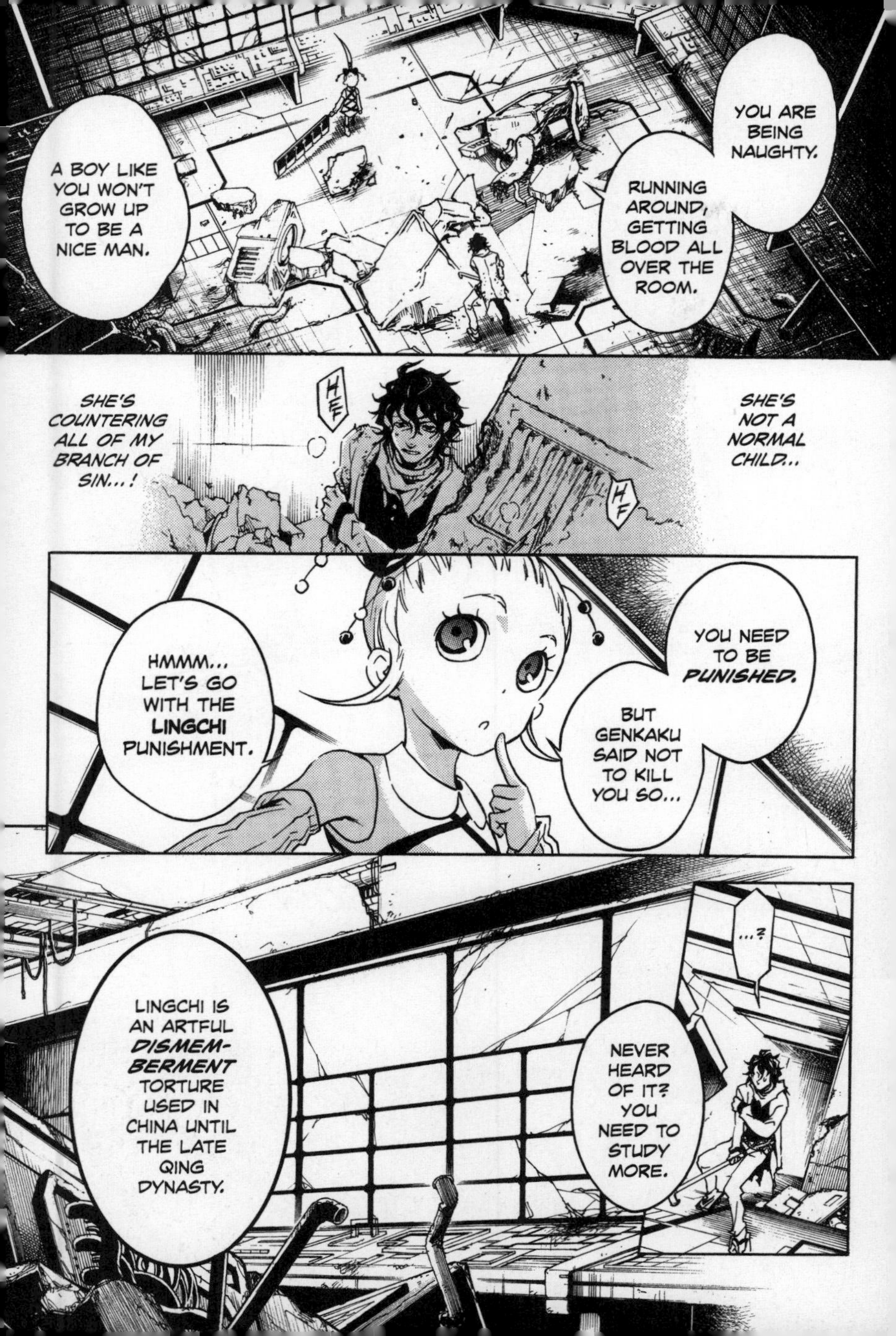

YOU ARE BEING NAUGHTY.
RUNNING AROUND, GETTING BLOOD ALL OVER THE ROOM.
A BOY LIKE YOU WON'T GROW UP TO BE A NICE MAN.
SHE'S NOT A NORMAL CHILD...
HF
HF
SHE'S COUNTERING ALL OF MY BRANCH OF SIN...!
YOU NEED TO BE PUNISHED.
BUT GENKAKU SAID NOT TO KILL YOU SO...
HMMM... LET'S GO WITH THE LINGCHI PUNISHMENT.
...?
NEVER HEARD OF IT? YOU NEED TO STUDY MORE.
LINGCHI IS AN ARTFUL DISMEM-BERMENT TORTURE USED IN CHINA UNTIL THE LATE QING DYNASTY.

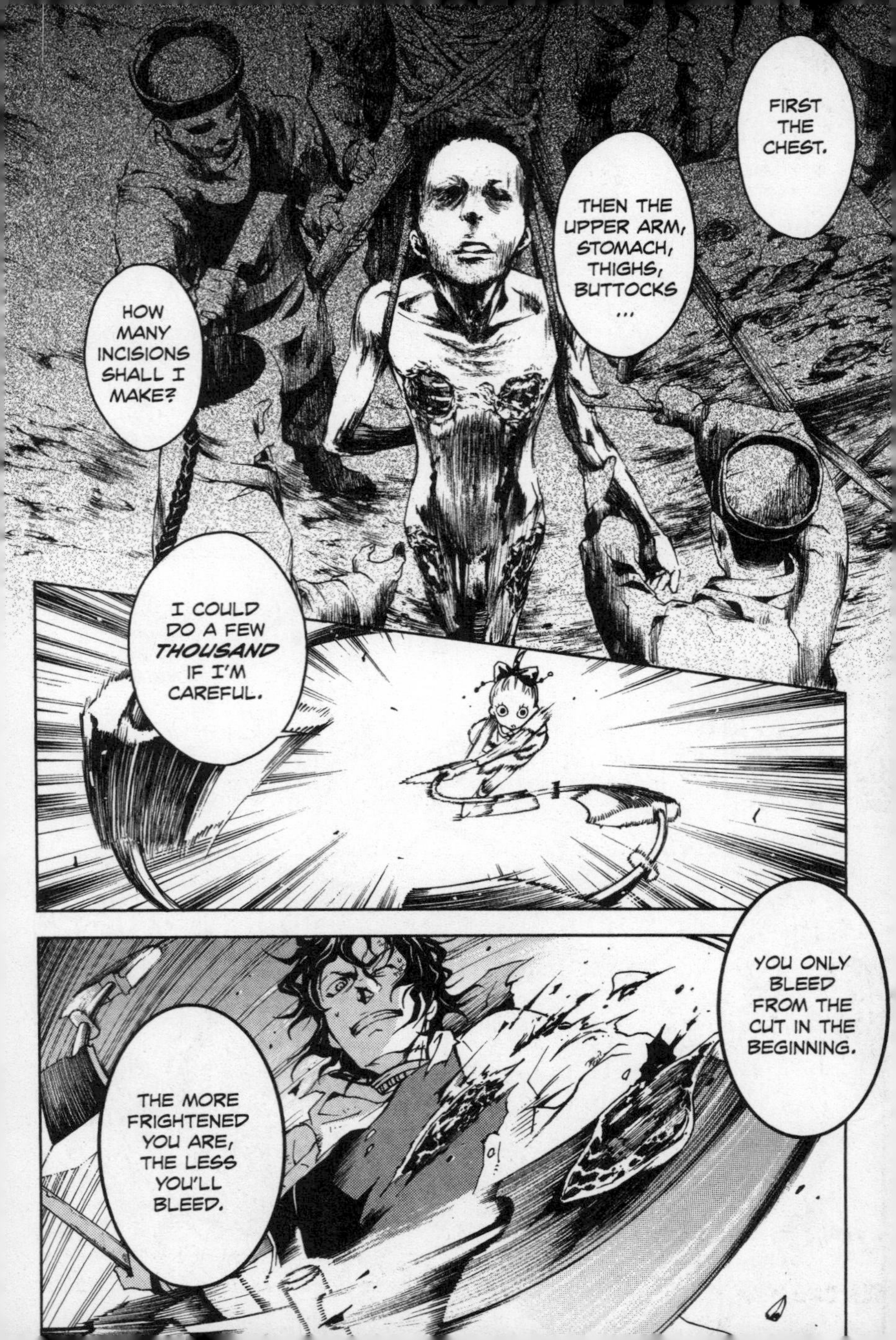
FIRST THE CHEST.
THEN THE UPPER ARM, STOMACH, THIGHS, BUTTOCKS ...
HOW MANY INCISIONS SHALL I MAKE?
I COULD DO A FEW *THOUSAND* IF I'M CAREFUL.
YOU ONLY BLEED FROM THE CUT IN THE BEGINNING.
THE MORE FRIGHTENED YOU ARE, THE LESS YOU'LL BLEED.

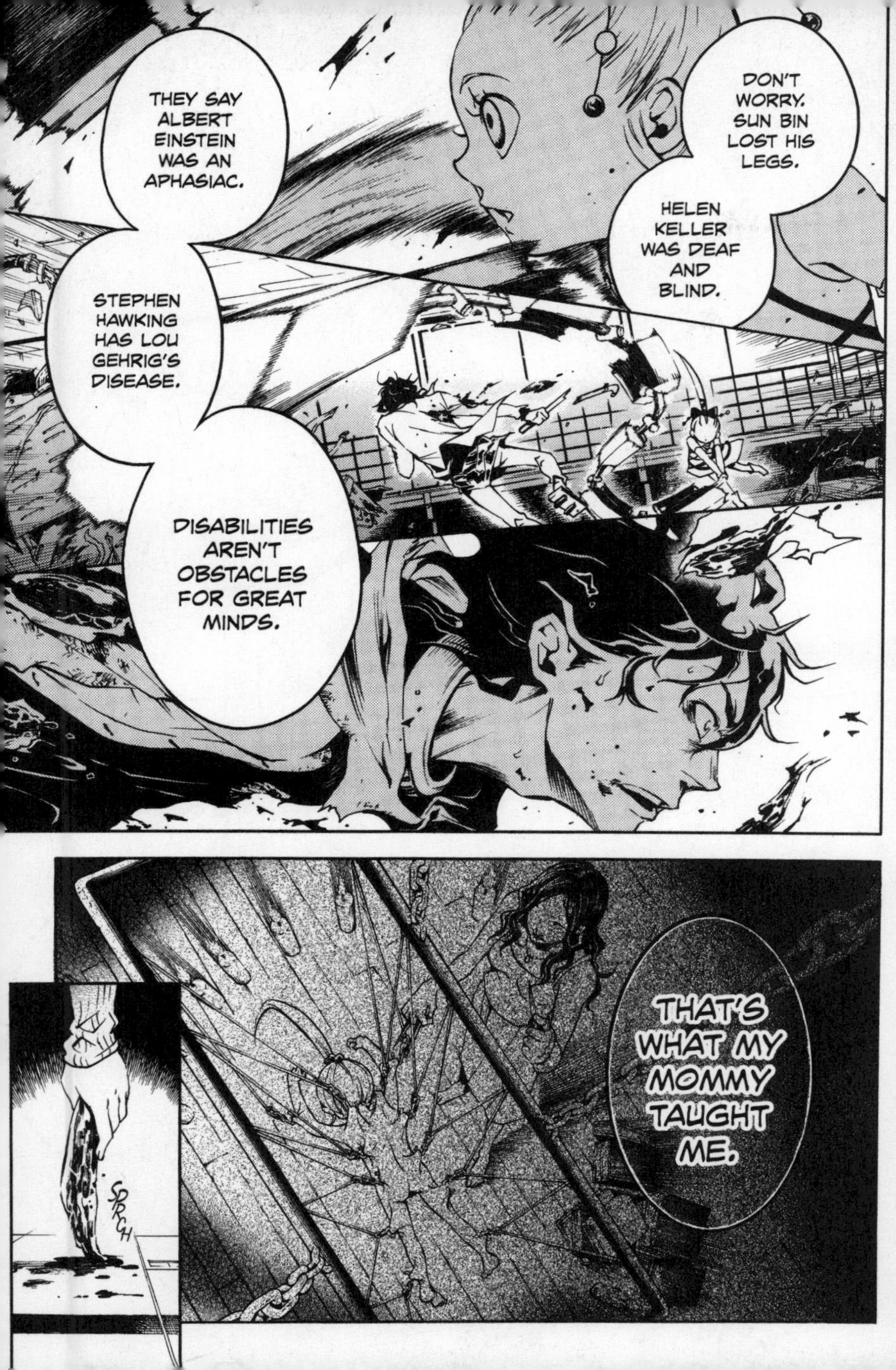
DON'T WORRY. SUN BIN LOST HIS LEGS.
HELEN KELLER WAS DEAF AND BLIND.
THEY SAY ALBERT EINSTEIN WAS AN APHASIAC.
STEPHEN HAWKING HAS LOU GEHRIG'S DISEASE.
DISABILITIES AREN'T OBSTACLES FOR GREAT MINDS.
THAT'S WHAT MY MOMMY TAUGHT ME.
SPRCH

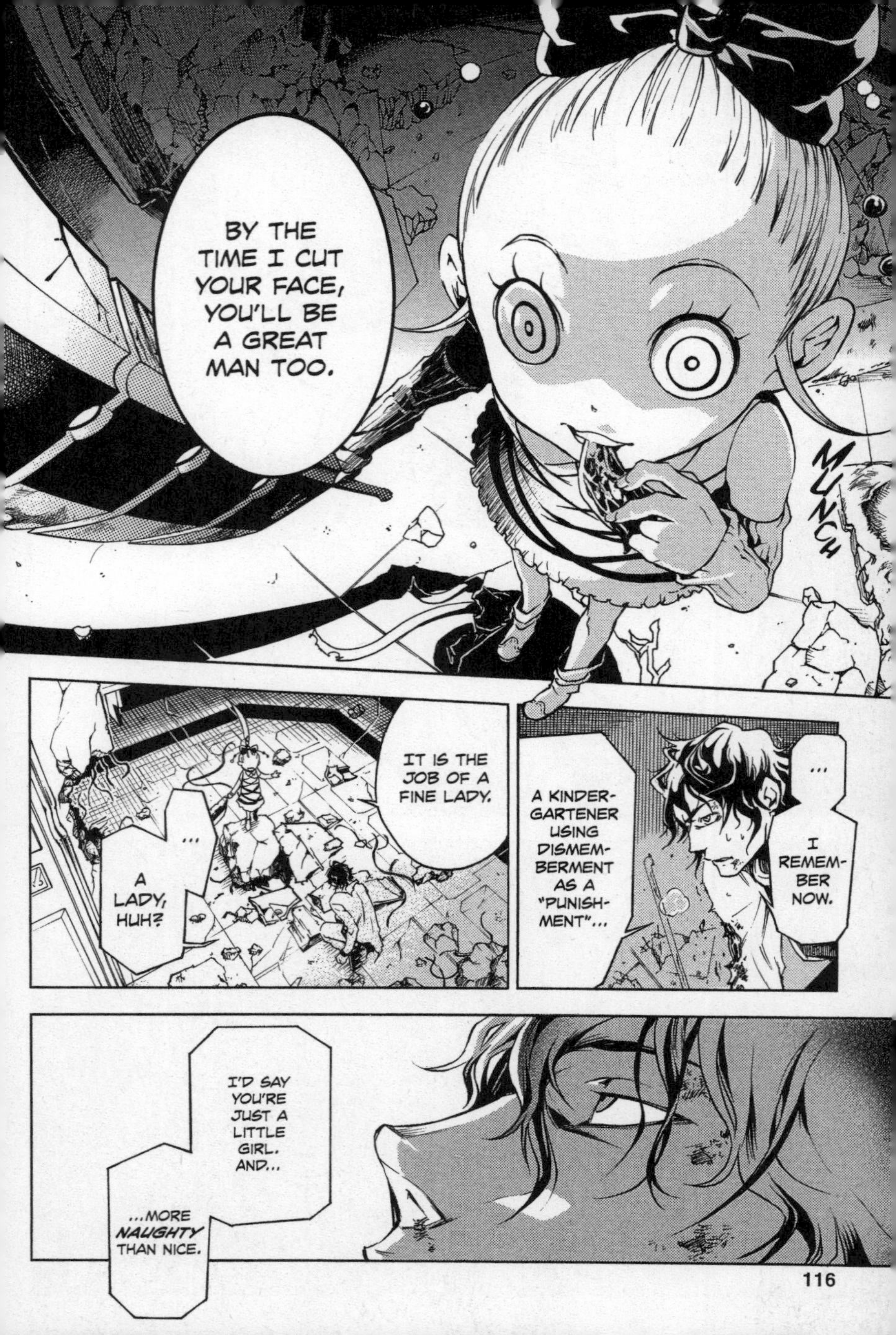
BY THE TIME I CUT YOUR FACE, YOU'LL BE A GREAT MAN TOO.
MUNCH
...
I REMEMBER NOW.
A KINDERGARTENER USING DISMEMBERMENT AS A "PUNISHMENT"...
IT IS THE JOB OF A FINE LADY.
...
A LADY, HUH?
I'D SAY YOU'RE JUST A LITTLE GIRL. AND...
...MORE *NAUGHTY* THAN NICE.

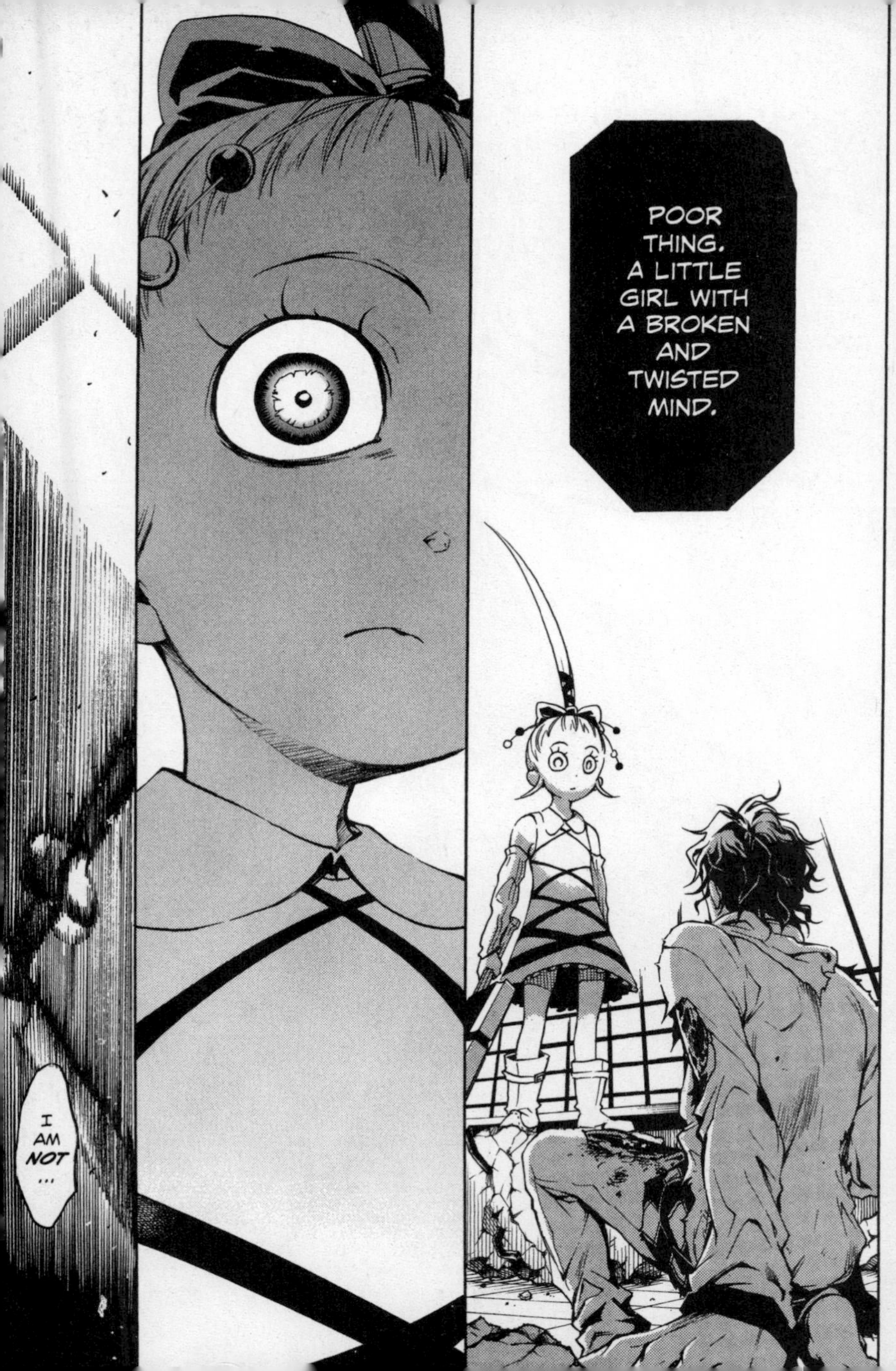
POOR THING. A LITTLE GIRL WITH A BROKEN AND TWISTED MIND.
I AM *NOT* ...

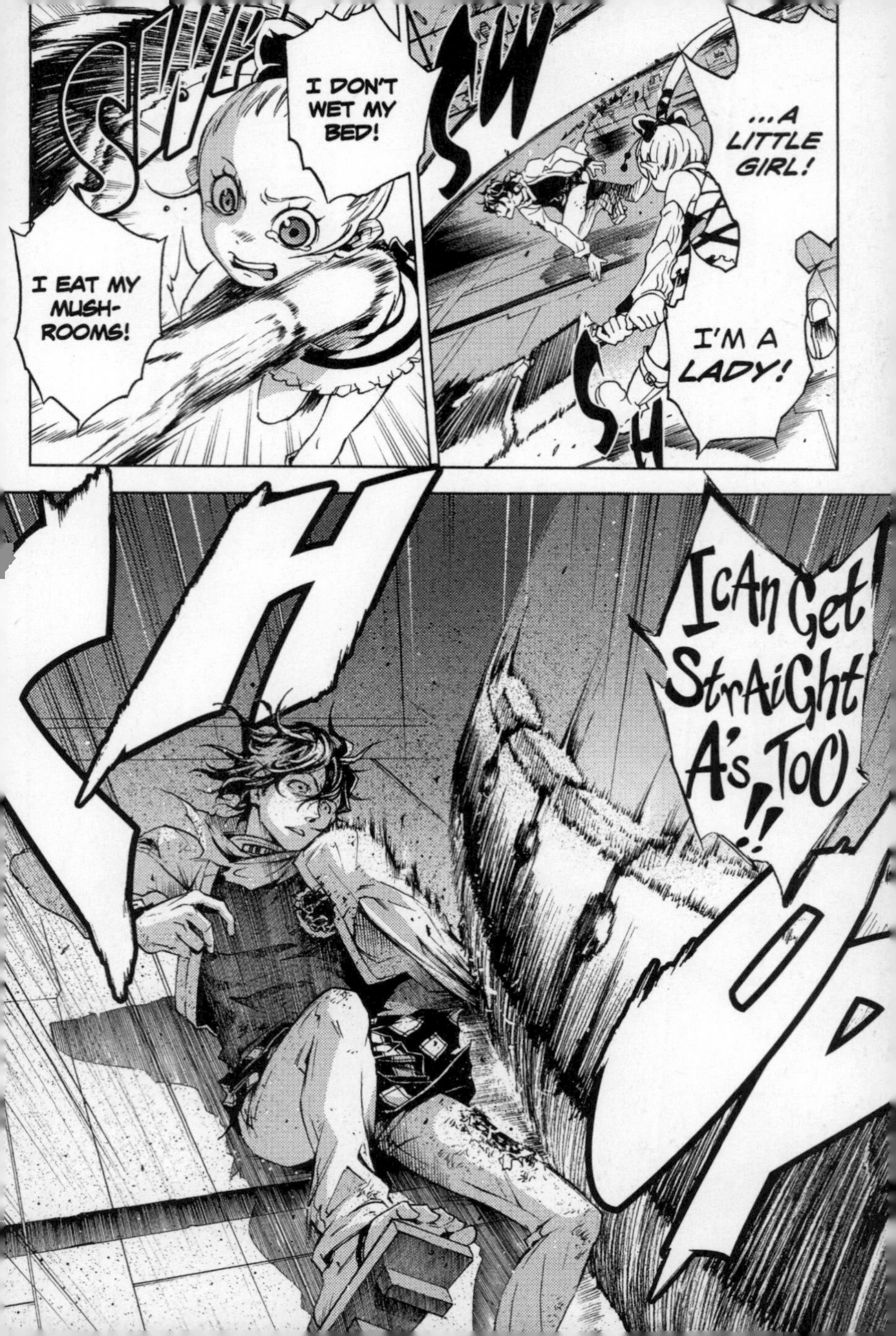
...A LITTLE GIRL!
I'M A LADY!
I DON'T WET MY BED!
I EAT MY MUSH-ROOMS!
I CAN GET STRAIGHT A'S TOO!!

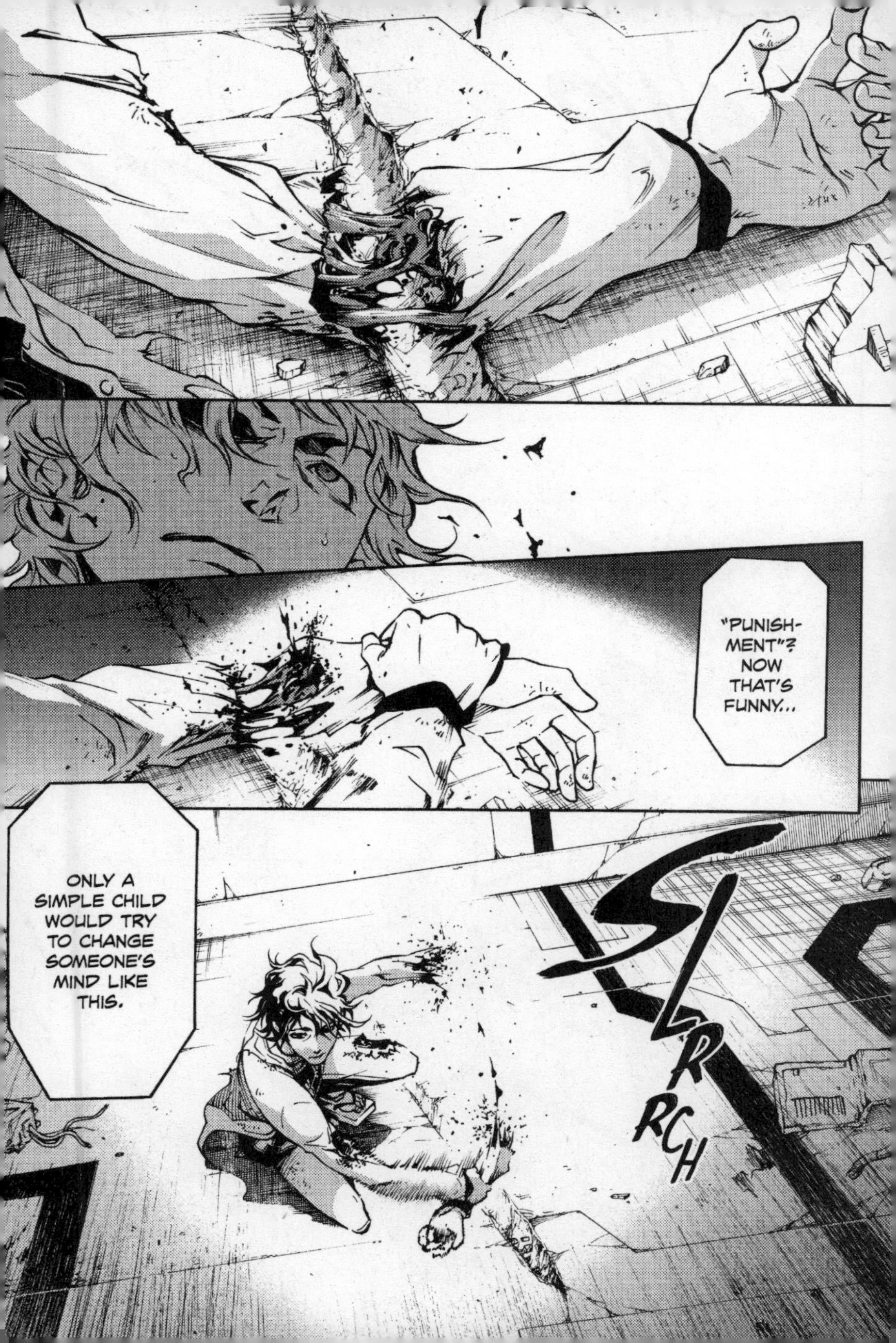
"PUNISH-MENT"? NOW THAT'S FUNNY...
ONLY A SIMPLE CHILD WOULD TRY TO CHANGE SOMEONE'S MIND LIKE THIS.
SLRRCH

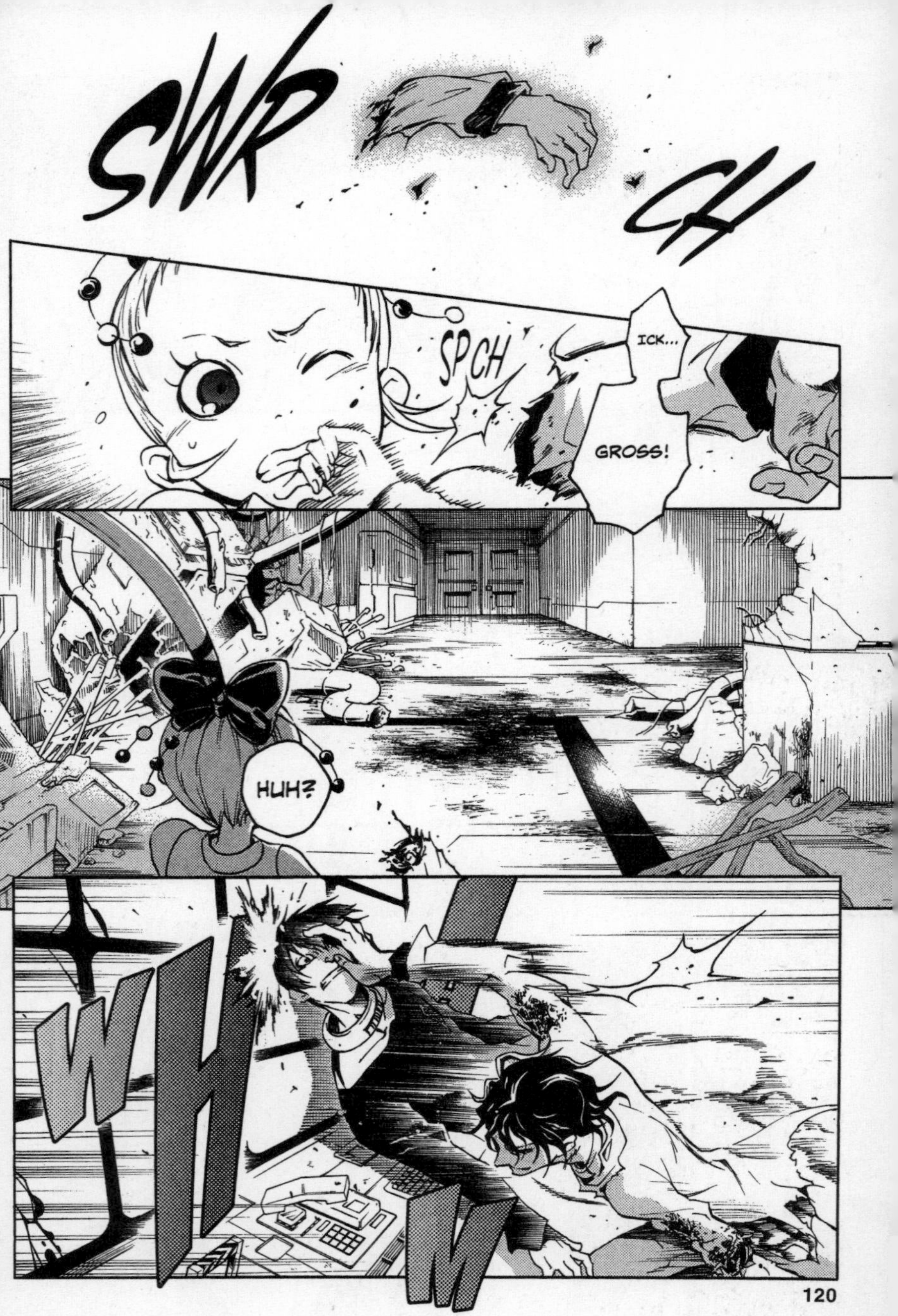
SWRCH
ICK...
GROSS!
SPCH
HUH?
WHM

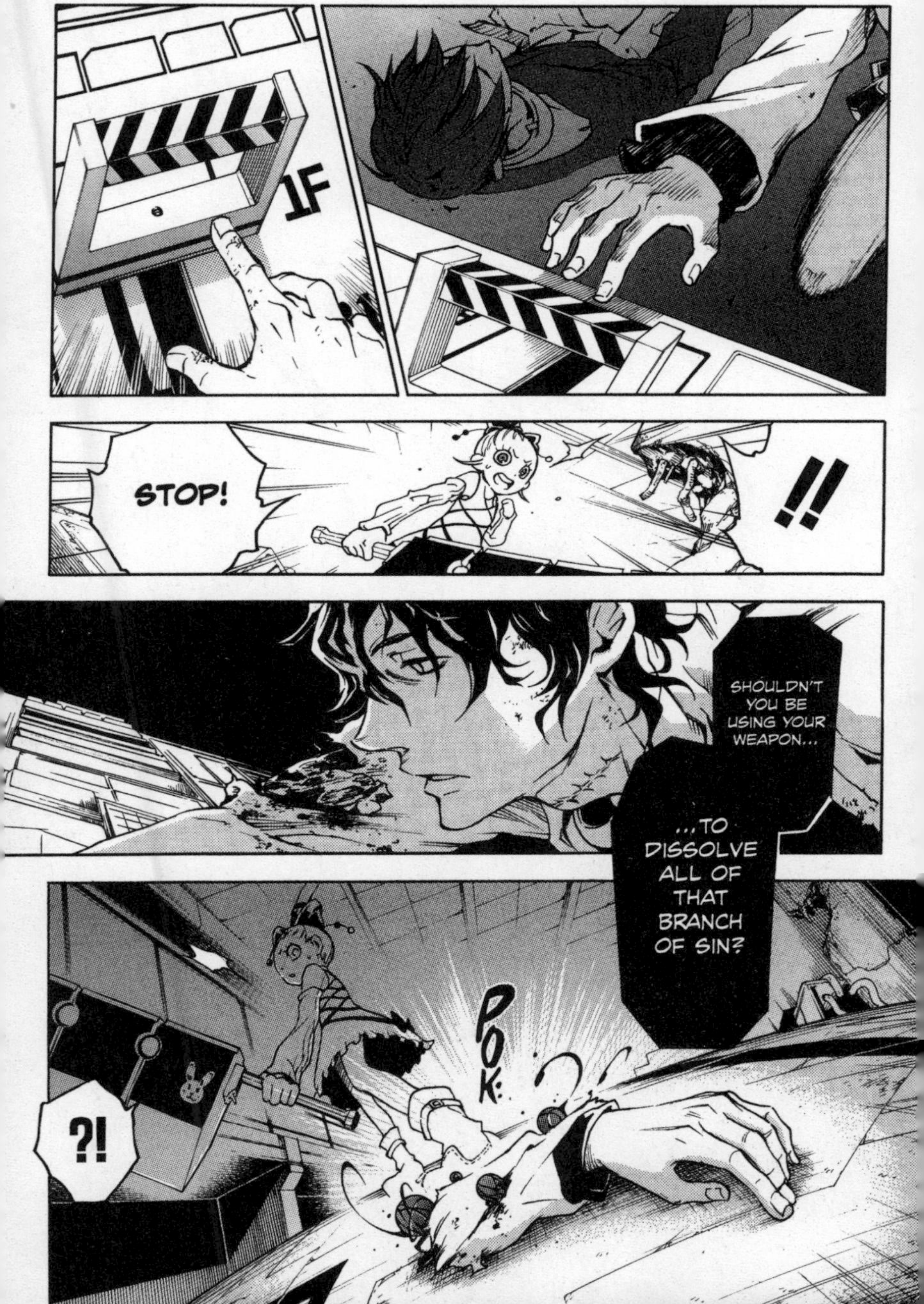

!!
STOP!
SHOULDN'T YOU BE USING YOUR WEAPON...
...TO DISSOLVE ALL OF THAT BRANCH OF SIN?
POK
?!

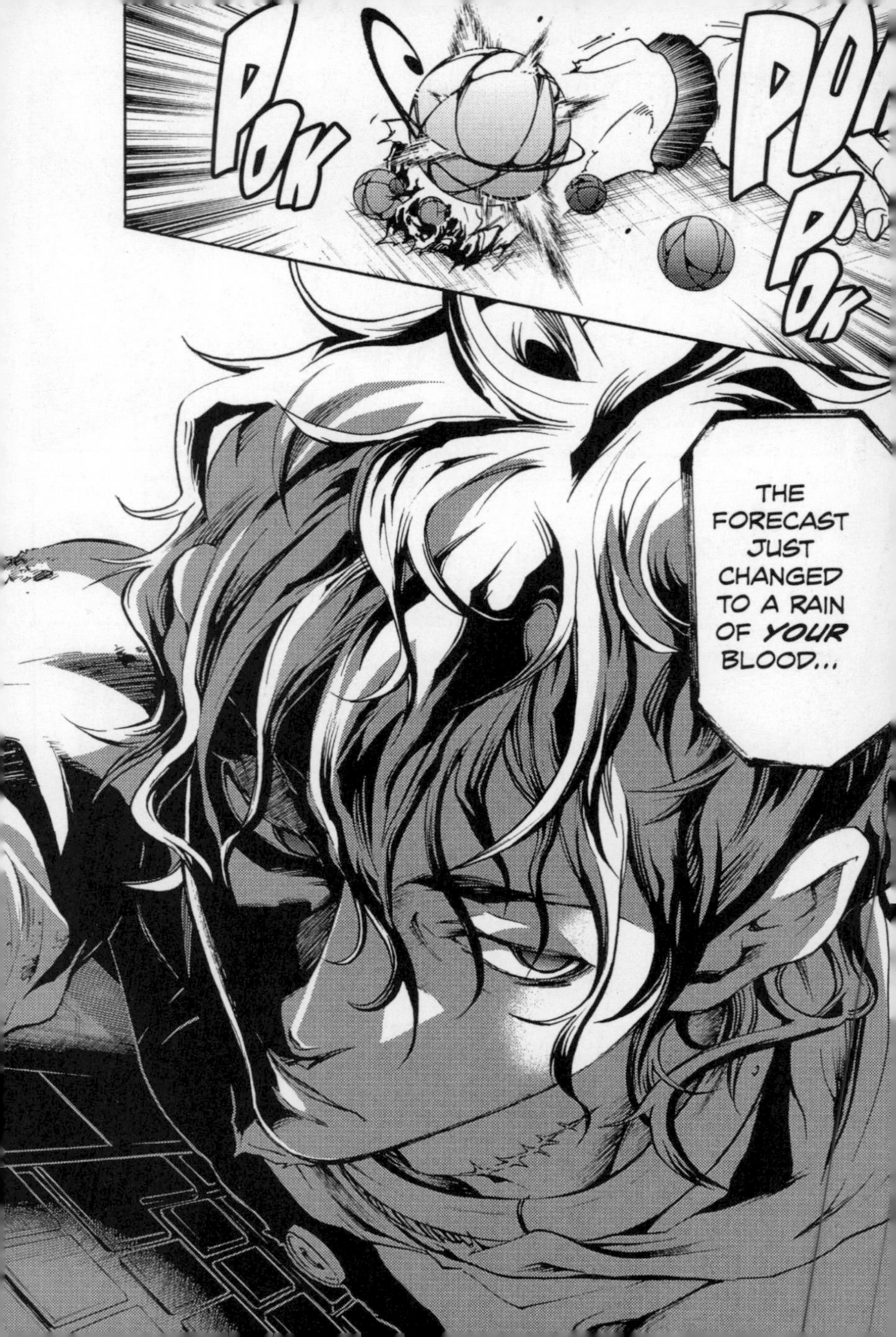
POK
POK
POK
THE FORECAST JUST CHANGED TO A RAIN OF *YOUR* BLOOD...

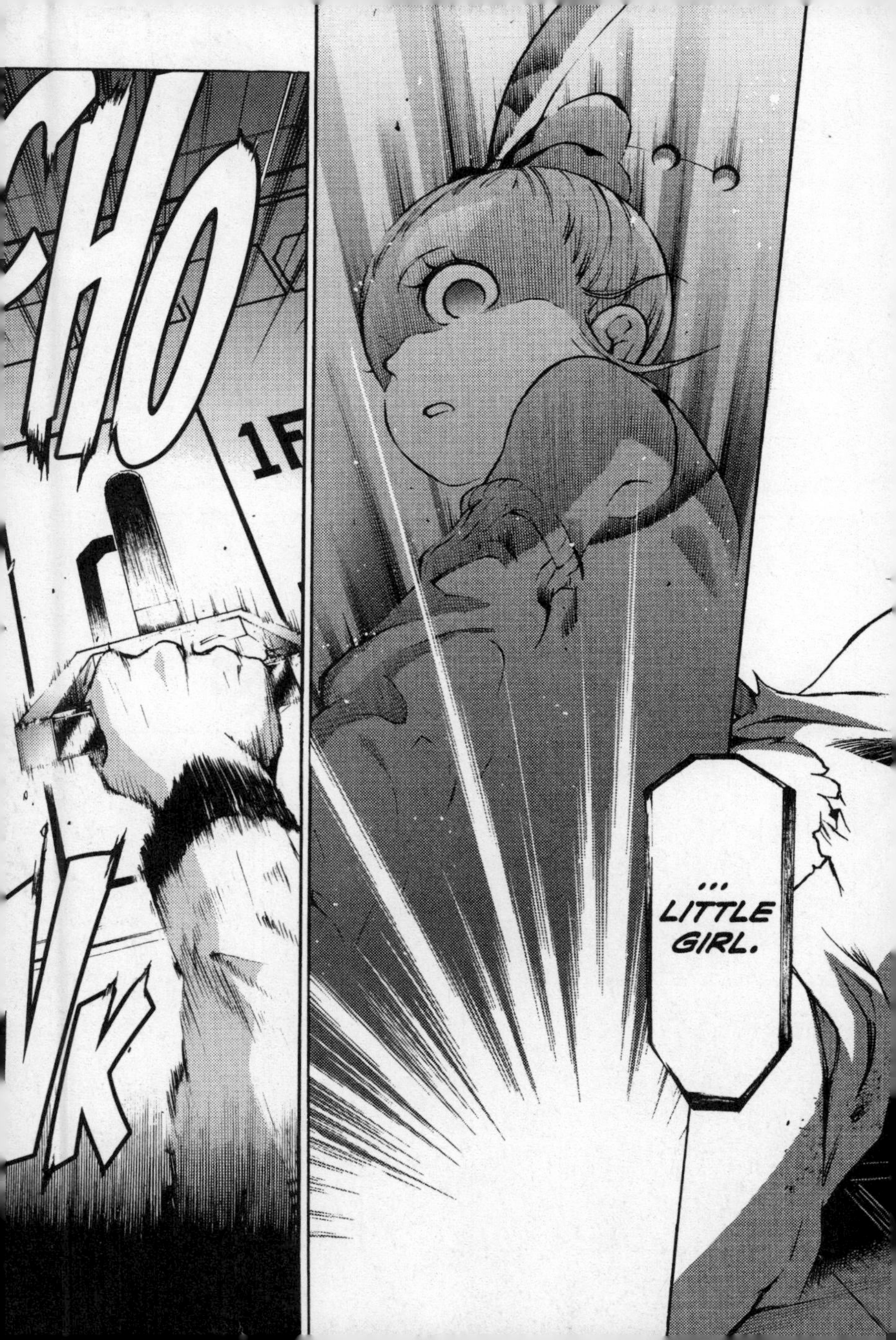
... LITTLE GIRL.
CHO
K
1F

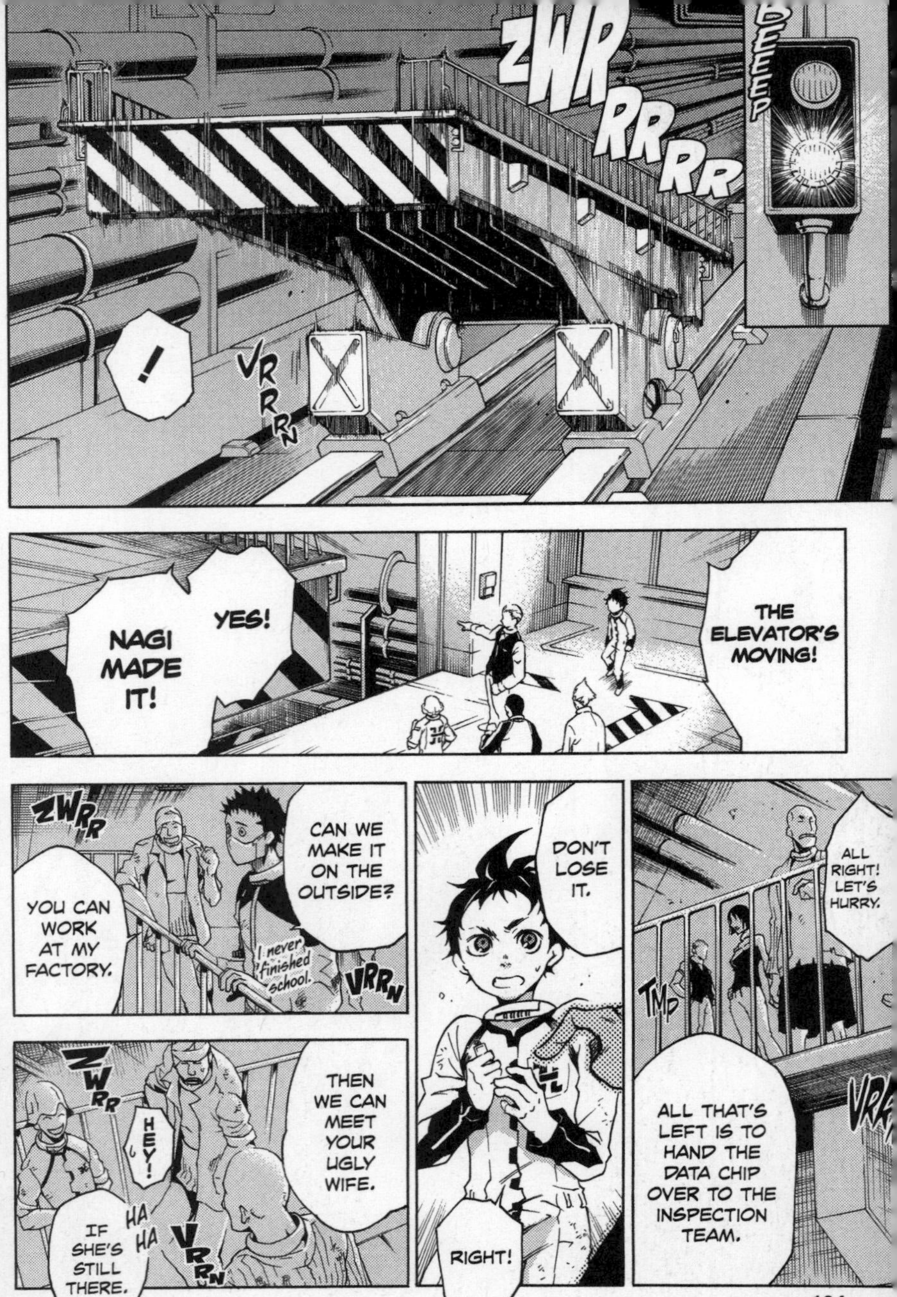
BEEEP
ZWRRRRRR
!
VRRRN
THE ELEVATOR'S MOVING!
YES!
NAGI MADE IT!
ALL RIGHT! LET'S HURRY.
TMP
ALL THAT'S LEFT IS TO HAND THE DATA CHIP OVER TO THE INSPECTION TEAM.
DON'T LOSE IT.
RIGHT!
CAN WE MAKE IT ON THE OUTSIDE?
ZWRR
I never finished school.
YOU CAN WORK AT MY FACTORY.
VRRN
THEN WE CAN MEET YOUR UGLY WIFE.
ZWRR
HEY!
HA HA
VRRN
IF SHE'S STILL THERE.

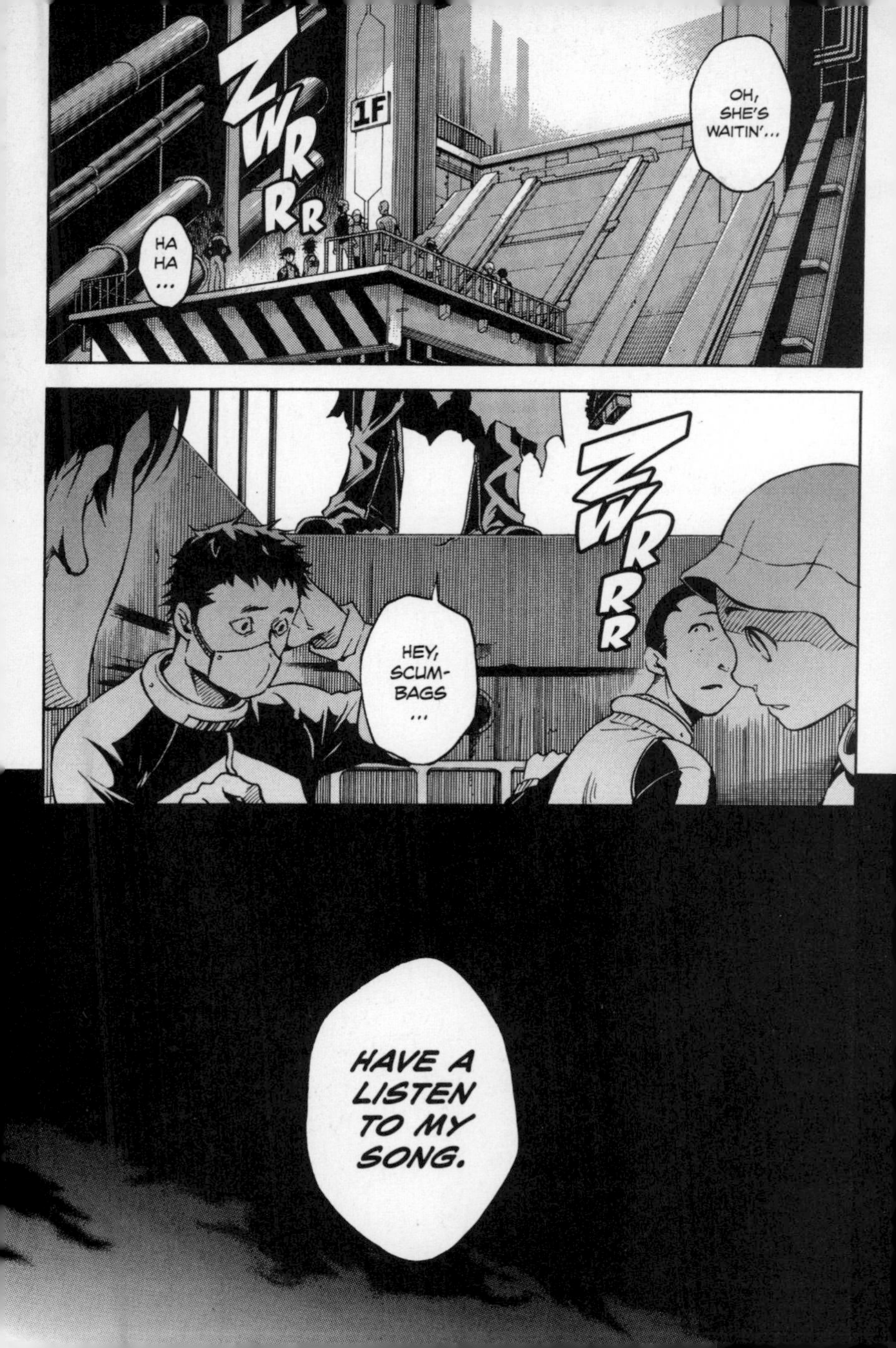
OH, SHE'S WAITIN'...
ZWRRR
HA HA ...
ZWRRR
HEY, SCUM-BAGS ...
HAVE A LISTEN TO MY SONG.

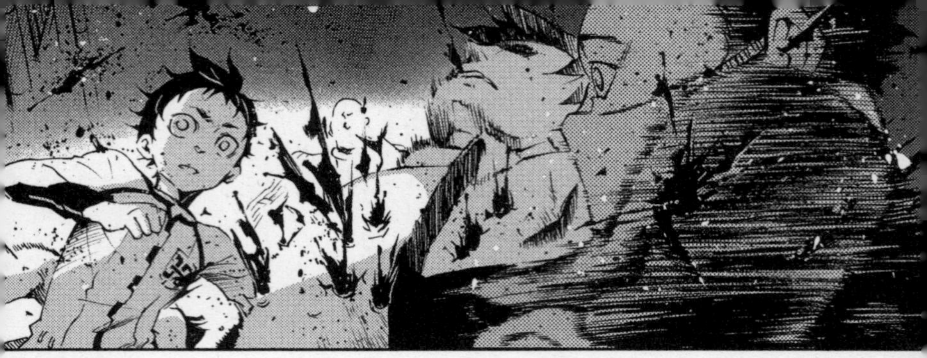
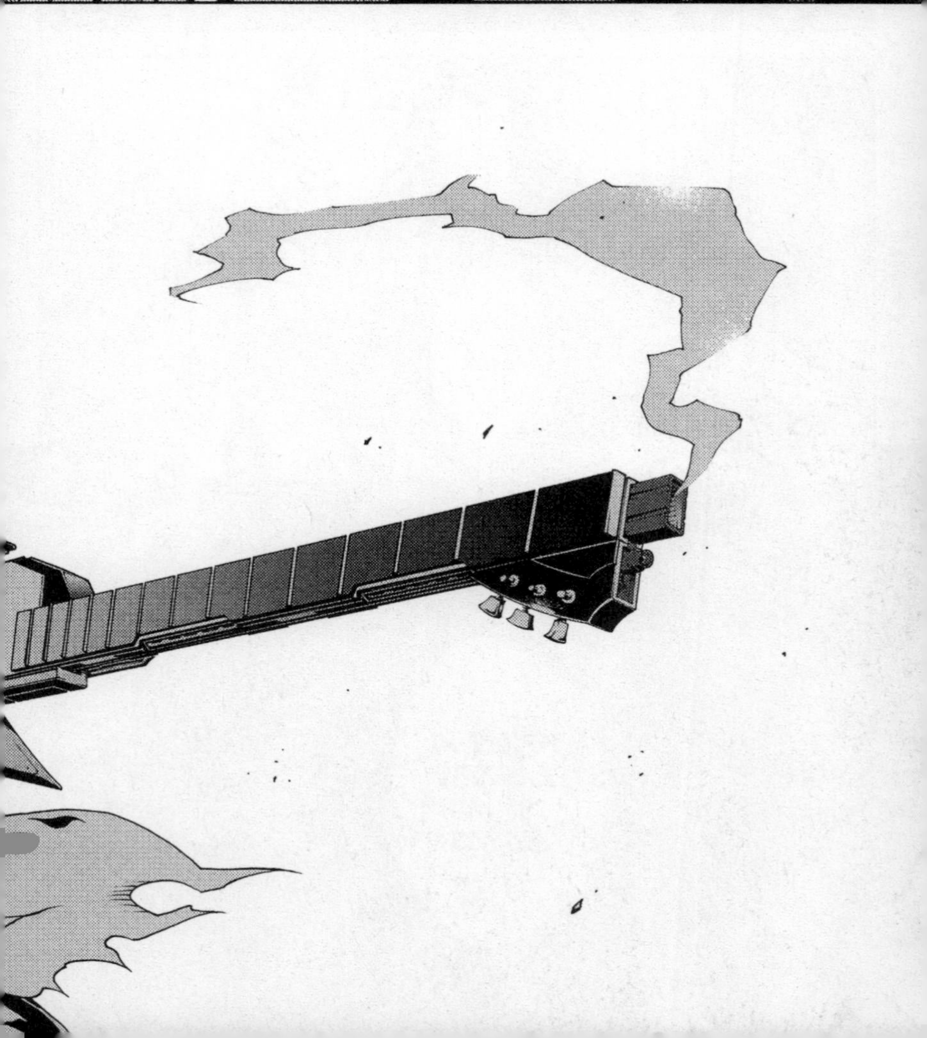

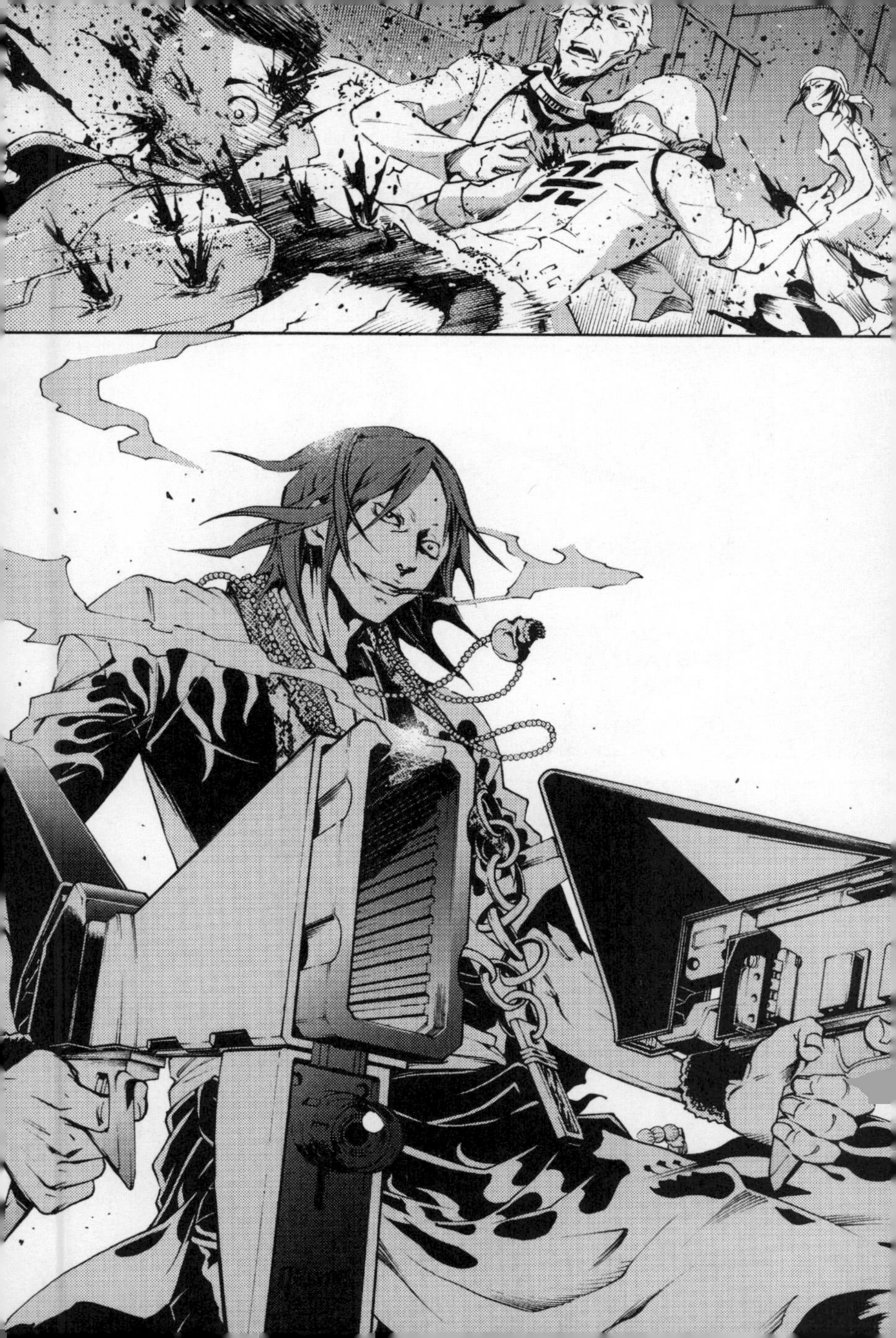

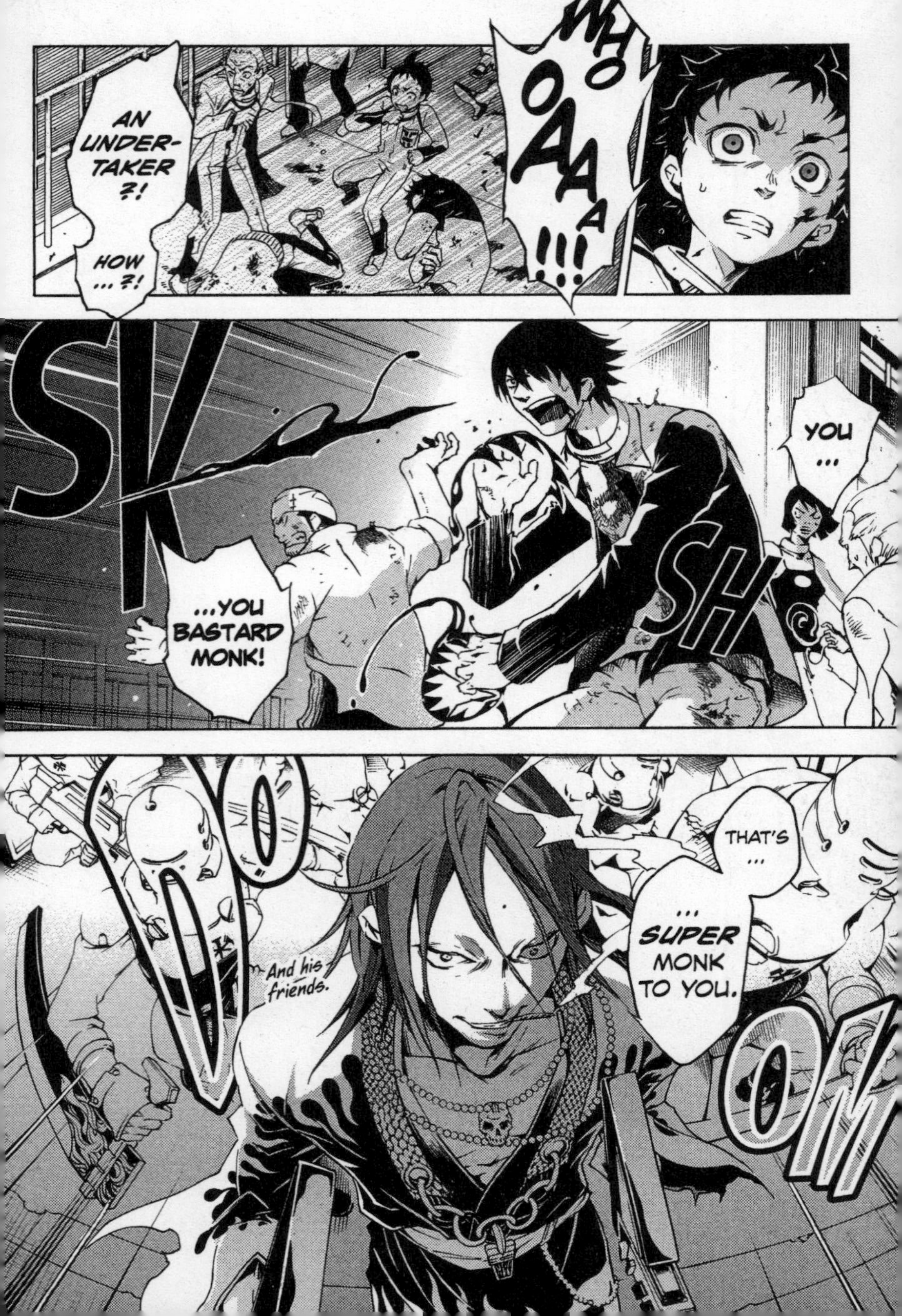
WHOOAAAA!!!
AN UNDER-TAKER?!
HOW ...?!
SK
SH
YOU ...
...YOU BASTARD MONK!
THAT'S ...
... SUPER MONK TO YOU.
And his friends.
VO
OM

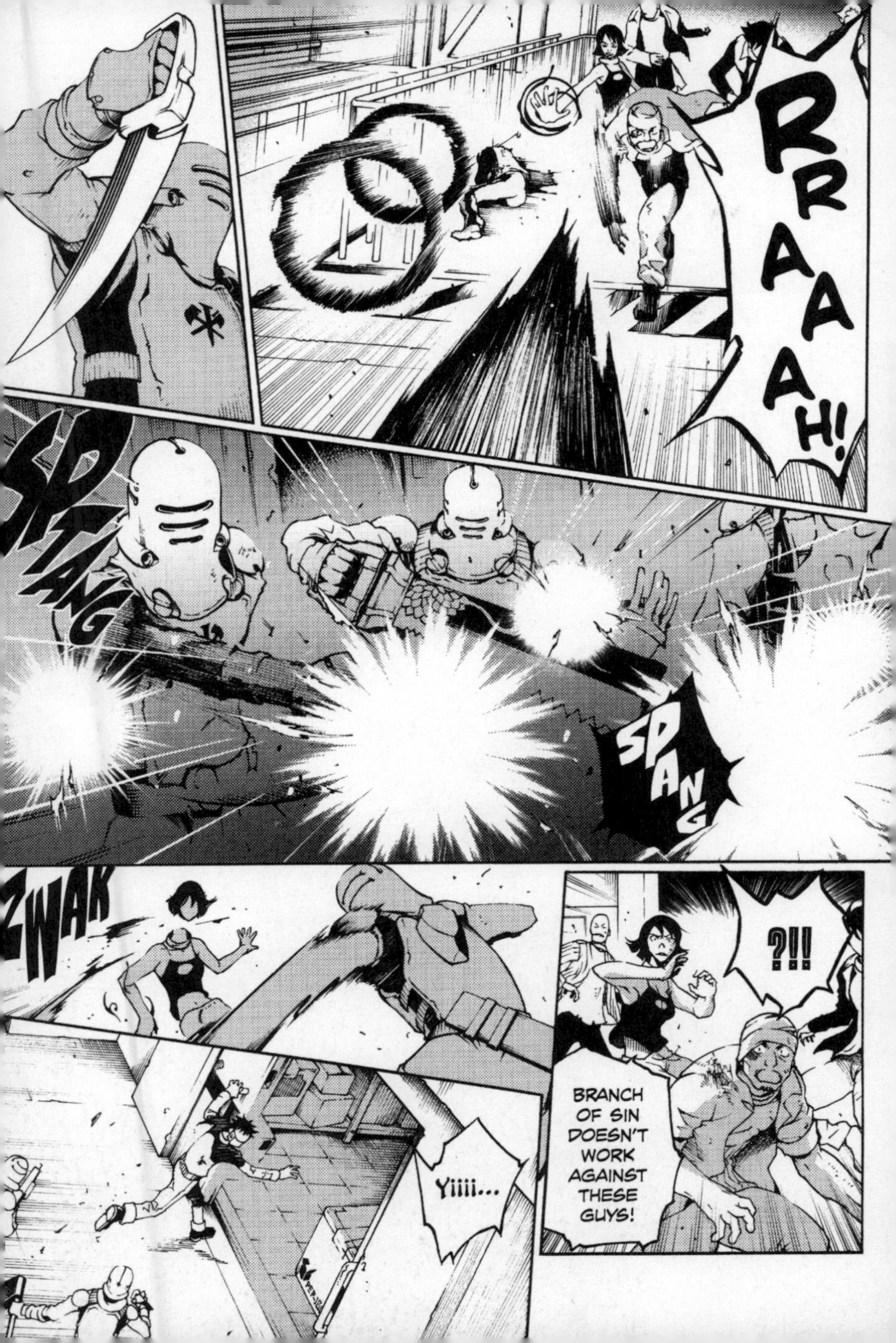
RRAAAH!
SPANG
SPTANG
?!!
BRANCH OF SIN DOESN'T WORK AGAINST THESE GUYS!
ZWAK
Yiiii...

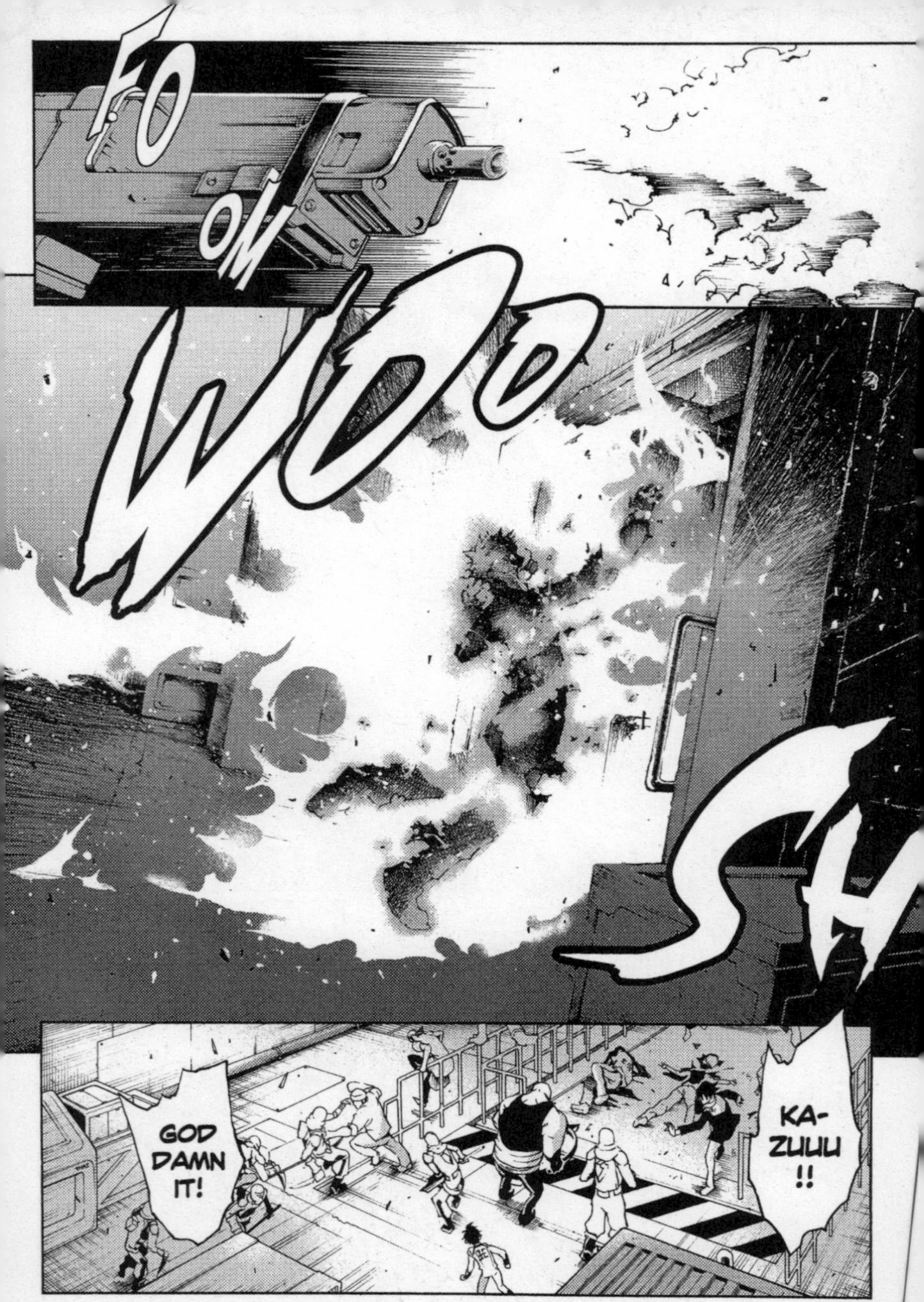
FOOM
WOOSH
KA-ZUUU!!
GOD DAMN IT!

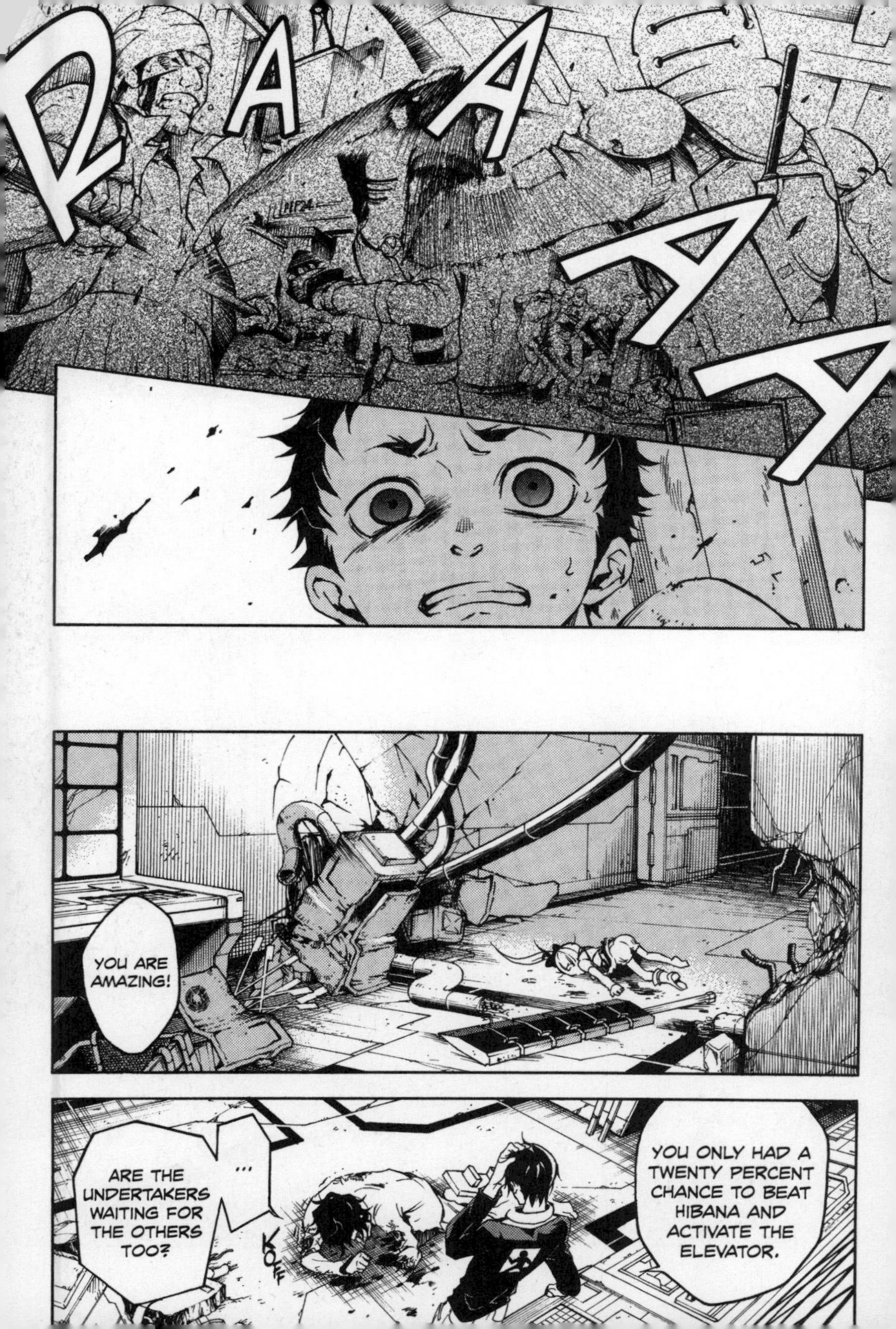
RAAAA
YOU ARE AMAZING!
YOU ONLY HAD A TWENTY PERCENT CHANCE TO BEAT HIBANA AND ACTIVATE THE ELEVATOR.
...
ARE THE UNDERTAKERS WAITING FOR THE OTHERS TOO?
KOFF

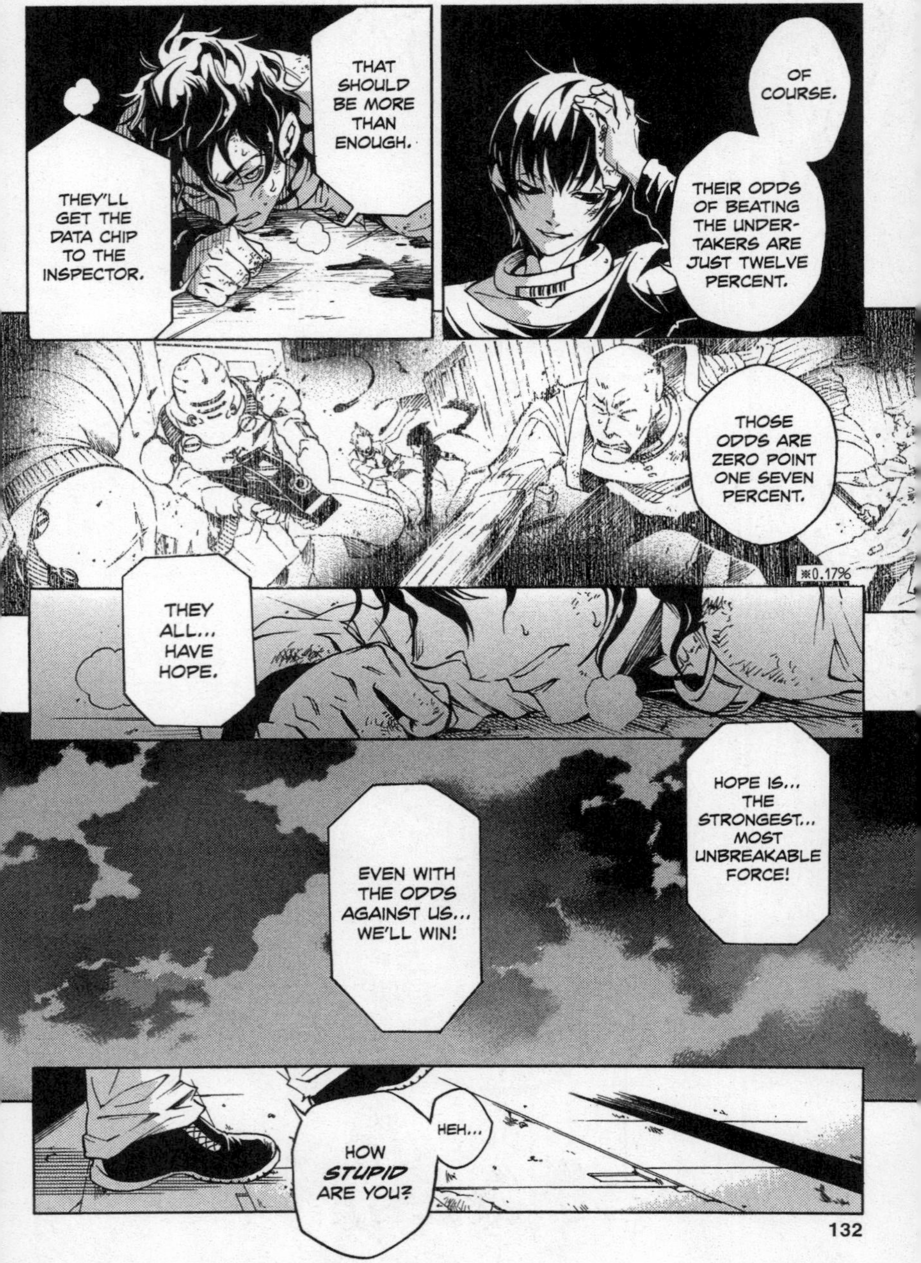
OF COURSE.
THEIR ODDS OF BEATING THE UNDER-TAKERS ARE JUST TWELVE PERCENT.
THAT SHOULD BE MORE THAN ENOUGH.
THEY'LL GET THE DATA CHIP TO THE INSPECTOR.
THOSE ODDS ARE ZERO POINT ONE SEVEN PERCENT.
※0.17%
THEY ALL... HAVE HOPE.
HOPE IS... THE STRONGEST... MOST UNBREAKABLE FORCE!
EVEN WITH THE ODDS AGAINST US... WE'LL WIN!
HEH...
HOW *STUPID* ARE YOU?

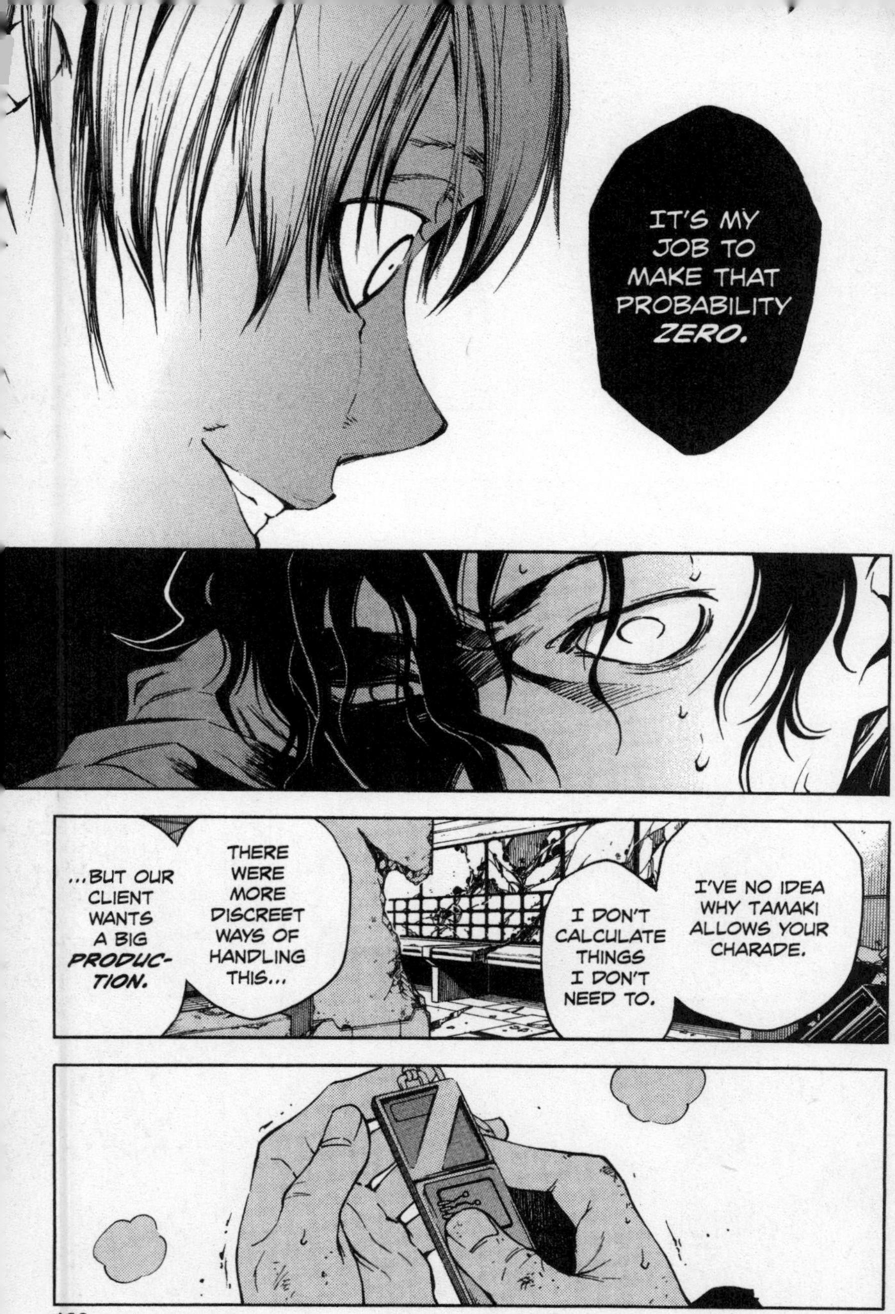
IT'S MY JOB TO MAKE THAT PROBABILITY *ZERO.*
I'VE NO IDEA WHY TAMAKI ALLOWS YOUR CHARADE.
I DON'T CALCULATE THINGS I DON'T NEED TO.
THERE WERE MORE DISCREET WAYS OF HANDLING THIS...
...BUT OUR CLIENT WANTS A BIG *PRODUC-TION.*

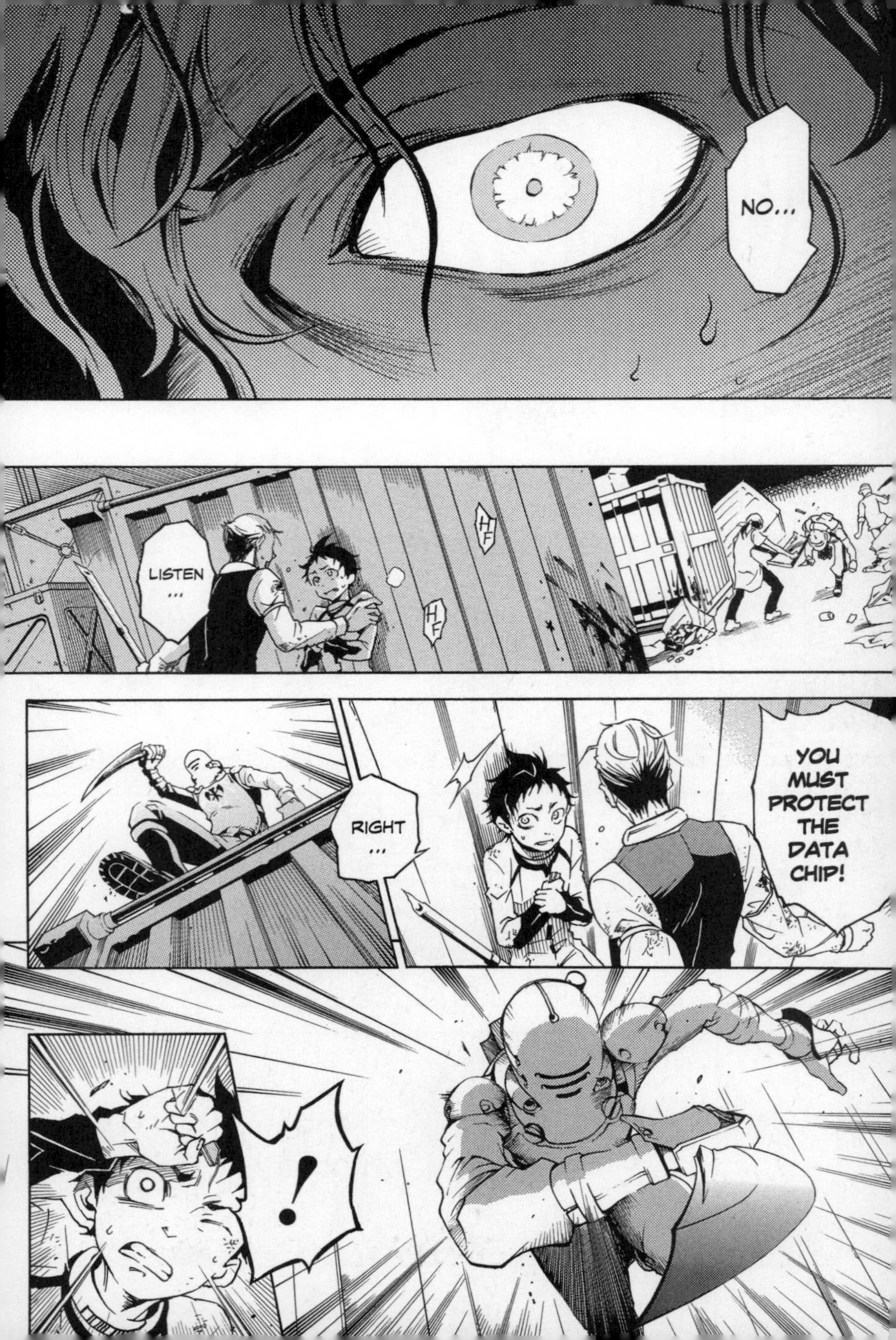
NO...
H F
H F
LISTEN ...
YOU MUST PROTECT THE DATA CHIP!
RIGHT ...
!

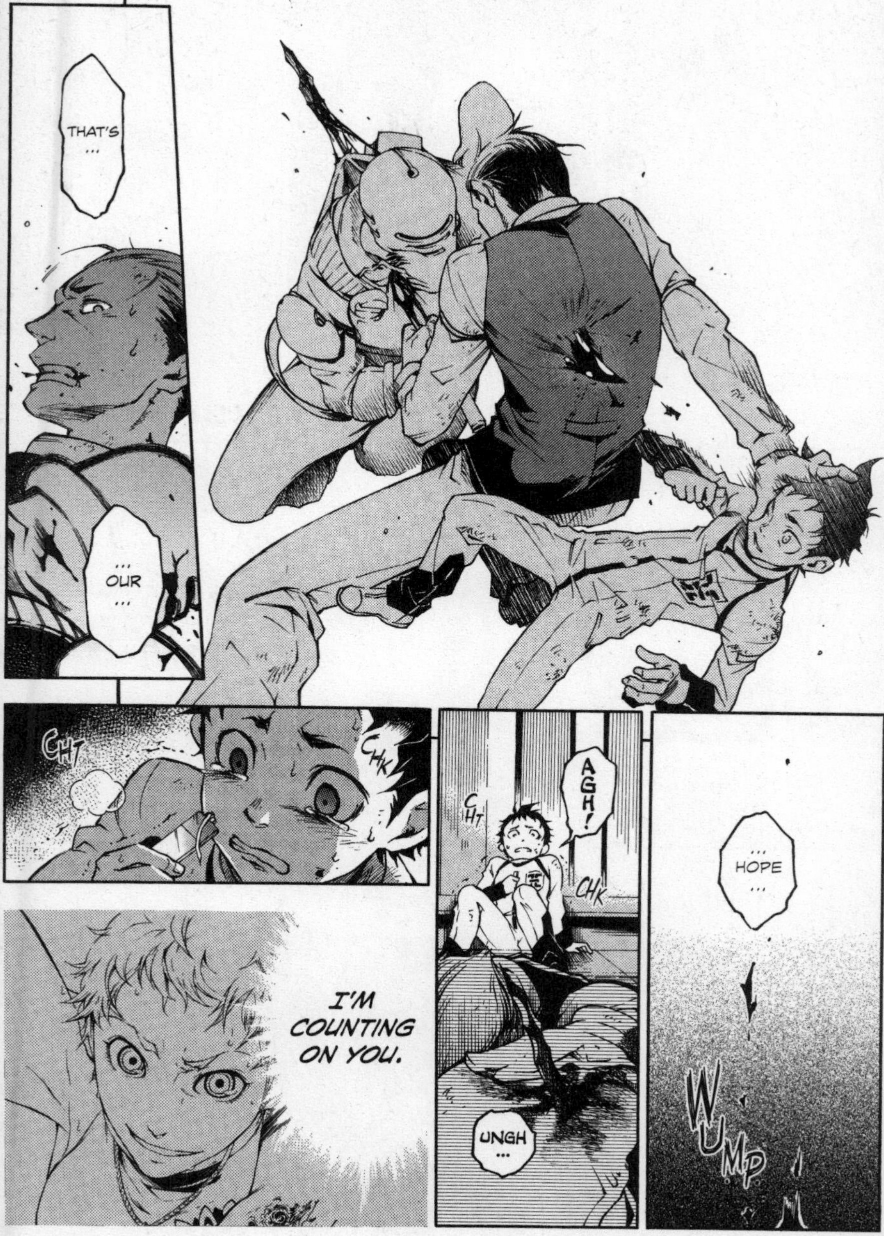
THAT'S ...
... OUR ...
... HOPE ...
WUMP
AGH!
CHT
CHK
UNGH ...
CHT
CHK
I'M COUNTING ON YOU.

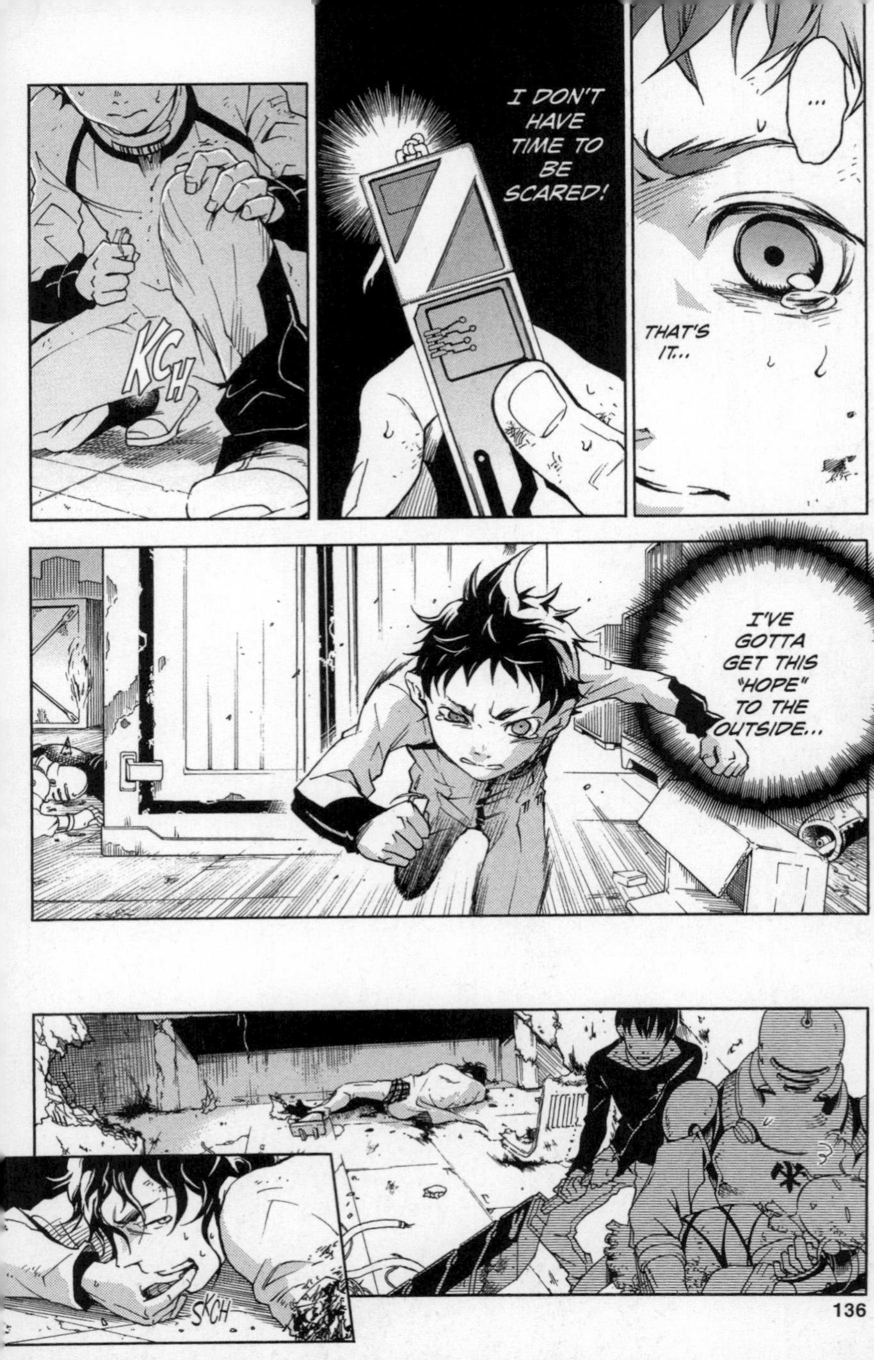
...
THAT'S IT...
I DON'T HAVE TIME TO BE SCARED!
KCH
I'VE GOTTA GET THIS "HOPE" TO THE OUTSIDE...
SKCH

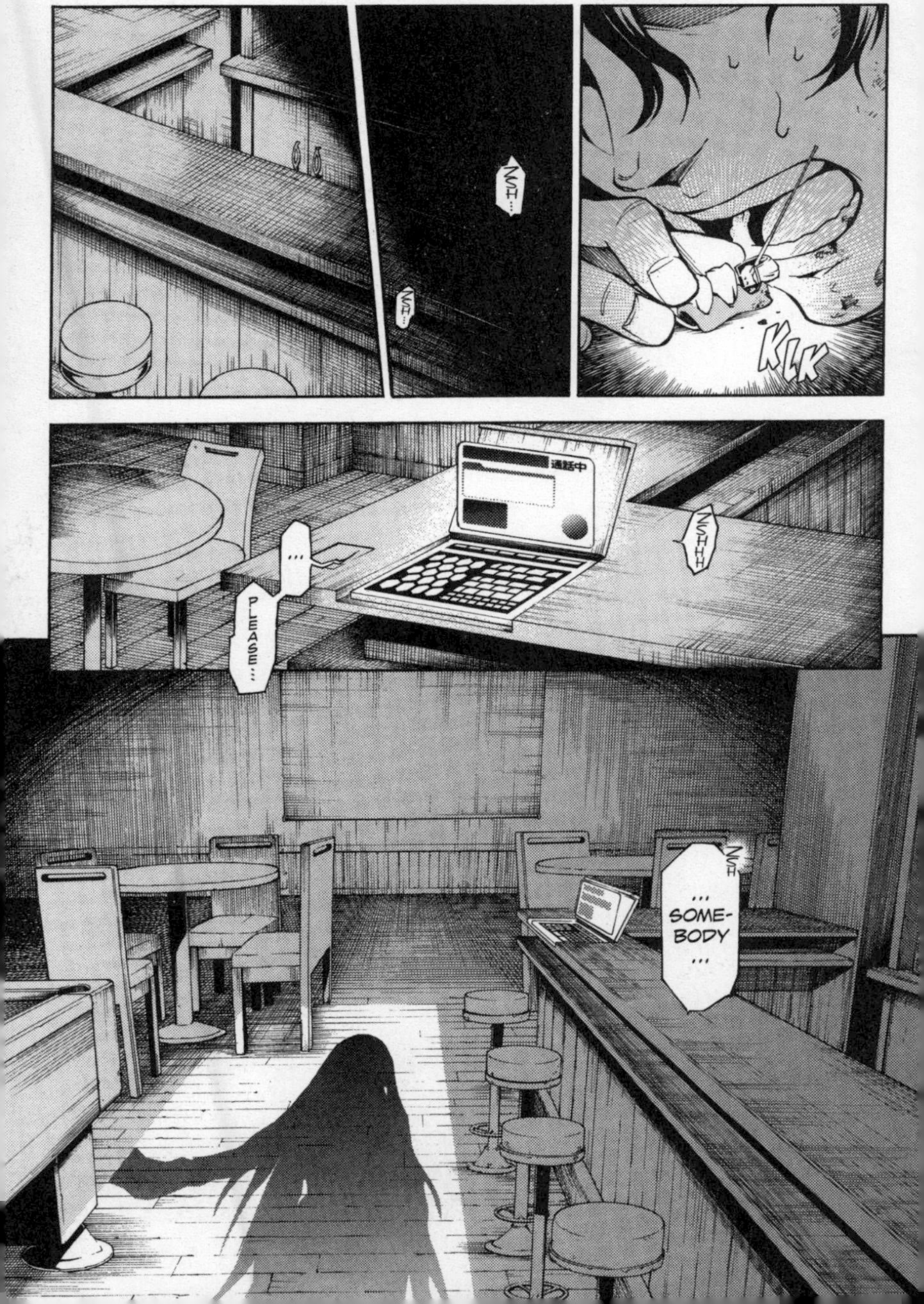
KLK
ZSH...
ZSH...
通話中
ZSHHH
...
PLEASE...
ZSH
...SOME-BODY...

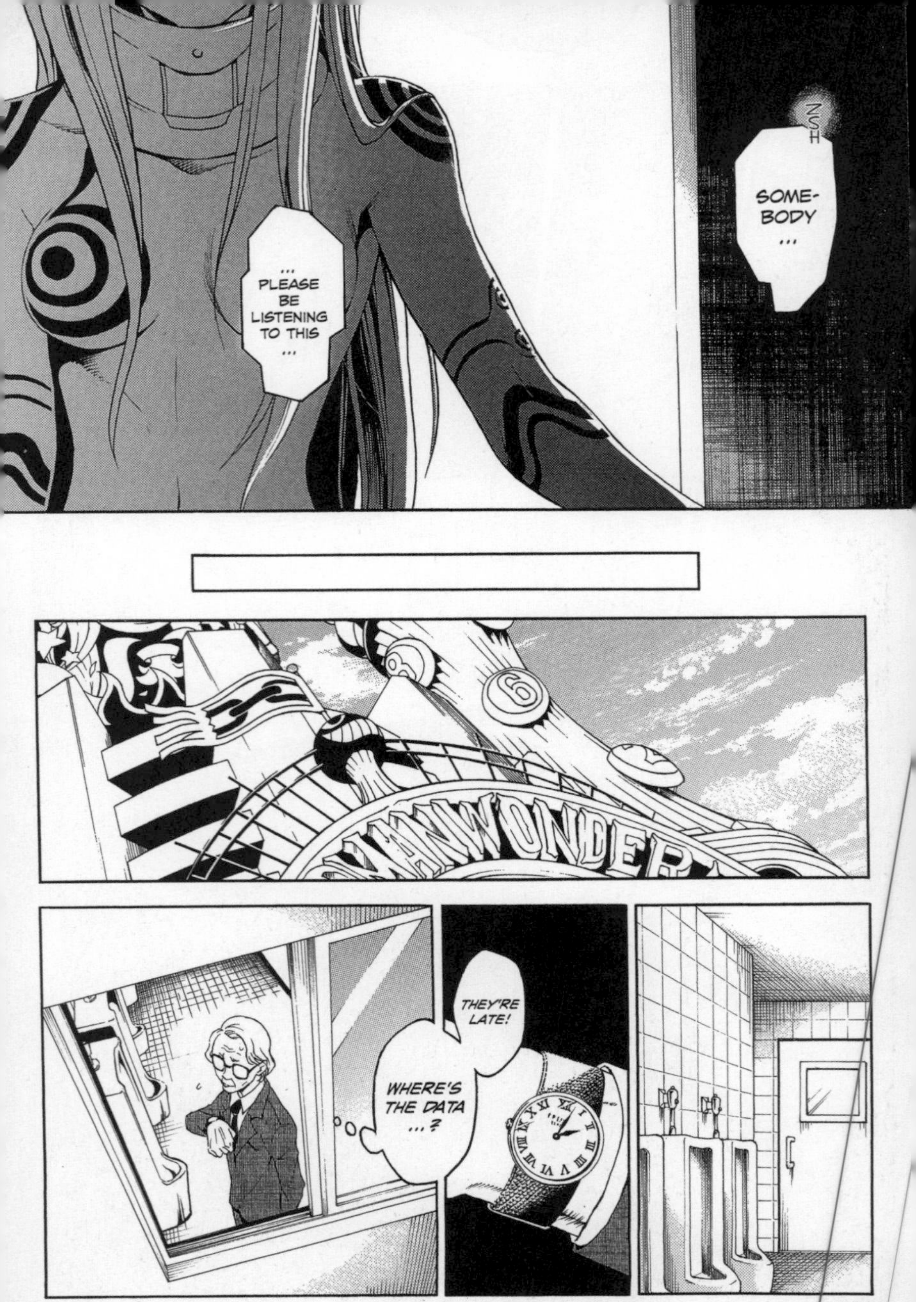
ZSH
SOMEBODY...
...PLEASE BE LISTENING TO THIS...
THEY'RE LATE!
WHERE'S THE DATA...?

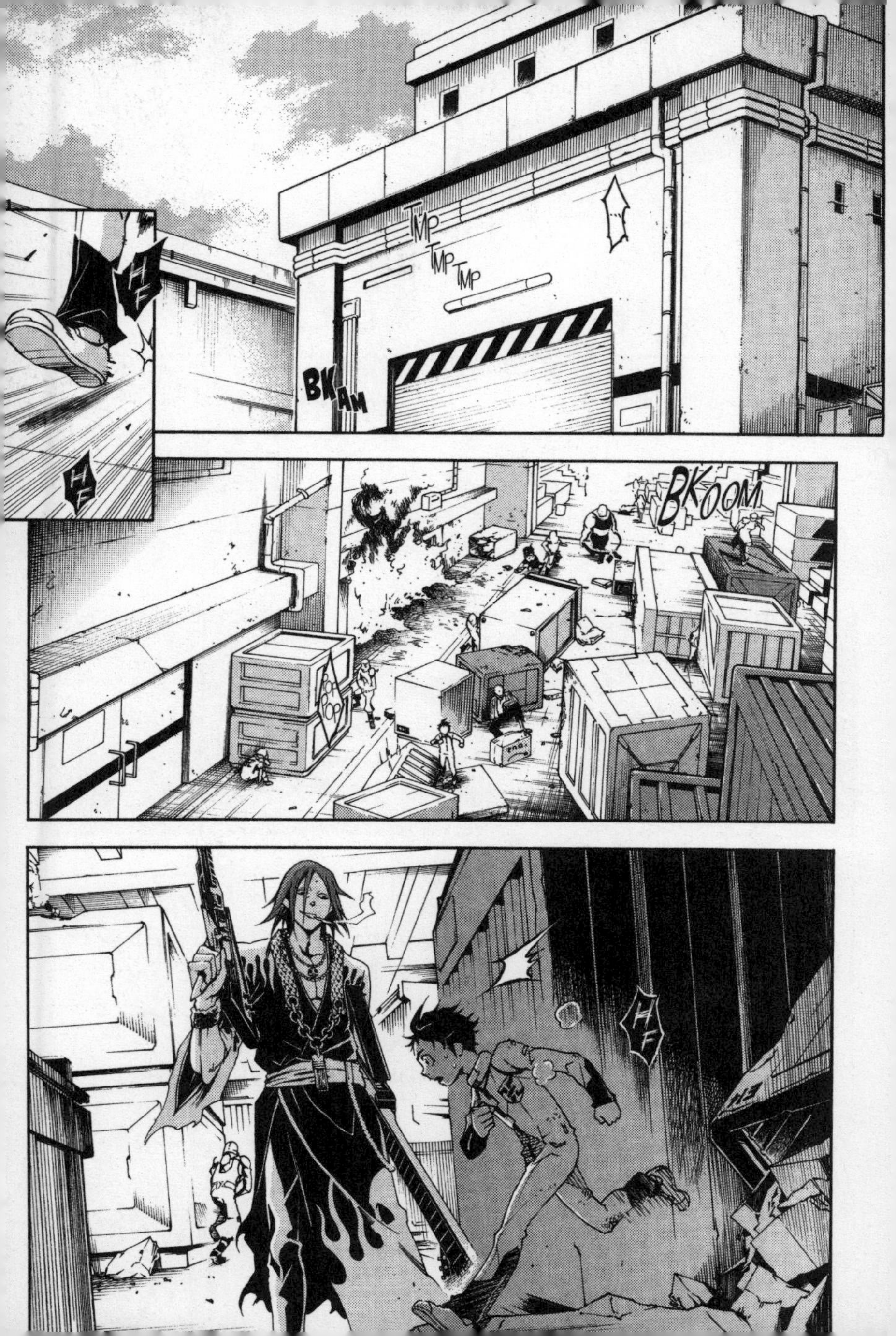
TMP
TMP TMP
BKAM
HF
HF
BKOOM
POP POP
HF

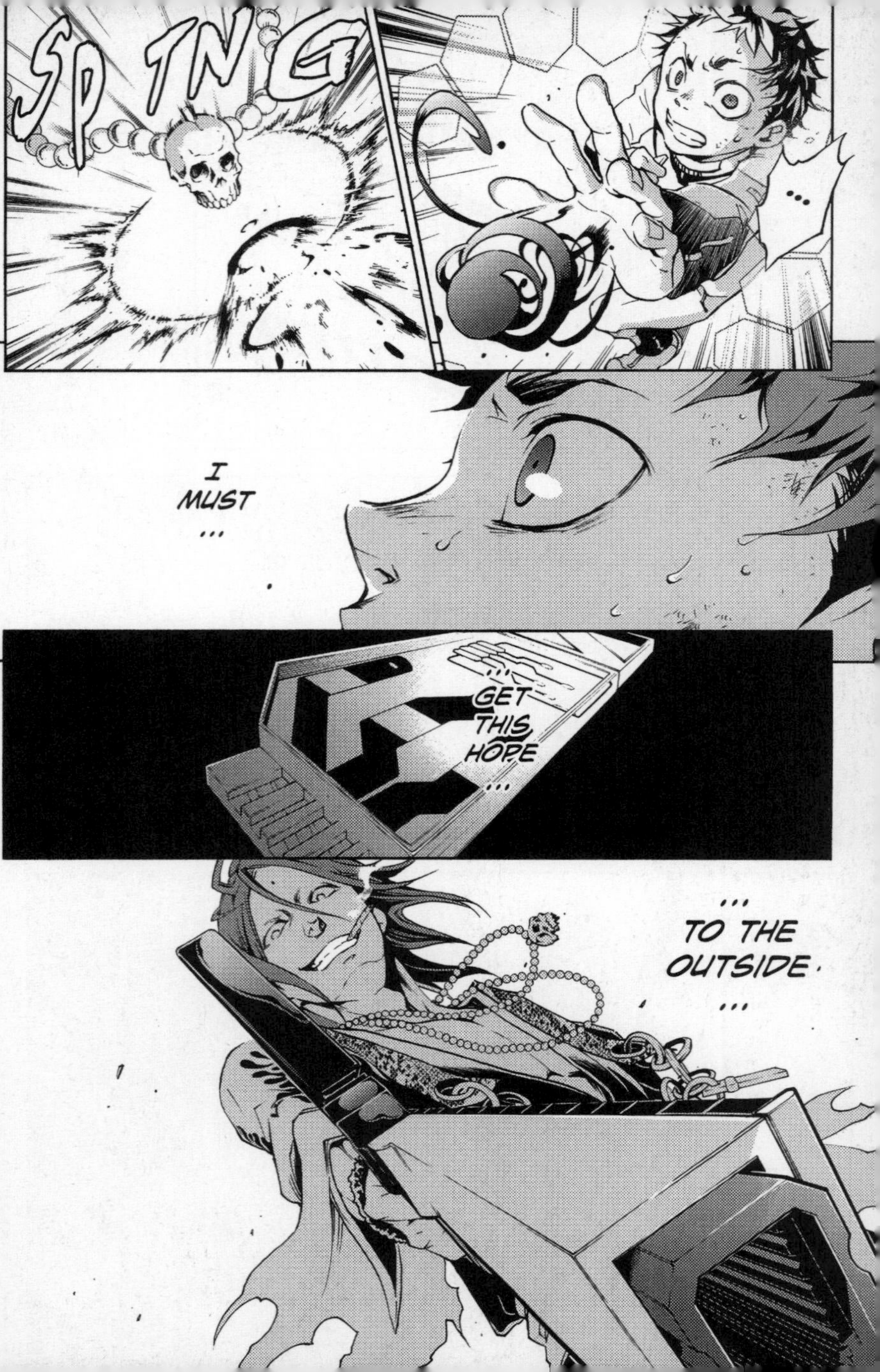
...
SPING
I MUST ...
... GET THIS HOPE ...
... TO THE OUTSIDE ...

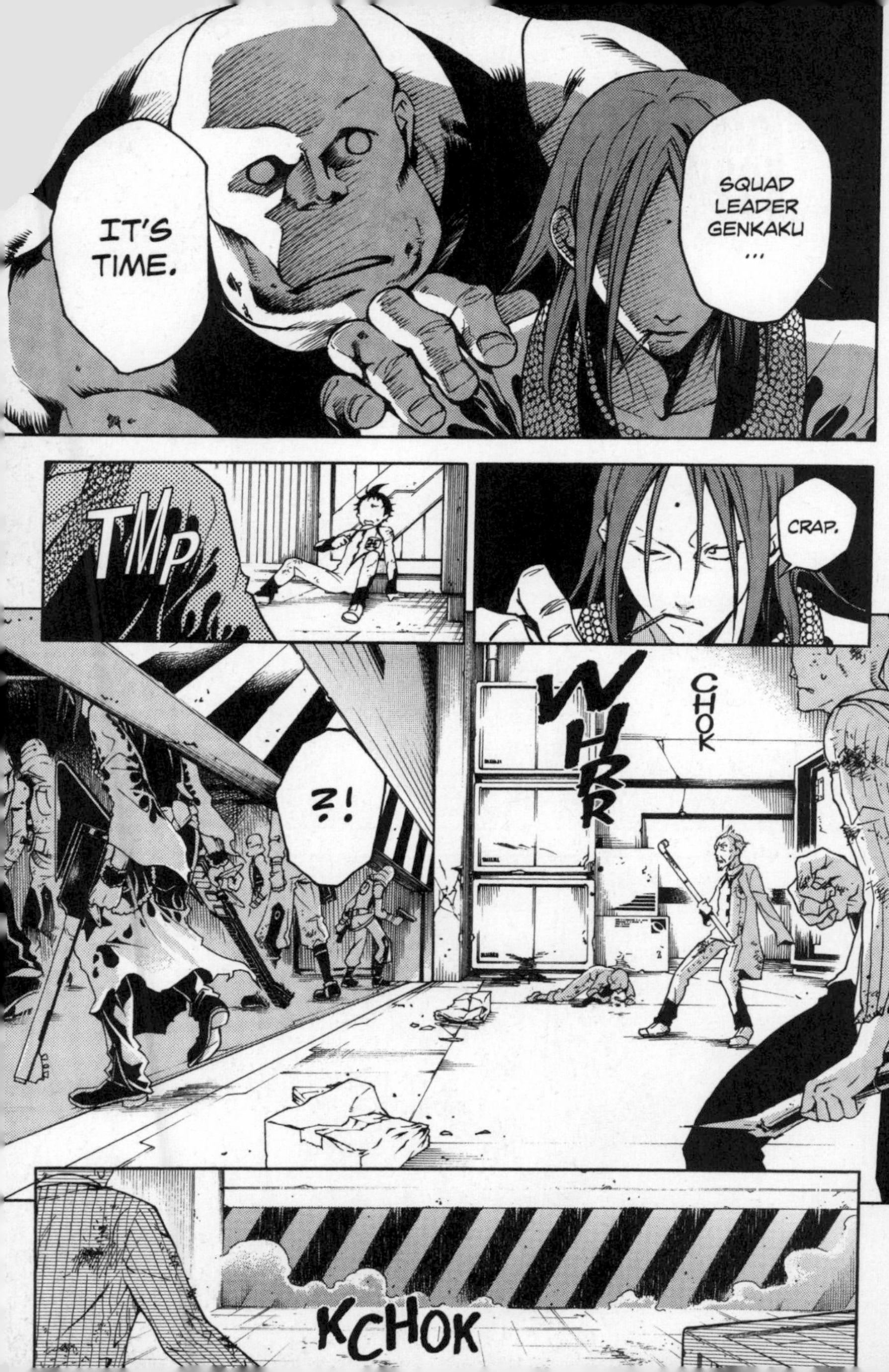
SQUAD LEADER GENKAKU ...
IT'S TIME.
CRAP.
TMP
CHOK
WHRR
?!
KCHOK

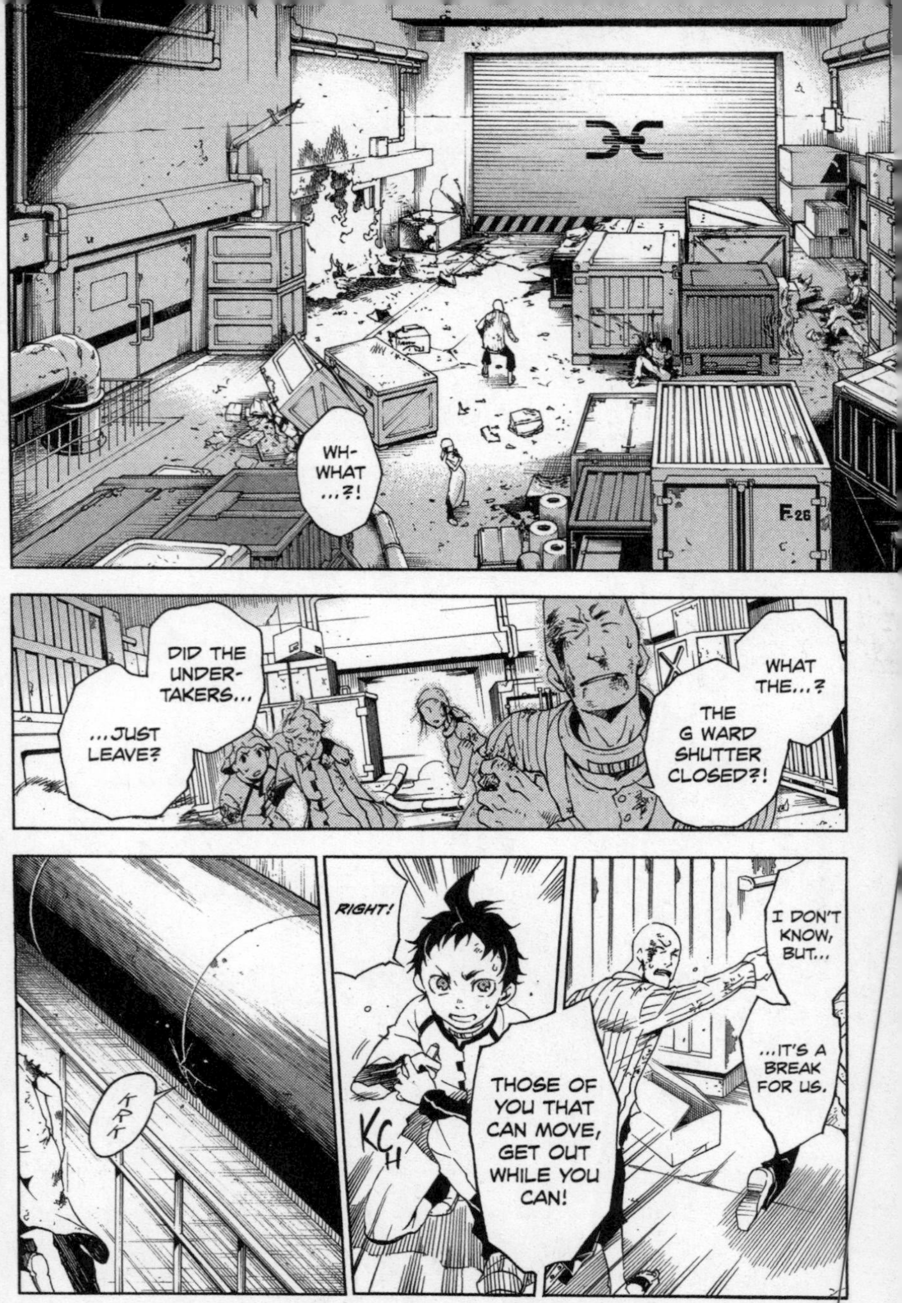
F-26
WH-WHAT...?!
WHAT THE...?
THE G WARD SHUTTER CLOSED?!
DID THE UNDER-TAKERS...
...JUST LEAVE?
I DON'T KNOW, BUT...
...IT'S A BREAK FOR US.
THOSE OF YOU THAT CAN MOVE, GET OUT WHILE YOU CAN!
RIGHT!
KCH
KRK

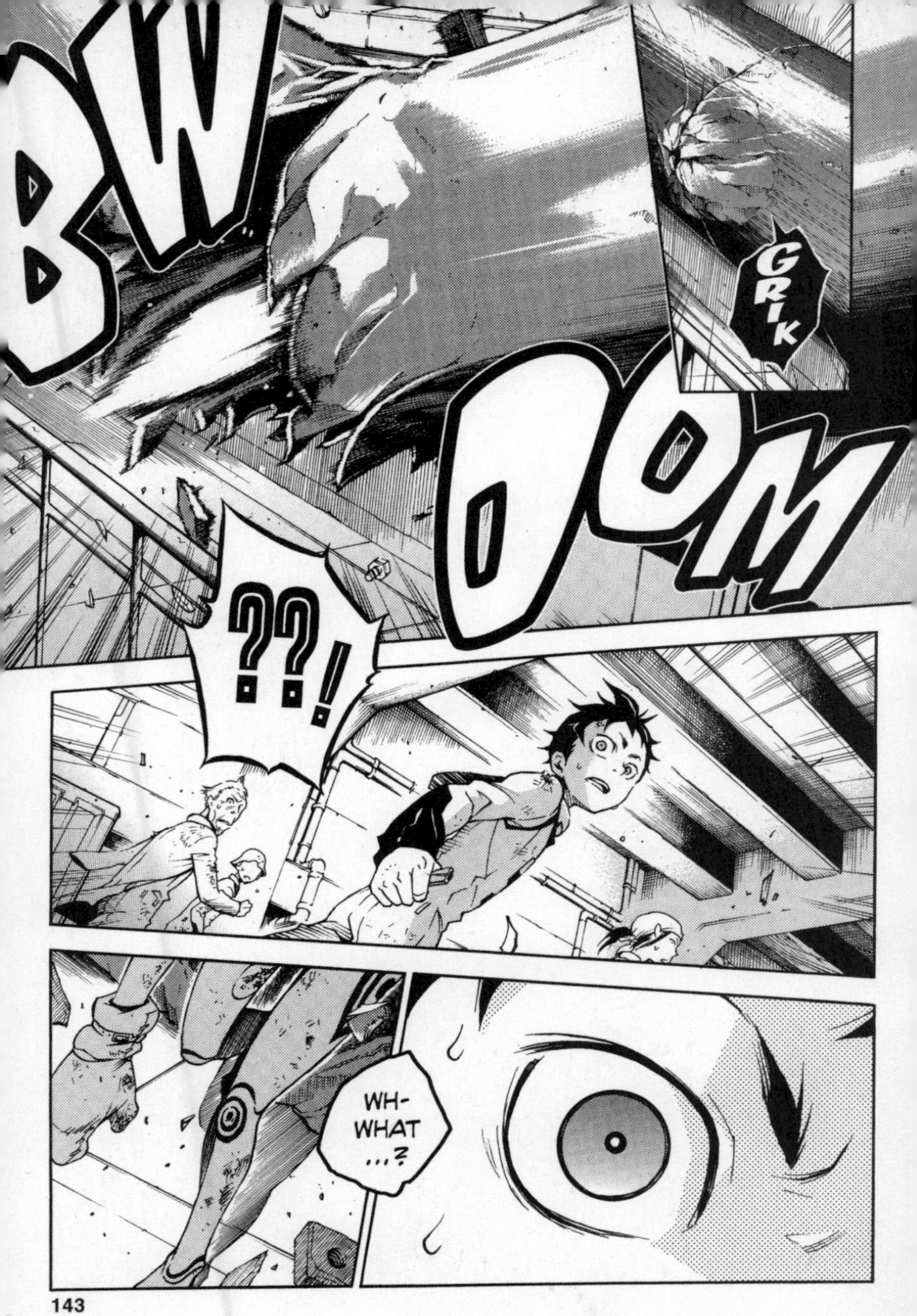
BADOOM
GRIK
??!
WH-
WHAT
...?

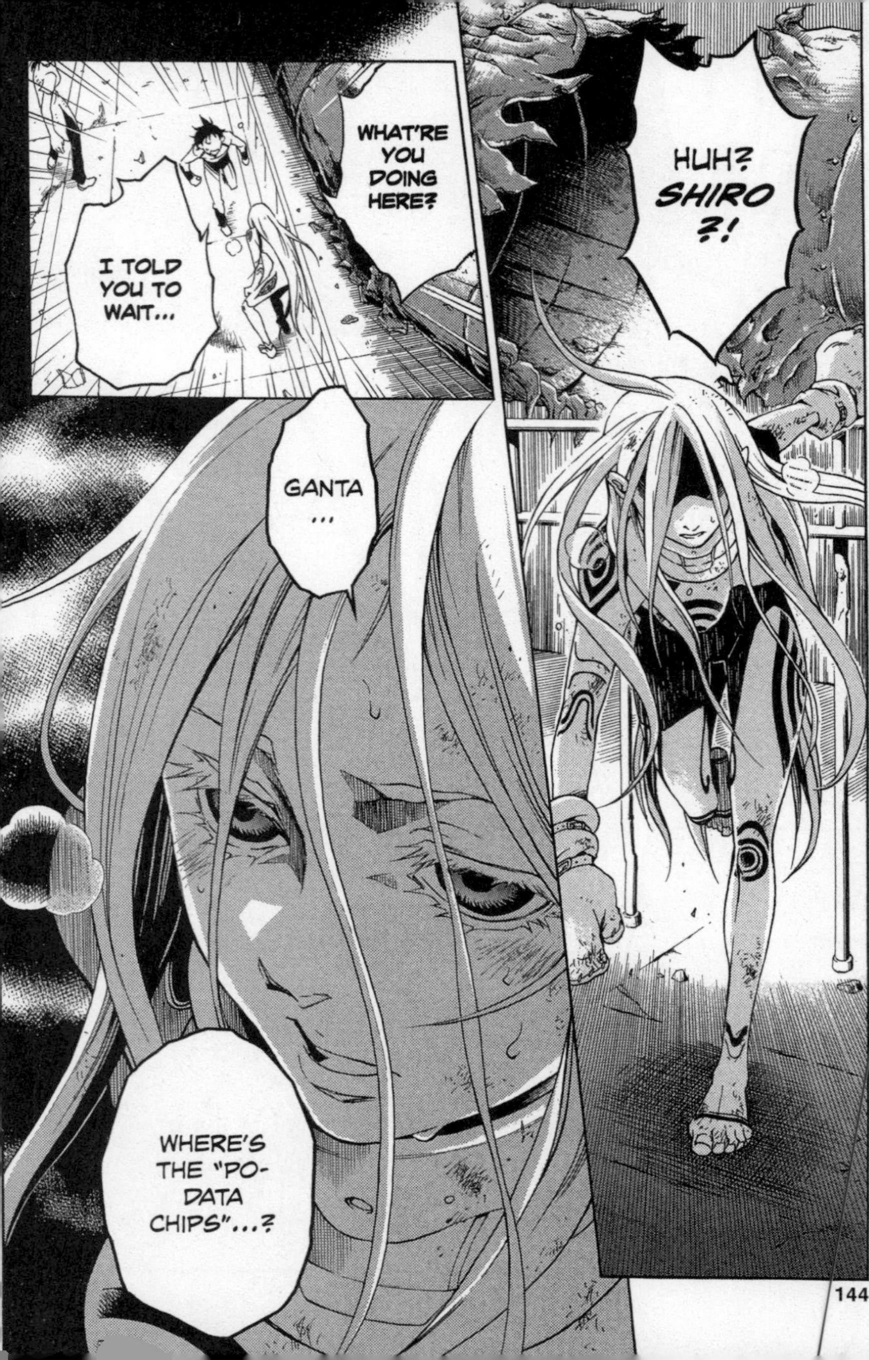
HUH? SHIRO ?!
WHAT'RE YOU DOING HERE?
I TOLD YOU TO WAIT...
GANTA ...
WHERE'S THE "PO-DATA CHIPS"...?

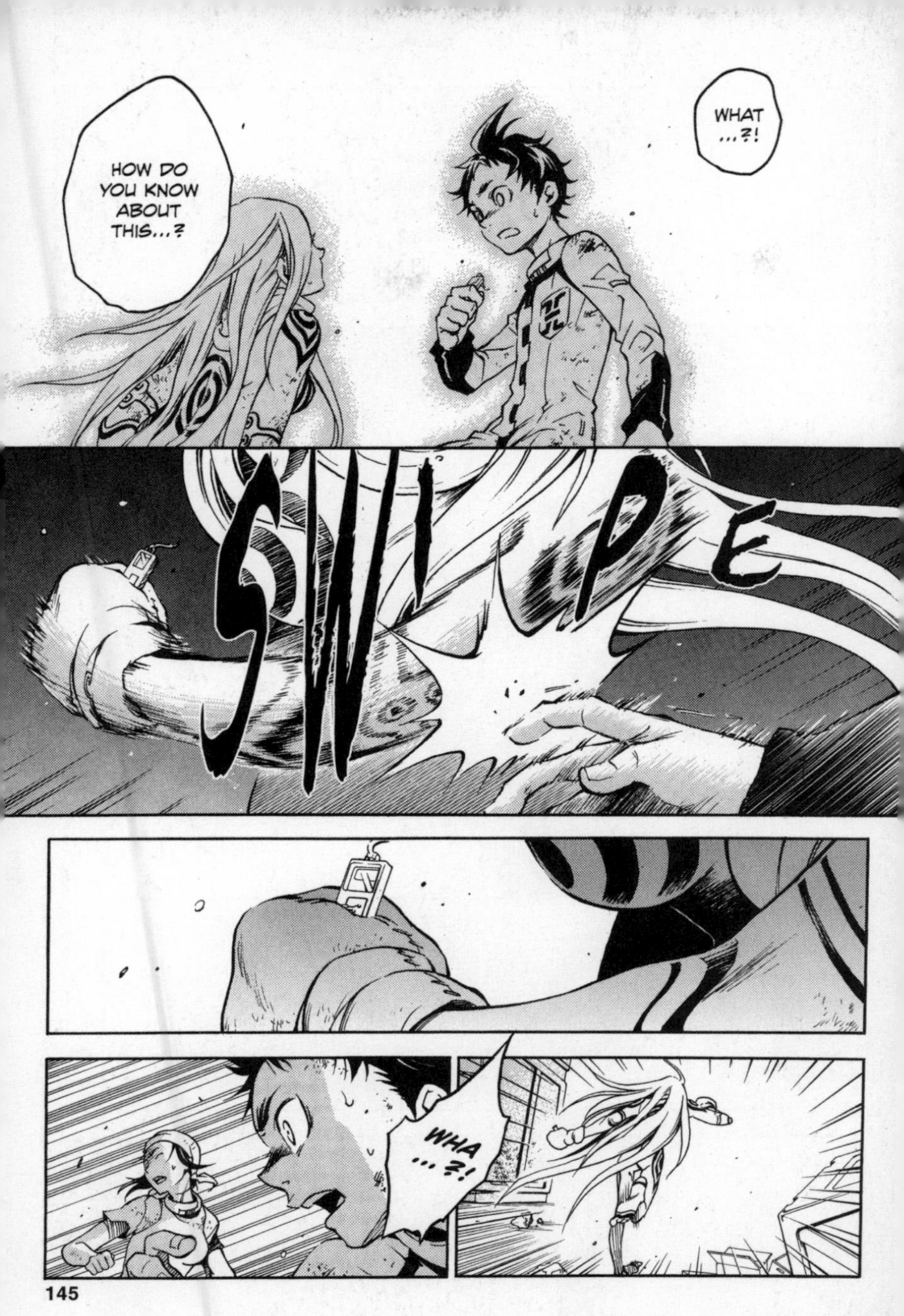
WHAT ...?!
HOW DO YOU KNOW ABOUT THIS...?
SWIPE
WHA ...?!

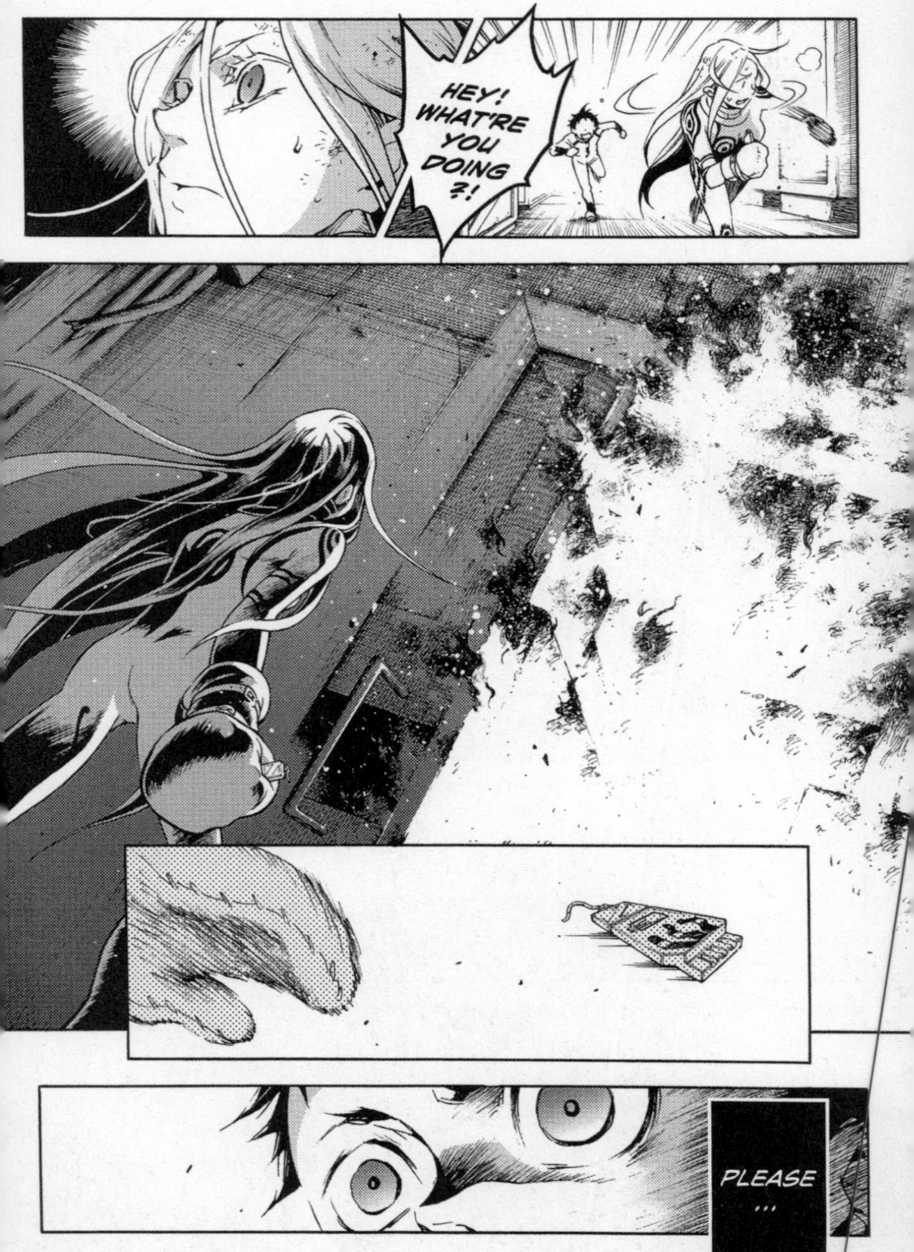
HEY! WHAT'RE YOU DOING ?!
PLEASE ...

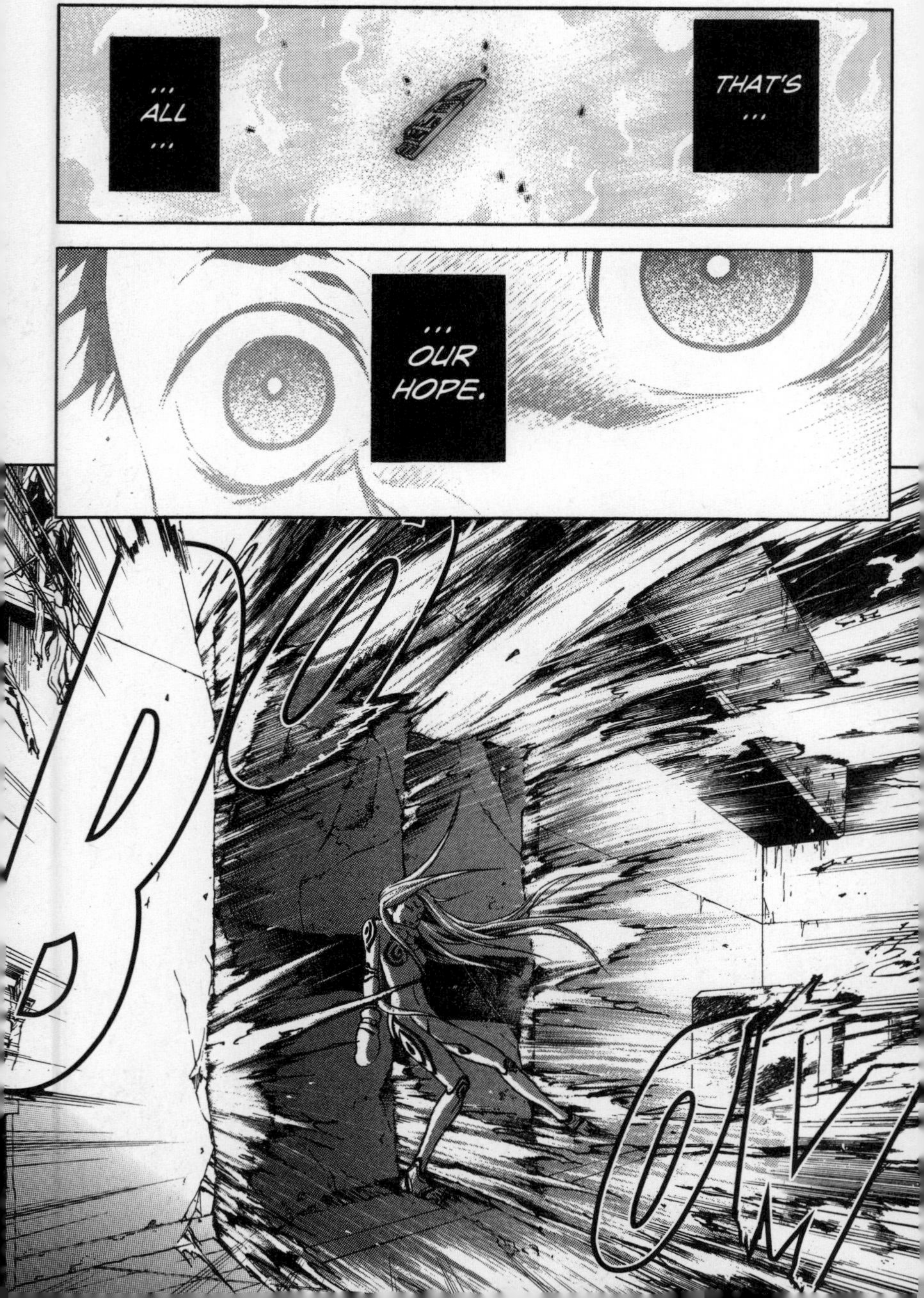
THAT'S ...
... ALL ...
... OUR HOPE.
BOOM

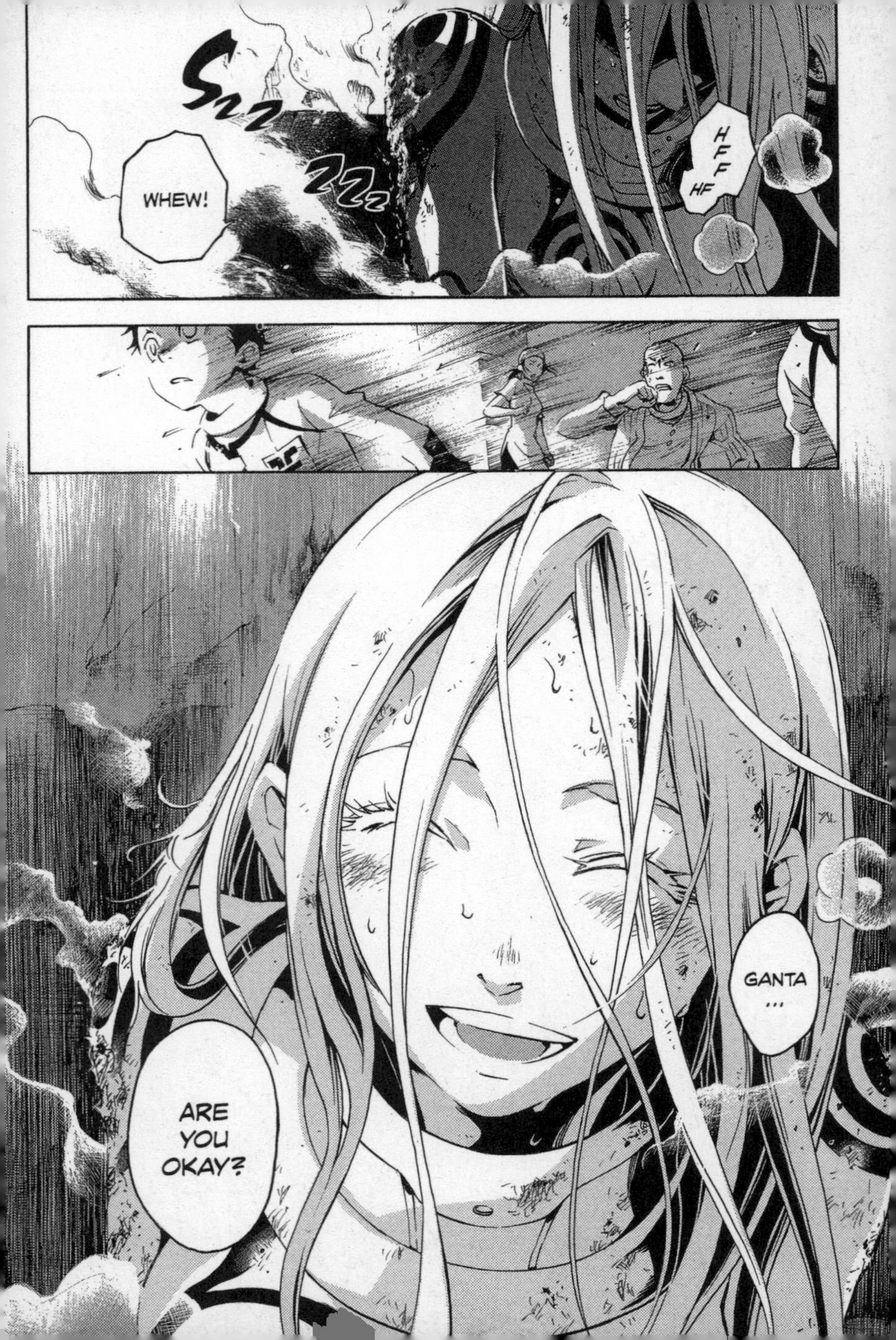
HFF HF
Szzz
Zzzz
WHEW!
GANTA ...
ARE YOU OKAY?

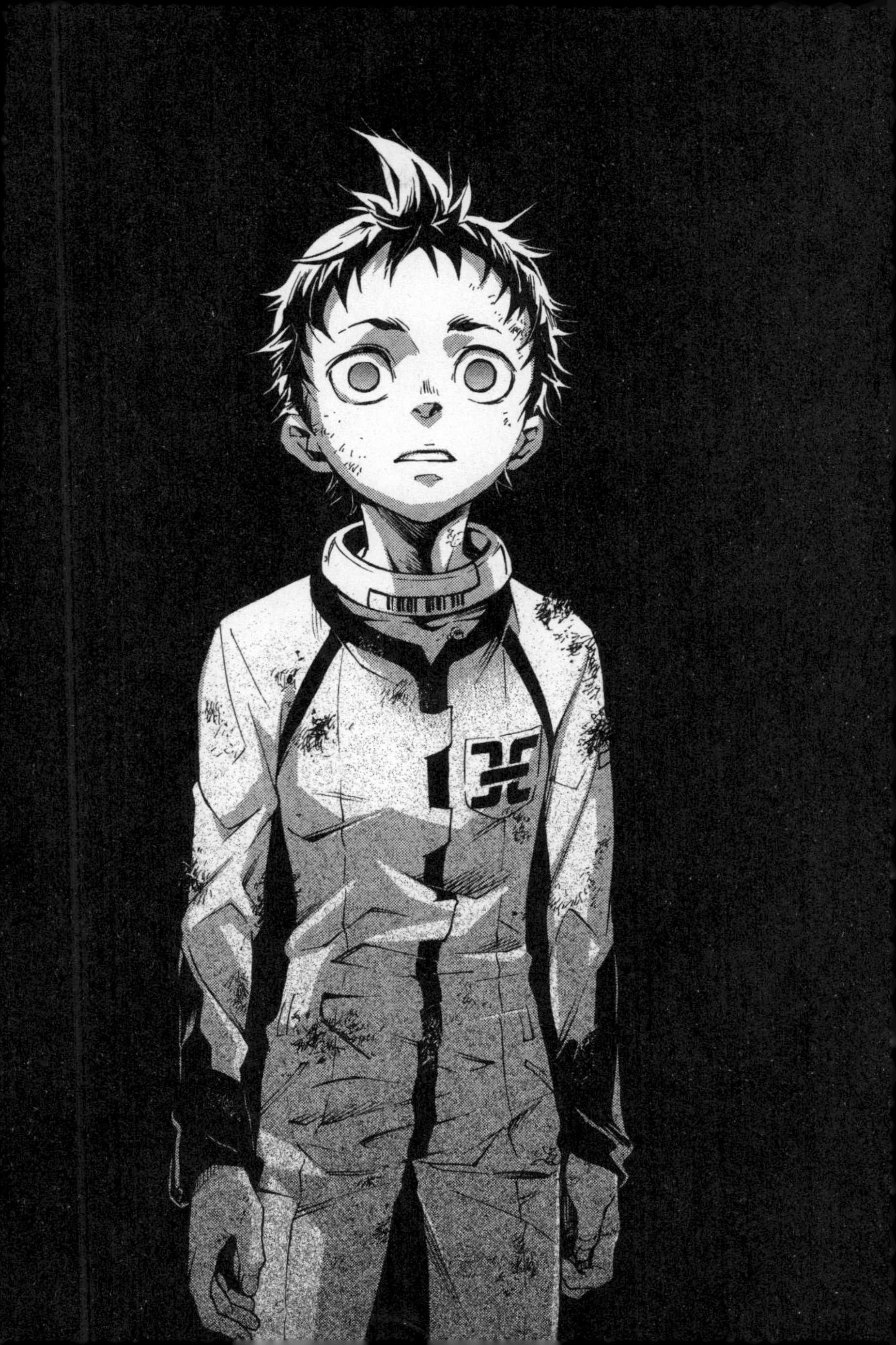

DEADMAN WONDER LAND

DWL

16 Salty Cookies

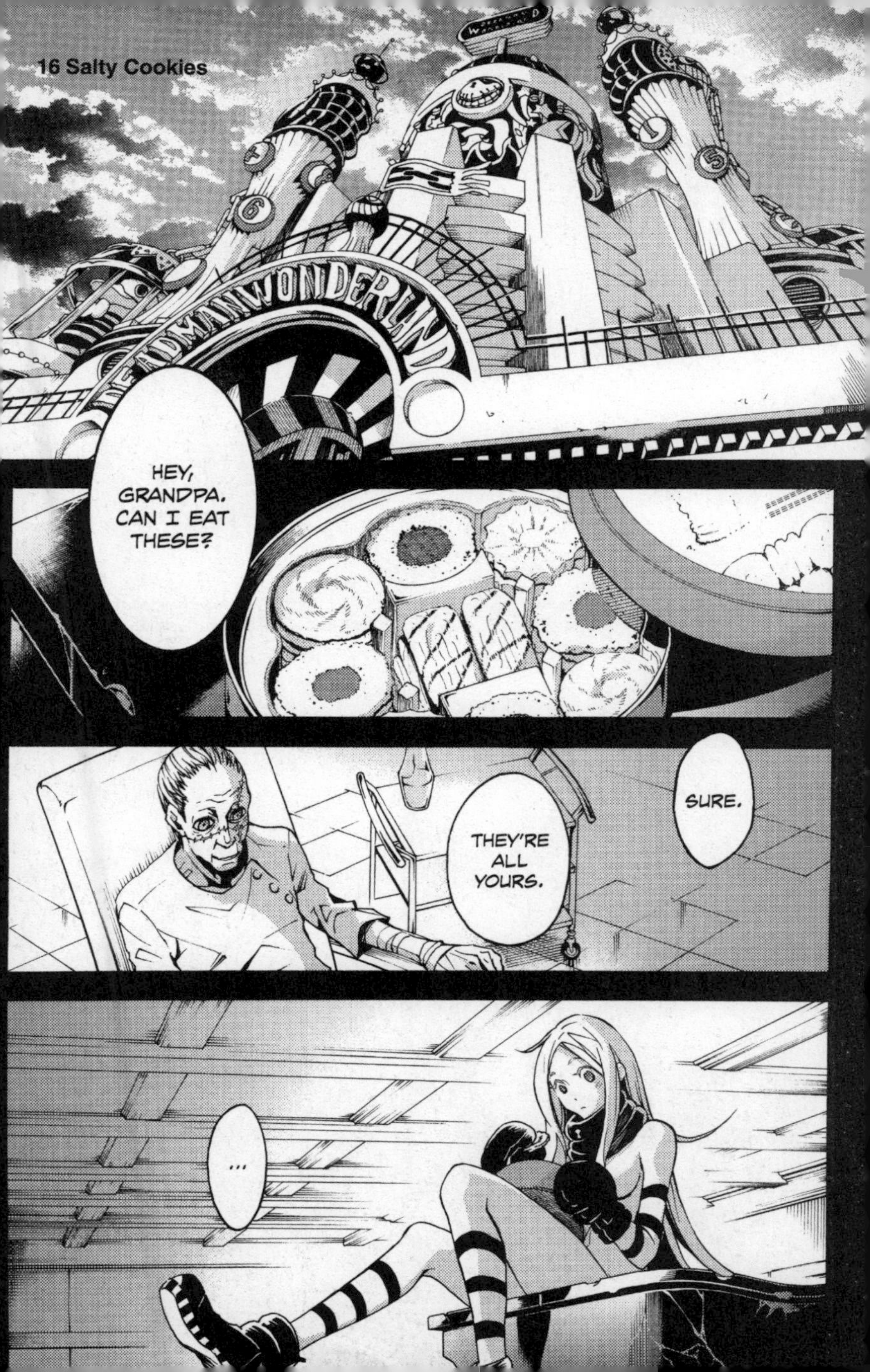

DEADMAN WONDERLAND
HEY, GRANDPA. CAN I EAT THESE?
SURE.
THEY'RE ALL YOURS.
...

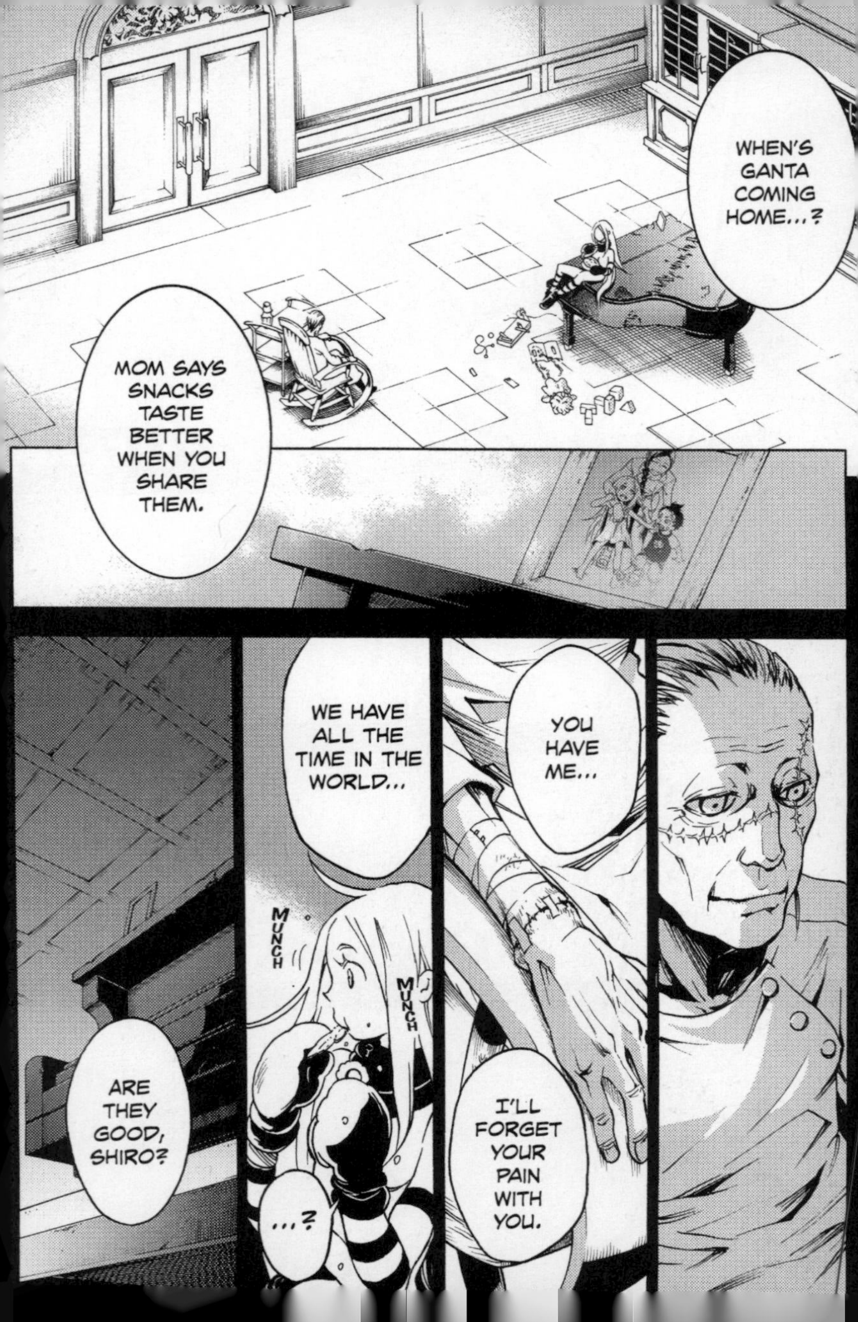
WHEN'S GANTA COMING HOME...?
MOM SAYS SNACKS TASTE BETTER WHEN YOU SHARE THEM.
YOU HAVE ME...
I'LL FORGET YOUR PAIN WITH YOU.
WE HAVE ALL THE TIME IN THE WORLD...
MUNCH
MUNCH
...?
ARE THEY GOOD, SHIRO?

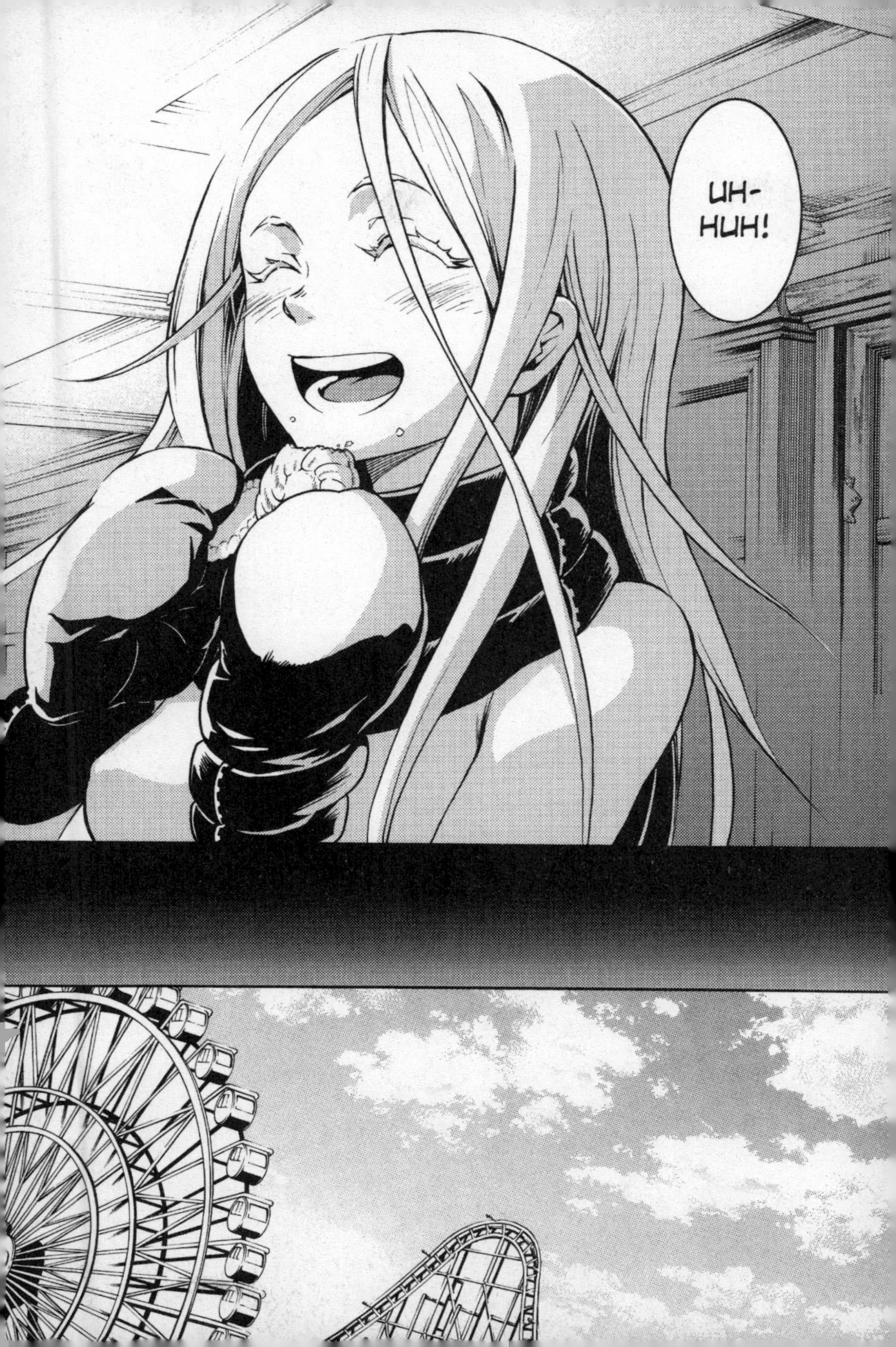
UH-
HUH!

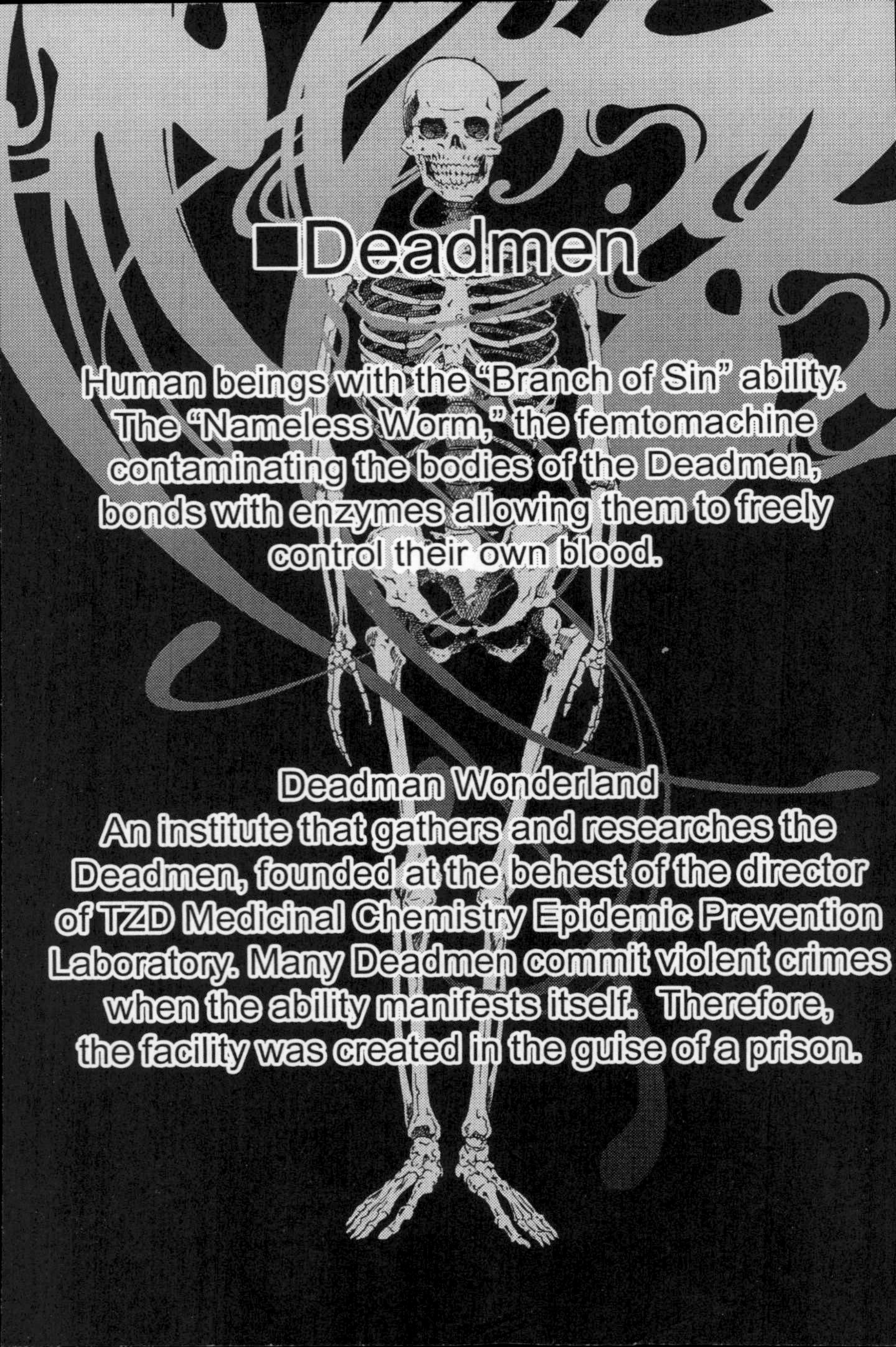

□Deadmen

Human beings with the "Branch of Sin" ability. The "Nameless Worm," the femtomachine contaminating the bodies of the Deadmen, bonds with enzymes allowing them to freely control their own blood.

Deadman Wonderland

An institute that gathers and researches the Deadmen, founded at the behest of the director of TZD Medicinal Chemistry Epidemic Prevention Laboratory. Many Deadmen commit violent crimes when the ability manifests itself. Therefore, the facility was created in the guise of a prison.

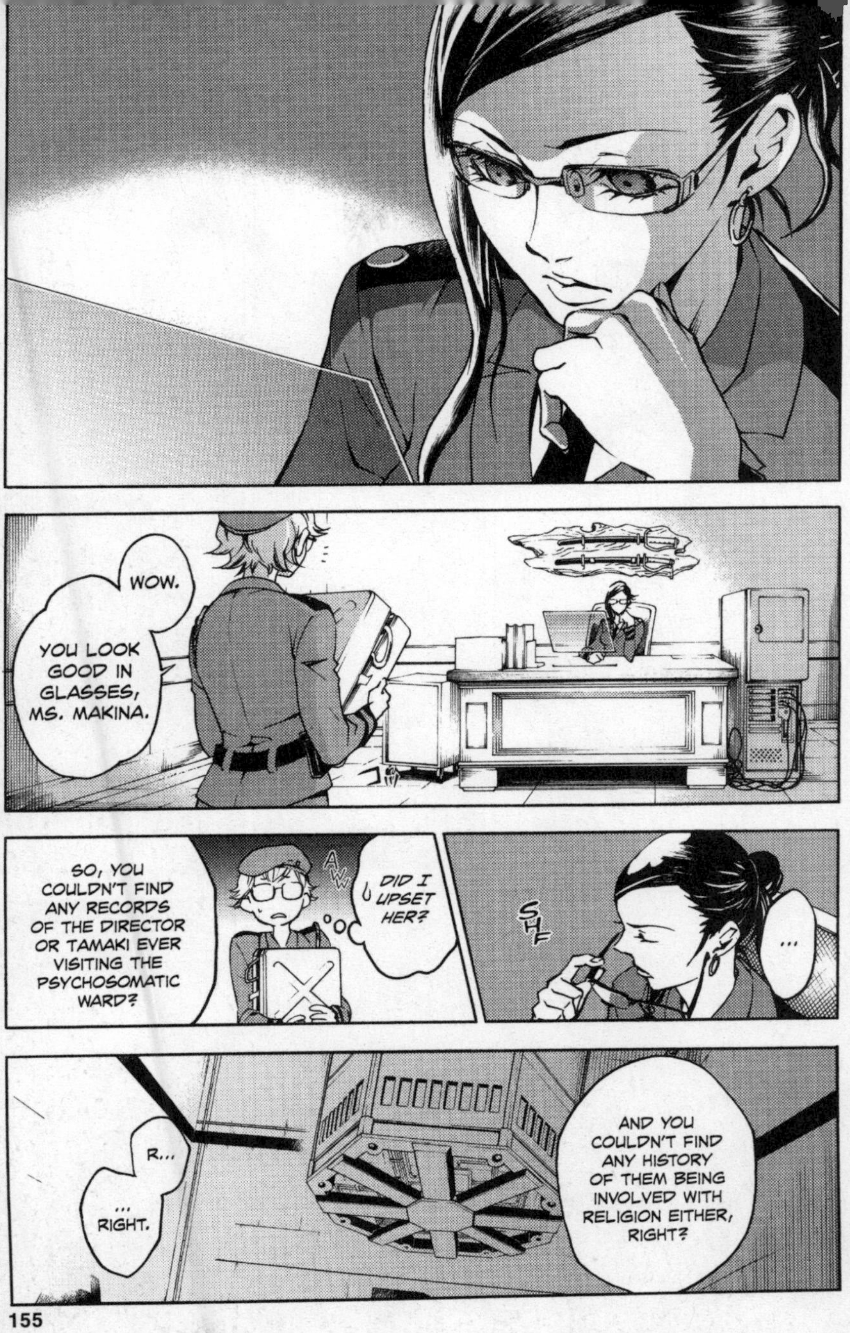
WOW.
YOU LOOK GOOD IN GLASSES, MS. MAKINA.
SHF
...
DID I UPSET HER?
AW
SO, YOU COULDN'T FIND ANY RECORDS OF THE DIRECTOR OR TAMAKI EVER VISITING THE PSYCHOSOMATIC WARD?
AND YOU COULDN'T FIND ANY HISTORY OF THEM BEING INVOLVED WITH RELIGION EITHER, RIGHT?
R...
... RIGHT.

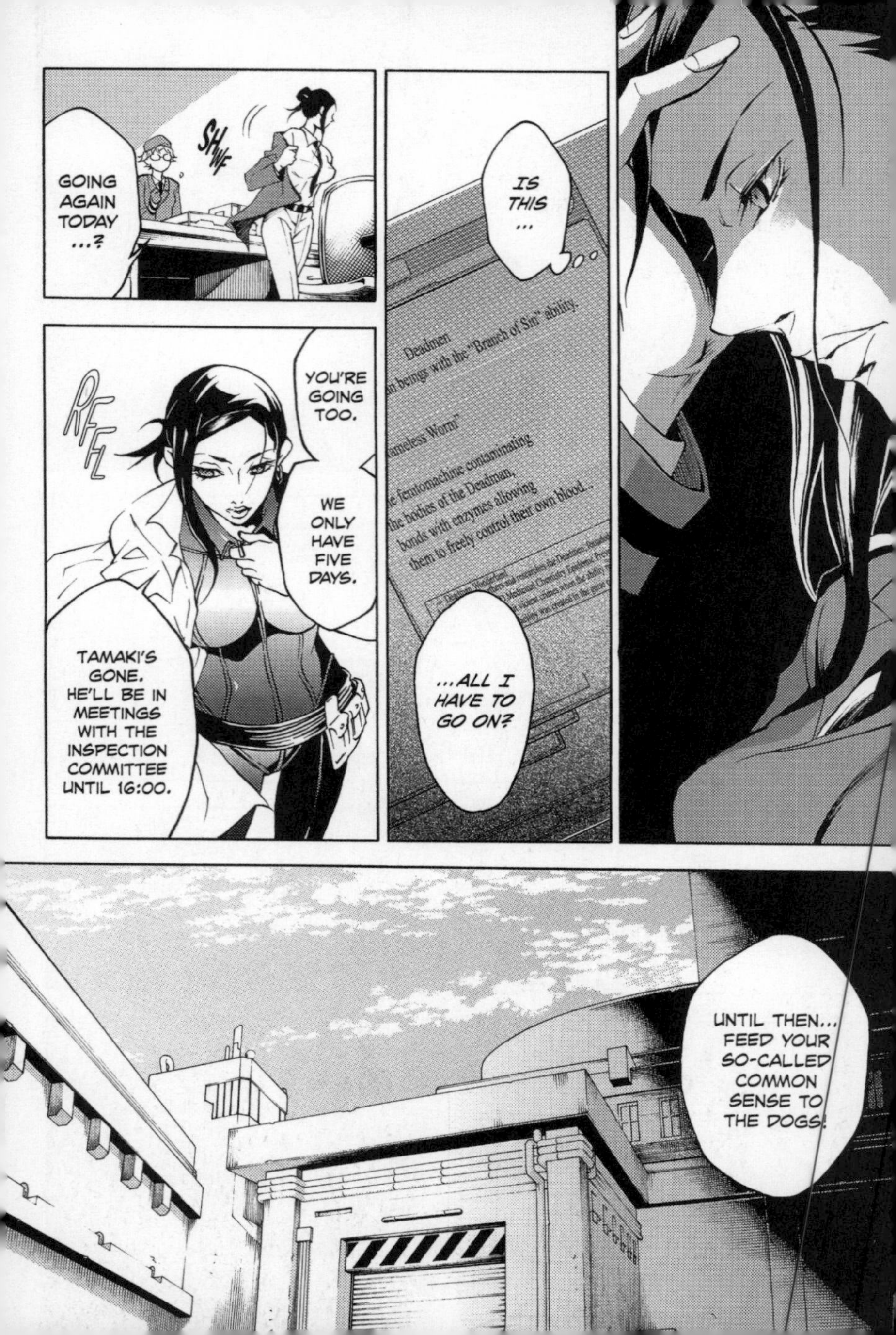
IS THIS...
Deadmen
n beings with the "Branch of Sin" ability.
ameless Worm"
e femtomachine contaminating
the bodies of the Deadman,
bonds with enzymes allowing
them to freely control their own blood...
...ALL I HAVE TO GO ON?
SHWF
GOING AGAIN TODAY...?
RFFL
YOU'RE GOING TOO.
WE ONLY HAVE FIVE DAYS.
TAMAKI'S GONE. HE'LL BE IN MEETINGS WITH THE INSPECTION COMMITTEE UNTIL 16:00.
UNTIL THEN... FEED YOUR SO-CALLED COMMON SENSE TO THE DOGS!

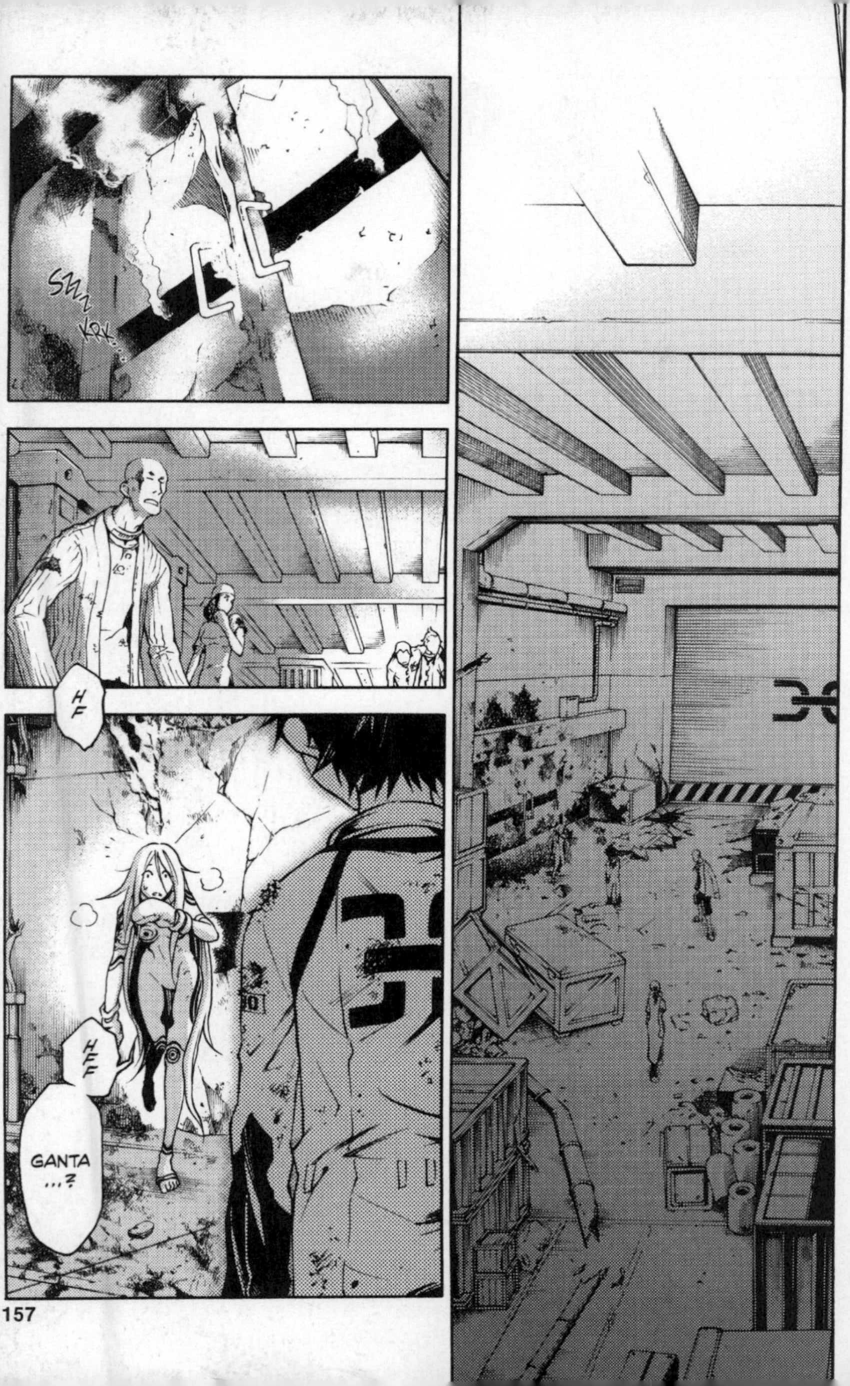
SZZZ
KRK...
HF
HEF
GANTA ...?

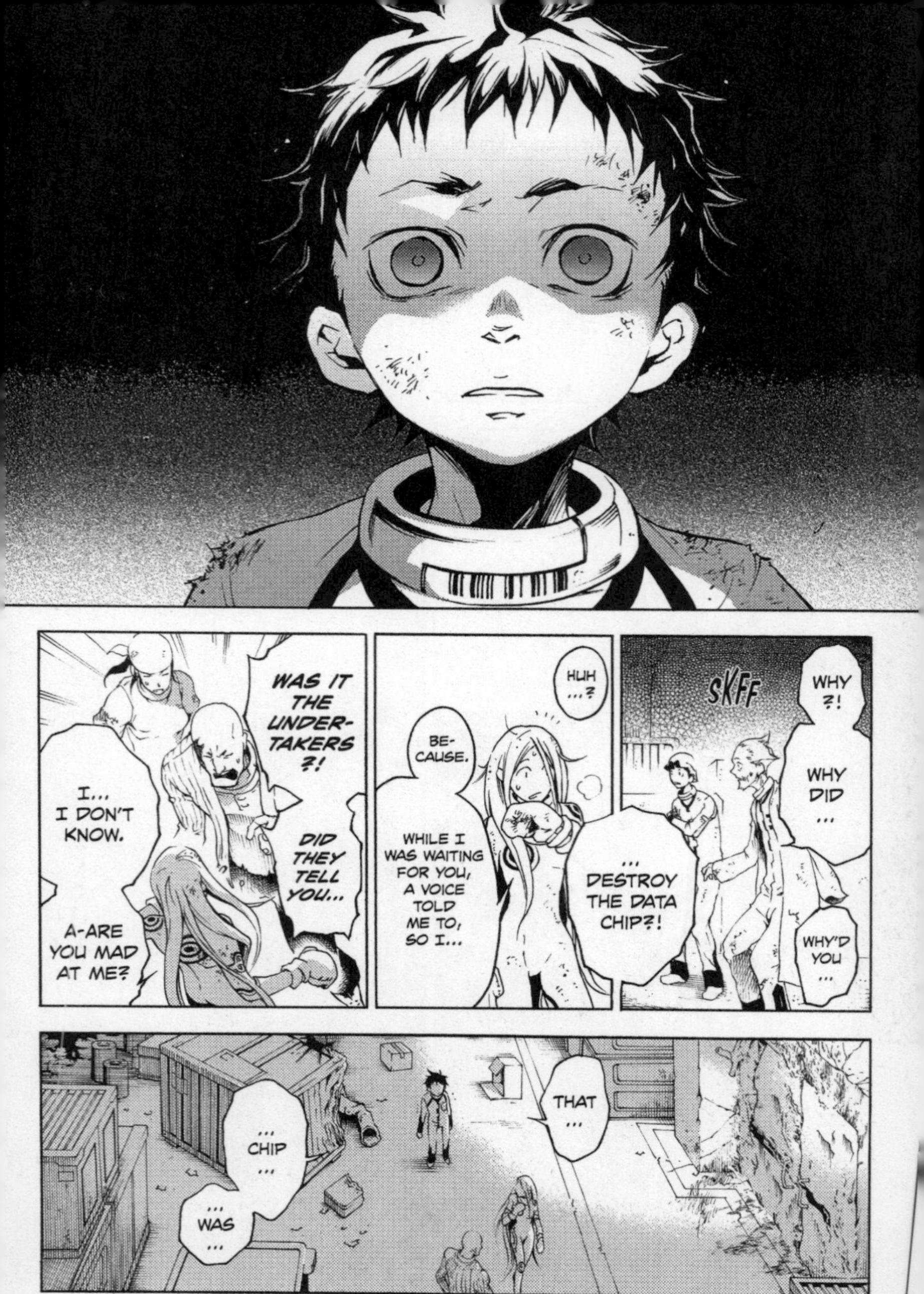

WHY ?!
WHY DID ...
SKFF
WHY'D YOU ...
... DESTROY THE DATA CHIP?!
HUH ...?
BE- CAUSE.
WHILE I WAS WAITING FOR YOU, A VOICE TOLD ME TO, SO I...
WAS IT THE UNDER- TAKERS?!
DID THEY TELL YOU...
I... I DON'T KNOW.
A-ARE YOU MAD AT ME?
THAT ...
... CHIP ...
... WAS ...

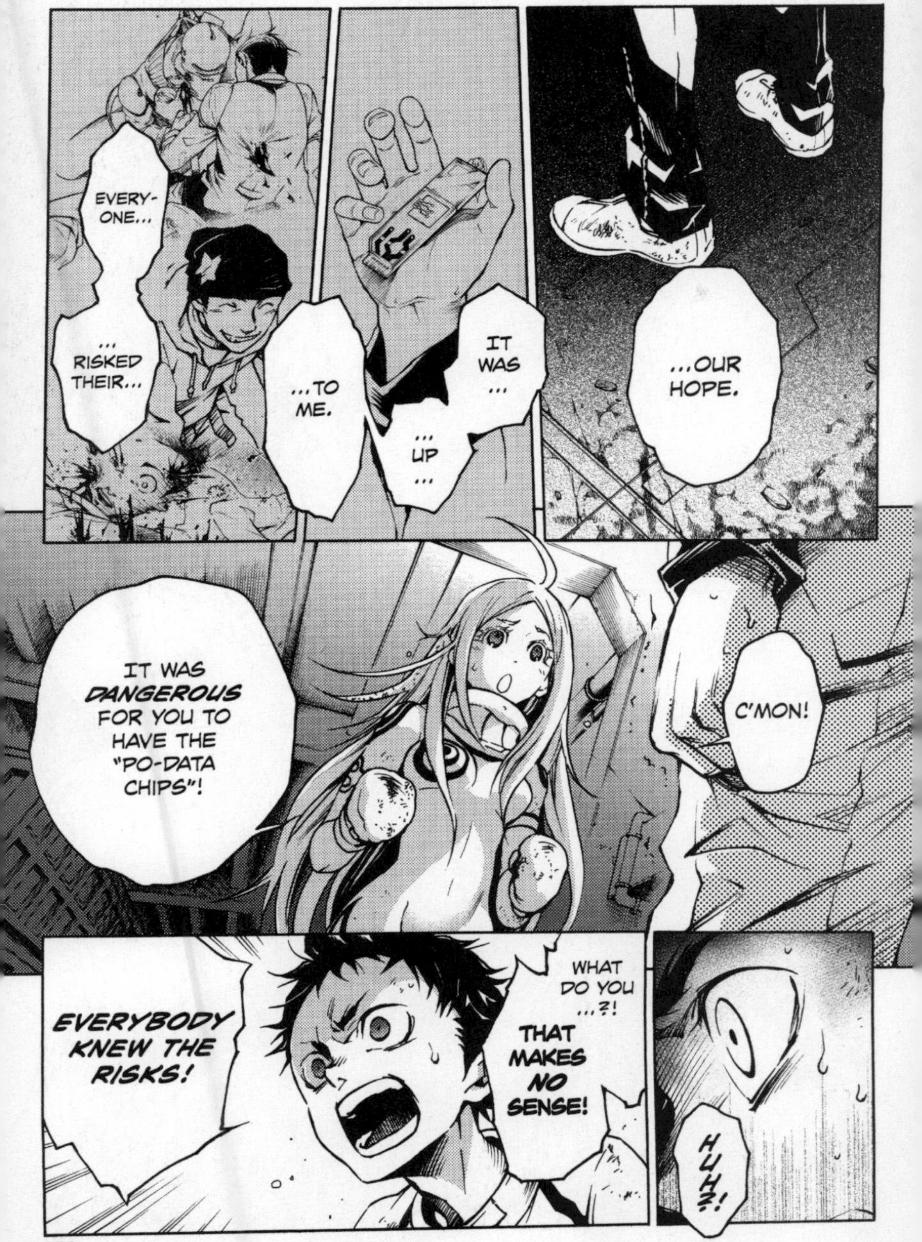
...OUR HOPE.
IT WAS ...
... UP ...
...TO ME.
EVERY-ONE...
... RISKED THEIR...
C'MON!
IT WAS *DANGEROUS* FOR YOU TO HAVE THE "PO-DATA CHIPS"!
HUH?!
WHAT DO YOU ...?!
THAT MAKES *NO* SENSE!
EVERYBODY KNEW THE RISKS!

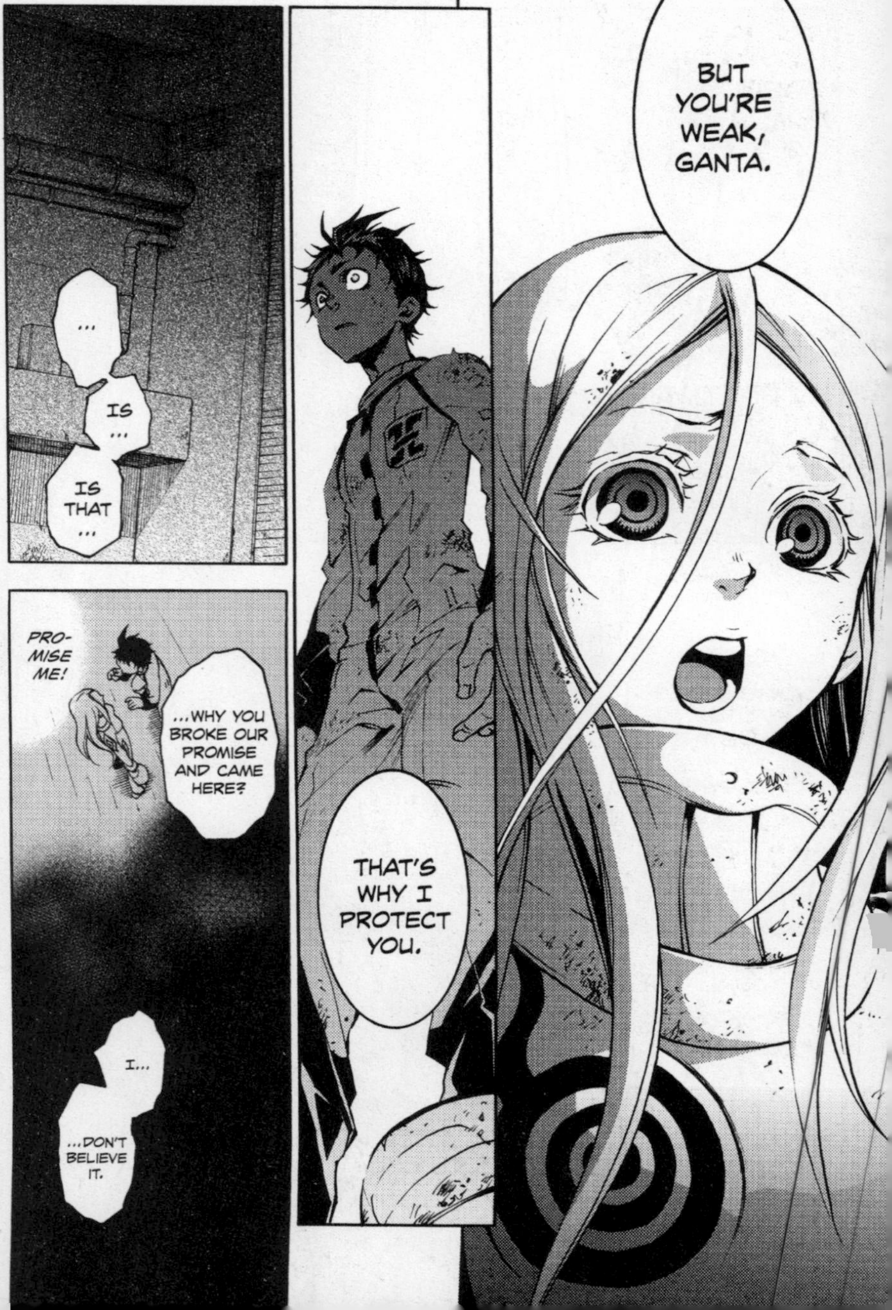
BUT YOU'RE WEAK, GANTA.
THAT'S WHY I PROTECT YOU.
...
IS ...
IS THAT ...
PROMISE ME!
...WHY YOU BROKE OUR PROMISE AND CAME HERE?
I...
...DON'T BELIEVE IT.

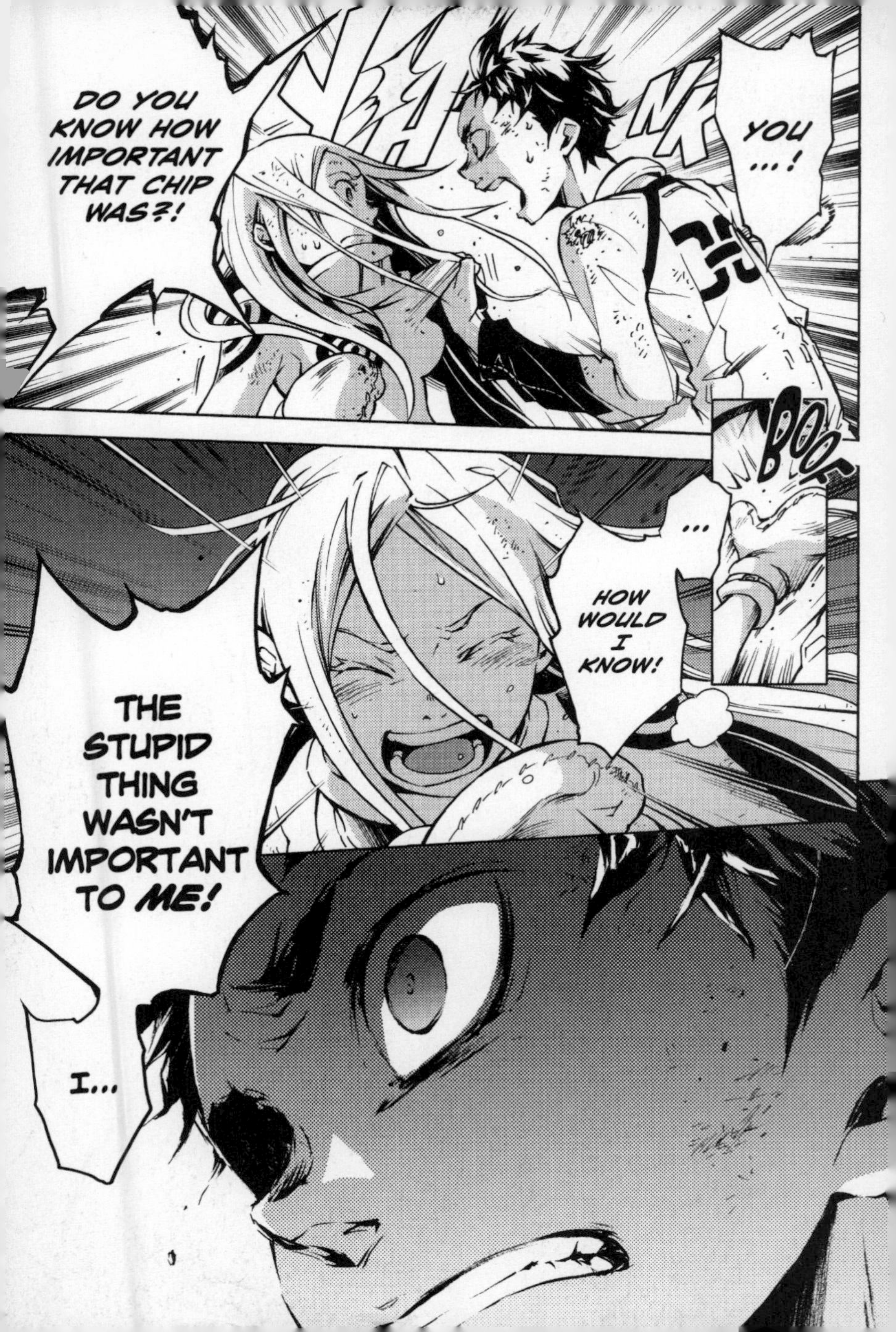
YOU ...!
DO YOU KNOW HOW IMPORTANT THAT CHIP WAS?!
BOOF
...
HOW WOULD I KNOW!
THE STUPID THING WASN'T IMPORTANT TO ME!
I...

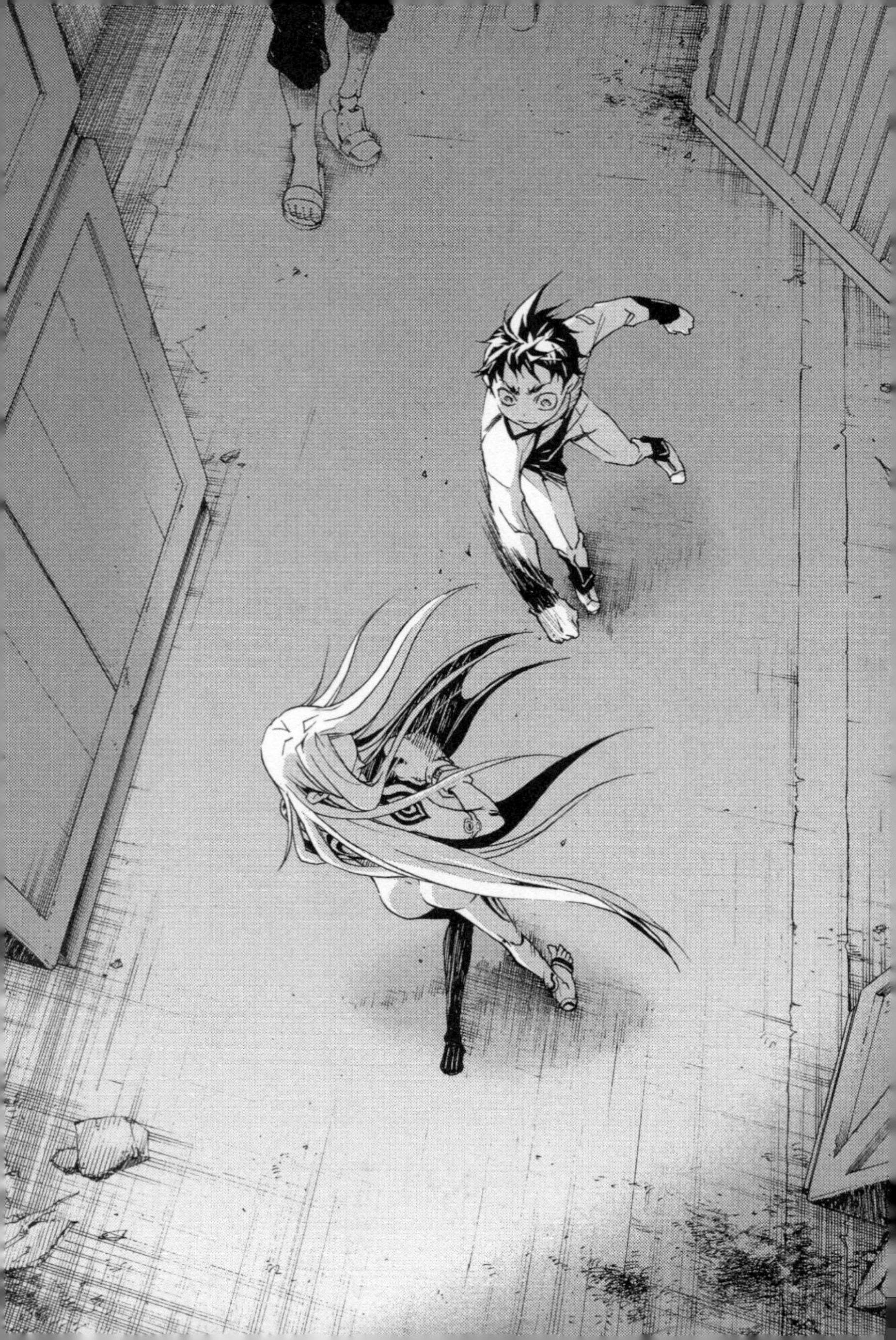

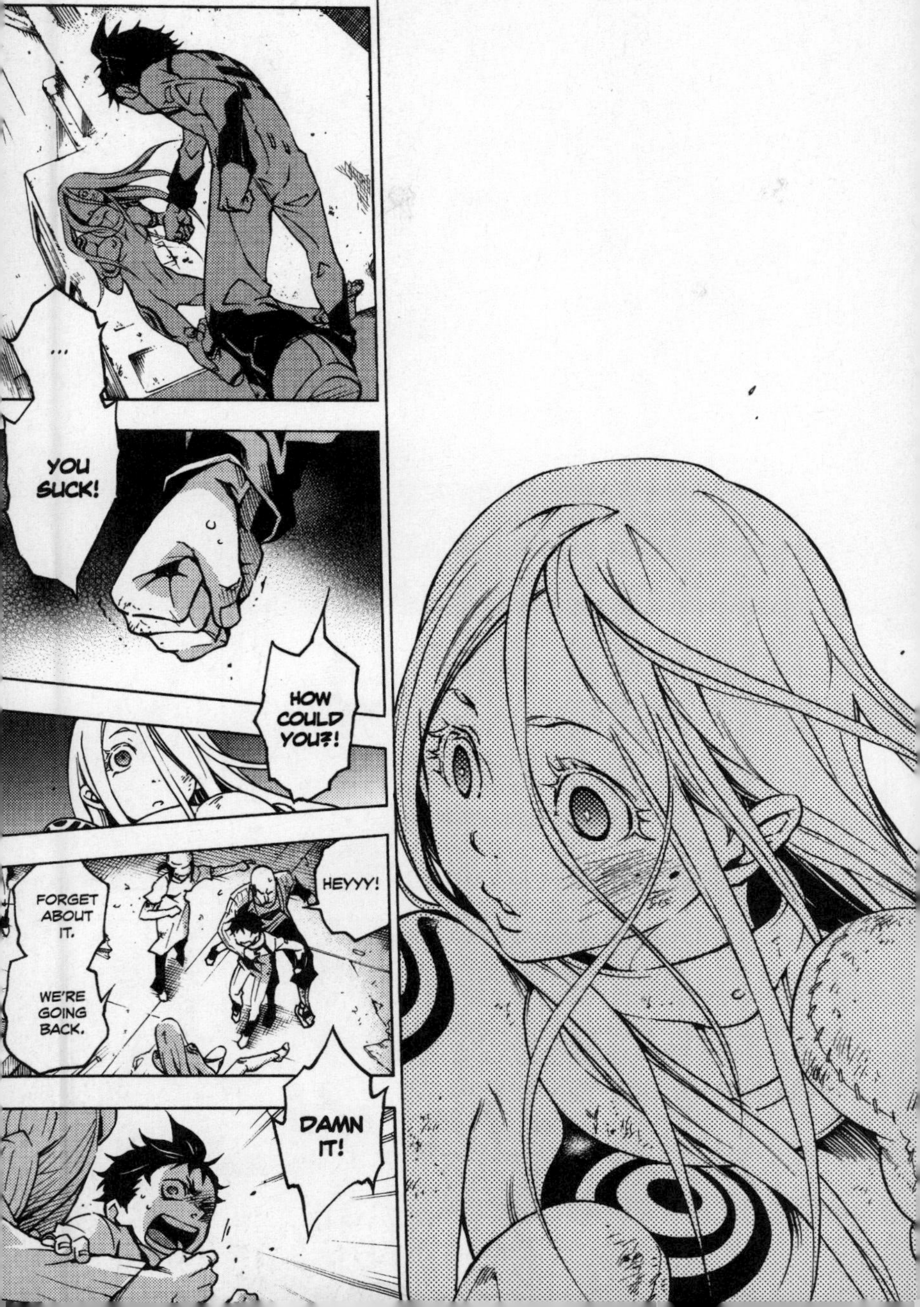
...
YOU SUCK!
HOW COULD YOU?!
HEYYY!
FORGET ABOUT IT.
WE'RE GOING BACK.
DAMN IT!

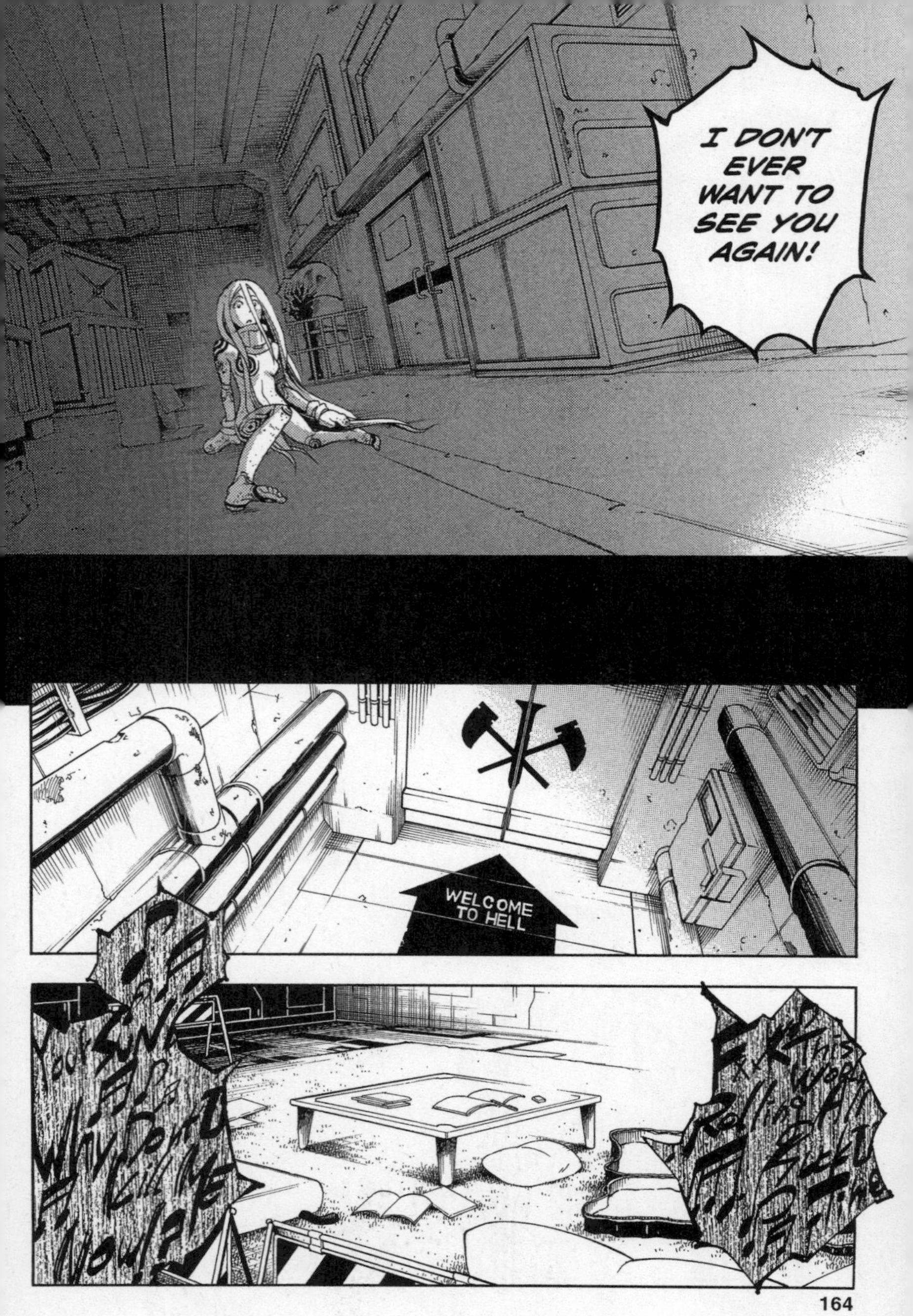
I DON'T EVER WANT TO SEE YOU AGAIN!
WELCOME TO HELL
This world
You're
Why don't
kill me now!?

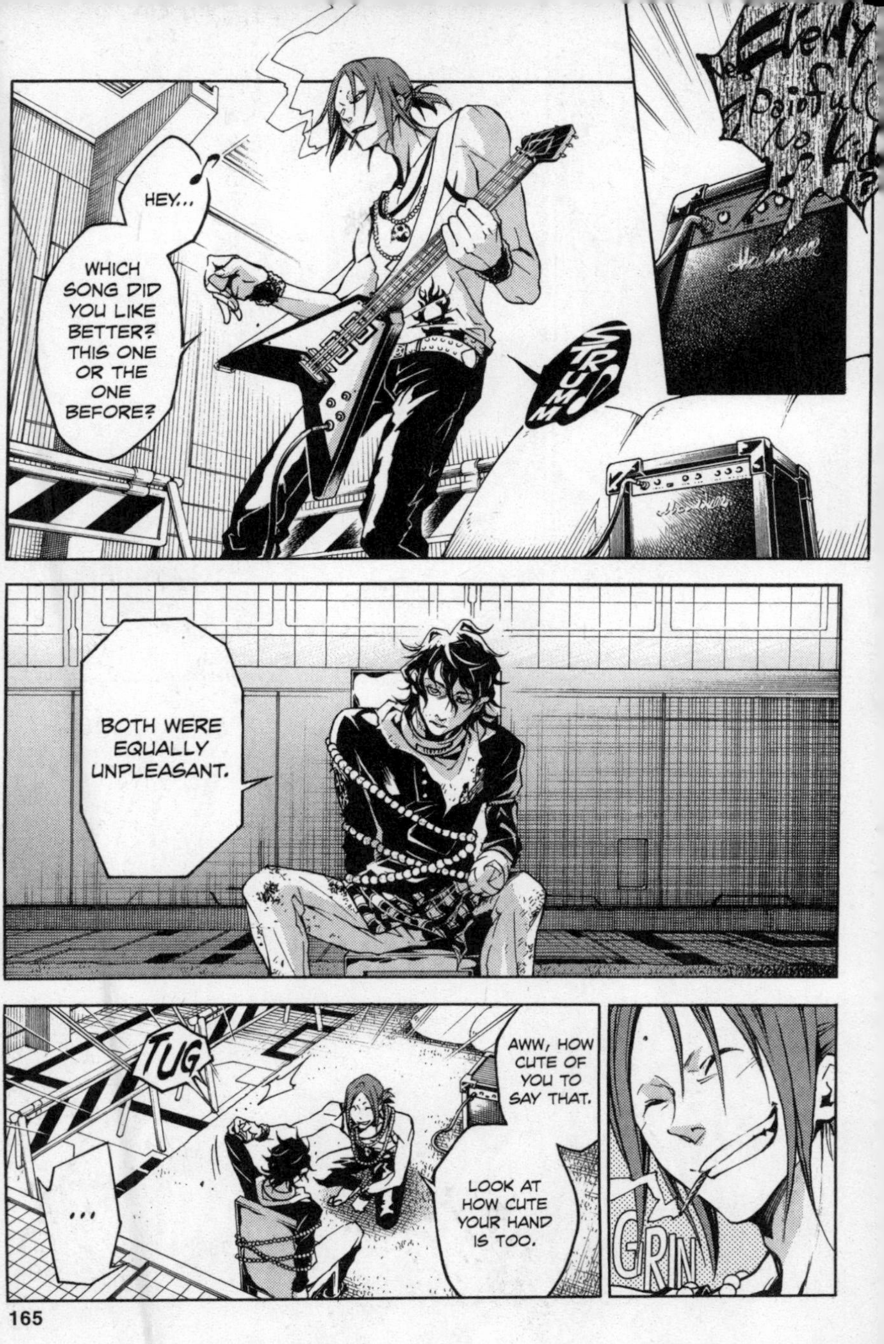
HEY...
WHICH SONG DID YOU LIKE BETTER? THIS ONE OR THE ONE BEFORE?
STRUMM
BOTH WERE EQUALLY UNPLEASANT.
GRIN
AWW, HOW CUTE OF YOU TO SAY THAT.
LOOK AT HOW CUTE YOUR HAND IS TOO.
TUG
...

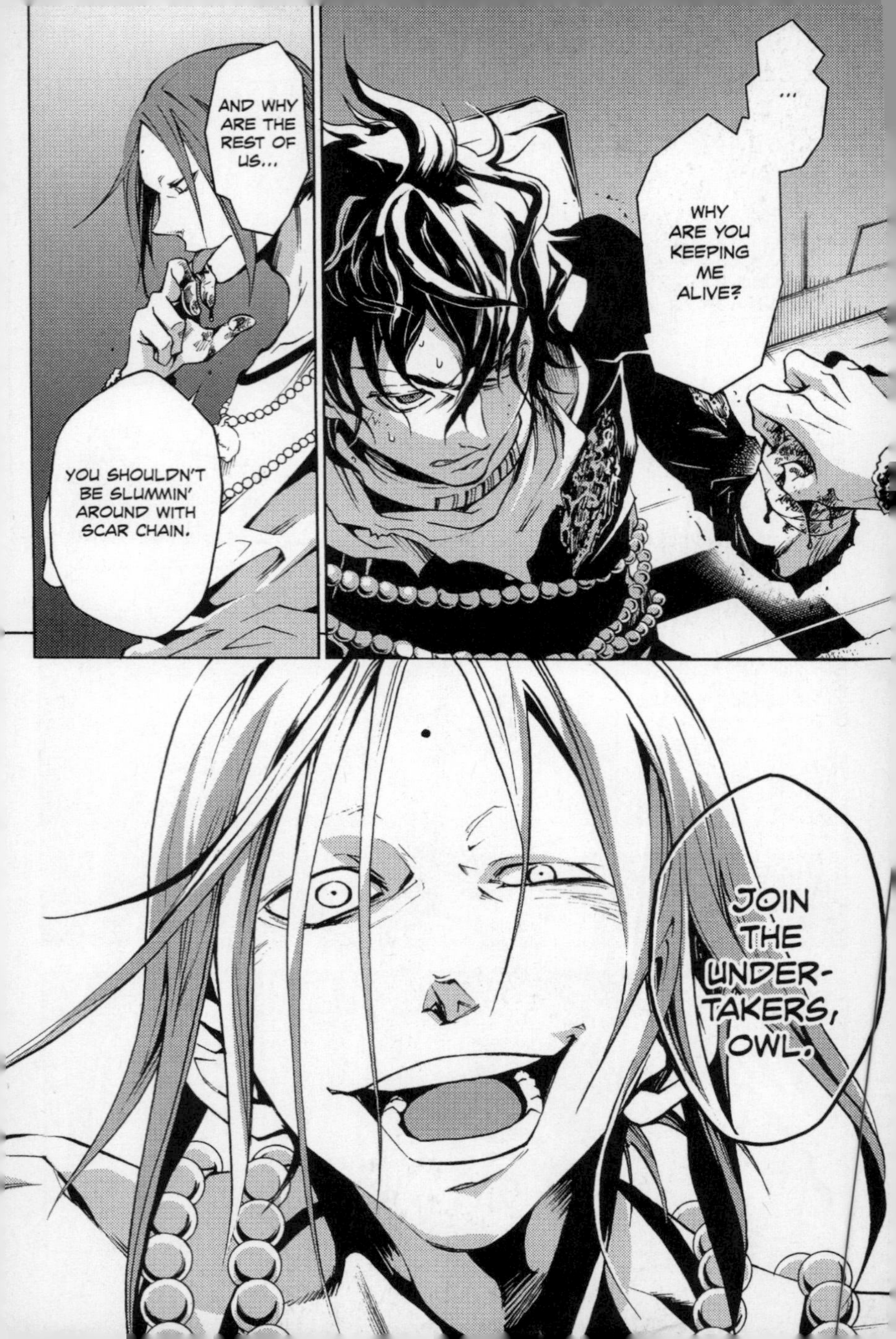
...
WHY ARE YOU KEEPING ME ALIVE?
AND WHY ARE THE REST OF US...
YOU SHOULDN'T BE SLUMMIN' AROUND WITH SCAR CHAIN.
JOIN THE UNDER-TAKERS, OWL.

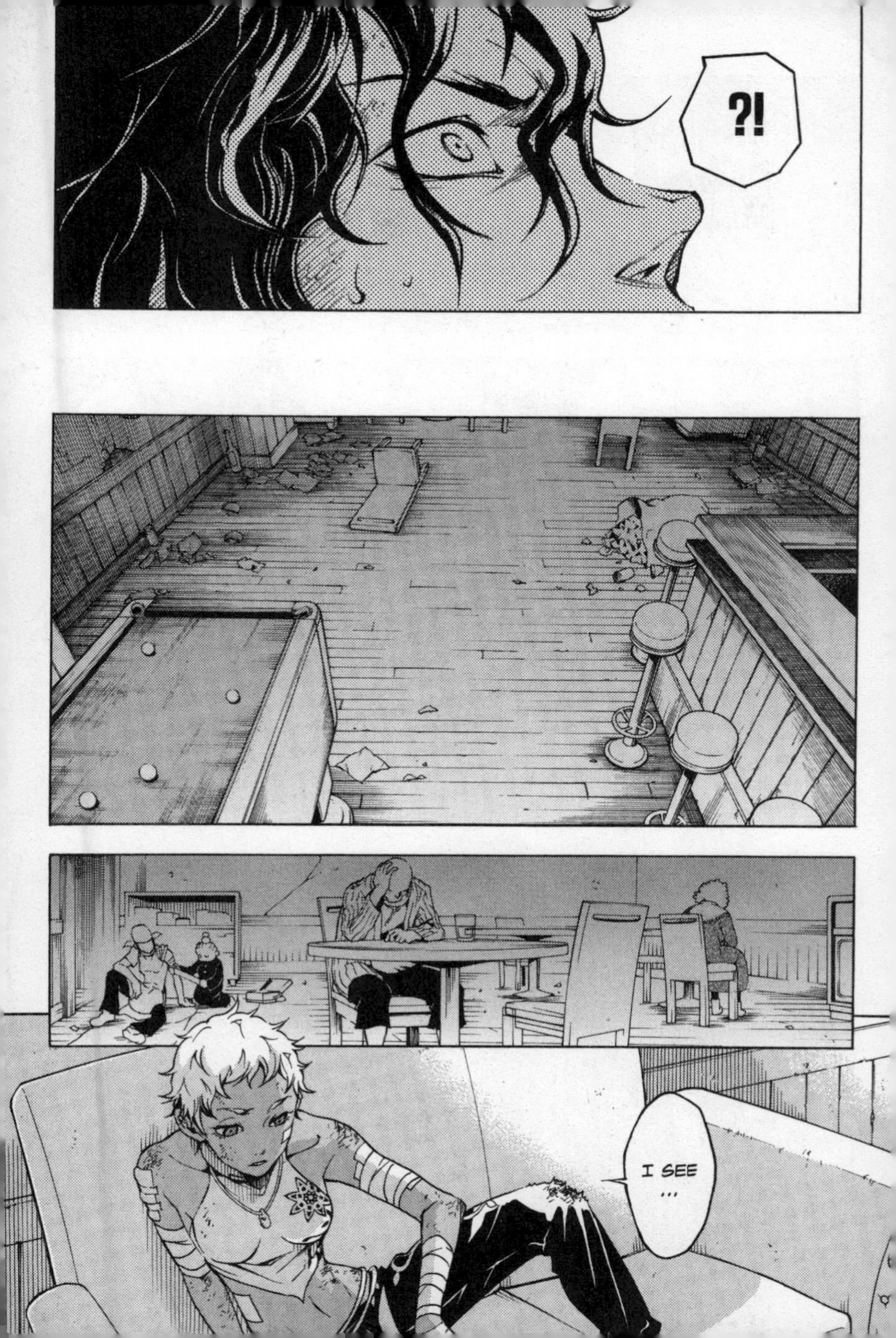
?!
I SEE ...

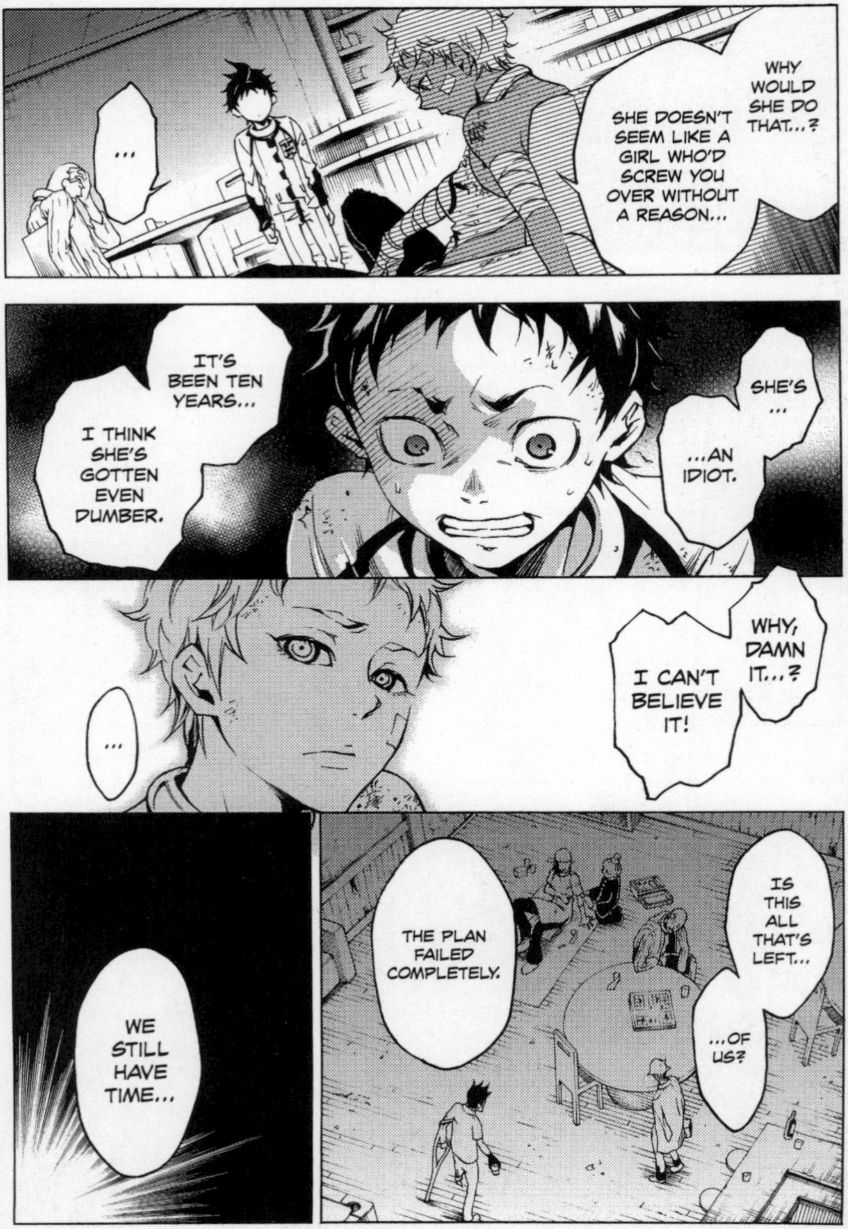
WHY WOULD SHE DO THAT...?
SHE DOESN'T SEEM LIKE A GIRL WHO'D SCREW YOU OVER WITHOUT A REASON...
...
SHE'S ...
...AN IDIOT.
IT'S BEEN TEN YEARS...
I THINK SHE'S GOTTEN EVEN DUMBER.
WHY, DAMN IT...?
I CAN'T BELIEVE IT!
...
IS THIS ALL THAT'S LEFT...
...OF US?
THE PLAN FAILED COMPLETELY.
WE STILL HAVE TIME...

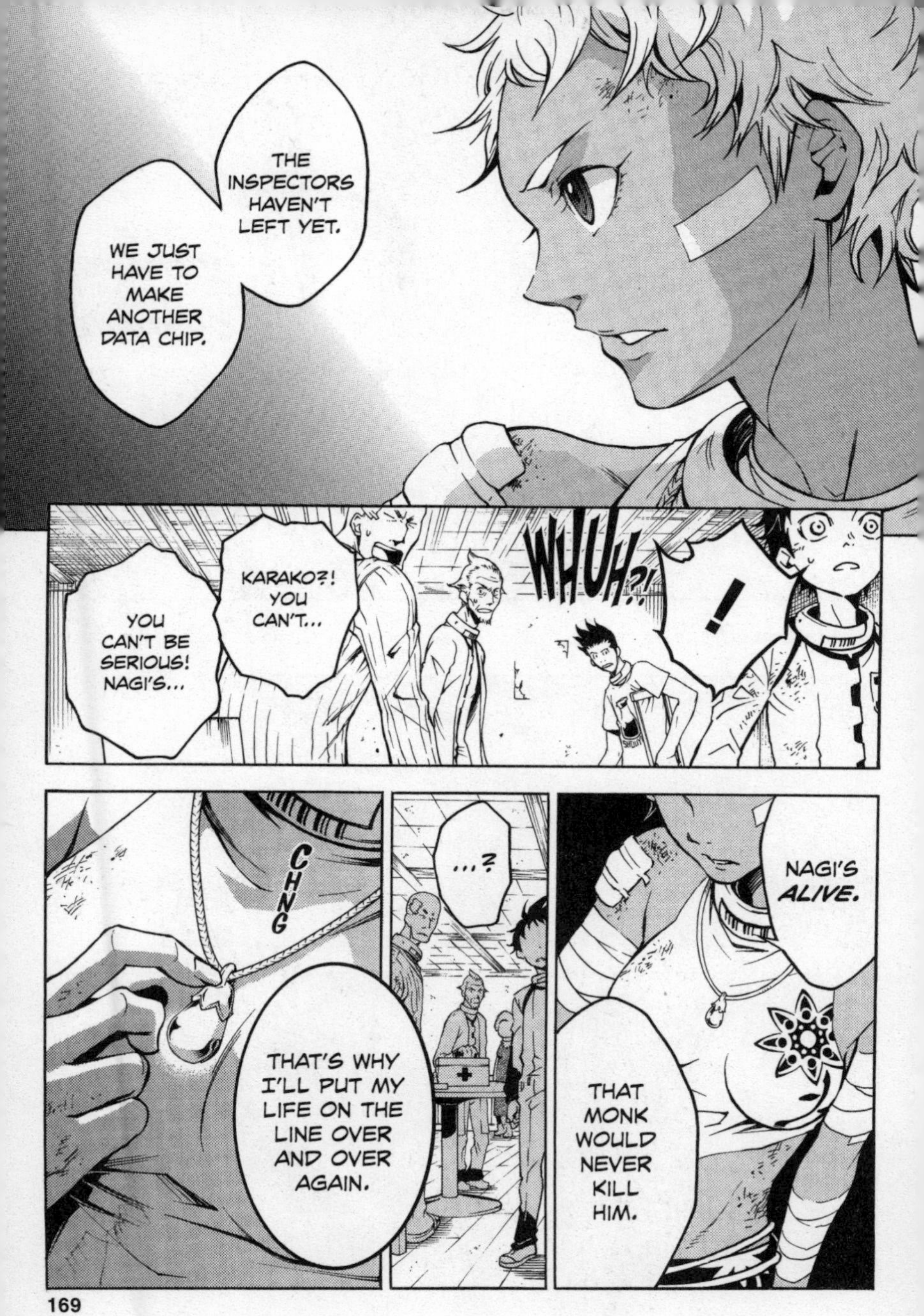
THE INSPECTORS HAVEN'T LEFT YET.
WE JUST HAVE TO MAKE ANOTHER DATA CHIP.
WHUH?!
!
KARAKO?! YOU CAN'T...
YOU CAN'T BE SERIOUS! NAGI'S...
NAGI'S *ALIVE.*
THAT MONK WOULD NEVER KILL HIM.
...?
CHNG
THAT'S WHY I'LL PUT MY LIFE ON THE LINE OVER AND OVER AGAIN.

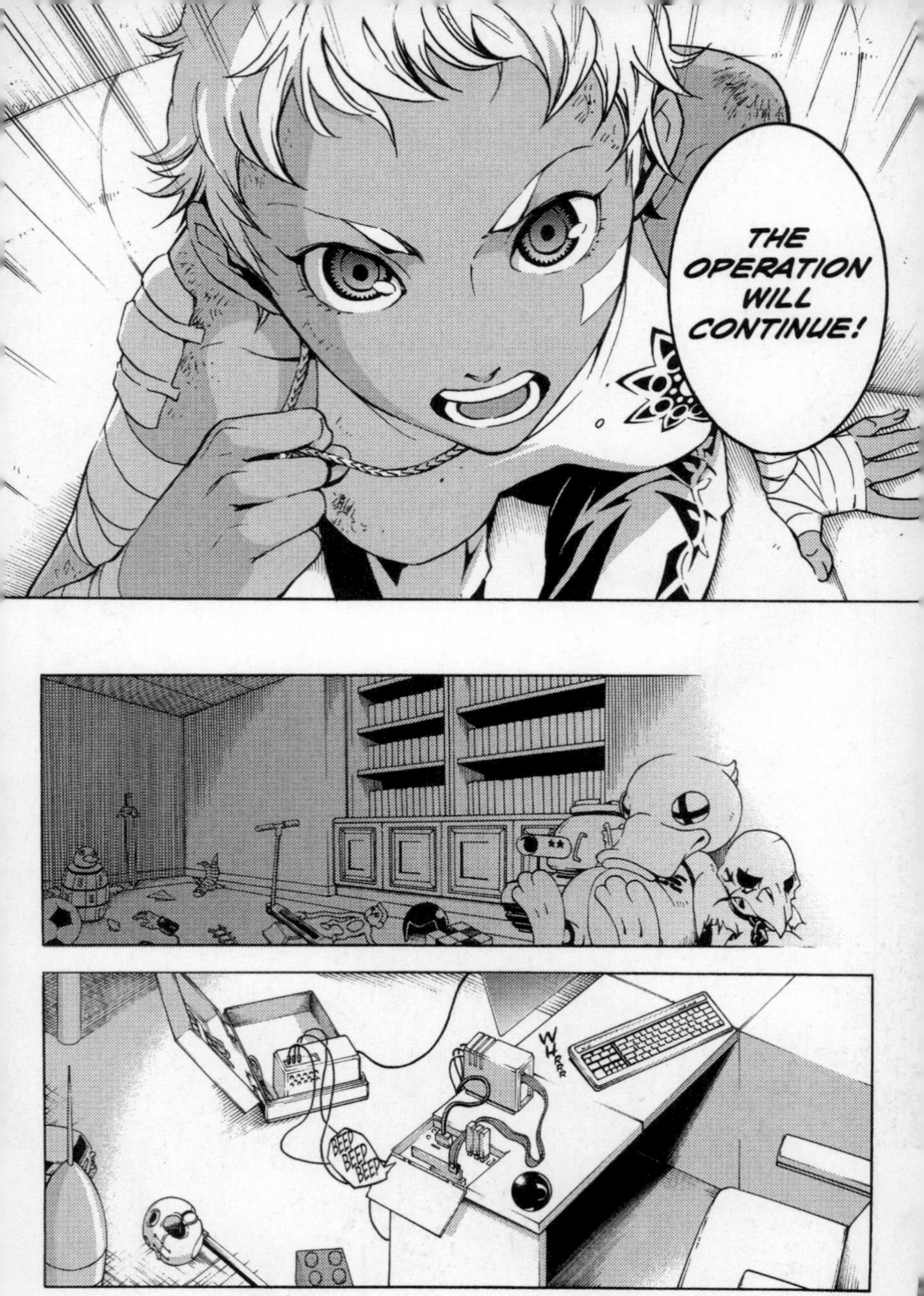
THE OPERATION WILL CONTINUE!
WHRRR
BEEP BEEP BEEP

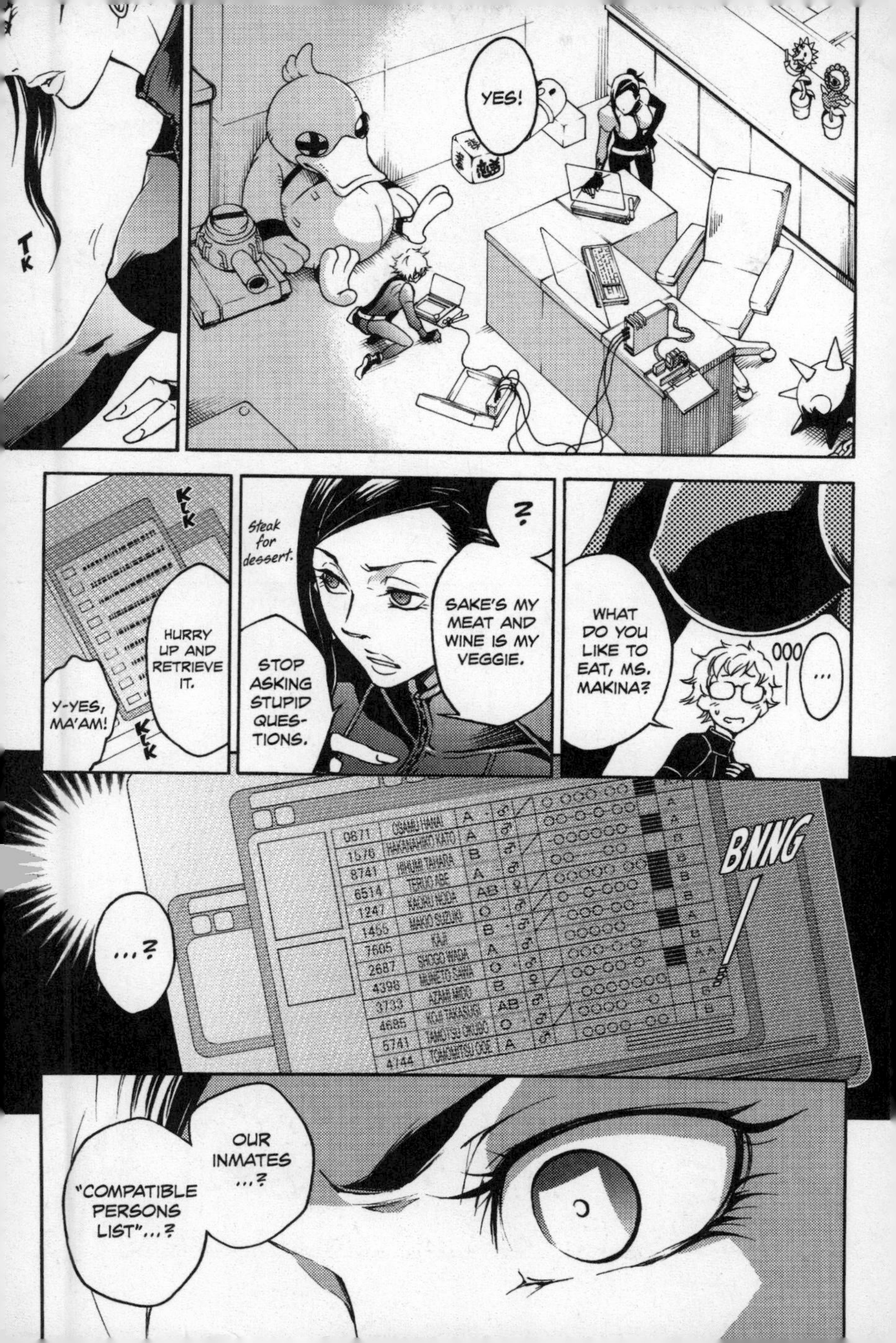
YES!
TK
K
WHAT DO YOU LIKE TO EAT, MS. MAKINA?
OOO
...
SAKE'S MY MEAT AND WINE IS MY VEGGIE.
Steak for dessert.
?
STOP ASKING STUPID QUES-TIONS.
KLK
HURRY UP AND RETRIEVE IT.
Y-YES, MA'AM!
KLK
BNNG
0871 OSAMU HANAI A ♂
1576 HAKANAHIKO KATO A ♂
8741 MIHUMI TAHARA B ♂
6514 TERUO ABE A ♂
1247 KAORU NODA AB ♀
1455 MAKIO SUZUKI O ♂
7605 KAJI B ♂
2687 SHOGO WADA A ♂
4398 MUNETO SAWA O ♂
3733 AZAMI MIDO B ♀
4685 KOJI TAKASUGI AB ♂
5741 TAMOTSU OKUBO O ♂
4744 TOMOMITSU OUE A ♂
...?
OUR INMATES ...?
"COMPATIBLE PERSONS LIST"...?

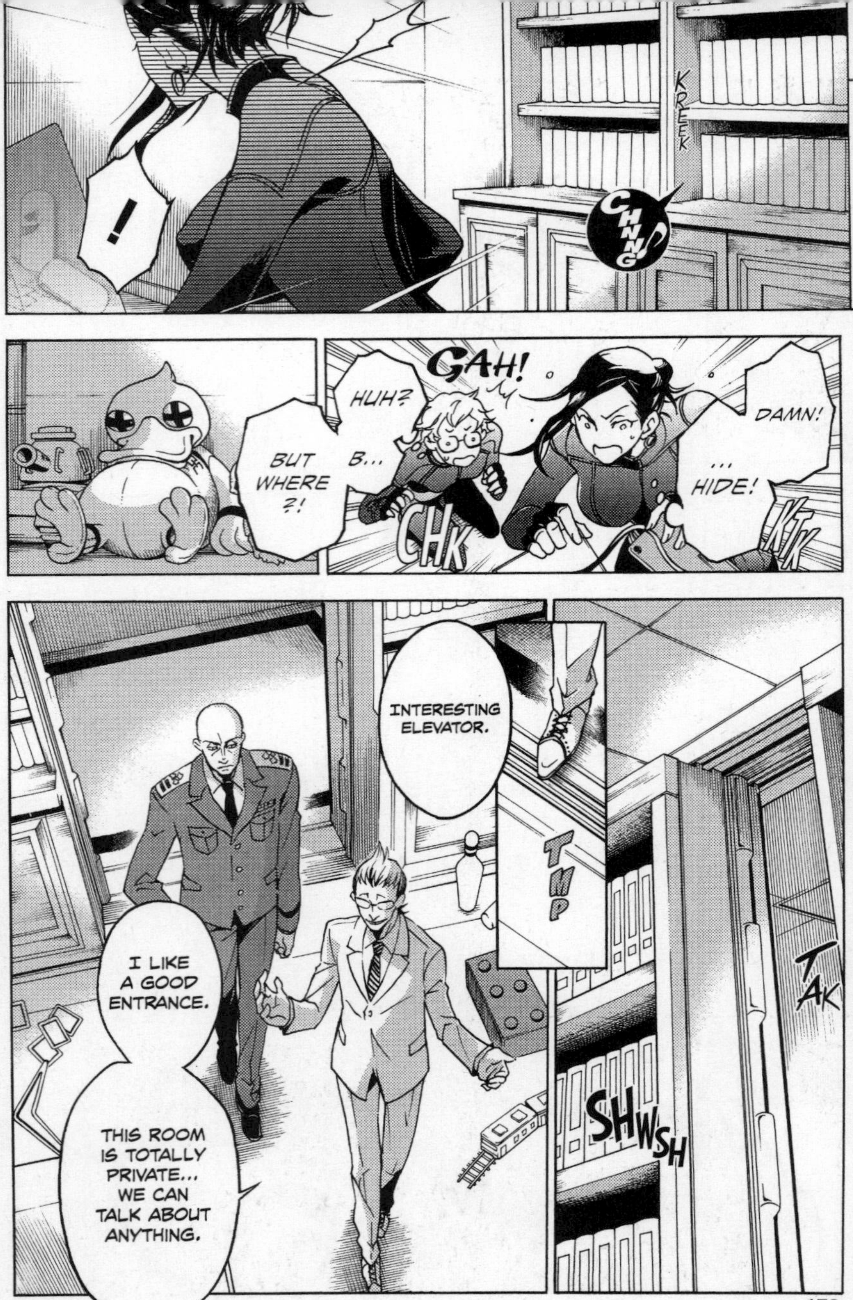
KREEK
CHNNG
!
DAMN!
GAH!
HUH?
... HIDE!
B...
KTK
CHK
BUT WHERE?!
TAK
SHWSH
TMP
INTERESTING ELEVATOR.
I LIKE A GOOD ENTRANCE.
THIS ROOM IS TOTALLY PRIVATE... WE CAN TALK ABOUT ANYTHING.

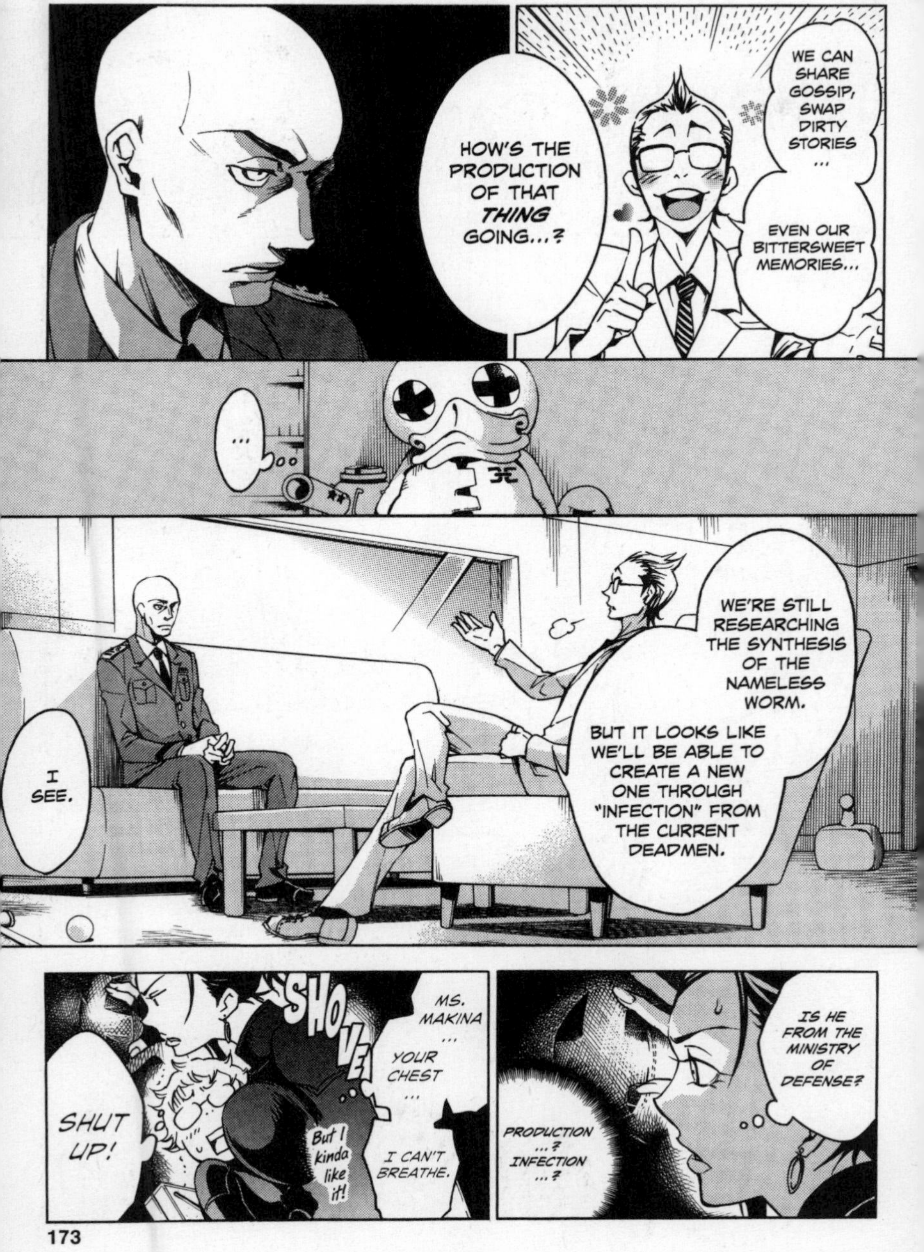
WE CAN SHARE GOSSIP, SWAP DIRTY STORIES ...
EVEN OUR BITTERSWEET MEMORIES...
HOW'S THE PRODUCTION OF THAT *THING* GOING...?
...
WE'RE STILL RESEARCHING THE SYNTHESIS OF THE NAMELESS WORM.
BUT IT LOOKS LIKE WE'LL BE ABLE TO CREATE A NEW ONE THROUGH "INFECTION" FROM THE CURRENT DEADMEN.
I SEE.
IS HE FROM THE MINISTRY OF DEFENSE?
PRODUCTION ...? INFECTION ...?
MS. MAKINA ... YOUR CHEST ...
SHOVE
I CAN'T BREATHE.
But I kinda like it!
SHUT UP!

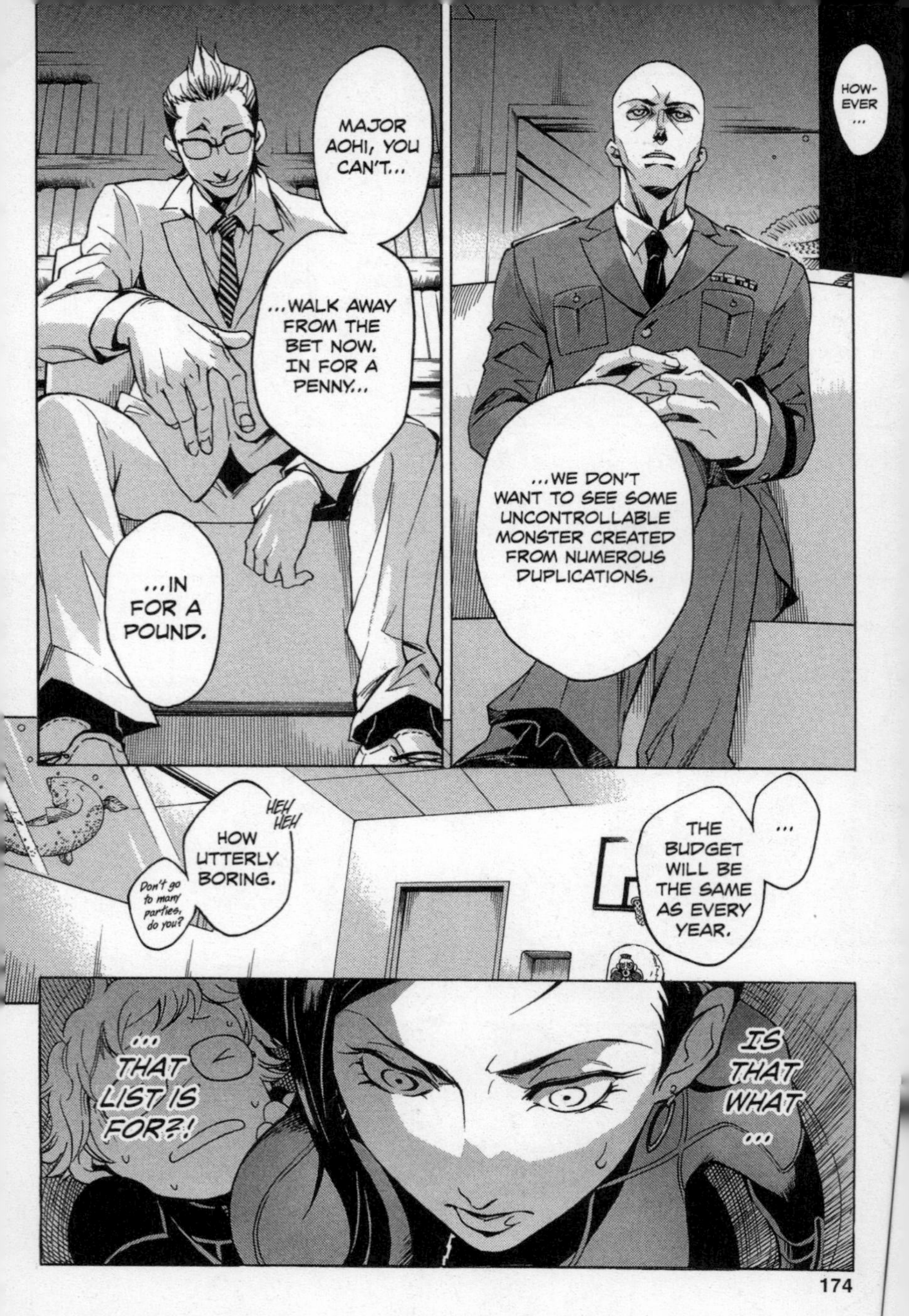

HOW-EVER...
...WE DON'T WANT TO SEE SOME UNCONTROLLABLE MONSTER CREATED FROM NUMEROUS DUPLICATIONS.
MAJOR AOHI, YOU CAN'T...
...WALK AWAY FROM THE BET NOW. IN FOR A PENNY...
...IN FOR A POUND.
...
THE BUDGET WILL BE THE SAME AS EVERY YEAR.
HEH HEH
HOW UTTERLY BORING.
Don't go to many parties, do you?
IS THAT WHAT...
...THAT LIST IS FOR?!

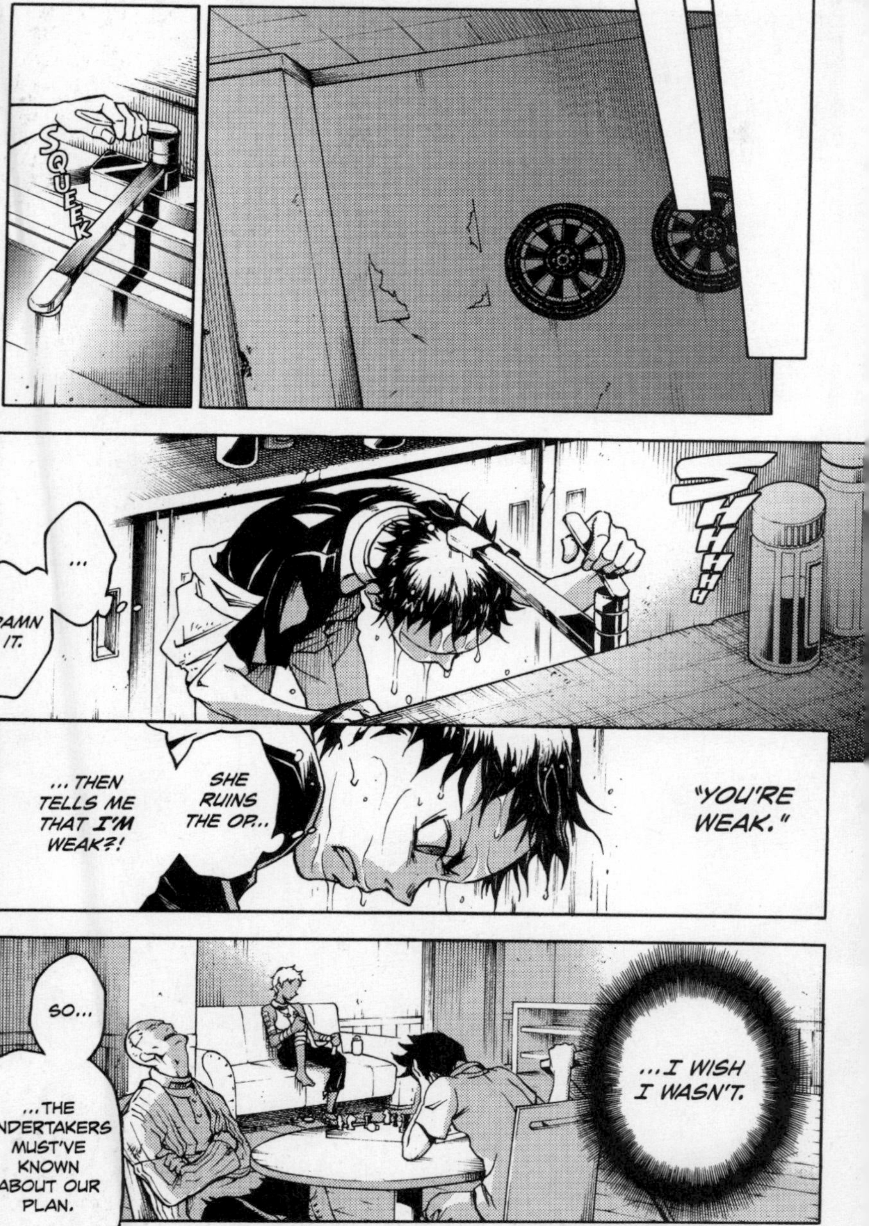
SQUEEK
SHHHHHH
... DAMN IT.
"YOU'RE WEAK."
SHE RUINS THE OP...
...THEN TELLS ME THAT I'M WEAK?!
...I WISH I WASN'T.
SO...
...THE UNDERTAKERS MUST'VE KNOWN ABOUT OUR PLAN.

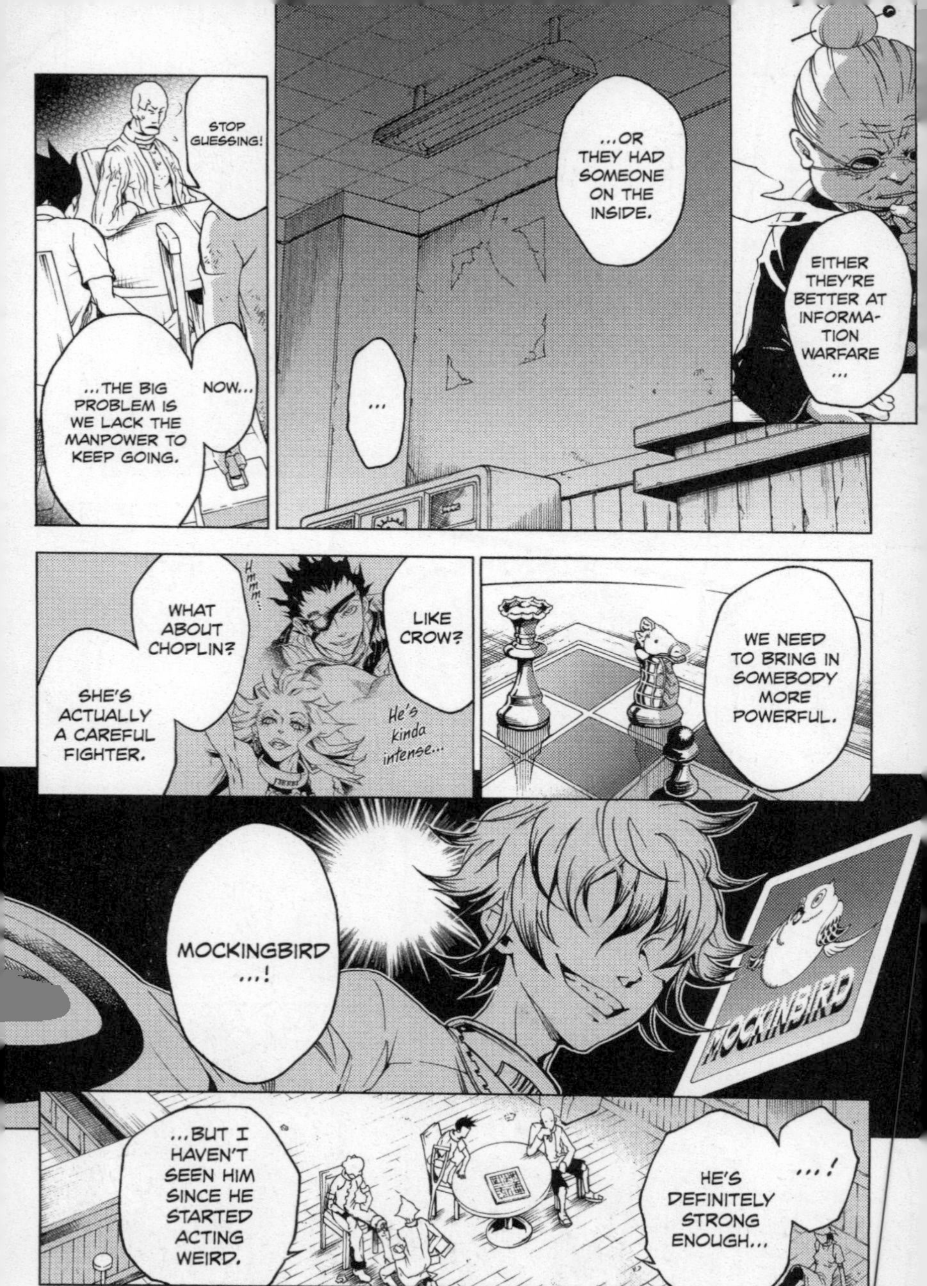
EITHER THEY'RE BETTER AT INFORMATION WARFARE...
...OR THEY HAD SOMEONE ON THE INSIDE.
...
STOP GUESSING!
NOW...
...THE BIG PROBLEM IS WE LACK THE MANPOWER TO KEEP GOING.
WE NEED TO BRING IN SOMEBODY MORE POWERFUL.
LIKE CROW?
Hmmm...
He's kinda intense...
WHAT ABOUT CHOPLIN?
SHE'S ACTUALLY A CAREFUL FIGHTER.
MOCKINGBIRD ...!
MOCKINBIRD
...!
HE'S DEFINITELY STRONG ENOUGH...
...BUT I HAVEN'T SEEN HIM SINCE HE STARTED ACTING WEIRD.

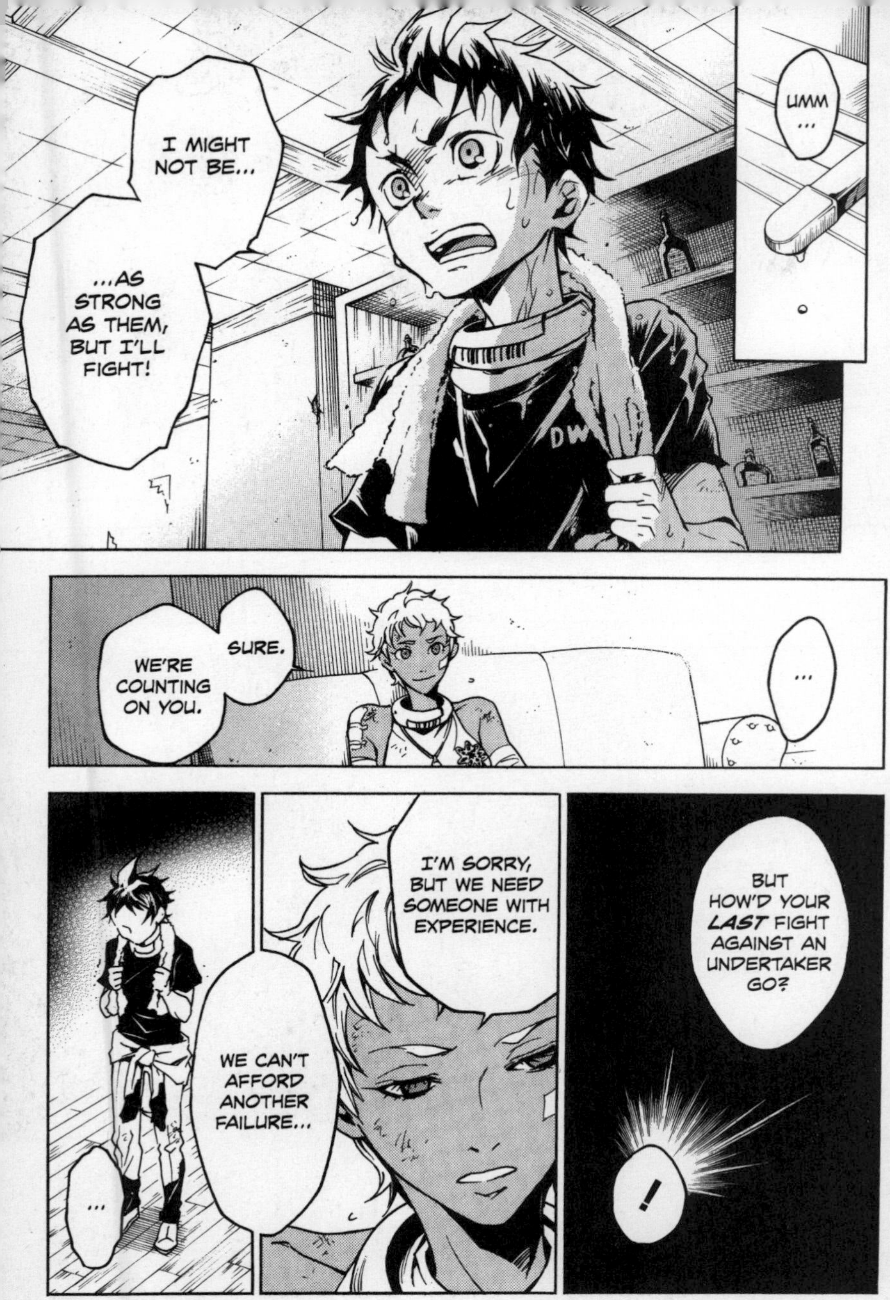
UMM ...
I MIGHT NOT BE...
...AS STRONG AS THEM, BUT I'LL FIGHT!
...
SURE.
WE'RE COUNTING ON YOU.
BUT HOW'D YOUR *LAST* FIGHT AGAINST AN UNDERTAKER GO?
!
I'M SORRY, BUT WE NEED SOMEONE WITH EXPERIENCE.
WE CAN'T AFFORD ANOTHER FAILURE...
...

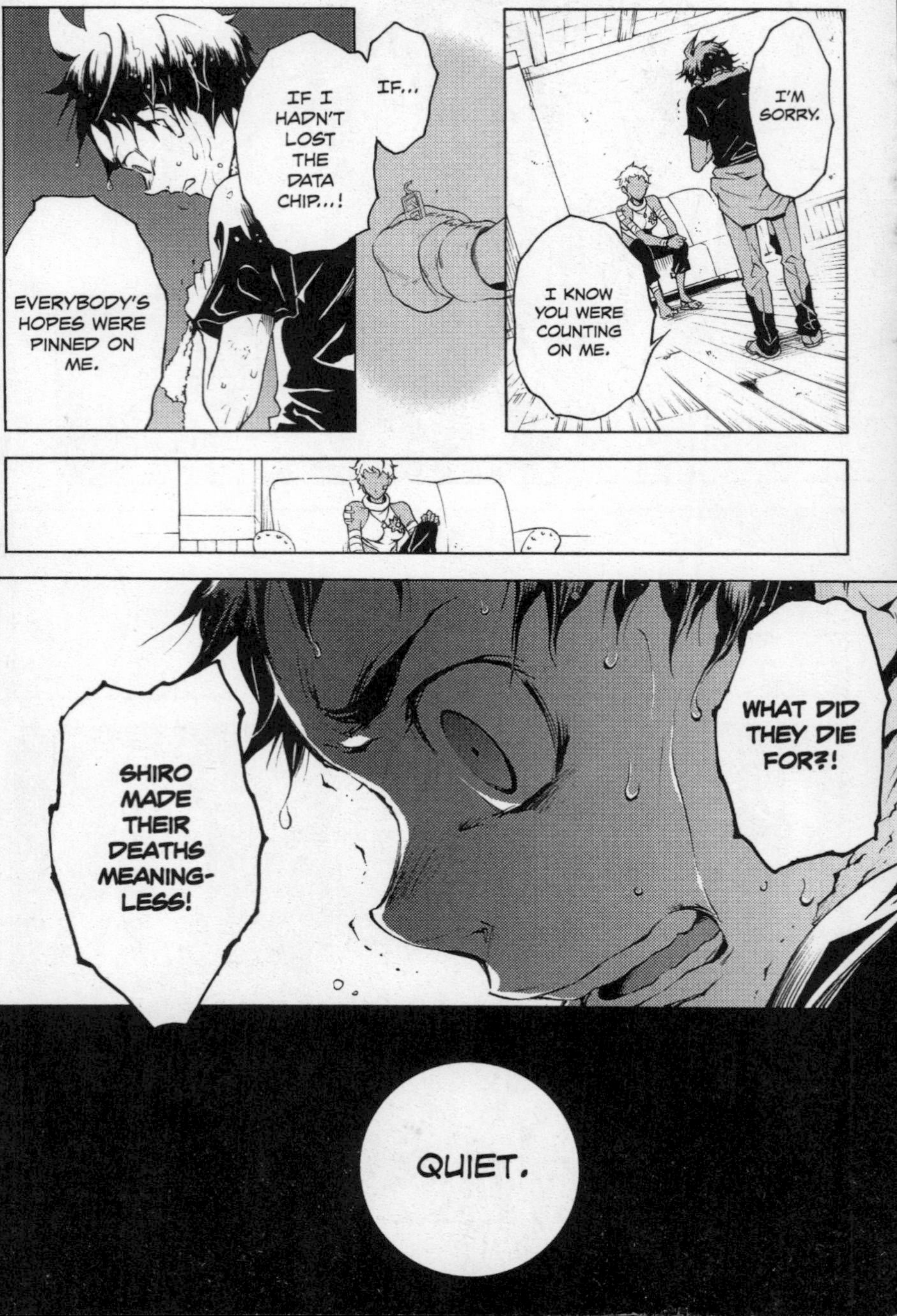
I'M SORRY.
I KNOW YOU WERE COUNTING ON ME.
IF...
IF I HADN'T LOST THE DATA CHIP...!
EVERYBODY'S HOPES WERE PINNED ON ME.
WHAT DID THEY DIE FOR?!
SHIRO MADE THEIR DEATHS MEANING-LESS!
QUIET.

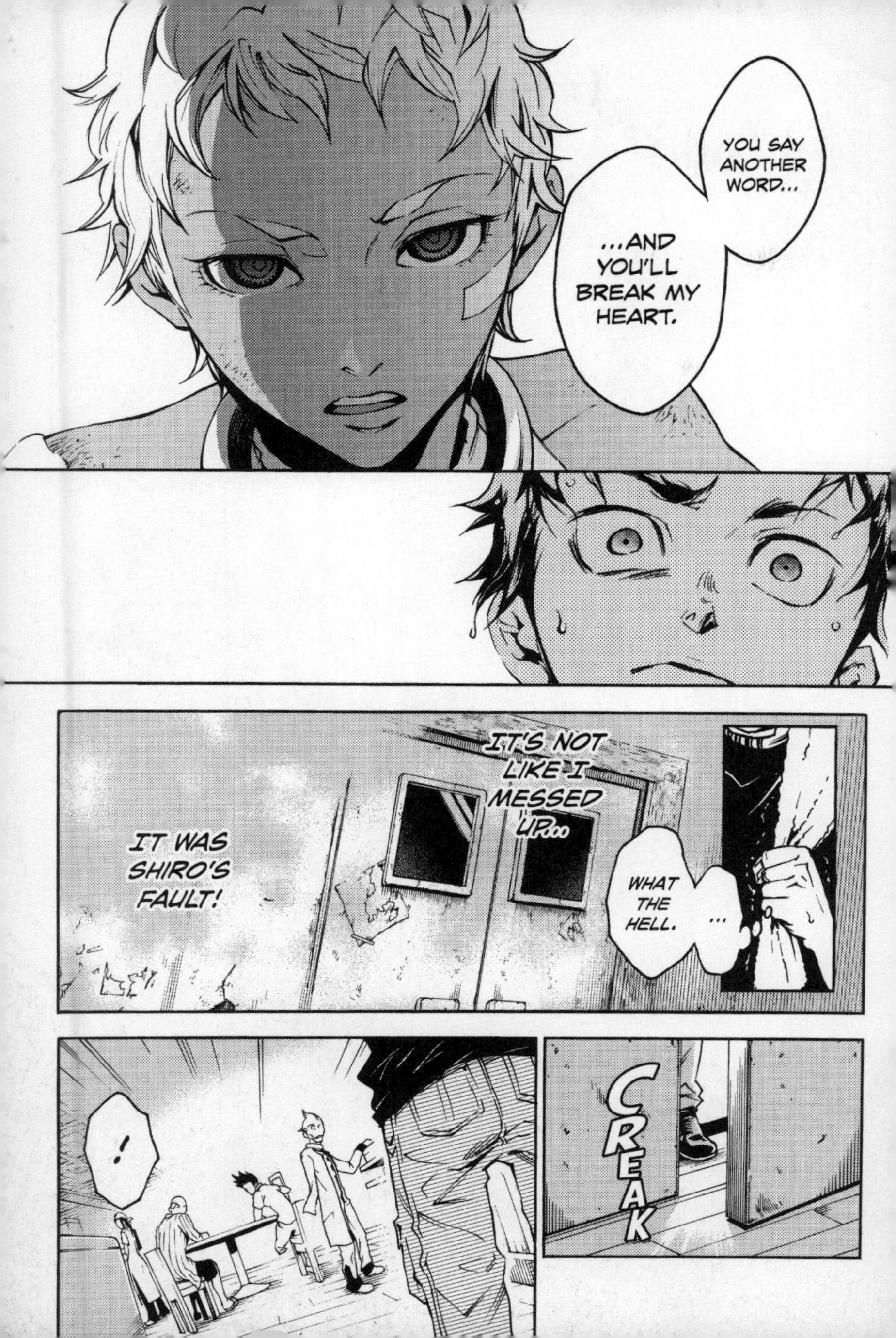
YOU SAY ANOTHER WORD...
...AND YOU'LL BREAK MY HEART.
WHAT THE HELL. ...
IT'S NOT LIKE I MESSED UP...
IT WAS SHIRO'S FAULT!
CREAK
!

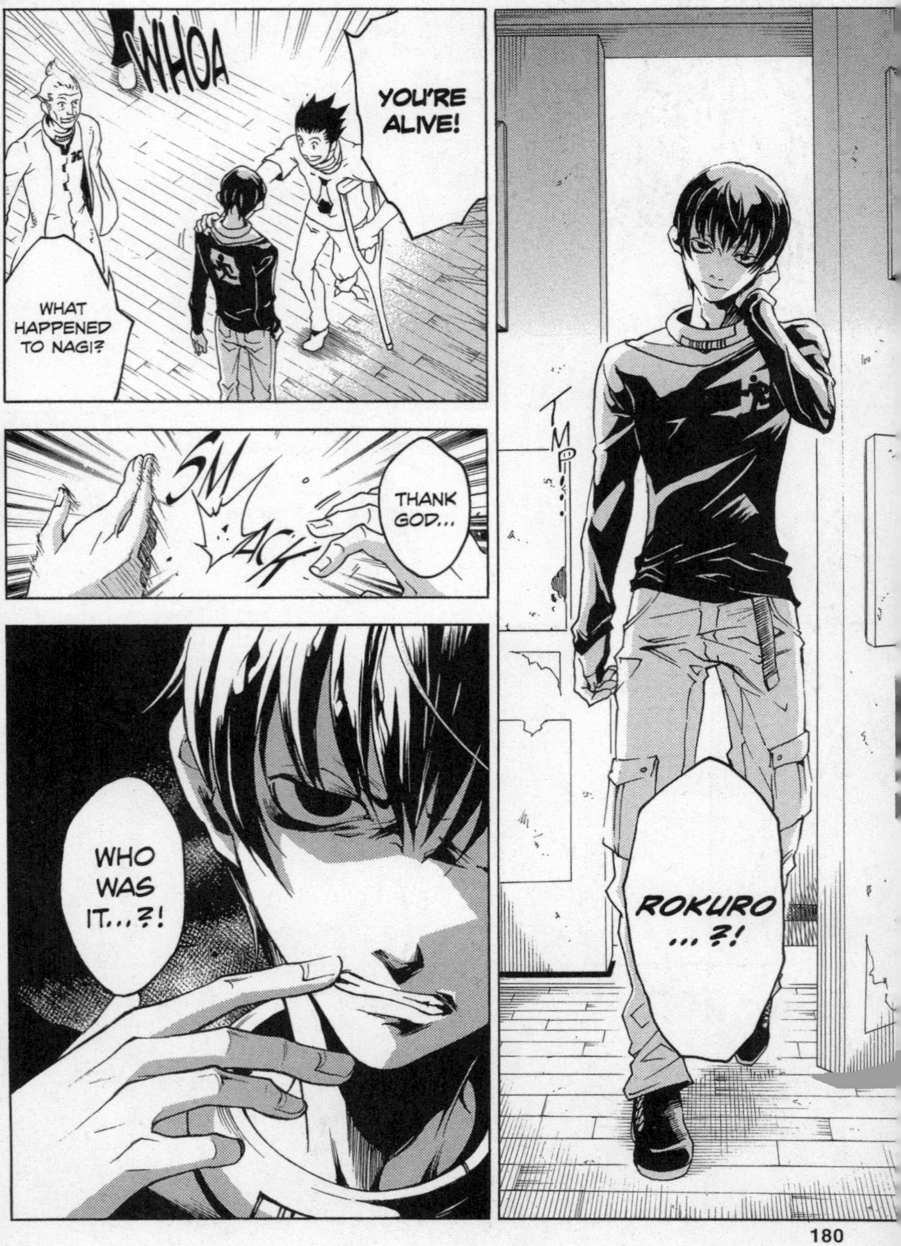
TMP
ROKURO ...?!
YOU'RE ALIVE!
WHOA
WHAT HAPPENED TO NAGI?
THANK GOD...
SMACK
WHO WAS IT...?!

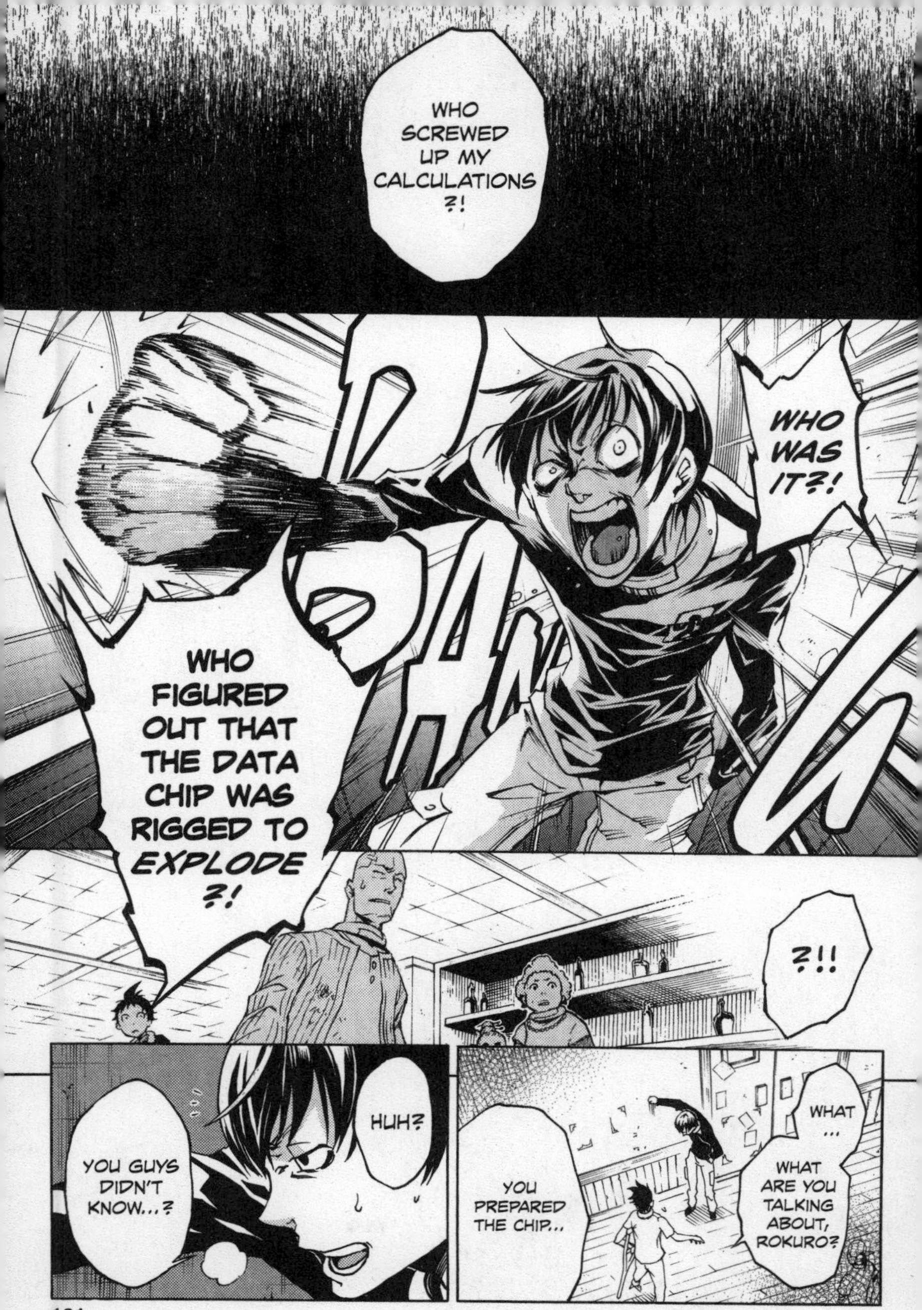
WHO SCREWED UP MY CALCULATIONS ?!
WHO WAS IT?!
WHO FIGURED OUT THAT THE DATA CHIP WAS RIGGED TO EXPLODE ?!
?!!
WHAT ... WHAT ARE YOU TALKING ABOUT, ROKURO?
YOU PREPARED THE CHIP...
HUH?
YOU GUYS DIDN'T KNOW...?

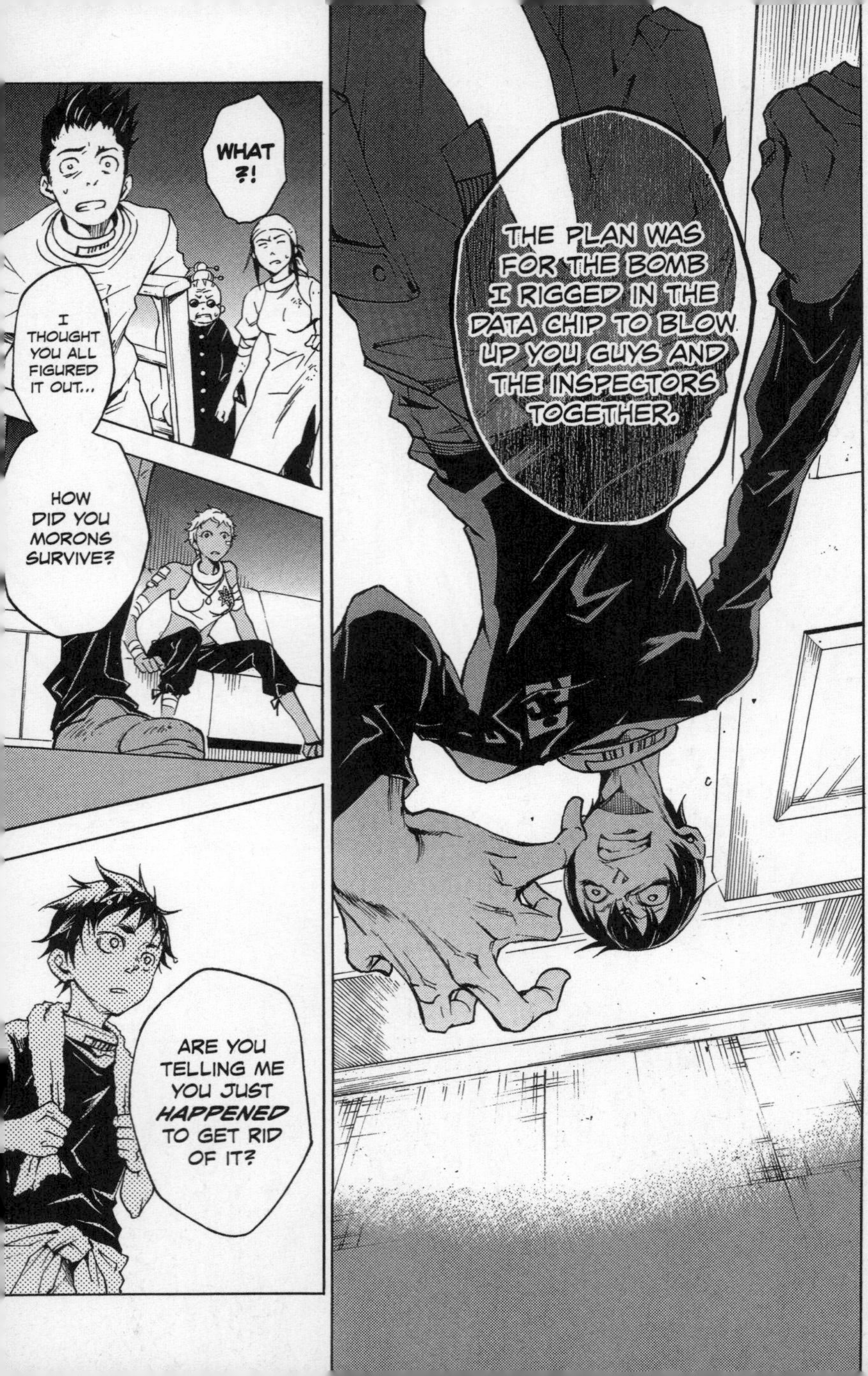
THE PLAN WAS FOR THE BOMB I RIGGED IN THE DATA CHIP TO BLOW UP YOU GUYS AND THE INSPECTORS TOGETHER.
WHAT?!
I THOUGHT YOU ALL FIGURED IT OUT...
HOW DID YOU MORONS SURVIVE?
ARE YOU TELLING ME YOU JUST *HAPPENED* TO GET RID OF IT?

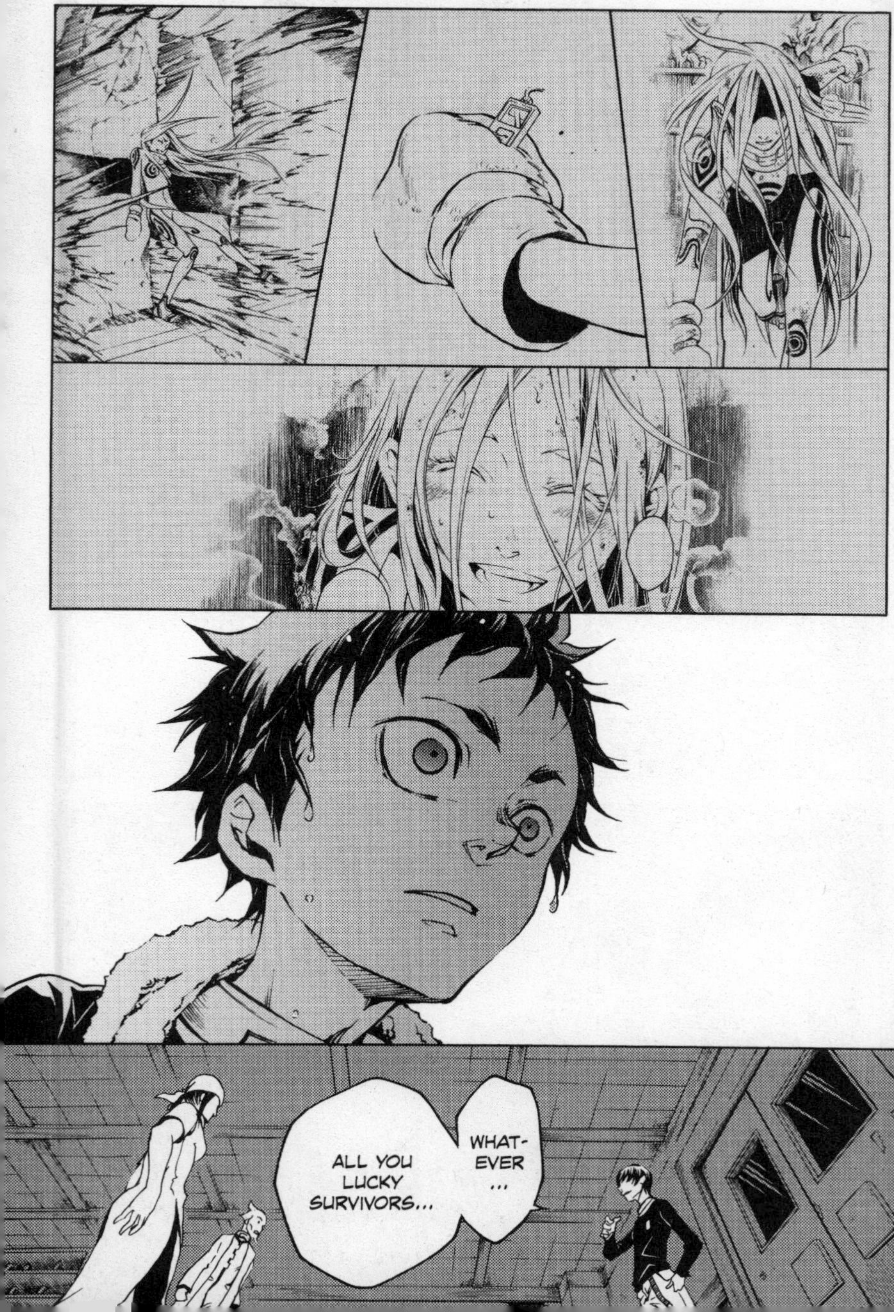
WHAT-EVER...
ALL YOU LUCKY SURVIVORS...

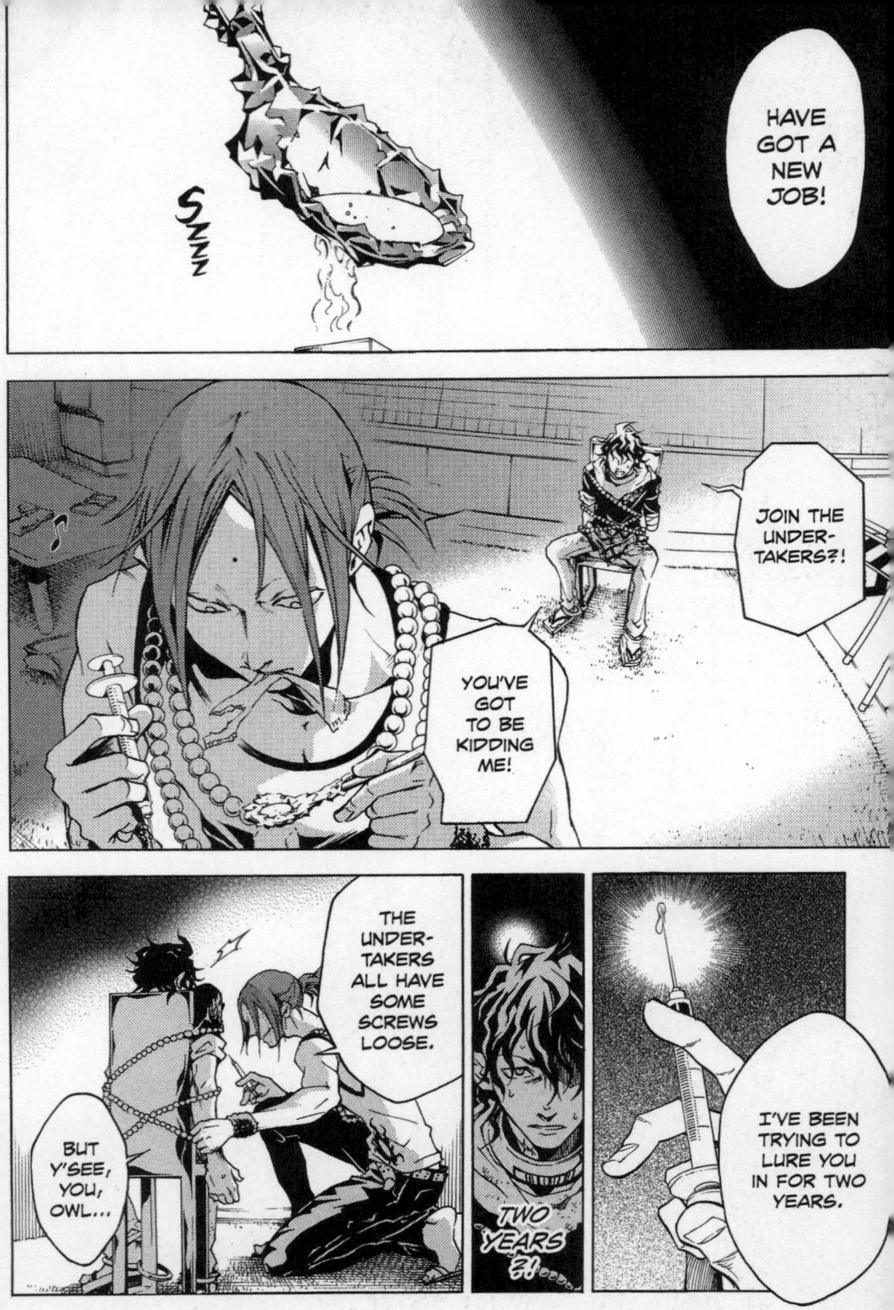
HAVE GOT A NEW JOB!
SZZZ
JOIN THE UNDER-TAKERS?!
YOU'VE GOT TO BE KIDDING ME!
I'VE BEEN TRYING TO LURE YOU IN FOR TWO YEARS.
TWO YEARS ?!
THE UNDER-TAKERS ALL HAVE SOME SCREWS LOOSE.
BUT Y'SEE, YOU, OWL...

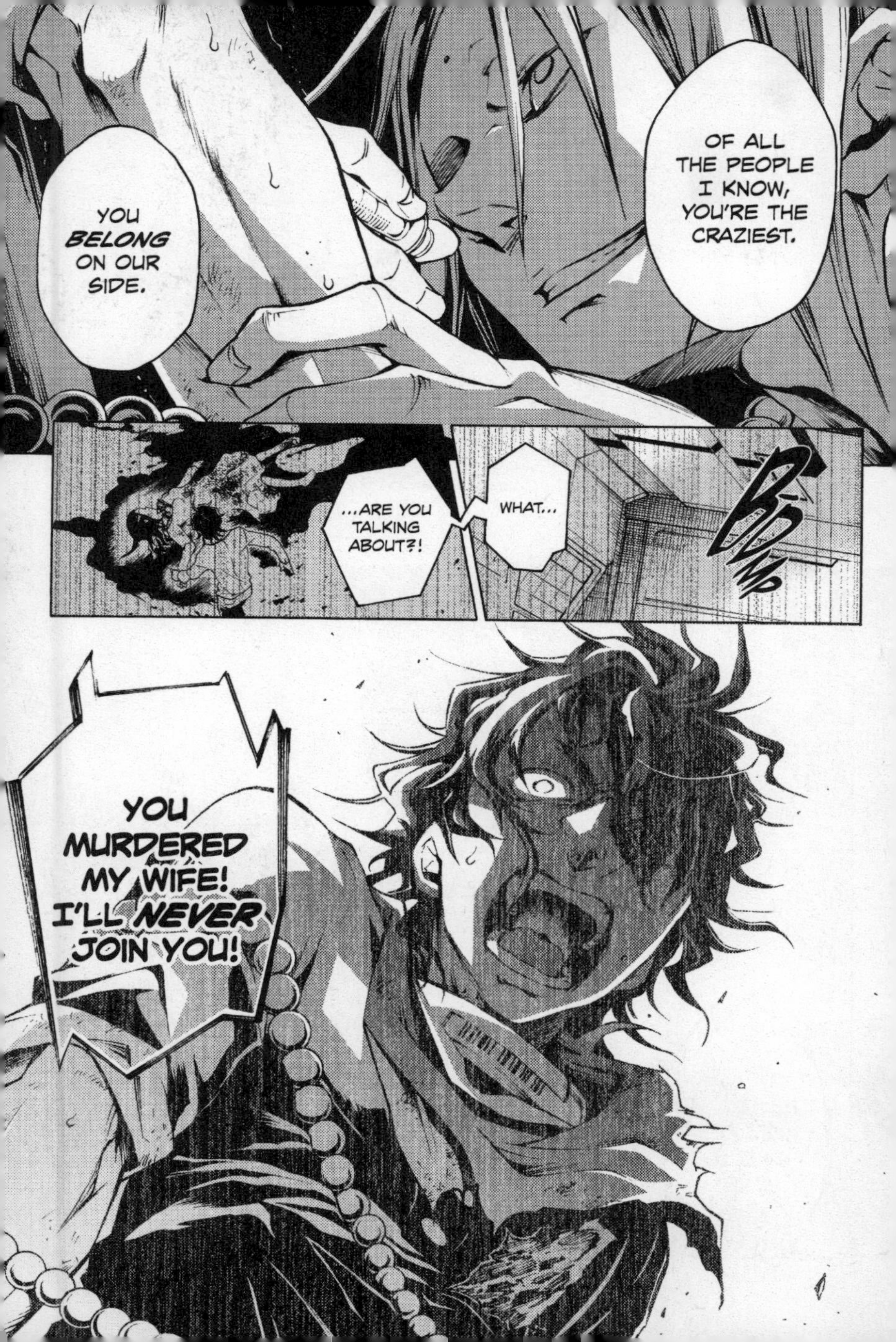
OF ALL THE PEOPLE I KNOW, YOU'RE THE CRAZIEST.
YOU BELONG ON OUR SIDE.
BDUMP
WHAT...
...ARE YOU TALKING ABOUT?!
YOU MURDERED MY WIFE! I'LL NEVER JOIN YOU!

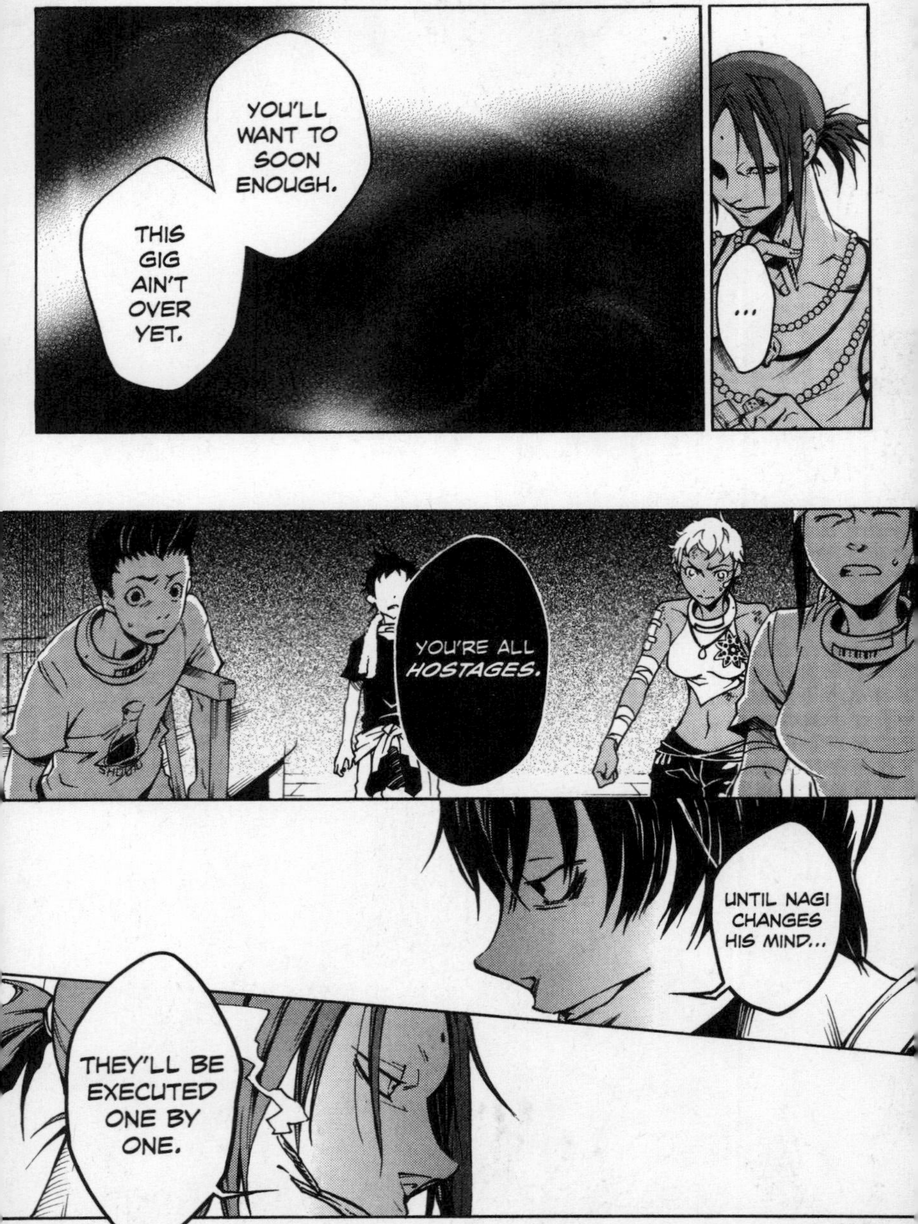
...
YOU'LL WANT TO SOON ENOUGH.
THIS GIG AIN'T OVER YET.
YOU'RE ALL *HOSTAGES.*
UNTIL NAGI CHANGES HIS MIND...
THEY'LL BE EXECUTED ONE BY ONE.

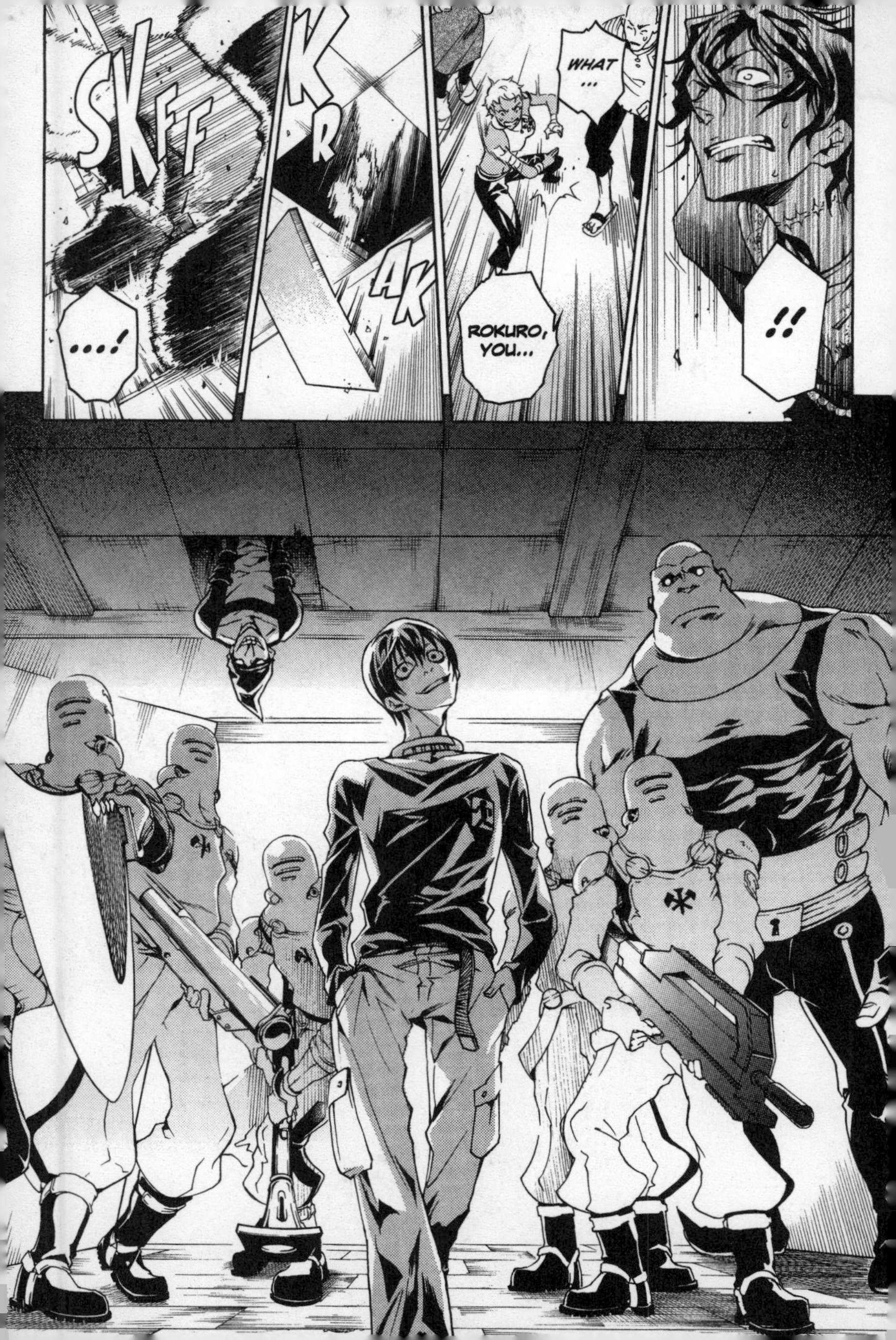
!!
WHAT ...
ROKURO, YOU...
KR
AK
SKFF
...!

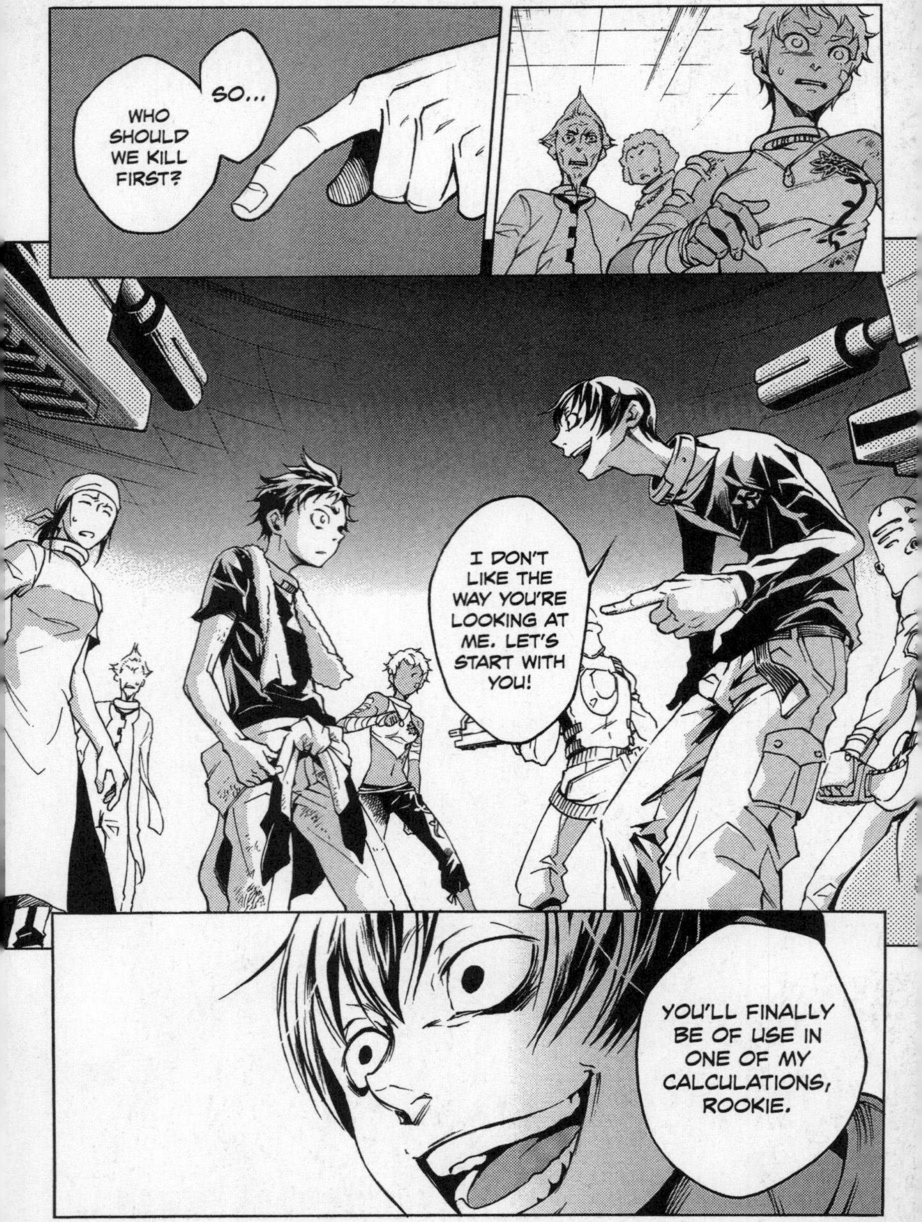
SO...
WHO SHOULD WE KILL FIRST?
I DON'T LIKE THE WAY YOU'RE LOOKING AT ME. LET'S START WITH YOU!
YOU'LL FINALLY BE OF USE IN ONE OF MY CALCULATIONS, ROOKIE.

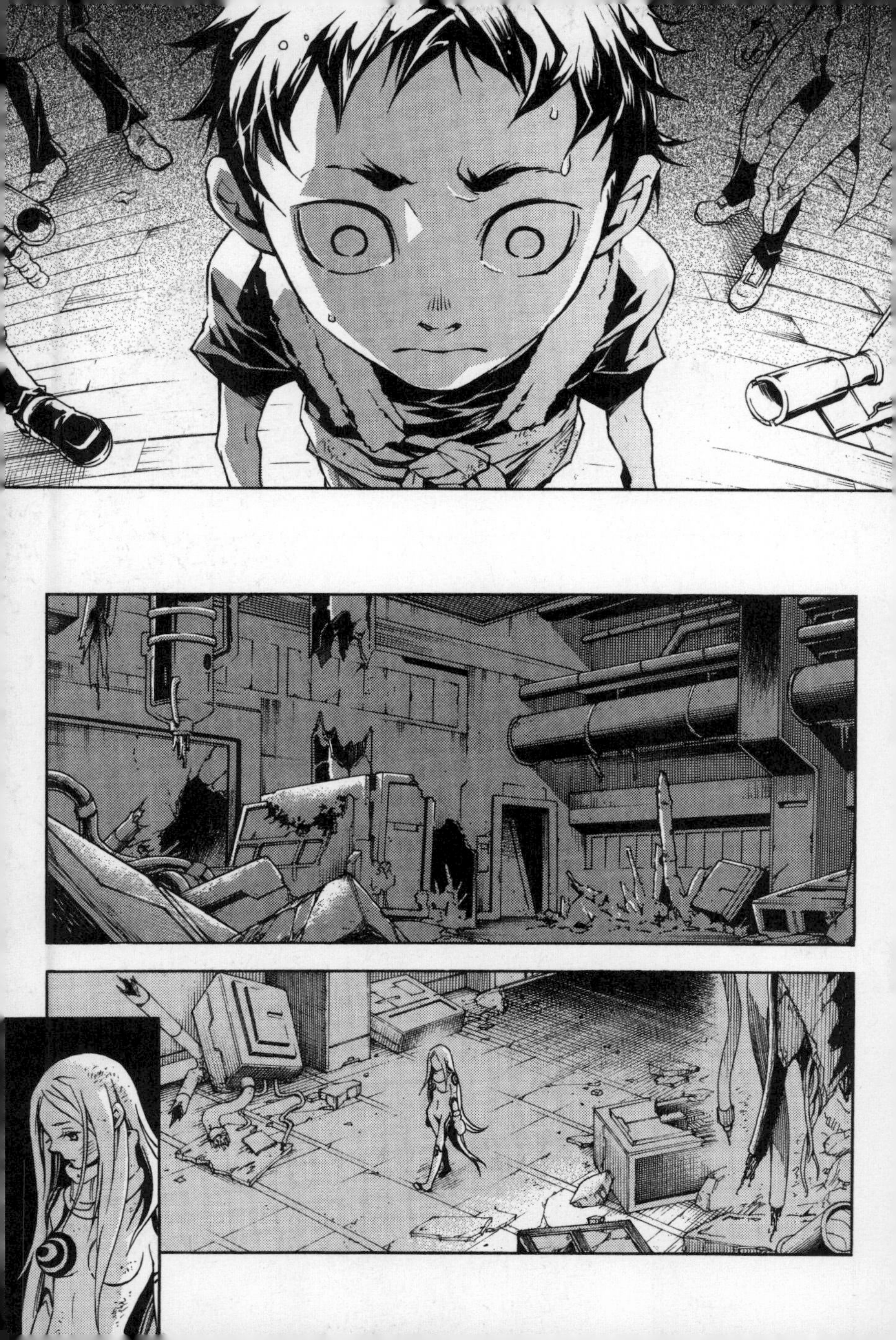

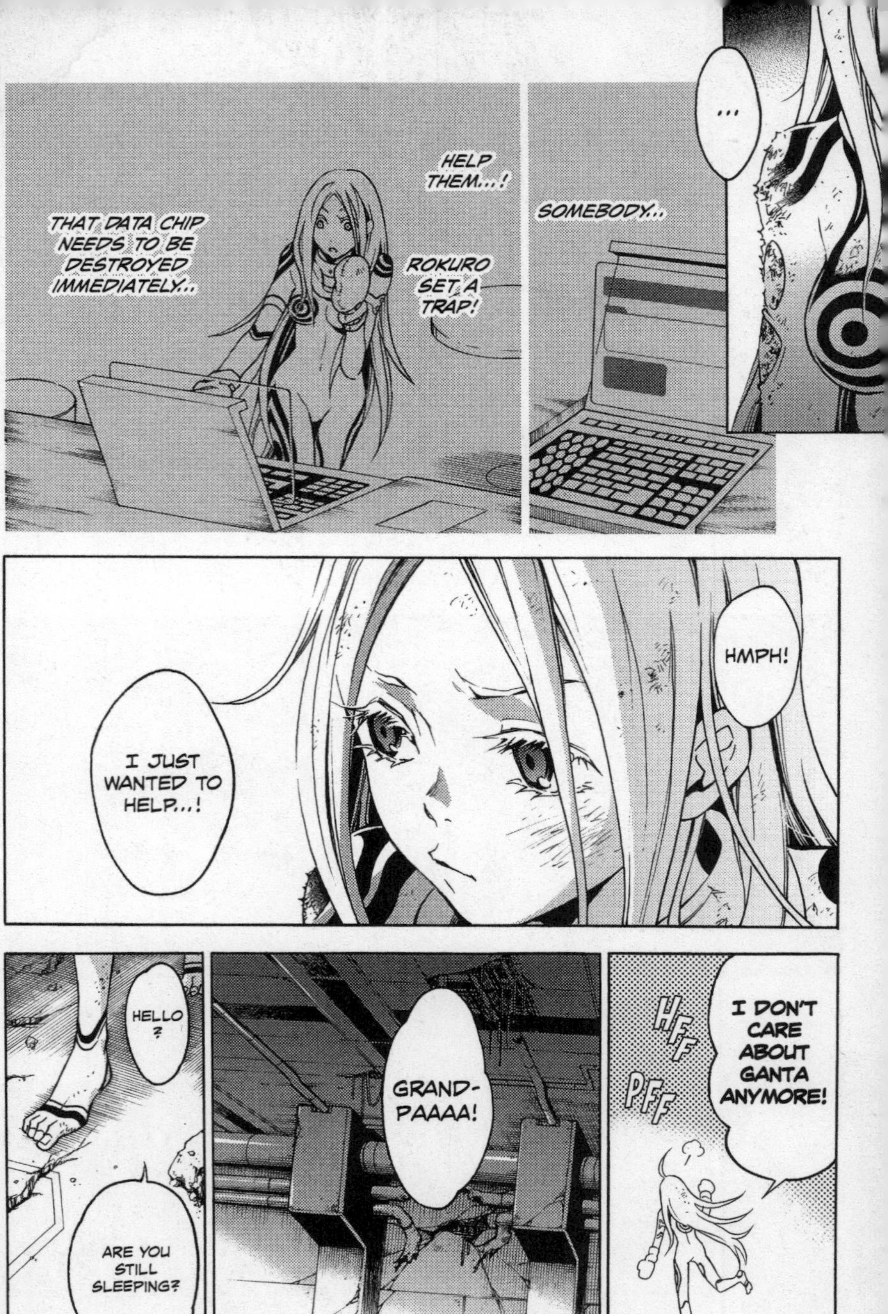
...
SOMEBODY..
HELP THEM...!
ROKURO SET A TRAP!
THAT DATA CHIP NEEDS TO BE DESTROYED IMMEDIATELY..
HMPH!
I JUST WANTED TO HELP...!
HFF
PFF
I DON'T CARE ABOUT GANTA ANYMORE!
GRAND-PAAAA!
HELLO?
ARE YOU STILL SLEEPING?

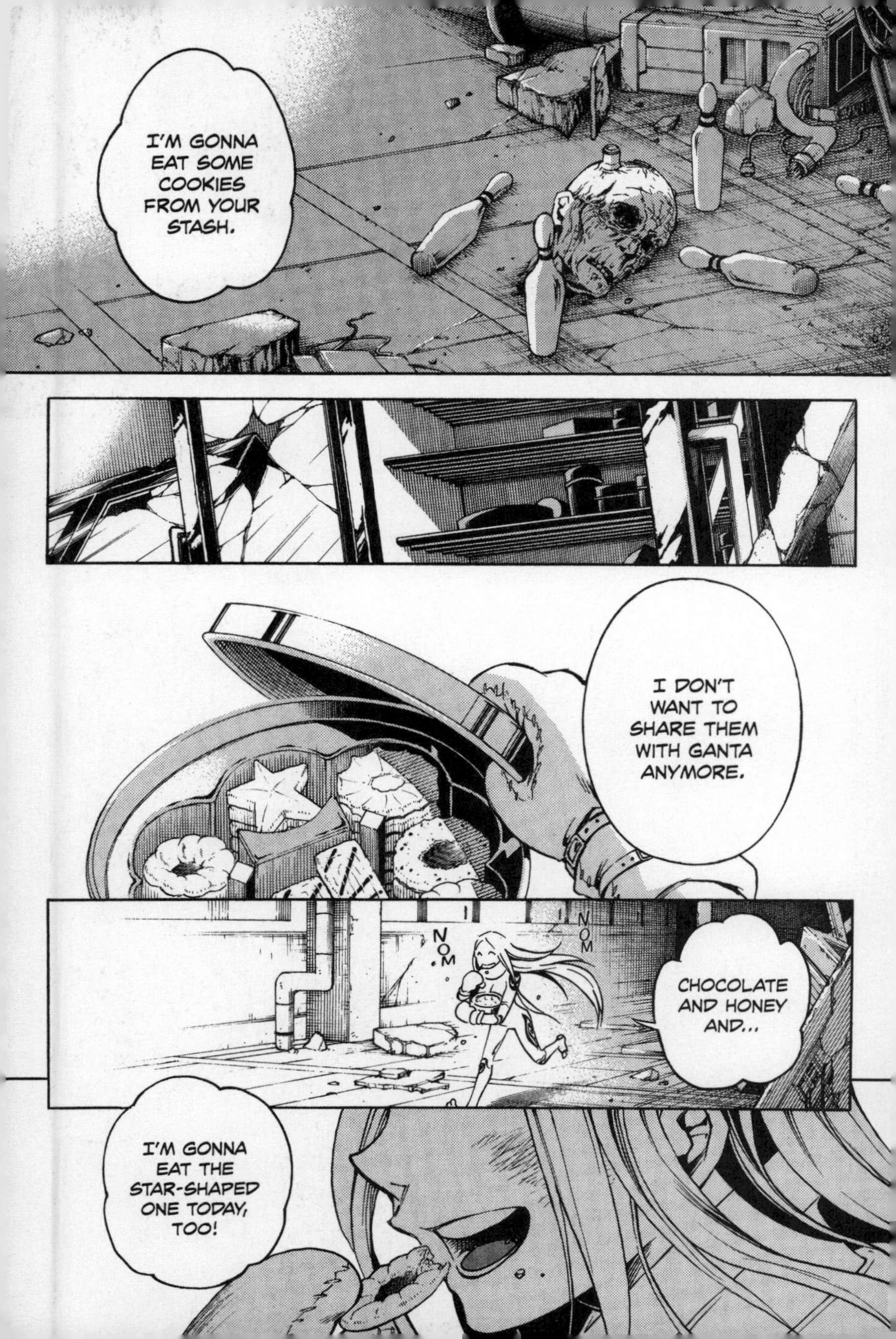
I'M GONNA EAT SOME COOKIES FROM YOUR STASH.
I DON'T WANT TO SHARE THEM WITH GANTA ANYMORE.
CHOCOLATE AND HONEY AND...
NOM
NOM
I'M GONNA EAT THE STAR-SHAPED ONE TODAY, TOO!

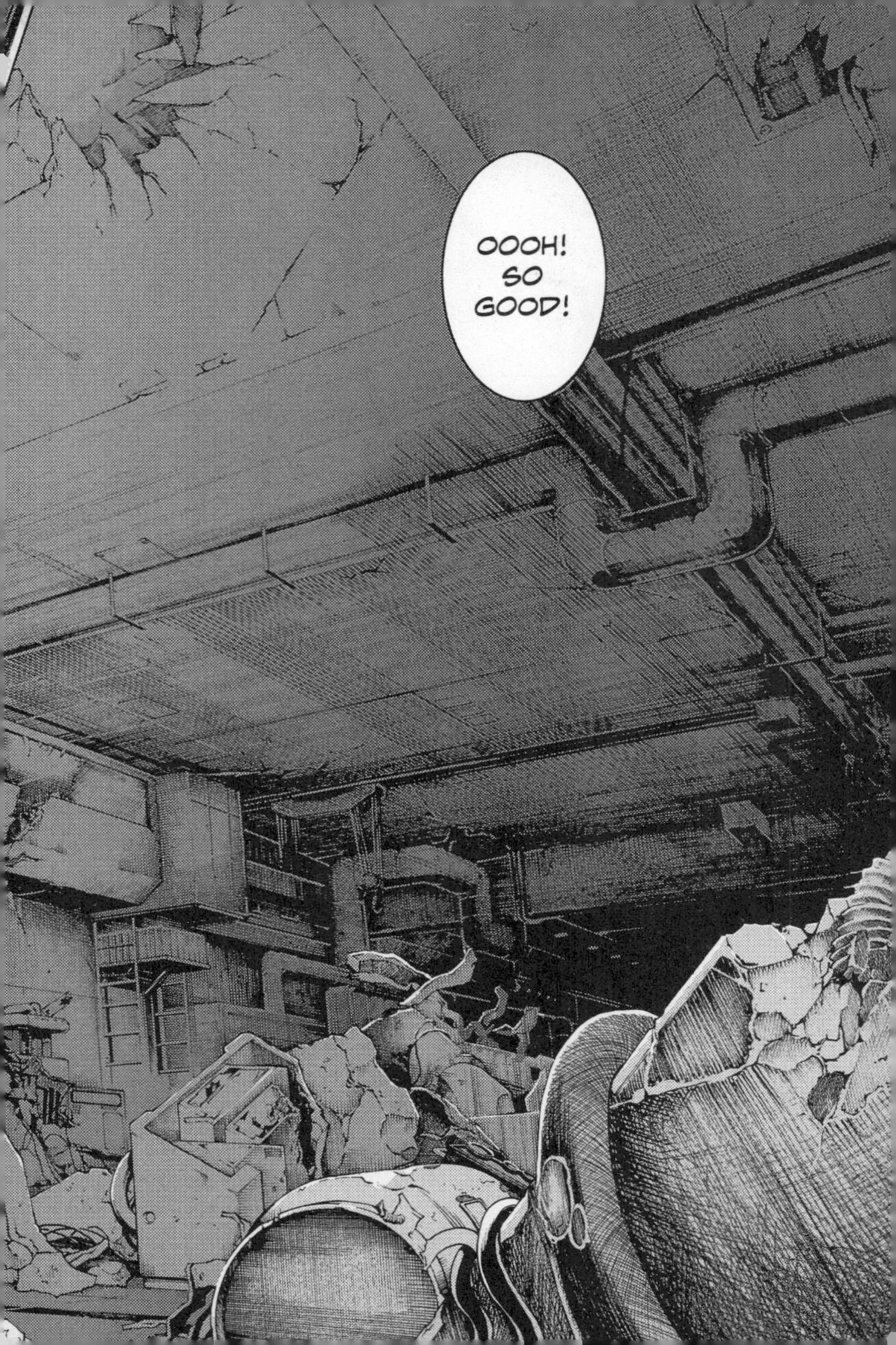
OOOH! SO GOOD!

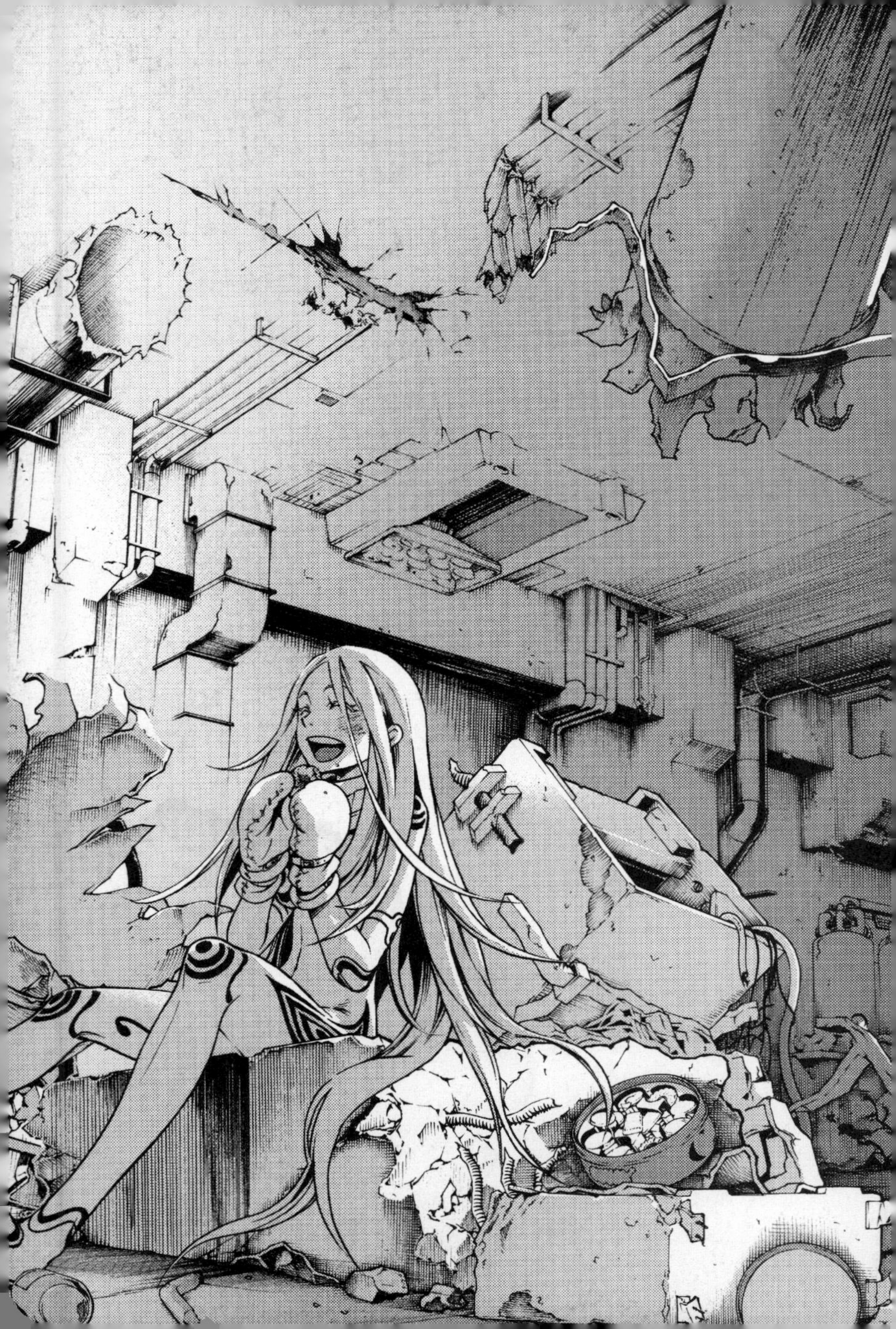

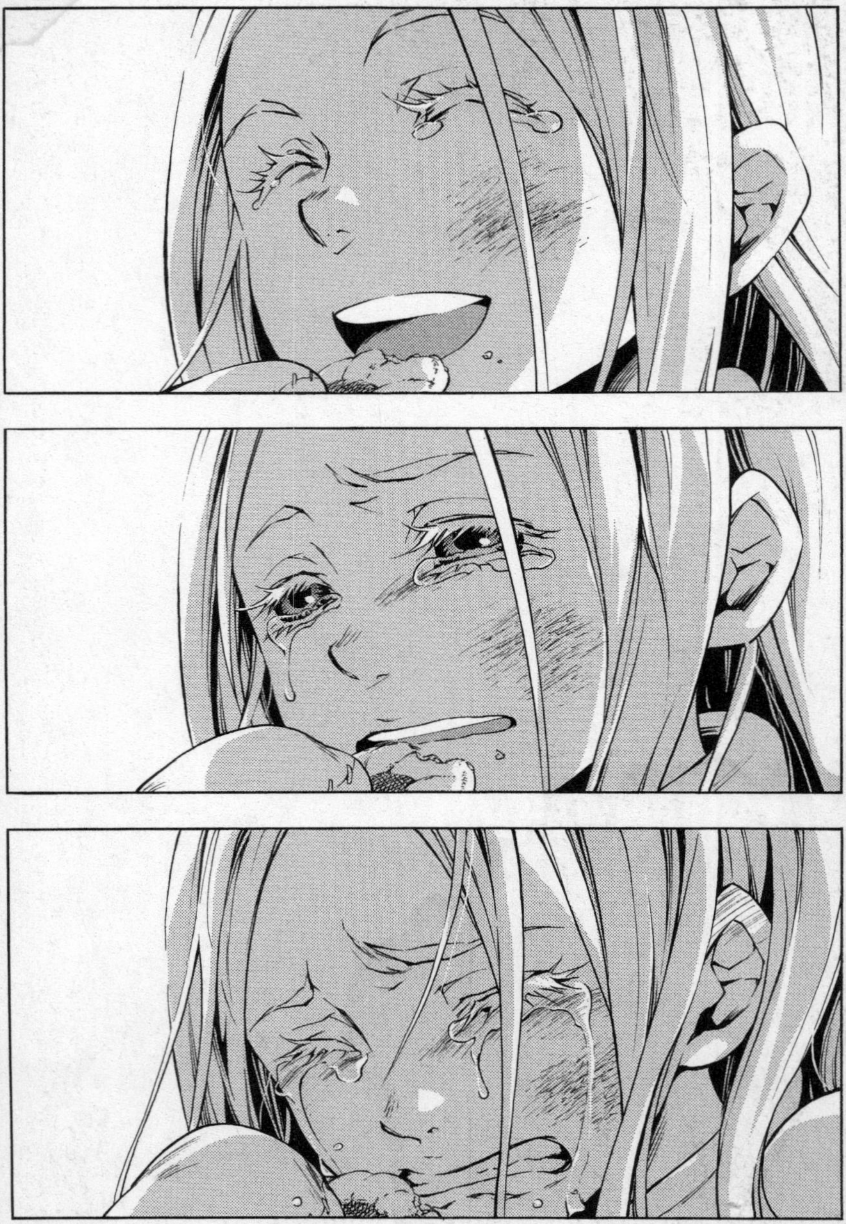